THE COMPLETE IDIOT'S GUIDE® TO

Cashing In on Your Inventions

by Richard C. Levy

ALPHA

A member of Penguin Group (USA) Inc.

Fairy tales can come true. To Sheryl and Bettie, the bright and beautiful ladies who enrich my life and keep me young at heart. I love you muchisimo.

Copyright © 2002 by Richard C. Levy

International Standard Book Number: 0028642201
Library of Congress Catalog Card Number: 2001094711

05   04   8   7   6   5

Interpretation of the printing code: The rightmost number of the first series of numbers is the year of the book's printing; the rightmost number of the second series of numbers is the number of the book's printing. For example, a printing code of 02-1 shows that the first printing occurred in 2002.

Printed in the United States of America

Publisher
Marie Butler-Knight

Product Manager
Phil Kitchel

Managing Editor
Jennifer Chisholm

Acquisitions Editor
Mike Sanders

Development Editor
Amy Gordon

Production Editor
Billy Fields

Copy Editor
Cari Luna

Illustrator
Chris Sabatino

Cover Designers
Mike Freeland
Kevin Spear

Book Designers
Scott Cook and Amy Adams of DesignLab

Indexer
Angie Bess

Layout/Proofreading
John Etchison
Gloria Schurick

Contents at a Glance

Part 1: How to Get Your Great Ideas on the Road   **1**

   1 How to Realize Your Full Potential   3
      There is no future in the word impossible.

   2 Beware of Invention Marketing Flimflam Artists   21
      How to identify and sidestep unscrupulous invention marketing services and other pitfalls.

   3 Licensing vs. Venture Capital   43
      An analysis of commercialization options.

Part 2: Getting High Marks   **59**

   4 How to Find a Home for Your Brainchild   61
      Reach companies with the right stuff.

   5 Knock. Knock. Buy My Invention, Please!   79
      Getting through the door and being invited to stay.

   6 How to Turn a Proposal into a Marriage   89
      Life's a pitch! How to play the big room and not come off like a lounge act.

   7 How to Negotiate Your Deal   101
      Crafting contracts is a skill that can be learned.

   8 Key Deal Points   113
      It's all about relationships, not transactions.

Part 3: Goin' for the Gold   **125**

   9 The United States Patent and Trademark Office   127
      Ways to protect your intellectual property.

   10 It All Begins with a Search   145
      What to do when the mother of all ideas hits.

   11 How to Hire a Patent Attorney.   161
      Yes, you will need a patent attorney. Here's why.

Part 4: Uncle Sam Wants (to Help) YOU!   **171**

   12 How to Apply for a Utility Patent   173
      Protect a new and useful process, machine, manufacture, composition of matter, or any new and useful improvement thereof.

   13 Flower Power. How to Apply for a Plant Patent   189
      Money can grow on trees and on flowers, too.

14 How to Apply for a Design Patent 203
Design patents are a method to protect ornamental and cosmetic aspects of your inventions—NOT their function.

15 Mark Your Words 219
Do not underestimate the contribution a good trademark can make to your licensing effort.

16 Securing Your Copy Rights 239
Copyright protection is free, and you don't need a lawyer to obtain it.

17 I've Got a Secret 251
Loose lips sink ships. The definition and value of trade secrets.

18 Say, Ah! The Patent Examination Process at the USPTO 257
What goes on with your application behind the scenes at the USPTO.

Part 5: People Who Share, People Who Dare **273**

19 Hidden Treasures in Uncle Sam's High-Tech Closets 275
Where to find federal funding for some types of inventions and establish partnerships.

20 Yes, Inventors, There Is a Santa Claus 295
The toy industry is one of the most potentially lucrative frontiers for the independent inventor.

21 Inventor Organizations 307
Join a vibrant social network comprised of individuals who share a community and are striving for a similar goal.

Appendixes

A Agreements 317

B Resources 329

C Political Letter 349

Index 351

Contents

Part 1: How to Get Your Great Ideas on the Road 1

1 How to Realize Your Full Potential 3

Overcoming Naysayers 4
The First Pitch 5
America, the Land of Opportunity 7
   Towering Examples of American Ingenuity 8
   Other Fields of Dreams and Dreamers from Other Fields 8
   Who's Witcomb L. Judson? 9
Answering the Call 9
Investing in Your Invention 9
Education Isn't Everything 11
Levy's 10 Commandments for Success 12

2 Beware of Invention Marketing Flimflam Artists 21

Attack of the Killer Patent Attorney 22
Flimsy Firms 23
Operation Mousetrap 26
   Foreign Affairs 27
The Price Is Not Always Right 27
Inventors Awareness Group 27
A Step in the Right Direction 28
What Comes After the Pitch 28
Heads Up 30
Before You Contract for Services ... .31
Who Are These Parasites? 32
How to Tell the Pros from the Cons 32
New Twist to an Old Scheme 36
How Do They Get Your Name? 37
Profile of an Honest Broker 37
What to Do if You Are a Victim 37
States (Inventor) Rights 38
   Minnesota (Invention Services 325A.02) 38
   Virginia, Chapter 18, 59.1-209 39
How to Find an Honest Broker 40

3 Licensing vs. Venture Capital 43

Business Options 44
The Licensing Option 46
   Reinventing Inventors 46
   Manufacturers Seek Risk Reduction 47

You Scratch My Back, I'll Scratch Yours 47
Know How + Know Who = Success 48
The MBA Syndrome...48
The Advantages of Licensing 49
The Disadvantages of Licensing 50
Whoooah, Not So Fast! 50
Doing It Yourself: The Venturing Strategy 51
The Advantages..51
The Disadvantages 54
Prerequisites Common to Licensing and Venturing 55
Other Factors in Choosing a Commercialization Strategy........56
Think About Costs, at All Costs 57
If You Are Still Not Sure 57

Part 2: Getting High Marks

4 How to Find a Home for Your Brainchild   61

Finding a Licensing Partner 62
Attend Trade Shows...64
One-Stop Shopping...64
Meet 'n' Greet 65
Worth the Price of Admission...65
How to Locate the Right Trade Show 65
Conferences and Meetings: Networking Meccas 66
Finding Conferences in Your Area..66
Big Companies vs. Small Companies 67
Large Companies..67
Small Companies..69
So, What's the Answer? 71
Public Companies vs. Private Companies.........................71
Finding Information on Public Companies 72
Private Companies...75
Where to Find Product and Corporate Profiles 76
The Thomas Register 77
Standard & Poor's 77
Does the Shoe Fit? 77

5 Knock. Knock. Buy My Invention, Please!   79

First Impressions 80
N.I.H. Syndrome 81
Choosing Your Target and Making Your Mark 83
The Corporate Culture 85
Lookin' to Hook 'Em 85
Sign on the Dotted Line 87

6 How to Turn a Proposal into a Marriage 89

Honesty Is the Only Policy 90
You Should Hear a Pin Drop 90
The Three Ps 92
Elements of a Proposal..*93*
Between the Covers *94*
Pitching Isn't Enough. Pitch In, Too. *97*
Multiple Submissions 98
Unfavorable Odds 99
Your Champion 99

7 How to Negotiate Your Deal 101

On Lawyering—One Man's Opinion 102
Should You Use a Lawyer to Approach the Company? 102
Do You Need a Lawyer for Contracts? 103
Do You Need a Lawyer for Patents? 104
Conducting Business 105
Winning at What Cost? 105
Agreeing to Agree 106
Advances 107
Royalties..107
Guarantees 107
The Option Agreement 108
Levy's 10 Commandments of Contract Negotiation 108
Terms of Endearment 110
Patents. Trademarks. Who Pays?..111

8 Key Deal Points 113

I Do Not Have All the Answers..114
Show Me Yours, I'll Show You Mine....................................114
Fairness and Flexibility Rule 115
Management by Objectives..116
The Spirit of Agreement 117
Setting the Scene and the Mind 118

Part 3: Goin' for the Gold 125

**9 The United States Patent and
Trademark Office 127**

The Big Three in IP 128
Keepin' a List and Checkin' It Twice 129
Definition of a Patent 131
The Patent Law 131

What Is Patentable?..132
The Examiners (Say Ah!) 133
Established by Law, Built by Innovation—The USPTO 133
Only Inventors Need Apply 135
Copy Documents, Not Ideas, Please! 136
Disclosure Documents...136
Submarine Patents (Periscope Up!) 139
Office of Independent Inventor Programs 141
Coming Attractions...142

10 It All Begins with a Patent Search   145
Looking for a Green Light 146
How to Conduct a Patent Search 147
Patent Attorney Directed Search.................................147
Direct Hire Professional Search..................................148
The Do-It-Yourself Patent Search 149
Patent and Trademark Depository Libraries 152
Electronic Databases 154
PTDL Publications 155
Patent Search Steps 156
Patent Classification System 157
How to Order Copies of Prior Art 158
What to Do with Your Search Results........................159
Searching Trademarks 159
The Last Word ... .160

11 How to Hire a Patent Attorney   161
Do You Need a Patent Attorney? 162
Is That Your Final Answer? 164
Levy's Rules for Hiring a Patent Attorney.................165
Another Money Saver 169

Part 4: Uncle Sam Wants (to Help) YOU!   171

12 How to Apply for a Utility Patent   173
Provisional Application for a Patent...........................174
Filing Date 174
Nonprovisional Application for a Utility Patent 175
Models Not Generally Required 180
Solamente Ingles, Por Favor 181
The Rules of the Game 182
I Do Solemnly Swear ... .183
Patentability of Computer Programs 185
Just the Fax, Please 186

13 Flower Power: How to Apply for a Plant Patent 189

Interest in Plant Patents, a Growing Business 190
Beyond the Garden Walls 191
Who Can Apply for a Plant Patent? 192
No Trespassing—Patent-Protected Grounds 192
Infringement 193
Turning to Trademarks 194
The Cost of Doing Business 194
Making Application 195
   The Application *195*
   Specification *195*
   The Claim *197*
   The Oath: I Do Solemnly Swear *197*
   Drawings *197*
   Specimens—Send Me No Flowers *197*
   Cost: Green Fees *198*
Inquiries...198
Provisions and Limitations 198
Inventorship 199
Asexual Reproduction 199
Helpful Hints 201

14 How to Apply for a Design Patent 203

Insurance Against Me-Too Competitors 204
Form over Function...204
Putting the Competition on Notice 205
Lawyers Need Not Apply..206
How to Find a Draftsman 206
Design Patents Can Be Valuable 207
Defining Design..209
Types of Designs and Modified Forms 209
Claims 209
Improper Subject Matter for Design Patents 210
The Difference Between Design and Utility Patents 210
Elements of a Design Patent Application 211
The Preamble..212
The Figure Descriptions...213
A Single Claim..213
Drawings or Photographs 214
   The Views *215*
   Surface Shading and Drafting Symbols............................*216*
   Broken Lines *216*
   Photographs..*217*

15 Mark Your Words   **219**

There Is Nothing Like a Brand, Nothing in the World 220
Trademarks Can Take Many Forms 221
Dollars & Scents 221
Supreme Court Makes a Colorful Decision.........................222
Lost in the Translation 222
United States Patent and Trademark Office 224
Correspondence and Information 225
What Kinds of Marks Are Available? 225
Function of Trademarks 227
Do You Need a Federal Trademark Registration? 227
Marks Not Subject to Registration 228
Registerable Marks...229
Searches for Conflicting Marks 230
Law Firm Trademark Search 230
Professional Trademark Search 230
  Making Application 232
Do-It-Yourself Trademark Search................................232
Searching the USPTO via the Internet 232
Establishing Trademark Rights 232
Terms of a Trademark 234
Types of Applications for Federal Registration 234
Who May File an Application? 234
Foreign Applicants...235
Where to Send the Application and Correspondence 235
Use of the "TM," "SM," and "®" Symbols 235
Examination 235
Publication for Opposition 236
Issuance of Certificate of Registration or
  Notice of Allowance 236

16 Securing Your Copy Rights   **239**

Copyrights—They're Different 240
The Copyright Office 240
What Would an Inventor Copyright?..............................241
How Do You Secure a Copyright?.................................241
Who May File an Application? 243
Notice of Copyright 243
How Long Does Copyright Last? 245
What Is Not Protected By Copyright? 245
Striking the Right CORDS 246
How to Submit Registrations 247
In Search of Copyright Records 247
For Further Information 248
How to Investigate the Copyright Status of a Work 248

Individual Searches of Copyright Records 249
Application Forms 249

17 I've Got a Secret   251

In the Court...252
Can Independent Inventors Have Trade Secrets?......................254
Uniform Trade Secrets Act...255
Keep a Tight Lip 255

**18 Say, Ah! The Patent Examination Process
      at the USPTO   257**

First Office Action 258
Your First Response 259
Final Rejection..260
Amending Your Application 260
Time for Response and Abandonment 263
How to Make Appeals 263
What Are Interference Proceedings?..264
What Rights Does a Patent Give You? 265
Maintenance Fees 266
Can Two People Own a Patent? 266
Can a Patent Be Sold? 267
Assignment of Patent Applications..267
Infringement of Patents 267
To Sue or Not to Sue 268
Patent Enforcement Insurance 269
Abandonment of Patents 271

Part 5: People Who Share, People Who Dare   273

**19 Hidden Treasures in Uncle Sam's
      High-Tech Closets   275**

National Institute of Standards and Technology 276
Advanced Technology Program (ATP) 277
  Partnerships 278
  Portfolio 278
  Proposals...279
Manufacturing Extension Partnership (MEP).............................280
In Search of Innovation at USG Labs 281
Open for "Your" Business 281
  Department of Defense 281
  National Aeronautics and Space Administration.....................282
  Department of Health and Human Services 282
  National Science Foundation 283
Department of Energy...283

Office of Industrial Technologies (OIT) 283
OIT Success Stories 284
Be Nice and Maybe You'll Get a Grant......................................285
DOE's Inventions and Innovation (I&I) Program 286
Notable Achievements 288
Small Business Administration 288
Small Business Innovation Research (SBIR) Program 288
How SBIR Works *290*
State-Supported SBIR Programs...*290*
Scoring and Selection Process *291*
SBIR Success Stories *292*
Small Business Technology Transfer (STTR) Program..............293
Federally Funded Research and Development
Centers (FFRDC'S) 293

20 Yes, Inventors, There Is a Santa Claus   295
An Industry Overview 296
The Toys Legends Are Made From 297
New York Toy Fair: A Networking Mecca 299
The Professional Edge 300
Questions for Self-Analysis 302
A Degree in Toy Design...305
TIA Freebie..305
The Hit Parade..305

21 Inventor Organizations   307
Expanding Your Network 308
Care to Share? 308
Inventor Organizations Thrive on American Soil 309
Truth in Packaging—Caveat Emptor...310
Take Your Pick 311
National Organizations 311
United Inventors Association (UIA) *311*
Intellectual Property Owners (IPO) *313*
The Value of State and Local Organizations.............................314
Informal Organizations *316*

Appendixes

A Agreements   317

B Resources   329

C Political Letter   349

Index   351

Foreword

Great ideas. Those are what drive our economy today. Great ideas form the framework of our future and may, in many cases, stand as cornerstones for new industries. But where do those powerful, great ideas come from?

Intuitively, we'd expect that most, if not all, significant inventions are actually the offspring of corporate R&D. Or we might assume that the bulk of really innovative technology emerges from those hundreds of federal laboratories across the country.

Not true.

You're not alone if you are surprised to learn that the majority of great ideas spring from the minds of independent inventors and entrepreneurs, most often working alone in garages or basement workshops. I'm talking about those ingenious commercial products and services we quickly come to demand—those remarkable innovations that change the way we live, how well we live, and even how long we live.

Independent inventors have always been America's most precious natural resource. But, while their ideas hold promise for helping us cope with our world, the inventors' own world remains one of constant struggle, and all too frequently, dismal discouragement.

It's a rocky path from idea to marketplace, and even the brightest of independent inventors are ill-equipped to make that journey on their own. They're quick to learn the harsh reality: Inventing is the easy part; *cashing in* on the invention is the far greater challenge. Realizing their limitations, where will they turn for help?

Bookstores, either brick and mortar or virtual style, are filled to capacity with *how-to-do-it* guides. Too few, however, deliver the wisdom of authors who have actually *done it* themselves. This is not a good thing. Imagine a fledgling airline pilot sharpening his cockpit skills by studying the sage advice of someone who *tried it once*; or worse, someone who simply likes airplanes.

More often than not, the ubiquitous inventor/writer relies on minimal idea commercialization experience—boasting of success more likely sparked by serendipity than marketing acumen. And, in most cases, it is evident that those self-proclaimed commercialization experts are banking on making their money from the reader (that's *you*), thus gaining in book sales the wealth that eluded them in the marketplace.

That's not the case with this book. Richard C. Levy brings a ray of sunlight to inventors everywhere who are struggling in the shadows.

In *The Complete Idiot's Guide to Cashing In on Your Inventions*, readers will discover a wealth of solid, down-to-earth advice delivered by a truly seasoned pro. Richard knows the business of commercializing new products. After all, he's *done it*; not just once, but many times.

Because he is passionate about extending a helping hand to other inventors and entrepreneurs, Richard has been sharing his rich experience for many years. As an author of several inventor-help books and a popular lecturer at conferences and seminars—frequently at his own expense—Richard tells his stories. He has a vast array of success stories to relate, yet he's quick to draw upon his nonsuccesses, as well. They often hold the most valuable lessons.

On many occasions, I've enjoyed the pleasure of sharing a podium with Richard, always marveling at his grasp of the art and nuances of commercialization. I envy his skill at keeping audiences riveted with insightful and entertaining dialogue—always on the edge of their seats. Happily, the following pages capture that same spirit and obvious passion for helping inventors reach their goals.

The *American Dream* lives, and Richard is here with this great book to help inventors and entrepreneurs learn how to be a part of it.

So, settle back, fasten your seat belt, and turn the page. Richard will be your skilled pilot as he helps *your* great idea take flight—while keeping your feet firmly planted on the ground.

Donald Grant Kelly, CEO, Academy of Applied Science

Founding Director, Office of Independent Inventor Programs, United States Patent Office

Introduction

"For more than 200 years independent inventors have been the backbone of America's economic strength. They don't have to be taught how to think "outside the box;" they do it naturally. From groundbreaking inventions, such as the laser, the MRI, imaging radar and sonar, the World Wide Web, and the personal computer, to everyday consumer products, such as Furby, the can opener, frozen pizza, the golf tee, and water skis, the contributions made by independent inventors dramatically change the way the world lives."

—Joanne M. Hayes-Rines, publisher, *Inventors' Digest.*

Of more than six and a half million patents granted in the United States since 1790, a few have had enormous impact on our lives while at the same time bringing fame and fortune to their inventors. The electric lamp, the transistor radio, the internal combustion engine, and the telephone come to mind quickly. Some inventions have had little or no impact on our lives, such as the Pet Rock and Cabbage Patch Kids, but have brought fame and fortune to their inventors. But the vast majority of inventions dreamed up during the last two hundred or so years has created no recognition or financial gain for their inventors. Why? These concepts were never commercialized. They have left no trace. You can bet that when the inventors applied for their patents, the inventions seemed like terrific ideas. But then something happened or, more accurately, did not happen.

What did not happen was the sale, and nothing happens until something is sold. Just as invention begins with resistance so does the sale. When resistance is overcome, the idea finds a successful structure, and the sale is made. *The Complete Idiot's Guide to Cashing In on Your Inventions* is about overcoming resistance, at myriad levels.

We are all laboratories, conducting experiments with thought and extending thought to function and utility. What we can accomplish is bewildering. All it usually takes is a jolt from outside to liberate one from inertia and the rut of habit. It is not enough to sit by and wait for things to happen; success comes to those who are proactive, not reactive, to people who possess the dare to go.

Some people say, if it's not broken, don't fix it. My mantra is *if it's not broken, break it.* Most successful products have typically been those that broke rules. For example, Monopoly was rejected by Parker Brothers in 1934. They told inventor Charles B. Darrow that his game took too long to play, the rules were too complicated, and players kept going around and around the board instead of ending up at a finish space. Monopoly was sent back because it had 52 fundamental playing errors. Darrow had such faith in the game that he published it himself. When news of its success reached Parker Brothers, the company licensed the game in 1935. Since then, it has sold over 200 million copies worldwide.

It is your birthright to break rules. It is your birthright to chase opportunities. It is your birthright to catch the imagination, try, fail, and try again, and again. It is your birthright to make mistakes as much as it is to succeed.

At the same time, while it's important to do things in a novel way, remember the advice of humorist Will Rogers: "If you're ridin' ahead of the herd, take a look back every now and then to make sure it's still there."

In this book, you'll learn how to ...

➤ Recognize your own potential.

➤ Avoid invention marketing rip-off schemes.

➤ Protect your invention through patents, trademarks, and/or copyrights.

➤ Pitch and license your concepts to manufacturers.

➤ Have prototypes made professionally.

➤ Make the best deal: a win/win.

➤ Dramatically reduce your legal expenses.

➤ Find expert advice and support via associations, publications, and the Internet.

In addition to learning how to license and protect your inventions, it is my hope that *The Complete Idiot's Guide to Cashing In on Your Inventions* will encourage you to ...

➤ Trust yourself more and recognize, accept, and take responsibility for the mutuality of events. Part of the adventure is accepting and capitalizing on consequences—even those that are unintended.

➤ Forbid yourself to be deterred by poor odds just because your mind has calculated that the opposition is too great. If making money from inventions was easy, everyone would do it. Remember, if Edison had stopped at, say, 30 filaments, we might still be in the dark.

➤ Do not fear the winds of hard times. Kites rise against the wind, not with it.

➤ Take your chances, not someone else's. The rewards are greater.

➤ Ask questions. If you do not ask a question, the answer is an automatic no.

➤ Have the courage to make mistakes. Mistakes are the byproduct of experimentation. Edison, asked if he was discouraged by failure, replied: "I have not failed. I am merely 500 ways closer to finding the solution."

➤ Remember that the best hitters fail 65 percent of the time. The price of never being wrong is never being right.

➤ Resist the herd instinct. Be yourself and be faithful to your own muse. Never give up your individuality.

➤ Look for opportunities, not guarantees.

➤ See a rejection as a rehearsal before the big event. There can be no success without failure.

➤ Learn the value of teamwork and how much people contribute to each other's success. There's no "i" in team.

➤ Pay attention to what author James Burke calls the *web of change*. Through it we are all linked to each other and to the future. No individual acts without causing the web to change. He talks about this phenomenon as The Pinball Effect.

➤ Do not fear pressure deadlines and situations. Diamonds are made under pressure, after all.

➤ Create change. Change is inevitable, except from vending machines.

➤ Enjoy the hunt. For it is here, in the moment of transition, in the rushing to a goal, that the power resides.

The Complete Idiot's Guide to Cashing In on Your Inventions is written for the ordinary person with the extraordinary idea and the yen to turn it into royalty income. It's a classic American landscape: Real fortunes being made by plain folks with an itch, courage, indefatigable entrepreneurial spirit, and, of course, the better idea.

A person's judgment cannot be better than the information upon which it is based. Information by itself is worthless. Information, when combined with insight, becomes the thing that greases wheels. I have based this book upon my personal empirical experiences in real world marketplaces. As such, it is based on business as it happens and not theoretical or hypothetical situations.

Once you have successfully taken an abstract concept through research, development, and licensing and forged it into a royalty-producing product, you will think it's a miracle that it happened at all.

My desire is that you will look upon this book as a chart, superimpose your own lines on it, and use it to navigate the stormy and hazardous waters of protecting, licensing, and commercializing inventions.

Important: The chapters in this book on the protection of your intellectual property are provided only as a primer. Intellectual property laws, regulations, filing fees, and so forth are in a constant state of change, pushed and pulled by technologies, marketplaces, and special interests. These chapters are not designed to take the place of competent legal counsel, which I encourage you to seek.

If you are going to play a sport, you need to have the right equipment. Baseball, for example, requires a ball, a glove, a bat, a cap, and a pair of spikes or athletic shoes. And so it is if you are going to engage in the enterprise of marketing your invention to potential licensees or investors. You need to be perceived as an athlete, and not a spectator. You need the uniform and the equipment if you want to be a pro. And you need to practice (read: experience multiple rejections).

It is a requirement today that you have the full gamut of tools, e.g., computer with high-speed Internet connection, e-mail account, fax machine, multiple-line phones for conferencing, voice mail/answer service, cellular phone, scanner/copier, and so on. This way you'll be able to keep pace with your companies.

How This Book Is Organized

I have designed this book to be a quick-access resource companion to accompany you throughout your journey from "What if?" to the deal and, hopefully, to riches (though financial reward must not be the only thing that drives you).

The sequence is a step-by-step blueprint for overcoming your fears, building your confidence, taking pride in your ideas, adapting to change, taking risks, and taking control.

Part 1: "How to Get Your Great Ideas on the Road" shares America's greatest traditions and visions as a center of innovation and free enterprise, home to the world's most prolific, daring, and successful inventors and entrepreneurs. Through all the wit, color, and home-spun truth I could muster, it asks you to look at yourself and realize that on any given day your dream can come true. But for this to happen, you must have the "Dare to Go," know where to go, and what to do when you get there.

The most important part of this book appears in Part 1. It instructs you in how avoid being ripped-off by carrion birds who toil under the guise of reputable invention marketing services. Part 1 helps you analyze whether it's better to license your invention or seek "adventure capital" and build a business.

By the time you finish reading Part 1, if I have done my job well, you will have started to highlight parts of these pages with a yellow marker.

Part 2: "Getting High Marks" assumes you have opted to go the licensing route. If, however, you want to establish your own manufacturing and marketing operation, then take four giant steps to Part 3.

Part 2 explains how to find the right company for your invention, get through the door, pitch the idea, and make a deal if you are fortunate enough to be afforded an opportunity. It's all about the hunt!

Part 3: "Goin' for the Gold" takes you to the U.S. Patent and Trademark Office. Learn what makes it tick and how you can take advantage of its invaluable services. You'll also learn ways to conduct a search for prior art.

It wraps on a very important issue—how to hire competent patent counsel.

Part 4: "Uncle Sam Wants (to Help) You!" explains the different kinds of ip protection—e.g., utility patent, plant patent, design patent, trademark, copyright, and trade secret. The information is designed as a primer, not to take the place of a patent counsel. The final chapter in Part 4 takes you behind the scenes at the U.S. Patent and Trademark Office for a look at how your application will be handled.

Part 5: "People Who Share, People Who Dare"; Uncle Sam has gone from being a principal customer of technology to wanting to share its technologies with private industry and build partnerships. There is a smorgasbord of delicious opportunities for you, and Chapter 19 is the appetizer.

Chapter 20 gives you a primer on the toy industry, one of the last great frontiers for the entrepreneurial inventor.

While I can do nothing to alleviate patent fees, I can help reduce your legal expenses. To that end, I have provided a confidential nondisclosure form and a licensing agreement that you can use as templates for your own transactions, potentially saving your lawyer hours of work and you thousands of dollars.

Extras

To add some additional perspective, inspiration, and a bit of off-road mental adventure, I have peppered this book with six different types of collateral information, which can be found in the following floating boxes.

Bright Ideas

This box gives you inspirational and frequently entertaining stories behind well-known inventions and their frequently not-so-well-known inventors.

Meet Your U.S. Patent Office

This box features short profiles of some key USPTO officials. I wish, alas, there was room to list even more bio sketches, but Mike, my editor, sets the limits.

Take My Words for It

What do you call a dictionary for inventors? How about an *inventionary*? Ouch! Well, whatever you call it, in these boxes you will find buzzwords, terms, and expressions used by inventors in the course of their enterprise.

Fast Facts

This box offers a *potpourri* of factoids and assorted trivia that will contribute to your greater understanding of the invention business.

411

Here you'll find important phone numbers, addresses, and Web sites.

Notable Quotables

This box provides inspirational nuggets and pearls of wisdom that I have collected over the years and stored in a drawer. You'll also find advice from successful inventors. It is based upon their empirical, nontheoretical experiences as front-line soldiers in the trench warfare of intellectual property development and licensing.

Wacky Patents

For a dash of humor and good cheer, in each chapter I have featured two wacky patents. But, though they may be off-the-wall to some of us, I have the greatest respect for their inventors. Who knows where an invention, such as a dust bag for a dog, will lead?

If you have researched inventors and inventions, you know that discrepancies, especially over inventorship, come with the territory. Ralph Waldo Emerson, 100 plus years ago, realized this, too. He explained it like this:

"'Tis frivolous to fix pedantically the date of particular inventions. They have all been invented over and over fifty times."

I choose to use the terms *inventor*, *developer*, and *creator* interchangeably, as does industry, to signify one or more of the independent creative forces behind an invention, usually a signatory to a license agreement and, as such, a participant in any advances and royalties.

John Melius, the program chair for Inventor's Network of the Capital Area (INCA), prefers to refer to himself as a product developer. He feels this designation puts him closer mentally to commercialized product. An inventor is typically dealing with something that is not a complete product ready for sale. It's an interesting approach.

Many inventors quoted in this book are extremely prolific. To be fair to everyone, including my editors, who need to deal with space considerations, I decided to list only one invention credit per inventor. The exception is A. Eddy Goldfarb, the dean of independent toy inventors, who has licensed more than 600 inventions since he left the Silent Service after World War II.

The process of invention and innovation is not easy to analyze. Therefore, I did not even attempt at listing co-inventing credits. Anyone who knows this business understands that it would be an impossible task. Therefore, if you see more than one person credited with the invention of a product, there is probably a good reason for it. Paul Saffo, a research fellow with the Menlo Park, California–based Institute for the Future, put it well when he told *Newsweek* that trying to understand the process of innovation is like shoveling smoke.

While my book focuses mostly on the independent inventor, this is not to imply that there is a lack of creativity or inventiveness at the corporate level. It is just the opposite. Many outstanding concepts come from in-house. Further, the contributions made by R&D and marketing executives to outside submissions often make the difference between success and failure. This has surely been the case with my products.

It is my most sincere hope that this book will intrigue, inform, entertain, and turn on a light bulb or two for even the most seasoned inventor.

This book is highly organized, so you'll be able to find what you're looking for. But you're an inventor, and when things are too organized, well, you get the picture. So, go ahead; just plunge in and browse around.

I am sure I have missed a few things here and there, but as Goethe noted: *"Incompleteness stimulates."*

Curtain up. Light the lights.

Richard C. Levy

Acknowledgments

The Complete Idiot's Guide to Cashing In on Your Inventions depended heavily upon the cooperation and assistance of a great many people. During the course of my research, I interviewed independent inventors, federal and state government officials, patent attorneys, corporate executives, editors of professional publications, educators, and members of inventor organizations. Their warm reception, hospitality, expertise, and good cheer made my assignment one that I'll always remember fondly.

Richard J. Apley, Director, Office of Independent Inventor Programs, United States Patent and Trademark Office, was an invaluable source of assistance. A 35-year USPTO veteran, Dick proactively led me through the ever-shifting bureaucratic landscape and its myriad arcane rules and regulations. When I told him about my desire to have the USPTO material fact-checked, he volunteered to personally read and comment on select chapters and enlist Supervisory Examiners and other officials to read the rest of it for currency and accuracy.

George Harvill, President, Greentree Information Services, a patent searcher *extraordinaire* and loyal friend, would fetch research material at the USPTO and run it to my office. When I had the idea to include wacky patents, the next morning a stack of them was on my desk. As always, George was there, on time, on point, informed, and organized.

Across the Big Pond in Melbourne, Australia, business associate and fairdinkum, ridgy-didge, dinky-di friend Malcolm Hall also volunteered to proofread the book. How could I pass up such a generous offer, especially from such a talented fellow? Mal had some terrific "catches."

At the U.S. Patent and Trademark Office, thanks also to Cathie Kirik, Program Analyst, Office of Independent Inventor Programs; Maria Hernandez and Ruth Nyblod, Public Affairs Specialists; John Cabeca, Supervisory Patent Examiner, Technology Center 2100; Bruce Campell, Supervisory Patent Examiner, Technology Center 1600; Lou Zarfas, Supervisory Patent Examiner, Design Technology Center 2900; and Amanda "Mandy" Putnam, Manager, Patent and Trademark Depository Library Program.

The list continues. Hans Petersen, Public Affairs Officer and Maurice Swinton, Director, SBIR Program, Small Business Administration; Michael Baum and Janice Kosko, Public Affairs Officers, National Institute for Standards and Technology; Howard Shapiro, Press Officer, Federal Trade Commission; Mary Berghaus Levering, Associate Register for National Copyright Programs Copyright Office; Zoran Franicevich, Program Analyst, OIT; Robert J. Marchick, Esq., Patent Counsel, Department of Energy; and William M. Welch, Assistant United States Attorney.

In private industry, among others: David Berko, Senior Vice President, Inventor Relations, Tiger Electronics, Inc.; Lawrence Bernstein, CEO, Plymouth, Inc.; Christa Brelin, Editor, Gale Research; Diane Cardinale, Public Information Manager, Toy Industry Association; Martin Connors, Publisher, Visible Ink Press; Tom Dusenberry, CEO, Call IT Entertainment, Inc.; Andy Gibbs, CEO, Patent Café.com, Inc.; Harold P. Gordon, Vice Chairman, Hasbro Inc.; Harvey Lepselter, Senior Vice President for R&D and Marketing, Babies 'n Things, Inc.; Joel M. Lerner, President, Environmental Design; Linda M. Long, CEO, Rainy Day Research; Cathy Meredith, Vice President, Licensing, Hasbro Games Group; Joanne M. Hayes-Rines, Publisher, *Inventor's Digest*; Dave Kapell, Chairman and Founder, Magnetic Poetry, Inc.; Ronald J. Riley, Executive Director, InventorEd, Inc.; Michael Ross, Executive Vice President and Publisher, *World Book*, Inc.; Sandy Schellhase, Senior Licensing Coordinator, Hasbro Games Group; Roger A. Shiffman, President and CEO, Tiger Electronics, Inc.; Dale Siswick, Senior Vice President, R&D, Hasbro Games Group; Barry Tunick, President and CEO, Centuri Corporation, Inc.; Lawrence J. Udell, Executive Director, California Inventor Center; Herbert C. Wamsley, Executive Director, Intellectual Property Owners, Inc.; and John K. Williamson, Assistant General Counsel, Intellectual Property, PPG Industries, Inc.

To Ronald O. Weingartner, thanks for allowing me to pull material from our book, *Inside Santa's Workshop* (Henry Holt, 1990).

Thanks to my agent, Jeff Davidson. He suggested Alpha Books, encouraged me to write an outline, and then sold it. At Alpha Books, heaps of gratitude to my editors: Mike Sanders, for his championship of this book, sound judgment, and patience with my telephone queries; Amy Gordon, a fellow Emersonian, for her sharp editorial skills; and Billy Fields, Cari Luna, and the rest of the team for their contributions.

A special note of gratitude to an inventor of the highest order, David Hampton (a.k.a. WACO Niner Seven Yankee Mike) for his vision, dedication, generosity, and genius in the creation of Furby and Shelby. And for their friendship, entrepreneurial spirit, business acumen, and unwavering confidence, thanks to Randy Rissman and Roger Shiffman, the former chairman and president, respectively, of Tiger Electronics, to whom we licensed Furby. I am appreciative to have had the opportunity to partner with you. It was dah/doo-ay all the way.

I also want to mention a few others whose friendship, creativity, and good cheer continue to make my work exciting and interesting: George C. Atamian, who combines scientific knowledge with prep school humor and knows how to travel; John Gray, best-selling author and interplanetary talent; Richard J. Maddocks, a world-class design engineer; Tim Moodie, a "driving force" in my games (Taxi!); and Michael Ross, who is as bright and clear as meticulously beveled crystal with a glinting edge.

Everything I do involves my family, and this book was no exception. My daughter, Bettie, a university senior and a talented writer, jumped in with her awesome editorial skills. She also impressed me with her ability to read and edit the manuscript while running on a treadmill.

There is no way to repay my wife, Sheryl, for tolerating the 18-hour days I spent at the computer while I wrote, and all the sacrifices my schedule required her to make. But, as with everything I tackle, she provided unqualified support and wise counsel, and kept our lives and business on track until the book gods released me from their grasp.

Last but not least, a special mention to SZL who's forever in my heart, Richie and Mimi in Paradox and Puerto Escondido, Monty in Brookline, Lady-girl in Hudson, The Kinky Man in Fairfax Station, Jeff in Hotlanta, and Haig der Marderosian, wherever you are.

The Beck Rules!

Trademarks

Part 1

How to Get Your Great Ideas on the Road

There is nothing more difficult, more risky, or more uncertain than to take the lead in anything. This is because people eschew change. Change makes them nervous. It brings in elements of the unknown. I call these people the Gottas. Gotta do it this way. Gotta do it that way. Well, this section is, in part, about how not to let the Gottas get you.

These chapters are designed to tighten up your mental bolts, fill your tanks with verbal fuel, and rev your self-confidence until it redlines and sends you out full throttle to meet and win over strangers—and build lasting relationships.

There are no stop signs along the road to cashing in on your invention, just an occasional yield right of way. There are no one-way streets. There are only wide, five-lane freeways with no speed control.

Along the way, you can expect to be ambushed by road pirates who will attempt to pull you over and steal your money and intellectual property. These chapters will show you how to avoid them.

Lastly, you will learn the advantages and disadvantages of licensing your invention, vis-à-vis seeking venture capital to commercialize it.

Ready? Engine purring? If so, buckle up, release the brake, and prepare yourself for an exciting ride.

Chapter 1

How to Realize Your Full Potential

In This Chapter

➤ Makin' it happen

➤ Overcoming the naysayers

➤ America, start your engines

➤ Genius, insight, and passion

➤ Levy's 10 Commandments of Business

"There is not one industry that could house and sustain all the inventors that could add value with their creativity. Many inventors flourish because they are independent with all that entails. Independent inventors are and will remain a vital element for industry."

—Harold P. "Sonny" Gordon, Vice Chairman, Hasbro, Inc.

Heavier-than-air flying machines are impossible, the well-known British mathematician and physicist William Kelvin assured everyone in 1895.

Man can never tap the power of the atom, said Nobel Laureate and physicist Robert Andrews Millikan, credited with being the first to isolate the electron and measure its charge.

Everything that can be invented has been invented, stated another man of vision, Charles H. Duell, Director of the U.S. Patent Office, in 1899.

TRW, Inc., the global technology, manufacturing, and service company, listed these observations in a *Wall Street Journal* ad that was tagged with the line: *There's no future in believing something can't be done. The future is in making it happen.*

What the people just quoted did not understand, quite obviously, is what inventors in high-tech labs to basement workshops across America are proving each day:

➤ There is no future in the word impossible.

➤ Results first. Theory second.

➤ Alert optimism beats conservative skepticism.

➤ Failure breeds success. Celebrate it!

Pessimism arrests growth and sensitivity. It has the same effect on you that leaving the cap off a bottle of Coke has on the pop. You become flat. What you need in order to have any chance at success is tons of energy, or in soda terms, high carbonation. You will never reach your limits without being fully charged.

Overcoming Naysayers

In his first three years in business, Henry Ford went broke three times. Dr. Seuss' first children's book was rejected by 23 publishers. The twenty-fourth publisher sold six million copies. In 1902, a young poet had his poems rejected by *Atlantic Monthly* as being *"too vigorous ..."* but Robert Frost persevered. Michael Jordan was cut from his high school basketball team. The University of Bern rejected a Ph.D. dissertation, saying that it was irrelevant and fanciful. Albert Einstein was disappointed but not down for the count.

Richard Hooker's book *M*A*S*H* was turned down by 21 publishers. Then Morrow released it in 1968, and it became a barn-burning best-seller, and a movie, then one of the most popular television series of all time.

In 1966, Yale University student Fred Smith wrote his thesis on a business that moved packages overnight through a central hub in Memphis. "The concept is interesting and well-formed," responded his professor. "But in order to earn better than a C, the idea needs to be feasible."

In each of the aforementioned instances, innovation, innovators, and positive thinking met, challenged, and overcame negative and myopic people—the type that go through life blocking light and avoiding anything that sounds iffy. Not every idea deserves to be supported. But I am driven to total distraction when ideas are blown off because they do not follow a well-known business model, scientific or engineering principle, proven pattern, or are flippantly labeled as not being feasible by people who are experts in keeping up with the art of yesterday.

My friend Ceil Hughes up in northeastern Pennsylvania has the right idea. She approaches life every day knowing that there are no guarantees no matter how many yesterdays proved something to be right or wrong. She wears a small gold scroll locket on a necklace that has a piece of paper inside that says: "Yesterday is history. Tomorrow is a mystery."

By the way, just because an idea is not worthy of pursuit, the inventor might be an asset. You know the old saw about not tossing out the baby with the bath water. I have lost track of how many times I was shown a technology that was inappropriate for my purposes, and to which I replied, "Please introduce me to the genius who came up with this."

WACKY PATENTS

Animal Ear Protectors
Patented November 18, 1980
United States Patent 4,233,942

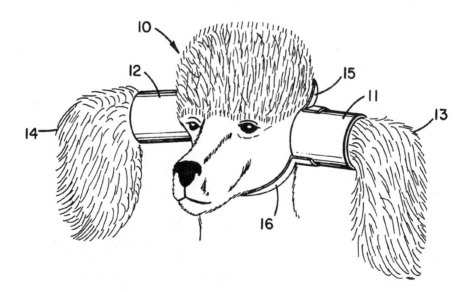

The First Pitch

Before pitching an idea, realize it will be shot down by at least a few companies, if not all of them. Like batters in baseball, many executives do not swing at the first pitch. Only once or twice in my career has a concept sold to the first looker.

Bright Ideas

Tired of the stains made by his fountain pen, Hungarian journalist, painter, and inventor Laszlo Biro (1899–1985) and his brother, George, developed a pen with a ball point that wrote without leaving ink blotches. Laszlo is credited as the pen's inventor although not the inventor of the first ballpoint pen, or the best design.

During World War II, the ballpoint pen became standard equipment in military aircraft—it would work at high altitudes—and with this capability came recognition for this innovative writing instrument.

In 1945, a New York City department store introduced a ballpoint pen and sold 10,000 units in one day at $12.50 each. Today billions are sold worldwide, many for pennies apiece.

Our *Adverteasing* game was rejected by Milton Bradley, Parker Brothers, and other companies before Cadaco, a small, family-owned publisher from Chicago, licensed it.

The game required players to recall slogans, jingles, and advertising trivia. It went on to sell over one million units. Our Hot Lixx electronic guitar, hugely successful for Tyco Toys, was first shown to and rejected by Mattel, Hasbro, Kenner, Matchbox, and others who claimed that musical instruments would not sell. It became an instant bestseller.

In the early '80s, there was not a single publisher willing to take on the self-help book *Richard C. Levy's Secrets of Selling Inventions*, so the 200-page, soft cover was self-published and sold by mail order. Once it had proven itself, earning in the area of $120,000, an enhanced edition was licensed to Gale Research. It received national distribution. The proposal for what became this book was seen by no less than a dozen publishers before the editors at Pearson Education saw its potential, put their tray tables and seat backs into the upright position, fastened their seat belts, and signed on for this ride. It was just right for them.

Fast Facts

In 2000, inventors from California were issued 19,844 patents, making it number one out of the 50 states in patent awards. The least number of patents, 57, was issued to residents of Alaska. Two patents were awarded to inventors living in Guam.

The aforementioned stories are just a few of more than a couple hundred such instances in my own career. The moral? Never give up. Follow the light of faith. It alone can trample underfoot the status quo, smite yes-but-isms, and devitalize onslaughts of skepticism and negativism.

America, the Land of Opportunity

We Americans invented free enterprise. Nowhere in the world do people have more freedom and encouragement to innovate and be different than from sea to shining sea. A visitor to this country in the late 1820s observed that the moment an American hears the word invention he pricks up his ears.

It is said that we Americans are men and women with "new eras in our brains." Our history is replete with examples of independent and courageous individuals who succeeded by doing things differently, people who believed in themselves and their ideas.

Alexis de Tocqueville, the French writer who visited America in 1831, wrote about Americans: "They have all a lively faith in the perfectibility of man, they judge that the diffusion of knowledge must necessarily be advantageous, and the consequences of ignorance fatal; they all consider society as a body in a state of improvement, humanity as a changing scene, in which nothing is, or ought to be, permanent; and they admit that what appears to them today to be good, may be superseded by something better tomorrow. America is a land of wonders in which everything is in constant motion and every change seems an improvement. The idea of novelty is there indissolubly connected with the idea of amelioration. No natural boundary seems to be set to the efforts of man; and in his eyes what is not yet done is only what he has not yet attempted to do." On the occasion of the 150th anniversary of the Patent Act of 1836, then vice president George Bush, speaking at the National Museum of American History, said, "It takes a special kind of independence to invent something. You put yourself and your ideas on the line. And maybe some people will say that you're crazy or that you're impractical, but for [over] two centuries, millions of Americans have ignored the ridicule. They've worked on ideas. From those ideas, they've started businesses. And many of those businesses have grown and are our greatest industrial companies, companies like Xerox, Ford Motor Company, American Telephone and Telegraph, and Apple Computer. Think of what America would be like if the skeptics had silenced the inventors."

411

Inventor's Digest, billed as America's only inventors' magazine, first appeared in 1985. Serious inventors should read this excellent publication. It delivers information by the shovel load. The Web site is www.inventorsdigest.com.

This independence was never truer than in the cases of the following inventive Americans, people who dared to be different and refused to swap incentive for security. Many of their names have become well known.

Towering Examples of American Ingenuity

In 1923, Clarence "Bob" Birdseye, the Father of Frozen Food, got a patent on quick-freezing. Dr. William "Billy" Scholl patented his first arch support in 1904 at the age of 22. Beginning in 1896 and over a 47-year career, one-time slave George Washington Carver developed more than 300 products from peanuts alone. On a cold day in January 1839, Charles Goodyear vulcanized rubber. Yankee tinker Eli Whitney transformed the South with the cotton gin he invented in 1792. New Englander Edwin H. Land demonstrated his first instant cameras in 1947.

Many inventors are known for more than one product. William Lear, best known for the Learjet, also received a patent on the first car radio and the eight-track tape system. His company eventually became Motorola. In 1845, Peter Cooper, inventor of the famous locomotive Tom Thumb, was awarded the first patent for a gelatin dessert, which later became known as Jell-O. George Westinghouse not only invented air brakes for railroad cars, but he is also credited with a type of gas meter and a pipeline system that safely conducted natural gas into homes.

Bell Telephone was named for Alexander Graham Bell, a former Boston University professor, who received his first patent for the telephone and a telephone system in 1876.

Other Fields of Dreams and Dreamers from Other Fields

Some well-known Americans are famous for something other than their inventions. Actress Hedy Lamarr patented a sophisticated anti-jamming device to foil Nazi radar during World War II. After the patent expired, Sylvania adapted the invention, and it is still used in satellite communication. Author Samuel L. Clemens (a.k.a. Mark Twain) patented a pair of suspenders. Zeppo Marx patented a wrist-worn heart alarm. Novelist John Dos Passos is listed as co-inventor of a toy pistol that blows bubbles. Actress Julie Newmar patented a type of pantyhose. Singer Edie Adams patented a ring-shaped cigarette and cigar holder. Confederate General James E. B. Stuart patented a method of attaching sabers to belts. Escape artist Harry Houdini held a patent on a diver's suit that permitted escape. Bette Nesmith, mother of Michael Nesmith of The Monkees, invented Liquid Paper typewriter correction fluid.

Notable Quotables

"An invasion of armies can be resisted, but not an idea whose time has come."

—Victor Hugo, French author

Who's Witcomb L. Judson?

Other Americans are not as well known as their inventions. In 1893, Witcomb L. Judson of Chicago filed the first patent on a slide fastener for shoes ("Clasp Locker Or Unlocker For Shoes"), known today as the zipper. During the Civil War, Martha Coston invented a safety flare for which the U.S. government paid her $20,000. Northam Warren, after graduating from Detroit College of Pharmacy, originated the first liquid cuticle remover (Cutex) in 1911. Newspaper editor Carlton Magee invented the parking meter in Oklahoma City in 1932. Walter Hunt patented the safety pin in 1849. Joseph F. Glidden protected his idea for barbed wire in 1874. Alonzo D. Phillios struck a bright idea in 1836 when he patented the friction match.

Not all inventions are so conventional. Two virtually unknown American inventors, Philip Leder of Chestnut Hill, Massachusetts, and Timothy A. Stewart of San Francisco, California, made history on April 12, 1988 when U.S. Patent No. 4,736,866, entitled *Transgenic Non-Human Mammals* was issued. The Harvard University researchers were awarded the first patent covering an animal. Their technique introduced activated cancer genes into early-stage mice embryos. The resulting mice were born with activated cancer genes in all their cells. These mice, extremely sensitive to cancer-causing chemicals, developed tumors quickly if exposed to small amounts of such chemicals. The resulting value to medical and scientific research is considerable.

There are plant inventors, too, an example of whose work is covered by U.S. Patent No. 4,092,145. John Wesley Willard Sr. protected a method of prolonging the life or beauty of cut flowers. The patent abstract reads, in part: "Cut flowers are intimately contacted with water containing a catalytically effective amount of a novel catalyst to prolong their life or beauty. In a preferred variant, the water may also contain water soluble catalyst treated lignite." This invention has 22 claims of invention.

Answering the Call

As diverse as the aforementioned inventions are, the inventors share many things in common, characteristics that you too will need to fulfill your aspirations and see your inventions patented, licensed, manufactured, and commercialized. Perhaps the most important characteristic shared by these people is that, while others reflected on their ideas, these inventors answered the call.

Investing in Your Invention

The biggest barrier facing you is not the amount of money in your bank account, but the amount of time you have to invest in what it takes to

Take My Words for It

Kill Fee: A negotiated payment made to an inventor by a manufacturer if an agreement is prematurely terminated prior to the start of production and through no fault of the inventor.

commercialize your invention. You won't read this book, research a company, prepare a proposal, walk in with a prototype, pitch it, hammer out a license, and start cashing advance and royalty checks. This is a long, tough road. You have heard this old saw by Thomas Edison before, but it's worth repeating: "Genius is one percent inspiration and 99 percent perspiration."

Whether you are a clerk, plumber, psychologist, sailor, lawyer, dentist, priest, travel agent, or university president, if you are the best at what you do, it has taken your full-time focus and hands-on experience. You did not reach the height of success working part-time. Nothing great was ever achieved without blood, sweat, and tears.

Common denominators that appear in the stories of each and every successful individual are sacrifice and risk. People who have reached the top of their game did not do it by standing back shivering and contemplating the cold waters of uncertainty, but they jumped right in with both feet, and scrambled through as best they could.

Bud Grant, the former head coach of the Minnesota Vikings, said it well: "You practice hard all week long so that when the ball bounces your way on Sunday afternoon, you will know what to do with it." It's no different for you. You'll play as you practice.

I am not suggesting that you give up your day job tomorrow, but that you prepare yourself for a change of attitude, pace, and routine. If you work hard enough at it, even if you are not the most creative inventor, you will position yourself within the lightning-strike zone.

WACKY PATENTS

Substance Dispensing Headgear
Patented October 19, 1999
United States Patent 5,966,743

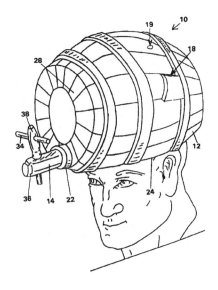

Education Isn't Everything

Thomas Alva Edison received 1,093 patents, four posthumously. Perhaps the greatest inventor in history, Edison was a grammar school dropout who had just three months of formal education. Edwin H. Land, inventor of the Polaroid camera; Bill Gates, founder and CEO of Microsoft and one of the nation's richest individuals; and R. Buckminster Fuller, the social theorist, all dropped out of Harvard. So, the fact that you do not have a formal education shouldn't stop you. The world is full of intelligent people who have not had the benefit of a formal education. Conversely, just because you may have graduated from a top university, I would not put too much emphasis on it. When my dad, a former assistant attorney general for the Commonwealth of Pennsylvania, interviewed job candidates, he would remind them that just because they graduated from Harvard, Yale, or another prestigious law school, it did not impress him. He would tell the young lawyers, "I'll be impressed when the school brags about you."

In the end, product is king in the world of inventing and licensing.

An exceptionally high IQ may mean something in some fields, but studies show that the threshold for creativity is an IQ of about 130. After that, *Business Week* reports, IQ doesn't make much difference—such nonintellectual traits, such as values and personality, become more important.

Bright Ideas

In May of 1849, when Abraham Lincoln was a Congressman from Illinois, he received Patent No. 6,469 for "A Device for Buoying Vessels over Shoals." It consisted of a set of bellows attached to the hull of a ship just below the waterline. On reaching a shallow place the bellows were inflated, and the ship, thus buoyed, was expected to float clear. Lincoln whittled the prototype of the invention with his own hands.

Lincoln's appreciation of inventions was later to be of great service to the nation. John Ericcson's *Monitor*, the ironclad ship that defeated the *Merrimac*, would never have been built except for Lincoln's insistence, nor would the Spencer repeating rifle have been adopted for use by the Army.

Lincoln had high praise for the patent office, reflecting on the institution's beginnings: "The Patent System added the fuel of interest to the fire of genius."

My philosophical and social wiring were installed primarily by three people: Daddy, who was bright, well-reasoned, honest, and cool under fire; and Mother and Nana, two strong, savvy, and creative liberated ladies. Their taste and social skills had no equal. In college, my wrestling coach, Jim Peckham, taught me that to win was not enough, one had to *"earn the right to win."* Add to this the gifts bestowed upon me by my wife, Sheryl, and our daughter, Bettie, and I was good to go the distance. I was always encouraged to try things, even at the risk of failure. I was brought up to believe that I could accomplish anything that I put my mind to doing.

Bright Ideas

On December 19, 1871, Mark Twain received Patent No. 121,992 for "An Improvement in Adjustable and Detachable Straps for Garments," otherwise known as suspenders. Twain, who later lost a fortune investing money on the inventions of others, actually received three U.S. Patents: The second was in 1873 on his famous *Mark Twain's Self-Pasting Scrapbook*, and the third was in 1885 for a game to help people remember important historical dates.

In Twain's novel, *A Connecticut Yankee in King Arthur's Court*, his character Sir Boss remarks that "a country without a patent office and good patent laws is just like a crab and can't travel any way but sideways and backways."

Levy's 10 Commandments for Success

To be successful in the exciting, frequently gut-wrenching enterprise of product development and commercialization, it takes a lot more than a good idea, a strong patent, and luck. In fact, the idea is about 10 percent of the equation. You need to understand the following concepts if you want to beat what can sometimes seem like insurmountable odds.

1. *Do not take yourself too seriously.* Do not take your idea too seriously either. The world will probably survive without your idea. Industry will probably survive without your idea. You may need it to survive, but no one else does.

2. *The race is not always to the swift, but to those who keep running.* It is a mistake to think anything is made overnight other than baked goods and newspapers. My

first corollary is—*Nothing is as easy as it looks*. My second corollary is—*Everything takes longer than you think*. You win some, you lose some, some are rained out, but always suit up for the game and stick with it.

When the Convair Company could not find a way to stop San Diego's night fog from rusting Atlas missile parts they were manufacturing, it put out a public plea for assistance. Norm Larsen, a local chemist, responded with 39 formulas. But it was his fortieth that held the answer, producing a petroleum-based chemical that gets under water and displaces it through the pores of metal. Larsen's invention became WD-40; sales for this product topped $100 million. By the way, WD-40 stands for Water Displacement-40th formula.

Notable Quotables

"If you start to take Vienna—take Vienna."

—Napoleon

It is not speed that separates winners from losers. It is perseverance. The salesperson driving 30 miles at 4:15 P.M. to make one last sales call before 5:00 P.M., the actor auditioning for the hundredth time, the writer facing a keyboard every day creating 25 pages to get four or five that are keepers, and the athlete never quitting the team all show perseverance. That is the quality required to hit the heights of personal achievement.

3. *You can't do it all yourself.* My success continues to be the result of unselfish, highly talented, and creative partners and associates willing to face the frustrations, rejections, and seemingly open-ended time frames that are inherent to any product development and licensing exercise. I have also been lucky to meet and work with very creative, understanding, and courageous corporate executives willing to believe in me and gamble on our concepts. When they work well together, nothing can stop the combo of entrepreneurs and the corporate *intrapreneurs*.

It is the cross-pollination and subsequent synergism of these two forces that result in success, success in which all parties share. For if any link in this complex and often serpentine chain breaks, an entire project could flag.

A good way to put it all into perspective is to sit through the credit crawl that runs following a television show or feature film. It becomes immediately evident how many more people than the stars, and/or a celebrated director, were involved to get the show on the air or screen.

While not disclaiming the telephone, Alexander Graham Bell noted that "great discoveries and improvements invariably involve the cooperation of many minds. I may be given credit for having blazed the trail but when I look at the subsequent developments, I feel the credit due to others rather than myself."

Bright Ideas

Alfred Nobel, a Swedish chemist and industrialist, while trying to find a way to make nitroglycerin safe to handle, patented the dynamite stick in 1867. He combined the powerful liquid with a fine, chalky powder and packed it into a paper cylinder. The term dynamite is derived from the Greek word meaning *power*.

The Nobel Prizes were established using money from the sales of his chemical explosives.

Fast Facts

The USPTO maintains all patent applications in the strictest confidence until the patent is issued. After the patent is issued, however, the Office file containing the application and all correspondence leading up to issuance of the patent is made available in the Files Information Unit for inspection by anyone. Copies of these files may be purchased from the Office.

It's perhaps summed up best by advertising industry legend Bill Bernbach, who said an idea can turn to dust or magic, depending on the talent that rubs against it.

4. *Keep your ego under control.* Creative and inventive people, according to profile, hate to be rejected or criticized for any reason. They are usually critical of others. They are also extremely defensive where their creations are concerned.

An out-of-control ego kills more opportunities than anything. While we inventors need a healthy ego to serve as our body armor, it can quickly get out of hand and become arrogance if not governed. Great mistakes are made when we feel that we are beyond questioning.

I have always found that my concepts are enhanced by the right touch. Working together or in competition, others contribute time and time again to making an idea more useful or marketable. Share an idea, get back a better one.

I have worked with many egomaniacs, and most ended up as lonely as the survivors of Ft. Zinderneuf. Unchecked egocentricity can be a major source for failure. Arrogance has no place in the process. So, if ego is a problem, check it here before you read on.

5. *You will always miss 100 percent of the shots you do not take.* Do not be afraid to make mistakes. If you do not put forth the effort, you will not fail, but you will not succeed either. Inaction will keep opportunities from coming your way.

Nobel Prize-winner William Shockley, known as the father of the transistor, described the process of inventing the transistor at Bell Labs as *creative failure methodology*.

Trust yourself. Never permit yourself to be deterred by poor odds because your mind has calculated that the opposition is too great. I once asked Dr. Erno Rubik, inventor of Rubik's Cube, why children are so good at solving his puzzles and adults often do not even try. "Because no one has told the children that they cannot do it," he explained.

6. *Do not invent just for the financial rewards.* We all want to make money. This is only natural. It is what we are taught from the earliest age in America. But you should be motivated by the gamesmanship as well. It may sound trite, but people who do things just for money usually come up shortchanged. Or to put it another way, pigs get fat, while hogs get slaughtered.

Although I have negotiated and received seven-figure advance and guarantee packages, there were times that I took a small advance against higher royalties and earned seven figures on the other end. And sometimes I didn't earn anything.

As important as money is, you need to use common sense and judge cases on their own merits. Each industry has its own standards that you will use as a baseline.

From time to time, I do paid corporate consulting. I charge by the hour plus out-of-pocket expenses. I insist upon first-class travel, top of the line hotels, etc. On the other hand, I do not charge the licensees of my products for my time when it involves a product of mine. I just ask for out-of-pocket costs. I look at it as a marketing expense. I analyze everything in terms of risk-reward. But most of the time, I see it as my obligation and pleasure to do what it takes. If successful, I will benefit on the other end through royalties and more business, hopefully.

Bright Ideas

In 1948, George de Mestral, a Swiss engineer, took a hunting trip into the Alps. As he picked burrs off his socks and pants, De Mestral wondered why they stuck to his clothing. When he looked closely at the burrs, he realized that tiny hooks on them were catching to thread loops in the clothing.

A light bulb went off in de Mestral's head. Eight years later Velcro was born. The patent on Velcro has expired, but the trademark is alive and the technology is used in all kinds of applications from shoes to space suits.

I believe one of the shortcomings of the independent inventor is that he or she insists upon being paid for every hour of labor. If you feel this way, get over it. Look at the bigger picture. Learn to trade short-term security for long-term goals. Except when

I worked in the kitchen and bookstore at college, I cannot recall ever being paid by the hour. My corporate and government jobs were not based upon hourly rates. Executives are not paid by the hour.

If all you want to do is make money, and take no risk, Will Rogers has some advice: "The quickest way to double your money is to fold it over and put it back in your pocket."

7. *If you bite the bullet, be prepared to taste gunpowder.* Not every idea or decision works, whether they involve an invention or a method of presenting product to a potential licensee. So often do I find myself victimized by the Law of Unintended Consequences. One day you get the gold mine, another day you get the shaft. It's easy for people who live by their creative wits to go from drinking wine to picking grapes. But I find the risks and gambles are what I love most about a career with no safety net. Knowing how hard the business of invention development and licensing is keeps my feet moving and me on the *qui vive.*

For every action, there is an equal and opposite criticism. The odds are that you will encounter far more criticism than acceptance. This is simply the way it is. Do not whine about mistakes. Learn from them. Do not blame someone else. Take responsibility for your actions. Fix the problem, not the blame.

8. *Learn to take rejection.* Do not be turned off by the word "no" because you will hear it often, as in, "No, we're not looking for that at this time." "No, you will have to do better than that for us to consider it." "No, your idea isn't original."

Bright Ideas

Your tax dollars at work. NASA Ames scientists developed a padding concept for a better airplane seat. Today it has all kinds of additional applications including wheelchairs, X-ray table pads, off-road vehicle seats, ski boots, and football helmet liners. The material is an open-cell polyurethane silicone plastic foam that takes the shape of impressed objects but returns to its original shape even after 90 percent compression. It absorbs sudden impacts without shock or bounce. For instance, the manufacturer claims a three-inch-thick pad can absorb all the energy from a 10-foot fall by an adult.

Rejection can be positive if it is turned into constructive growth. Do not let it shake your confidence. My experience is that products get better the more times they are presented.

Rejection is a rehearsal before the big event. I define the word "No" to mean "not yet." It is the shakedown period similar to the practice of taking a play out of town before it opens on Broadway. Remember that the finest steel goes through the hottest fire.

I rarely license a product to the first manufacturer that sees it. And for every product I've licensed, there are many more that never made it off the drawing board, and probably should not have.

Bottom Line: Rejection of ideas is part of the invention licensing business. If you are going to live by the crystal ball, sometimes you will have to eat glass.

9. *Believe in yourself.* One of the first steps toward success is learning to detect and follow that gleam of light that Emerson says flashes across the mind from within. We tend to dismiss without notice our own thoughts because they are ours. In every work of genius, we recognize our own rejected thoughts; they come back at us with a certain alienated majesty.

It is critical that you learn to abide by your own spontaneous impression. Permit nothing to affect the integrity of your own mind.

If you stand for something, you will always find some people for you and some against you. If you stand for nothing, you will find nobody against you and nobody for you. Take your choice.

Remember the advice of Winston Churchill: "Never, never, never, never, never give in—except to dictates of conscience and duty."

10. *Sell yourself before you sell your ideas.* Be concerned about how you are perceived. You may be capable of dreaming up many ideas, but if you cannot command the respect and attention of corporate executives, associates, and perhaps investors, your product will never get off the mark, and you may not be invited back for an encore.

Take My Words for It

The terms **patent pending** and **patent applied for** are used by a manufacturer or seller of an article to inform the public that an application for patent on that article is on file in the Patent and Trademark Office. The law imposes a fine on those who use these terms falsely to deceive the public.

Ideas come, ideas go. Know how much to push. Know when to disappear. Do not wear out your welcome. (Some people suffer from *sellitus*!) You cannot put a dollar value on access to a corporate executive's valuable space and time. I cannot tell you how hard I have worked over the years to gain and maintain access to companies.

Independent inventors who have corporate experience understand the fragility of ideas much better than people who have never worked inside. Former corporate types realize the pressures of such work and people without this experience do not have a clue how to conduct themselves. There is an unwritten code of conduct. Inventors with corporate experience understand that there are territorial imperatives, lines one must not cross, manners that must be displayed. Alas, many great ideas never see the light of day because their inventors personally burn up on the launch pad.

And for good measure, let's add …

➤ *Know Your Market:* Identify your market—both consumer and manufacturer—and know it backward and forward. One of the inventor's greatest downfalls is that he or she is inventing in a vacuum and not in the marketplace.

Just like an athlete, you will play as you practice. Nothing beats good preparation. It will help equalize your position *vis-à-vis* the professionals to whom you are pitching. The more you know your product and its market, the more confident you will become and able to handle people who may attack your arguments. A residual benefit of confidence is that it tends to be contagious. You want to make believers out of everyone. You want to enlist in-house champions for your concepts, people who will support it when you are no longer on the front line.

Bright Ideas

Elijah McCoy, son of runaway slaves, invented the oil lubricator. Born in Canada, he studied engineering in Scotland, and then worked for a railroad in Michigan as an oilman.

Back then, trains had to stop at regular intervals to be lubricated. Crews would run around squirting oil between the train's moving parts. Without periodic lubrication, parts would rub together, overheat, and come to a halt.

It was expensive and wasteful to stop the train every time it needed lubrication. Therefore in 1872, he invented the oil lubricator, a device that oiled engine parts while the train was under power.

McCoy designed lubricators for lots of machines. People insisted on McCoy lubricators—they wanted *the real McCoy.*

➤ *The Paranoids Are Chasing Me!* There are two kinds of amateur inventors, the paranoid and the more paranoid. If you are worried about getting ripped off by potential licensees, do not deal with them. Better yet, if you are worried about being ripped off, go into another business.

The quickest turn off is when a company feels that the inventor is distrustful of it. We have all heard about inventors who were ripped off by major corporations. Remember the Sears wrench and the hidden windshield wiper stories? But there are far more stories about honorable executives and great win/win deals.

Rather than go in paranoid, I follow the advice of former President Ronald Reagan, who, when asked what it was like to work with the USSR, counseled, "Trust, but verify."

The road to success is always under construction, and there are no short cuts. There is simply no way to avoid the ache and pain of hard work. Longfellow put it well when he wrote in *The Ladder of St. Augustine*: "The heights by great men reached and kept, were not attained by sudden flight, but they, while their companions slept, were toiling upward in the night."

The Least You Need to Know

➤ Trust yourself and your instincts. They are anchors in a storm.

➤ Realize that what you can accomplish is truly amazing if you keep your feet on the ground and your eyes on the stars.

➤ Do not be afraid to make mistakes. The price of never being wrong is never being right.

➤ Do not follow where the path leads, but rather go where there is no path and leave a trail.

➤ Enjoy what you do!

Chapter 2

Beware of Invention Marketing Flimflam Artists

In This Chapter

➤ Tips from the Federal Trade Commission

➤ Operation Mousetrap

➤ American Inventor's Corporation executives indicted in $60 million invention promotion scam—over 34,000 victims

➤ How to tell the pros from the cons

➤ What to do if you are victimized

➤ How to find the honest agents and consultants

"My rule is simple. Never deal with invention marketing firms or agents that reach you through T.V., radio, newspaper, and magazine ads or unsolicited direct mail appeals. It is as simple as that. No ifs, ands, or buts. You can remember it like this: Ad equals bad."

—Richard C. Levy

This is the most important chapter in this book because this phase of your invention commercialization adventure is a real minefield for rookies. It is here that you are most vulnerable to having your intellectual and physical pockets picked. At this point, you are apt to be swindled by smooth talking flimflammers in the guise of marketing services and even patent attorneys who overcharge. The marketing types are many. The unprincipled attorneys are fewer and far between, but nonetheless pernicious to your business and bank account.

What do advertised invention marketing services and some patent attorneys share in common? Both take advantage of your inexperience. The advertised marketing services charge up-front fees and have no skill or track record in product placement. The business model for such companies is based entirely upon fees and not royalty income. In other words, they will do slipshod market research, marketing plans, patent searches, patent applications, and other assorted initiatives that rarely result in product placement. In fact, invention services that cater to nonindustry-specific inventors rarely make an effort at licensing. They leave you with a pile of worthless paper—and a lot poorer for all of it.

Patent attorneys, on the other hand, can deliver a very valuable service as you will learn in Part Three. Alas, the occasional bad egg overcharges his or her clients and builds false expectations. You must be ever vigilant. Don't assume that advanced law degrees on the wall mean you have nothing to worry about.

Attack of the Killer Patent Attorney

I was talking to a novice inventor half way through writing this chapter. She was all excited about four design patents that were awarded to her for a juvenile health-related product. I explained the difference between a design patent and a utility patent. Note: The U.S. Patent and Trademark Office (USPTO) has issued over 6 million utility patents to date and just over 400,000 design patents. This tells you something about their worth. Based upon her patents, I said that I thought the chances of a major player licensing them were slim to none, though the patents might serve to attract and impress an investor. She took the news well. Then something she mumbled about her patent attorney prompted me to ask how much she was charged for the design patents.

"He charged me $7,500 each, plus some fees," she responded.

Arrrgh! I almost came unglued. Her total legal bill for the four design patents ran around $30,000. Since design patents can be done by inventors themselves, i.e. *pro se*, or a lot cheaper by a less opportunistic patent attorney (See Part Four), you can understand my reaction. This is the worst instance of overcharging that I have ever heard of. It is far from emblematic of most patent attorneys. I include it as an example because it is so dramatic.

Had she filed for the patents herself, she would have paid the USPTO a filing fee of $160 per patent, as a Small Entity. Add to this an issue fee of $220 per patent and the USPTO gets $380 each. The subtotal is $1,520. Let's say the drawings cost $100 each, though I have a hunch the cost would have been less. (If you would rather submit high quality photographs in lieu of drawings, this is now acceptable; see Part Four. And you might be able to shoot them yourself.) In any event, a rough and tough estimate for all this work is $1,920.00—nowhere near $30,000.

The next day, I called my patent searcher, George Harvill, president of Greentree Information Service, Bethesda, Maryland. I shared her story and patiently waited for his reaction, pen in hand. There was a long pause. Then he said:

"Each?! Holy moley. That's unconscionable. I can't believe it. That's thievery."

The following day, I called my patent attorney, Richard Besha of Nixon & Vanderhye, in Alexandria, Virginia. His reaction went like this:

"Each?! It's been a while since I have done a design patent but that's gouging. She got (expletive deleted)." Dick's fee for a design patent is $650 plus USPTO fees, drawings, etc.

And for good measure, I spoke to another patent attorney, Dinesh Agarwal.

"Each?! I guess that attorney doesn't need too many clients with fees like that."

Again, this is an extreme example and is meant to be a wake-up call to *each* and every one of you to be vigilant.

Flimsy Firms

After hearing an ad calling inventors to action, and a toll-free number (something like 1-800-GET-RICH), in the spirit of experimentation, I decided to give the invention marketing company a call.

I told the voice on the other end of the line that my idea was a device to keep individual strands of spaghetti fresh. My invention was a clear plastic tube capped off at both ends. "No pasta lover will be able live without it," I bragged.

"Terrific. Lots of potential," the voice assured me. All I had to do was pay $400 for an initial assessment. As he explained it, my investment gradually increased into the many thousands of dollars if I bought into various stages of the company's patenting and marketing program. Having had worms for breakfast, I did not go for the one on that hook.

The minute someone starts asking you for money, it's time to run for the hills. Money talks and if you give it to these kinds of companies, you'll hear it say "Good-bye."

According to *TIME* magazine, May 23, 2001, as many as 25,000 would-be inventors are ripped off each year. *TIME* reported that "virtually everyone"

Fast Facts

On December 10, 1999, 3Com Corporation received the six millionth United States patent at a special award ceremony hosted by the USPTO. 3Com received this landmark patent for its innovative HotSync technology, which allows users of handheld devices, based upon the Palm computing platform, to synchronize their information with a computer at the touch of one button.

who contacts invention marketing firms with dreams of riches "will in fact end up poorer." In 1996, federal authorities forced one such company, Invention Submission Corporation, with more than 70 offices around the world, to return $1.2 million to inventors for allegedly making false claims. Get this: ISC reported that of its 5,324 clients represented between 1997 and 1999, only 11 earned more money than they spent with the company. Consumer advocates told *TIME* that this number was inflated.

In January of 2000, Jay Nixon, the Attorney General of Missouri, announced that his office shut down Universal Consulting Service (a.k.a. Continental Ventures) for greatly misrepresenting the marketability, uniqueness, and patentability of customers' inventions. The company has been barred from doing business in the state and must refund more than $240,000 to inventors and pay $39,138 to the state.

One of the most infamous invention promoters was American Inventors Corporation (AIC). I say was because its management has been indicted for mail fraud, money-laundering, and tax evasion for allegedly bilking more than 34,000 inventors out of nearly $60 million.

On May 14, 2001, in the federal District Court presided over by Judge Michael Ponsor, in a precedence-setting action, three top executives of American Inventors Corporation officially changed their pleas to guilty in regard to the aforementioned crimes, according to William M. Welch, an Assistant United States Attorney for the District of Massachusetts. Attorney Welch told me in a telephone interview that he started his investigation in June of 1995 after reports about AIC aired on both "20/20" (ABC) and "48 Hours" (CBS) and complaints began to build up at the U.S. Postal Inspector's Office.

Welch and his team nailed AIC. He says Ronald Boulerice, owner and president of AIC, facing a maximum sentence of 53 years, pleaded guilty to conspiracy to commit mail fraud, money laundering, and filing false tax returns. As part of a prosecution deal, Boulerice will receive eight years in prison and forfeiture of all his assets. Here is the list with "very approximate" values. The assets include his personal residence with a private tennis court ($400,000) in Westfield, Massachusetts, a vacation home ($300,000) at Mt. Snow, Vermont, a beach house in Newport, Rhode Island, an as yet undeveloped property ($20,000) in Westfield, and an $80,000 marble mausoleum. Also part of the deal, his wife Judy would not be prosecuted. This arrangement still needs the approval of Judge Ponsor as of this writing. Sentencing will be September 28, 2001.

The Newport mansion sold in 1996 for $1.1 million. $600,000 went to his and Samson's criminal lawyers (which the feds will never be able to seize or forfeit), approximately $500,000 went to purchase a beach condo in Newport, subsequently sold in 1997. Welch and his team are still trying to trace and track down the disposition of all the money, but unfortunately most of it has been spent.

Codefendant John Samson, vice-president of AIC and president of American Institute for Research and Development (AIRD), also pleaded guilty to five counts of the 18-count indictment. Samson was facing a maximum sentence of 33 years in prison. Under the plea bargain agreement Samson would serve three years in prison, one year under house arrest, and forfeiture of 50 percent of his assets.

AIC salesman John Hoime pleaded guilty to one count of misprision of a felony. In December, 1997, Hoime was interviewed by criminal investigators and made a number of misleading and false statements, including denying that he took part in or had any knowledge of any criminal activities. At the time of his guilty plea, Hoime admitted that he knew that he had been part of a conspiracy to commit mail fraud while employed at AIC but did not report this fact to the criminal investigators in December 1997. As part of his guilty plea, Hoime agreed to serve 18 months in federal prison and six months under house arrest.

In total, 18 former AIC employees—including Boulerice, Samson and Hoime—have pled guilty or will plead guilty to mail fraud and/or tax fraud.

Personal Note: Congratulations to Bill Welch, his team of prosecutors, and the other federal officials who dragged these characters from behind their wet bars and put them behind the kind made out of cast iron. The entire independent inventing community owes these fine public servants a debt of gratitude.

These companies are not easy to charge. Welch talked about how such companies "morph" from one entity into another. For example, AIC had already set up the American Institute for Research and Development when the hammer came down on it. Further, in Florida in late 1994, these guys had something called Washington Financial Group ready to go should they have to close their doors up north.

When I asked if AIC had ever licensed any inventor product, he told me about a part of the scam that was totally new to me. AIC would go to a manufacturer, but rather than pitch the product as a royalty license, it would offer to give the so-called licensee x number of dollars that the licensee would pay back to the inventor as royalties. This way AIC could defend itself if claims were made that its inventors were not making any royalties. An example he cited involved a night sight for a gun that was sold to a company under this m.o. AIC gave the company $20,000 to channel back to the inventor. Unfortunately, the company went Chapter 11.

Richard Apley, director of the USPTO's Independent Inventor Program Office, says that these scams ring up about $200 million a year. The average loss per inventor is $20,000 for useless services.

I cannot say it too many times. Avoid invention marketing firms. They get rich and buy big homes and fast cars. They are slot machines that don't pay off.

WACKY PATENTS

Helium–Filled Sun Shades
Patented December 31, 1991
United States Patent 5,076,029

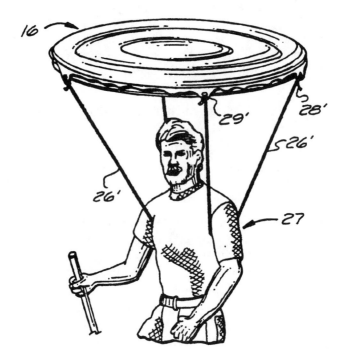

Operation Mousetrap

If you still have any doubt about how serious a problem this is, consider Operation Mousetrap, sprung on such land pirates in 1997 by Federal Trade Commission and state authorities. It was a sting to catch invention marketing scams that resulted in court actions against five companies who exploited tens of thousands of inventors to the tune of more than $90 million, according to the FTC.

I encourage you to visit the FTC Web site for the full list of defendants: www.ftc.gov/opa/1997/9707/mouse.htm

Then–USPTO Solicitor, Nancy Linck, said, "We are particularly concerned about the impact these disreputable firms have on independent inventors's confidence in the patent system. As a result of their dealings with unscrupulous invention developers, they come to see the system as frustrating rather than promoting the recognition and protection of their inventions."

One of the inventions that companies, under Operation Mousetrap, contracted to promote was a device that collects the shavings scratched off lottery tickets. Many scams are shut down, only to reappear under a new corporate guise.

Foreign Affairs

It's hard enough to control these characters here at home, but overseas it's impossible. Through foreign advertising campaigns, American invention marketing companies attract unsuspecting inventors from countries around the world. It is overseas where they really get away with murder. The long arm of American justice cannot reach that far.

The Price Is Not Always Right

"Necessity may be the mother of invention, but some of these marketing companies are nothing more than deadbeat dads," remarked U.S. Senator Joe Lieberman (D-CT), a former Connecticut attorney general, who chaired a hearing on invention marketing scams in 1994, the last Congressional hearing to date on the subject.

He told those attending the Government Affairs Subcommittee on Regulation and Government Information, "They praise all inventions, even those that stand no chance of being brought to market. They paint a rosy picture of huge profits, then do little or nothing to make that dream come true. They say they will make their money from royalties off the sale of the invention, when in reality their profits come from the inventor's up-front fee. And just when the inventor thinks the company is going to get rolling on their behalf, he or she has just been rolled, and the company has moved on to the next victim."

Notable Quotables

"Don't come up with a solution to which there is no problem."

—Larry Greenberg, co-inventor, Alphie

Inventors Awareness Group

Robert Lougher, founder of Inventors Awareness Group, Incorporated, and a former employee of American Inventors Corporation (AIC), Westfield, Massachusetts, told *The Wall Street Journal* that he quit AIC in disgust after concluding that the invention promotion concern was taking in millions of dollars from unsuspecting inventors, but rarely, if ever, getting its customers's ideas to market.

Lougher has become perhaps the most proactive and vocal inventor advocate in the battle to find and shutdown invention marketing scams. He said that when he was a marketing director for AIC …"I would ultimately witness widespread fraud, listen to horror stories from people who lost their homes, their cars and life savings, and sink to the lowest moral depths a human being can sink to."

Inventors Awareness Group is an all-volunteer consumer group formed in 1992. If you feel that you have been victimized by an invention con, send details to IAG. They say that your complaint will be forward to the appropriate law enforcement agency. IAG has represented the independent inventor community before the U.S. Senate, U.S. House of Representatives, and several other government agencies. Since 1992, IAG claims to have assisted over 10,000 inventors and saved them tens of millions of dollars.

If you wish to contact IAG, call (413) 568-5561. Its Web site is www.inventorworld. com.

A Step in the Right Direction

The American Inventors Protection Act of 1999 was signed into law (P.L. 106-113) on November 29, 1999. Two key provisions are …

> ➤ The title requires invention promoters to disclose in writing the number of positive and negative evaluations of inventions they have given over a five-year period and their customers' success in receiving net financial profit and license agreements as a direct result of the invention promotion services.

> ➤ Customers injured by failure to disclose the required information or by any material false or fraudulent representation by the invention promoter can bring a civil action to recover statutory damages up to $5,000 or actual damages. Damages of up to three times the amount awarded are available for intentional or willful violations.

411

The Patent and Trademark Office Public Search Library for trademarks is located at 2900 Crystal Drive, 2nd Floor, Arlington, Virginia 22202. The Public Search Library is open between 8:00 A.M. and 5:30 P.M., weekdays. Use of the Library is free to the public. Certain information may be searched at a Patent and Trademark Depository Library, too. For locations see Part Three. Searches may be conducted online, too, at www.uspto.gov.

What Comes After the Pitch

Here's what the FTC and USPTO recommend as follow-ups to the following pitch lines you may hear from an invention marketing company. They should set off alarms in your head that warm you to stay away.

> ➤ We think your idea has great market potential.

If a company fails to disclose that investing in your idea is a high-risk venture and that most ideas never make any money, beware.

➤ Our company has licensed a lot of invention ideas successfully.

If a company tells you it has a good track record, ask for a list of its successful clients. Confirm that the clients have had commercial success. If the company refuses to give you a list, it probably means they don't have any.

➤ You need to hurry and patent your idea before someone else does.

Be wary of high-pressure sales tactics. Simply patenting your idea does *not* mean you will ever make any money from it.

➤ Congratulations! We've done a patent search on your idea, and we have some great news. There's nothing like it out there.

Searches by fraudulent invention promotion firms, if done at all, usually are incomplete, conducted in the wrong category, or unaccompanied by a legal opinion on the results of the search from a competent patent attorney. Because unscrupulous firms accept virtually any idea or invention without regard to its patentability, they may market an idea for which someone already has a valid, unexpired patent. In that case, you could find yourself the subject of a patent infringement lawsuit—even if the promotional efforts on your invention are successful.

➤ Our research department, engineers, and patent attorneys have evaluated your idea. We definitely want to move forward.

This is a standard pitch. Many questionable firms do not perform any evaluation. In fact, many don't have the "professional" staff they claim. They want to move ahead with anything that will bring them cash fees.

➤ Our company has evaluated your idea, and now wants to prepare a more in-depth research report. It'll be several hundred dollars.

If the company's initial evaluation is positive, ask why it isn't willing to cover the cost of researching your idea further. Such reports are worthless.

411

The USPTO's Independent Inventor Program Office may be reached at (703) 306-5568; Fax: (703) 306-5570; or via e-mail: independentinventor@uspto.com

411

To file a complaint with the Federal Trade Commission or to get free information on inventor scams, call toll-free, 1-877-FTC-HELP (1-877-382-4357), or use the online complaint form at www.ftc.gov.

➤ Our company makes most of its money from the royalties it gets licensing clients' ideas. Of course, we need some money from you before we get started.

If a firm tells you this, but asks you for a large up-front fee, ask why they won't help you on a contingency basis. Unscrupulous firms make almost all their money from large up-front fees.

Heads Up

If you're interested in buying the services of an invention promotion firm, here's information from the Federal Trade Commission that can help you avoid making a costly mistake.

➤ Many fraudulent invention promotion firms offer inventors two services in a two-step process: one involves a research report or market evaluation of your idea that can cost you hundreds of dollars. The other involves patenting or marketing and licensing services, which can cost you several thousand dollars. Early in your discussion with a promotion firm, ask for the total cost of its services, from the "research" about your invention through the marketing and licensing. Walk away if the salesperson hesitates to answer.

➤ Many fraudulent companies offer to provide invention assistance or marketing services in exchange for advance fees that can range from $5,000 to $10,000. Reputable licensing agents rarely rely on large up-front fees.

➤ Unscrupulous invention promotion firms tell all inventors that their ideas are among the relative few that have market potential. The truth is that most ideas do not make any money.

➤ Many questionable invention promotion firms claim to have a great record licensing their clients' inventions successfully. Ask the firm to disclose its success rate as well as the names and telephone numbers of their recent clients. Success rates show the number of clients who made more money from their inventions than they paid to the firm. Check the references. In several states, disclosing the success rate is the law.

➤ Ask an invention promotion firm for its rejection rate—the percentage of all ideas or inventions that the invention promotion firm finds unacceptable. Legitimate firms generally have high rejection rates.

➤ Fraudulent invention promotion firms may promise to register your idea with the U.S. Patent and Trademark Office's Disclosure

Fast Facts

On September 3, 1969, Patent No. 3,400,371 issued with 495 sheets of drawings and 469 pages of specification. It had 16 joint inventors who worked for IBM.

Document Program. Many scam artists charge high fees to do this. The cost of filing a disclosure document in the USPTO is $10. The disclosure is accepted as evidence of the date of conception of the invention, but it doesn't offer patent protection.

➤ Unscrupulous firms often promise that they will exhibit your idea at trade-shows. Most invention promotion scam artists do not go to these tradeshows, much less market your idea effectively.

➤ Many unscrupulous firms agree in their contracts to identify manufacturers by coding your idea with the U.S. Bureau of Standard Industrial Code (SIC). Lists of manufacturers that come from classifying your idea with the SIC usually are of limited value.

Before You Contract for Services ...

Here are some things to do before you sign on with an invention marketer or agent.

➤ Question claims and assurances that your invention will make money. No one can guarantee your invention's success.

➤ Investigate the company before you commit. Call the Better Business Bureau, the consumer protection agency, and the Attorney General in your city or state and in the city and state where the company is headquartered. Ask if there are any unresolved consumer complaints about the firm.

➤ Make sure your contract contains all the terms you agreed to—verbal and written—before you sign. Ask an attorney to review the agreement.

➤ Remember, once a dishonest company has your money, it's likely you will never get it back.

Bright Ideas

In 1906, Ole Evinrude took his neighbor, Bess Cary, by rowboat in 90-degree heat to picnic on an island in his favorite Wisconsin lake. As he rowed, he watched their ice cream melt and wished he had a faster way to get to the island. At that moment, Evinrude realized that a car was not the only vehicle that could benefit from a gasoline engine. The next summer he conducted the field tests of the first outboard motor, a 1½ horsepower, 62-pound iron engine.

Who Are These Parasites?

About 80 percent of all people claiming to help inventors build a business, market their product, or raise capital are con-men, beggars, thieves, or incompetents, cautions Professor Mark A. Spikell, co-founder, Entrepreneurship Center, School of Business Administration, George Mason University.

Alan A. Tratner, founder of the nonprofit Inventor's Workshop International (IWIEF), describes most invention marketing companies as cancers on the inventing community, a disease that needs to be eradicated immediately. Too often, inventors lose large amounts of money and are derailed by the unfulfilled promises and the come-ons of these companies, he says.

This is a true story:

Dave Thomas created an improved joystick for video games. His wife, Susan, saw an ad in *USA Today*: "Have an invention? Need help?" They responded to the ad, and the company, located in Boston, was excited about promoting the device. There was just one hitch: It would take $10,000 to get it off the ground.

Then Susan's brother-in-law, who believed in the invention, was killed in an auto accident. His widow provided the needed $10,000 from the insurance settlement.

Dave and Susan flew to Boston. The account representative wined and dined them. They signed a contract and handed over a $10,000 cashier's check.

And then? The account representative disappeared. The Massachusetts Attorney General's Office didn't have any record of the company.

And Dave and Susan are $10,000 wiser.

Take My Words for It

NIH: Abbreviation for **Not Invented Here,** a term used to describe companies that do not welcome outside submissions from inventors.

How to Tell the Pros from the Cons

Separating the legitimate invention marketing companies and agents from the bad ones is not always easy. The image the fly-by-nights portray through false and misleading advertising in legitimate media (such as *USA Today, Entrepreneur, Popular Mechanics, Popular Science*, CNN, and so on) is compelling. Messages are tagged with toll-free numbers, paid actors deliver confidence-building call-to-action pitches, and slick four-color brochures picture well-known inventions that the invention marketer had absolutely nothing to do with (e.g., the tricycle, ballpoint pen, zipper, teddy bear, or radio). Often in print too small to read it will say "These products are not intended to represent success for inventors who have worked with our firm."

Does advertising ever show evidence of the company's own product placement? Rarely. And, if it does, you will not recognize the product, and inventor testimonials—if any—will be signed with a name and state only. Nothing is offered that would help you contact the inventor for a reference.

Here's the bottom line. There is no way any one company or individual could have enough meaningful contacts or expertise in enough fields of invention to find a home for the numbers of products that come in as a result of shotgun, mass-media advertising.

I specialize in the toy industry. It takes every bit of energy, and most of my waking hours, to keep up with the intercompany and intracompany movements of research and development and marketing executives and to stay ahead of what's in and what's out in terms of product trends. There is no way that I could track a multitude of industries simultaneously. No one could. The business of invention licensing depends too much on personal relationships, not unlike every business. Success is a combination of "know how" and "know who."

Here's a list of ways you can tell if a company is a pro or a con.

➤ **Up-front fees.** Reputable invention marketing services will not require up-front fees. You invested your ingenuity, time, and money to create and protect your invention. The marketer is obligated, in turn, to invest his or her ingenuity, time, and money to find it a home. What is fairer than that? The moment you pay for services, the carrot is removed; there is no risk for the marketer. With nothing to lose and your deposit in hand, the broker has little reason to display incentive.

➤ **Track record.** A reputable firm will be able to demonstrate a track record of successful product placement and a list of satisfied clients. A reputable company will crow about its accomplishments and urge you to call its inventor clients and industry references.

Notable Quotables

"Research is to see what everybody else has seen, and to think what nobody else has thought."

—Albert Szent-Gyorgyi

Fast Facts

The Patent and Trademark Office cannot give advice as to whether a certain patent promotion organization is reliable and trustworthy. The Office has no control over such organizations and does not supply information about them.

WACKY PATENTS

Fire Escape
Patented February 9, 1909
United States Patent 912,152

Direct mail pieces run the gamut from inexpensive postcards to envelopes bulging with slick brochures and official-looking paperwork. But whether the marketer has spent fifty cents or two dollars per mailer, it does not matter: The stuff isn't worth the paper it's printed on.

➤ **Postcards.** An inexpensive way to prospect for inventors, postcards from invention marketing companies usually go something like this:

IMPORTANT NOTICE

We have located six companies that produce, market, or sell products in a field to which your invention might apply. You may wish to contact these manufacturers if you are interested in one or more of the following:

A. Licensing your patent.

B. Finding a company to produce your invention.

C. Securing marketing, distribution, and/or sales help.

D. Hiring design or technical support.

Do they hit the hot buttons or what? Then comes the kicker. You are asked to remit a fee of $75 plus $1 for each name.

Once they get your money, all they do is pull names and addresses of appropriate manufacturers from the *Thomas Register* and send them to you. This satisfies their legal obligation. After you have paid for this service, you will be solicited about additional services.

" [Invention marketers] scare the living daylights out of me," James Kubiatowicz, former director of product development/toys at Spearhead Industries, told me. "They're leeches. They prey on the novices. Then pulling open his desk drawer, he adds, "I've got thirty-two post cards from these guys and I am saving the stamps. One of these days I'll steam them off and put them into a retirement fund.

"Anybody who is breathing and has a dollar can get strokes from these companies. They work on a person's ego."

➤ **Fat envelopes.** Other direct mail offers come in envelopes stuffed with slick flyers and official-looking confidential disclosure agreements with diploma-like borders. Rarely will you be able to make out the signature of the "authorized agent" who signs off on the *Dear Inventor* cover letter. Nor will you recognize any products they claim to have commercialized if any are shown at all.

Bright Ideas

Patsy Sherman and Samuel Smith were developing a substance for use on aircraft when they noticed that a lab assistant's shoe stayed clean where she had dropped some of the fluid. Scotchgard was born.

Most invention marketing companies wrap themselves in Old Glory and Uncle Sam. Names are made to sound government-sanctioned with words like American, Federal, and National. Logos incorporate the bald eagle, the stars and stripes, or another symbol of government. Often they use addresses and phone numbers that imply a Washington, D.C., presence. The addresses are typically nothing more than mail drops that forward correspondence on to the company's office elsewhere, and the phone numbers are routed through D.C., but answered in a boiler room somewhere else.

New Twist to an Old Scheme

Here is a novel way of getting money from inventors. A letter offers the inventor a free booklet on how to sell inventions. It invites a visit to the company's offices "… just to chat and to see what we look like." It is made clear that there is no obligation whatsoever.

The booklet is given away for free because, the letter states, "… inventions are our business." A visit is encouraged because "some inventors are reluctant to entrust their invention to people they have never seen and I [a company executive] cannot blame them for being cautious." A prepaid response card is enclosed.

The company goes on to build your confidence by separating itself from invention marketing companies. It claims not to neglect inventors after they pay a fee or steal or mishandle their invention. This company sticks to what it does best, *preparing invention descriptions and compiling lists of manufacturers.*

An Employment Agreement is enclosed through which you are asked to buy into the company's "technique" for writing descriptive material, preparing folios, and selecting manufacturers that it "believes" may "potentially" be interested in your invention. It asks for no rights to your invention. It does not seek to legally bind you or your invention in any way. The descriptive materials it sells you become your property.

The Agreement states that you understand "the company does no developing, promoting, or brokering." Its services are "strictly" to prepare invention descriptions and compile lists of manufacturers. It further claims to offer "no evaluation of the merits, practicability, feasibility, potential salability" of the invention.

What does it cost for this company to do a write-up of your invention and provide names of potential manufacturers? $589.50.

While I can see nothing dishonest in the service offered, the question you must ask yourself is, what is its value? In my opinion, it is a lot of money to pay for a technique in writing descriptive material, preparing folios, and selecting manufacturers that *might* be interested in your invention. The company exhibits neither "know how" nor "know who" in a particular field of enterprise.

Fast Facts

The Patent and Trademark Office can assist you in the marketing of your patent by publishing, at your request, a notice in the *Official Gazette* that the patent is available for licensing or sale. The fee for this is $25.

How Do They Get Your Name?

The odds are that if you have been awarded a patent, you have received an unsolicited letter that began with the fateful words, "Dear Inventor: A number of manufacturers have invited us to send them descriptions of your invention."

I can always tell when a patent is about to issue. Mailers from invention marketing companies flood my post office box. Often three or four will come from the same company on the same day. They are a harbinger of a new patent much as the robin is of spring.

When a patent issues, notice of it is automatically carried in the *Official Gazette* of the U.S. Patent and Trademark Office. This publication has come out weekly since 1872. It is mailed to subscribers and put on sale every Tuesday. The *Official Gazette* tells its readers the name, city, and state of residence of the applicant, with the mailing address in the case of unassigned patents, the patent number, title of invention, and lots of other information to help them appear to have given great consideration to your invention.

Take My Words for It

Marketing: Process of selling or offering something for sale based upon a plan.

Profile of an Honest Broker

As a general rule, reputable invention marketing companies or agents …

➤ Specialize in one industry where they are well known.

➤ Are eager to regale you with their success stories.

➤ Willingly introduce you to satisfied clients.

➤ Do not take up-front money for services.

What to Do if You Are a Victim

If you think that you have been victimized by a fraudulent invention marketing company, first contact the firm in writing and attempt to get your money back. If you are unsuccessful, report the problem to the FTC, your local consumer protection agency, the Better Business Bureau, the Attorney General (Consumer Protection Division) in your state and the state where the company is located, and any media you think might be interested in following up on your story.

You can report problems to the Federal Trade Commission by writing to Correspondence Branch, Federal Trade Commission, 6th and Pennsylvania Avenue NW, Washington, D.C. 20580. Or call the Complaint and Inquiry Branch at (202) 326-2222. You can also file complaints through the Commission's Web site at www.ftc.gov.

Bright Ideas

Patent leather got its name because the process of applying a polished black finish to leather was patented.

Notable Quotables

"Business has only two basic functions—marketing and innovation."

—Peter Drucker

If the invention marketing company is national, you may wish to tell your story to reporters who cover the consumer beat at network-level news-gathering operations, national daily newspapers, weekly and/or specialized magazines, and radio programs. You may wish to begin with local media just to get the story in play.

Depending upon the amount of money owed, Small Claims Court may be an option if the invention marketing company is local.

States (Inventor) Rights

More and more states are passing legislation that favors inventors. Some states are California, Connecticut, Illinois, Iowa, Kansas, Massachusetts, Minnesota, Nebraska, North Carolina, North Dakota, Ohio, Oklahoma, South Dakota, Tennessee, Texas, Utah, Virginia, Washington, and Wisconsin.

Unfortunately, most inventors who get ripped off by the paracreative slugs who operate under the guise of invention marketing services do not even realize that their state has protective legislation.

Here are some highlights from the laws of Minnesota and Virginia. I would encourage you to write to any of the aforementioned states for a complete copy of its legislation.

Minnesota (Invention Services 325A.02)

1. Notwithstanding any contractual provision to the contrary, inventors have the unconditional right to cancel a contract for invention development services for any reason at any time before midnight of the third business day following the date the inventor gets a fully executed copy.

2. A contract for invention development services shall be set in no less than 10-point type.

3. An invention developer who is not a lawyer may not give you legal advice with respect to patents, copyrights, or trademarks.

4. The invention marketer must tell you ...

   a. the total number of customers who have contracted with him up to the last thirty days; and

b. the number of customers who have received, by virtue of the invention marketer's performance, an amount of money in excess of the amount of money paid by such customers to the invention marketer pursuant to a contract for invention development services.

5. The contract shall state the expected date of completion of invention marketing services.

6. Every invention marketer rendering invention development services must maintain a bond issued by a surety admitted to do business in the state, and equal to either 10 percent of the marketer's gross income from the invention development business during the preceding fiscal year, or $25,000, whichever is larger.

Virginia, Chapter 18, 59.1-209

1. No invention developer may acquire any interest, partial or whole, in the title to the inventor's invention or patent rights, unless the invention developer contracts to manufacture the invention and acquires such interest for this purpose at or about the time the contract for manufacture is executed.

2. The developer must tell you if they intend to spend more for their services than the cash fee you will have to pay.

3. The Attorney General has the mandate to enforce the provisions of this chapter and recover civil penalties.

Fast Facts

George Washington signed the first patent bill on April 10, 1790, and for the first time in history, the intrinsic right of an inventor to profit from his invention was recognized by law.

Bright Ideas

The first Apple computer was born in the garage of Steve Jobs's parents in 1976. He and his partner, college bud Steve Wozniak, assembled computers for fellow students. Their first commercial order was for 50 computers. To raise the $1,300 needed to buy parts, Jobs sold his VW bus and Wozniak his Hewlett Packard calculator. In 1977, Apple sales soared to $800,000 and within five years it became a Fortune 500 company.

How to Find an Honest Broker

Here are three methods I endorse that, while not guaranteed, put the odds more in your favor that you will find competent and honest help.

➤ **Inventor Groups:** Call an inventor organization, preferably a local one, whose members may be able to recommend an agent. I think you will get a more complete picture of the situation and gain more confidence in the agent if you sit down with a satisfied customer.

➤ **Industry Referrals:** Ask the company to whom you would like to license your invention to recommend an agent. While not all companies are comfortable recommending invention brokers, many will. Some companies will even send you a list of names. You must, of course, talk to the agents and strike your own level of confidence and a fair deal; nonetheless, you know up-front that the door is open to them. Further, anyone recommended by one company likely has excellent relationships with other manufacturers, too.

➤ **Invention Consultants:** Do not confuse invention marketing firms with legitimate consultants. I strongly believe in paying consultants whenever their expertise can contribute to the progress and success of a project.

Notable Quotables

"Invention breeds invention."

—Ralph Waldo Emerson

What is consulting? England's Institute of Management Consultants defines consulting as "The service provided by an independent and qualified person or persons in identifying and investigating problems concerned with policy, organization, procedures, and methods; recommending appropriate action and helping to implement these recommendations."

There are as many types of consultants as there are problems to solve. These experts can bring new techniques and approaches to bear on an inventor's work. This contribution can range from helping to bridge a technological gap to the special knowledge and talent required to successfully license or market a particular innovation.

"I actually made my consultant a partner," says Richard Tweddell III, inventor of VegiForms, a device that press-molds vegetables, while still on the vine, into the likenesses of human faces. A former employee at Kenner Products, Cincinnati, Ohio, Tweddell credits his consultant with moving his company from ground zero. "He showed me how to license the product, he reviews all our licensing agreements, and he found companies that were interested in taking the rights to."

Advisors can provide impartial points of view by seeing challenges in a fresh light. They operate outside existing frameworks and free from existing beliefs, politics, problems, and procedures inherent in many organizations or situations.

Most consultants operate on the basis of an hourly rate plus expenses. You, however, as an inventor and by the nature of your work, may be able to make equity deals whereby in return for advice a consultant is given participation in any profits your invention might generate. You should think long and hard before doing something like this, because it is often less expensive to risk the cash and hold all the points possible in-house.

Do not think that consultants have all the answers. They do not. Consulting is very hard work and not everything can be solved as quickly as one would like. Do not look for miracle solutions.

Shop around. Get references on any consultant or research organization you are considering. Do not be impressed by a consultant's or organization's professional association alone (such as a university affiliation). Their success rate in fields related to yours is what matters. How much can they do with a single phone call? Results are what you want, not just paper reports.

One example of an inventor who took in consulting partners to make his project materialize is Seattle waiter Robert Angel, inventor of the popular game Pictionary. Angel knew that he had a terrific concept but needed some graphic support. He asked artist Gary Everson to help him design the game board in return for points in the venture. Everson agreed. The then 26-year-old inventor also needed assistance in making business decisions, so he gave points as well to an accountant named Terry Langston.

Pictionary went on to be the best-selling game of 1987, grossing more than $52 million at retail. In 1988, the product's sales soared to an astounding $120 million. To date, more than 14 million units of the quick-draw game have been sold, and the three partners have become wealthy, receiving royalties on every game sold.

Bright Ideas

While trying to create an extremely strong glue, Spencer Silver accidentally made an adhesive that was so weak it could barely hold two pieces of paper together.

"If I had thought about it, I wouldn't have done the experiment. The literature was full of examples that said you can't do this," remarked Silver on the work that led to the unique adhesives for 3M "Post-It" pads.

The Least You Need to Know

➤ Invention marketing companies that advertise on late night television and radio are mostly dishonest.

➤ The FTC can provide air coverage. Don't hesitate to complain if you have your pocket picked.

➤ If you are with an invention marketing company, get out while it's still a rescue. Don't wait until it becomes a body recovery.

➤ Empty barrels make the most noise. Verify everything you are told by an invention marketing company.

➤ There are honest brokers and services. They are just harder to find.

Chapter 3

Licensing vs. Venture Capital

In This Chapter

➤ Before you do anything, make sure you have something that people will want to buy

➤ Reinventing inventors

➤ Licensing your invention—the advantages and disadvantages

➤ Doing it yourself—the advantages and disadvantages

"I enjoy building businesses. New business development always begins with great innovation and fresh, new ideas. These ideas come from the independent thinker ... the person who has no rules or limitations. We must always find ways to let revolutionary new thoughts harvest."

—Tom Dusenberry, CEO, Call IT Entertainment

Before you reveal your invention to anyone—potential licensees or investors—you must be able to answer yes to all these questions:

1. Do you have a patent, a copyright, or some other form of legal protection?

2. Do you have a working model, or better yet, an engineering prototype?

3. Do you have credible data about the size of the market, including probable impact of selling price on quantity demanded?

4. Do you know what it will cost to produce your invented product at various levels of output?

Fast Facts

USPTO Today, an online magazine for the intellectual property community, made its debut in January 2000. Published monthly and available in hard copy twice a year, *USPTO Today* provides up-to-date news and in-depth coverage on issues of concern to USPTO external customers. The printed edition of this magazine has a subscription base of around 1,300.

To read the magazine online, you will first need to install Adobe's free Acrobat Reader on your computer. Then go to:

www2.uspto.gov/web/offices/ac/ahrpa/opa/ptotoday/jan2001.pdf.

For printed editions call 1-703-305-8341 or e-mail ruth.nyblod@uspto.gov, and you'll be put on the subscription list.

To get your invention to market, somebody has to sell it, and somebody has to produce it. As your invention moves toward the marketplace, business skills become more critical than technical skills. You will require more and more interaction with people who have these skills, and of course, your product will demand more and more money as it moves along to commercialization.

If you opt to go the licensing route—*always my choice*—your invention becomes more important than you in the corporate decision-making process. The manufacturer, in fact, may not feel you are necessary once it has an understanding of your invention.

Notable Quotables

"Assume any career moves you make won't go smoothly. They won't. But do not look back."

—Andy Grove, chairman, Intel Corp.

On the other hand, the inventor who seeks venture capital faces a maxim that says: *Better to take a chance on a first-rate manager with a second-rate product, than on a first-rate product in the hands of a second-rate manager.*

Business Options

There are two ways to commercialize your invention:

➤ You can license someone else to manufacture and market it.

➤ You can do it yourself.

Most other options are variations of these two possibilities.

When you license others to make and market your products, it does not require that you raise venture capital and dedicate yourself to a single enterprise. It limits your exposure to lawyers and bankers. Dealing with these people is akin to getting your oxygen shut off. And it frees you to dream up concepts, license and work to make them happen. However, this does not mean that licensing is the only option.

Some people thrive on building businesses, crunching numbers, and all that this entails. Others are control freaks, people who do not like giving up dominion over their inventions. The do-it-yourself option allows them to be the boss.

WACKY PATENTS

Flushable Vehicle Spittoon
Patented February 5, 1991
United States Patent 4,989,275

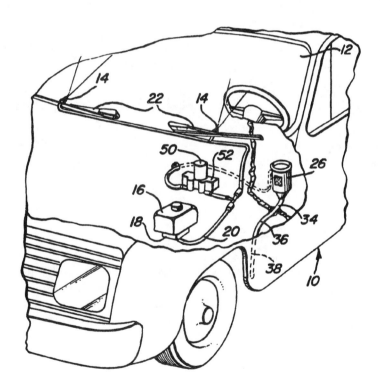

Licensing, the way I am now set up, has none of these aforementioned demands or requirements. It allows me to be free to create and develop concepts at my own pace and under conditions that I control. Of course, like everything in life, it's not perfect;

but at least I captain my destiny to a greater degree than when I was working within an organization. And my worries do not involve the kinds of issues one must handle running a company.

To help you make the decision on how best to commercialize your brainchild, here are some positives and negatives to consider about licensing versus the do-it-yourself. This information was prepared, in part, by the Argonne National Laboratory.

Bright Ideas

The exploits of deep-water divers were recorded as early as 475 B.C.E. when Xerxes of Persia sent people down to recover treasure.

Divers breathing through tubes are mentioned by Aristotle in 355 B.C.E. And Jules Verne's classic book, *Twenty Thousand Leagues Under the Sea*, describes divers breathing with iron tanks "fastened to their backs with straps."

In 1943, the modern aqualung was co-invented by Frenchmen Jacques Cousteau and Emile Gagnan. They called their invention the SCUBA (Self-Contained Underwater Breathing Apparatus) tank. Divers were suddenly able to swim underwater without an air supply from the surface.

The Licensing Option

Licensing is tempting because the amount of money, tasks, skills, and people required are considerably less than in running your own business. That does not necessarily mean it is the right alternative for you. Before I address the advantages and disadvantages of licensing, it is important that you understand the business climate within the licensing arena and what it will take from you to make things happen.

Reinventing Inventors

Since we licensed our first product, Star Bird, to Milton Bradley, January 1, 1978, industry has changed, pushed by technology and economics in a restless, volatile atmosphere. A dramatic paradigm shift has taken place, and inventors who do not understand and adapt will be left behind like last year's Christmas toys. Just as businesses are reinventing themselves, we inventors must do likewise or risk perishing.

The skill sets required to succeed today involve much more than technical talents. Manufacturers are no longer dependent upon the same kinds of products. Witness the explosion of new technologies; business models have changed. Marketing, not R&D (research and development), drives product. There are uncertain executive hierarchies.

While inventiveness remains a very critical element, I find myself depending more and more on business and marketing skills. You must be able to organize and inspire teams of creative people, provide leadership, navigate bureaucracy, analyze market opportunities, and narrow the focus while seeing the big picture.

Manufacturers Seek Risk Reduction

You must give more consideration to developing extensions of established lines. *The Complete Idiot's Guide* is an example of brand extension. There are over 400 titles in this line of books. I felt my work would fare better under a strong and successful brand like CIG than as a one-off title battling for shelf space.

Brand licensing is a $141 plus billion business. Except for Furby, which, as Kipling would say, *is another story*, many of my recent products are based on marquee brands: Men Are from Mars, Women Are from Venus (Mattel); Chicken Soup for the Soul (Cardinal); Warner Brother's Trivial Pursuit (Hasbro); Uncle Milton's Ant Farm Game (Great American Puzzle Factory); and Duncan Yo-Yo key chains (Basic Fun).

It is less risky for a manufacturer to launch a product within an existing brand than to dig out of a hole with something new.

You Scratch My Back, I'll Scratch Yours

We independent inventors must work closer with our licensees. We have to invest ourselves in our products far beyond the invention stage. It is important to take an active role in whatever needs to

Fast Facts

A U.S. patent for an invention is the grant of a property right to the inventor(s), issued by the U.S. Patent and Trademark Office (USPTO). The right conferred by the patent grant is, in the language of the statute and of the grant itself, "the right to exclude others from making, using, offering for sale, or selling" the invention in the United States or importing the invention into the United States. To get a U.S. patent, an application must be filed in the USPTO.

Notable Quotables

"It is curiosity, initiative, originality and the ruthless application of honesty that count in R&D."

—Julian Huxley, British biologist

be done—for example, finding engineering and design talent, sourcing components, conducting patent searches, pulling together research, writing and editing instruction manuals, creating package copy, and flying to R&D and marketing meetings, often in return for only expenses. Your eye should be on the larger prize if you want to make money as an independent. Position yourself as a *de facto* project manager and be the adhesive that holds things together and the oil that keeps things moving when problems arise, and people lose focus or worse, confidence.

Know How + Know Who = Success

To be so positioned, it takes *know how* and *know who*. The company must reach a level of comfort with you and have confidence in your capabilities. You must become a family member. Obviously, this relationship takes time to establish; just remember that you are always selling yourself first and your concept second. This way, if the idea is not accepted, you will be invited back.

Depth of involvement with the companies may mean fewer ideas generated and prototyped, but you will likely see a higher percentage of placements and introductions. This is because of the *value* your assistance adds to each project. It comes under the heading of taking care of your customers. My grandfather used to tell me that if you do not take care of your customers, somebody else will.

Bright Ideas

Twenty years ago, three young Canadians created Trivial Pursuit and licensed it for a reportedly astronomical royalty of 15.7 percent. (Industry average is five percent.) It has made its way into more than half the homes in this country. Over 30 million Trivial Pursuit games have been sold worldwide in 18 languages and 32 countries.

The MBA Syndrome

To further complicate matters, we once created concepts for people with a nose for product, risk takers passionate and genuinely excited by innovation. Today we see more and more companies run by financial types and MBAs whose logic and over-analysis deftly immobilize and sterilize ideas. They spend less time with the inventing community and more time with the investment community. They cannot grow evergreens because each year they cut down the forest and plant a new one. Alas, it is a very short-sighted, pump-and-dump, day trader mentality.

Not long ago, I addressed a prestigious business school. In the audience were 130 graduate students and professors. I asked the future MBAs: "How many of you have an idea you'd like to see commercialized, something for which you have passion?" Not a single hand was raised.

A few weeks later, a toy inventor to whom I told this story was talking to his son's fourth grade class. He asked the thirty-six 9 and 10 year olds the same question. Every hand went up.

I may make what happens between elementary and business school the subject of another book, because this transition has changed the way industry does business.

The Advantages of Licensing

As you know by now, I favor licensing. Here's why.

➤ Licensing multiplies resources to develop your invention. The licensee, if it is a dynamic firm—and you do not want to license any other kind—can put teams of professionals to work developing, producing, and marketing your idea. Insurmountable financial mountains to you may be petty cash molehills to them.

➤ They see things you do not. Licensees often perceive uses—and therefore markets—for your invention that you didn't see. One licensee turned a salt-water taffy machine into a new and highly efficient type of concrete mixer. The more markets, the more potential income.

➤ The licensee may pay you money up front, although probably not as much as you hope. In addition, they may agree to a minimum amount of guaranteed royalties for some period.

➤ Licensing frees you up. If what you want to do is retire, or return to inventing, then giving up control may serve your interests rather than defeat them.

➤ If you have a technology with a demonstrably strong potential, businesses may want your invention. Many large corporations regularly acquire new product, but smaller firms, though they may be less well known, offer possibilities as well. Many cannot afford expensive R&D departments but nonetheless need new product. Furthermore, smaller firms often operate much more dynamically than

411

Retailer Hammacher Schlemmer has been introducing its customers to innovative products for over 150 years. In 1930, it was first to sell the pop-up toaster; the steam iron came in 1948 and the microwave oven in 1968. In 1998, it claims to have introduced the first portable DVD player. If you think your invention is in this class of American lifestyle products, call 1-773-INVENT-1 and ask for the company's current Search For Invention entry kit, or download the forms from www.hammacher.com.

big ones, so do not write them off. I opted to pitch Furby to privately held Tiger Electronics and not majors Mattel or Hasbro. Tiger sold over 40 million Furbys, and then itself to Hasbro.

The Disadvantages of Licensing

No situation is perfect, and licensing is about as imperfect and unstable as it gets. But in spite of the following disadvantages licensing poses, for the way I like to live, I find it the best way to get product to market.

➤ You will lose control over your technology. Usually total control, for a long time, maybe forever.

➤ Your involvement is reduced. In most cases, you will have no further direct involvement at all. You may stick around as a consultant but usually for a limited time.

➤ Finding a licensee isn't easy. The right one may make you rich. The wrong one may bury your technology or butcher it. Even if you can eventually get it back, it may be too late.

➤ Protecting your interests is crucial. But it is also extremely difficult. Negotiating with licensees means playing with the big boys. They confront you with the immense staff resources of a corporation, lawyers, market analysts, and production engineers—a tough team for you to take on by yourself. Licensing agreements, when properly done, result from negotiations between two parties. The other side has pros to represent it, so you better have one of your own. If you're an amateur at the licensing game, you need the help of a lawyer or business type with experience in such negotiations.

Fast Facts

The USPTO is a noncommercial federal entity and one of 14 bureaus in the Department of Commerce. The office occupies a combined total of over 1,400,000 square feet, in numerous buildings in Arlington, Virginia. The office employs over 5,000 full-time equivalent staff to support its major functions—the examination and issuance of patents and the examination and registration of trademarks.

Whooah, Not So Fast!

As I mentioned at the beginning of this chapter, unless you have adequate legal protection for your invention, a working model—or better, an engineering prototype—market data, and cost estimates, get cracking at putting a package together. If you do not have these elements, how can you expect anyone to take you seriously?

Further, if you do not know what your invention will be worth to your licensee, you do not know what money you can reasonably demand. Your licensee will work up its version of all these figures. If the company is reputable, it won't cheat you, but its estimates of sales and profits will be on the low end and costs on the high side. You can count on it. You will struggle over the royalty, advance, and guarantee, if any.

In short, you not only have to show technical feasibility, you have to prepare a package of information about production and marketing that's close to a business plan. This document will help you decide whether you want to venture or license, and then execute that decision by supplying the data required to raise money for your own business—or to persuade a prospective licensee to talk you out of it.

At the very least, if you decide to license your invention, you will have to build a working model; reaching the engineering prototype stage would greatly increase both your chances of finding a licensee and the amount of money you may convince him or her to pay. By contrast, if you want to start your own business or develop the technology within a business you already operate, you will have to do even more than this.

Take My Words for It

Advance: Negotiated sum of money given to an inventor, usually against future royalties; typically nonrefundable.

Doing It Yourself: The Venturing Strategy

Starting your own business to make and market your product, or *venturing*, as it is often called, will require more from you, but has its own advantages and disadvantages to consider.

The Advantages

Here are some of the advantages to establishing your own enterprise.

➤ Running a company can be exciting. If you have the will and skill, you may enjoy it more than inventing. Some inventors are entrepreneurs by experience, some by instinct. The inventor/entrepreneur can achieve powerful things, as Edwin Land, inventor of the Polaroid 60-second camera, and Steven Jobs, inventor of the Apple operating system, have shown. But the combination occurs rarely.

➤ In the long run, you may make a lot more money. If your invention is a big success, your rewards could vastly exceed the royalties you could expect from any licensing agreement.

WACKY PATENTS

Saluting Device
Patented March 10, 1896
United States Patent 556,248

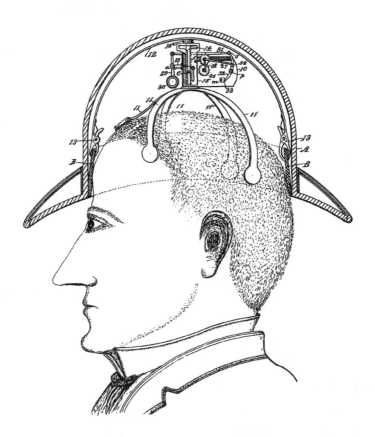

➤ Even if it is your company, you may not have to run it. Building a successful business involves hiring all kinds of people. There are plenty of examples of inventors who retained a large or controlling interest in their companies, but turned the management of it over to someone else.

➤ Obviously, being in business yourself can mean a lot of different things. You may decide you want to establish a company that offers the full monty, such as designing, manufacturing, and selling your product. More likely, you will focus on parts of the process while making arrangements with other firms to do the rest of it. After all, even General Motors buys a lot of its parts from independent suppliers, and lets franchised dealers do the retailing.

➤ As an inventor, you may already be in business formally. Even if you think you do not have a company in the legal sense, the day you commit yourself to making a financial success of your invention you start a business enterprise in the eyes of the IRS—however small and informal that enterprise may seem to you. So, if you haven't yet thought of the time and money you've invested getting this far in terms of a business proposition, start now, whether you think your business will stay small or grow. If you haven't created a structure that provides you limited liability (that is, a structure that legally insulates your personal assets against losses you may incur in your business), you should see a lawyer, soon. Prospective investors will concern themselves with this issue even if you haven't. And you may be asked to indemnify a licensee on the ip front.

➤ If you develop a business around your technology, experience suggests that your company will have to grow, even if it is sometimes possible to get an invention into the marketplace without involving yourself in the complexities of building a large company. If, for example, you've invented a specialized tool with a large profit per sale, you may be able to *bootstrap* your business by selling one, taking the proceeds and making two more, selling them and making four, and so on. Even in such rare cases, however, you will ultimately have to decide to stay small (running the risk that some larger firm, seeing your success, may invade the market with a competitive product) or to expand.

➤ If you run a growing business, you will eventually need capital from outside sources, which means you will need a formal business structure providing limited liability to investors—one in which tasks are subdivided functionally (manufacturing, marketing, etc.) and assigned to professionals. The two things intertwine, because no rational investor will put up the kind of money you will need for a company of even modest size unless you have at least a plan for a formal structure. Investors know, even if you won't admit it, that inventors generally prefer doing everything themselves; moreover, they know that building a

Notable Quotables

"When you do the common things in life in an uncommon way, you will command the attention of the world."

—George Washington Carver, botanist/inventor

Fast Facts

The USPTO projects that in Fiscal Year 2001 it will handle a record 335,400 utility, plant, and reissue patent applications. In Fiscal Year 1986, this number was 131,403.

successful enterprise absolutely requires genuine delegation of authority, something most inventors find extremely difficult to do. If you hope to grow a business, you must accept the ironic proposition that to keep overall control yourself, you will have to delegate a lot of specific authority to other people. You will have to learn to accept reflected glory.

➤ Successful management requires launching, mastering, and controlling a dynamic process and dealing with continuous change caused by growth, new technology, competitors, and so forth. A successful, growing, and dynamic business rests on a foundation of continuous planning, involving constant updating to reflect things like changing circumstances, goals, and human resources. The plan will keep you on track, and it is an invaluable tool with which to sell yourself and your business to prospective investors, customers, and suppliers—and to the people you want to recruit. The latter has crucial importance because you cannot grow without first-class help, and people worth hiring want to know what they're getting into, especially future opportunities.

411

More than six million patents have been granted since the patent system was established in the late eighteenth century. The number of patent and trademark applications keeps growing.

Uncle Sam Needs You! If you're a scientist or engineer and wish to become a patent examiner, call 1-800-786-9757. You may also access information about USPTO career opportunities via the Internet: www.uspto.gov/web/offices/ac/ahrpa/ohr/jobs/exam.htm

The Disadvantages

It is risky. Many new businesses fail. A new business built around a new product runs a double risk, especially since the list of reasons for new business failures reads like a catalog of many inventors' weaknesses. These include (among many, many others) …

➤ Undercapitalization. Typically, new start-up businesses do not have enough financing to go the distance or even do what needs to be done in the short haul. They base their business models on multiple stages of capital infusion. If things to not work in stage one, however, there is no future.

➤ Lack of management skills. Do you know how to build and run a business that involves employees, lawyers, bankers, accountants, et. al? You don't need a Harvard MBA to start a business, but there are skills and experiences you will need to possess or hire.

➤ Overestimating the market. In your enthusiasm, it is easy to overestimate the market for your concept. As a lone inventor, you may not have any checks and balances, i.e., others who have more experience than you, or at the very least another point of view.

➤ Inability to delegate responsibility. Are you able to lead by example and allow others to do their jobs? Or do you feel that only you know how to do things? If you do not understand "reflected glory," or if you are a one-man band, this can be dangerous to the health of a business.

➤ Resources remain limited. A major risk you run is to have too few resources. In the Army, they say never bring up the artillery until you have the ammo in place. It's no different in business. Without the resources, you'll have no fire-power.

➤ You will be spread increasingly thin. As the number of tasks and skills required multiplies—and it does, with a vengeance—you will spend more and more time either doing them or finding someone who can, and will. I call it the Law of Strawberry Jam. The wider something is spread, the thinner it gets.

➤ You probably won't make much money for quite a while. Building a business swallows cash, and a lot of it will be yours. If you can found a company and finance it adequately, you may be able to pay yourself a wage, but it'll probably be modest—your backers will expect you to be frugal with their money.

Prerequisites Common to Licensing and Venturing

Despite the apparently great differences between licensing and venturing as commercialization strategies, they have a lot in common—including certain prerequisites. Either way, somebody has to spend money, a lot of money. Whatever you may have spent so far will pale in comparison to what's required henceforth. So whether you want to market it yourself, or convince someone else to buy the rights to do it, you need a convincing package. This includes ...

➤ Proof that it works. This means a working model, or better yet, an engineering prototype. There's no substitute for showing investors or potential licensees something they can see, touch, and watch do its stuff. Without a *looks like, works like* model, you haven't much chance of interesting anyone beyond family and friends.

➤ Market analysis. This is a serious breakdown of potential customers, how many of them exist, how much they will pay, what the competition is, and how you will beat it. You need to know exactly what the market channels are through which products like yours reach the market. You should be able to show significant points of difference between your product and the competition. If you cannot, you've got a problem. You had better be sure your invention has no fatal flaws.

Above all, you have to be able to show why people will buy your product through statements from prospective customers and focus group results, backed up with believable figures in dollars and cents. The surest way to turn off a prospect who asks about the market is to respond, *When they see it, they will love it*. It ain't necessarily so. Your market analysis will determine whether it is worth going on with your invention, regardless of its technical elegance, and that analysis forms the basis for the next thing you need.

➤ Commercialization plan. This is a detailed analysis showing how you will develop, market, and sell your technology; the cost; and who will do the work—with all this information translated into a year-by-year, dollars and cents format, projected five years out. Investors (other than friends and family) will absolutely demand a plan; prospective licensees may insist, too. And even if they do not, you should have one.

Take My Words for It

Cannibalize: To use components from an existing product for the purpose of making a prototype.

Other Factors in Choosing a Commercialization Strategy

In deciding to license or venture, accept that, either way, you will have to give up a measure of ownership and/or control. In a sense, therefore, you're not deciding whether to get out but when, how completely, under what circumstances, and by what method. In other words, you're looking for an exit strategy at the same time you're looking for a commercialization strategy.

No matter which commercialization strategy you follow, you will increasingly have to involve yourself with people who wear suits. They have different imperatives, different expectations, and speak different languages. Many care nothing about you or your technology except as possible money-spinners. Like it or not, you will increasingly need such people, so learn to deal with them and pretty much on their terms. They're no more inclined to translate their professional language for you than Parisians are to speak English to American tourists.

If you decide that you aren't cut out to be an entrepreneur or that you do not want to be, that does not mean you cannot create a business around your invention. It does mean you will have to get an entrepreneur on your team. They do not come easy; you will have to work to turn up enough evidence to persuade one to cast his or her lot with you and your invention. And they do not come cheap; he or she will want a piece of the action, probably a big piece. But it may be worth it: Chester

Carlson was an inventor who couldn't balance his checkbook, much less run a company, but an entrepreneur named Joe Wilson made him a multimillionaire by building a company called Xerox.

Think About Costs, at All Costs

There are three kinds of costs: money, time, and personal. They are intertwined—to some extent interchangeable. If you think you cannot afford to hire a model-maker, for example, you may decide to save money by building it yourself at a cost of your time, which in turn often involves a personal cost to your health, your marriage, and so on, not to mention the fact that you may produce a poor model. Be guided by this reality: If you think a pro is expensive, hire an amateur.

If You Are Still Not Sure

To help you further analyze which route to commercialization is best for you and your invention, and for that matter, if your invention is efficacious, there are federal, state, and private organizations that can help you. Most of them can be found through the Small Business Administration or a similar state agency. The SBA's toll free number is (800) 827-5722.

From my experience, one of the most professional and effective places to go for help in assessing the marketability of your inventions is the Wisconsin Innovation Service Center (WISC), a cooperative effort between University of Wisconsin-Whitewater Small Business Development Center, UW-Extension, and the federal Small Business Administration. Run by a Debra Knox-Malewicki, a true friend to the independent inventor, the fee-based service just might make the difference if you are on the fence. Plus, you will obtain, through studies, all kinds of information you may never have seen otherwise.

Since it opened its doors in 1980, WISC has evaluated thousands of new product ideas at the request of inventors and small businesses. It has many success stories to share with you.

For information, write: Wisconsin Innovation Service Center, 402 McCutchan Hall, University of Wisconsin-Whitewater, Whitewater, Wisconsin 53190. Telephone: (262) 472-1365. Fax: (262) 472-1600. Or on the Internet, check them out at: academics.uww.edu/BUSINESS/innovate/innovate.htm.

Fast Facts

The laws of nature, physical phenomena, and abstract ideas are not patentable subject matter. Nor can a patent be obtained upon a mere idea or suggestion. The patent is granted upon the new machine, manufacture, etc. and not upon the idea or suggestion of the new machine. A complete description of the actual machine or other subject matter for which a patent is sought is required.

The Least You Need to Know

➤ However you commercialize your brainchild, protect it.

➤ License, and vary your mental gymnastics, spread the risk, and, frankly, have a life.

➤ Things fail no matter how well-researched and -intentioned. Remember Ford's Edsel and "New" Coke.

➤ If you're not sure, seek the counsel of an organization that can provide you with an assessment of your invention vis-à-vis the marketplace.

➤ Whichever road to commercialization you take, if it doesn't get you there, take the other road. Don't be afraid to change direction. Never stop trying.

Part 2
Getting High Marks

American business depends upon innovation and creative thought. Free enterprise is always dissatisfied with the status quo. It always wants the biggest, the best, and the newest. We are a "throw away" society. And like the oyster that is irritated by a grain of sand, America frequently produces the priceless pearl. This gives inventors seeking licensing opportunities or venture capital a target-rich environment.

In this part, we will discuss the advantages and disadvantages between large and small companies, public versus private. This will be followed up by pointers on how to get critical background information on each of the aforementioned units of business. Information is power, but only when properly utilized.

Even with the best and most accurate information at hand, there are no guarantees, just opportunities. In these chapters, you will learn how to take your best shots, make the pitch and, if you strike a nerve, close the deal.

In Part 1, we had ignition. In Part 2, we have forward motion.

Chapter 4

How to Find a Home for Your Brainchild

In This Chapter

➤ Finding companies with the right stuff

➤ Trading information at trade shows

➤ Conferences: networking meccas

➤ Big companies vs. small companies

➤ Public companies vs. private companies

➤ How to get the inside scoop

"Independent inventors tend to make the most radical innovations in technology because they are not held back by corporate group-think."

—Paul Herbig, author, *The Innovation Matrix*

Well, have you decided yet whether you want to go with my preferred direction and license your invention to a manufacturer, or start your own company to develop, produce, and bring it to market?

If you want to raise venture capital, skip to the chapters on how to protect your intellectual property, and find a nearby university or adult education center where how to raise venture capital is taught. To learn about state and federal programs, call the Small Business Administration's toll-free information line: 1-800-827-5722.

On the other hand, if you want to license, product, read on.

Finding a Licensing Partner

Keep in mind that until you have made personal contact with company executives, paid a visit to their offices, gotten to know them, and most importantly, talked with others who have licensed products there, you will not have a full picture of the situation. Here are some tips about how to find the right home for your invention.

Take My Words for It

Licensee: A term used in licensing agreements to designate the party buying the rights to commercialize an invention.

Licensor: A term used in licensing agreements to designate the inventor, or the person selling the rights to an invention.

411

Thomas Regional Directory Company publishes industrial buying guides that provide listings and advertising to help you find companies, in 19 regions of the USA, that make just about anything you can imagine. To see if you qualify for a FREE subscription, call 1-888-REGIONAL or visit the web site at www.thomasregional.com.

➤ Put a lot of time into researching and selecting which manufacturers to approach. Do not rush the process. Match your inventions with company capabilities and profiles. Remember that it is horses for courses.

➤ Do not make the error of insufficient options. Expect rejections—lots of them, so you will want as many candidates as possible.

➤ Find out if the company works with outside inventors. The best tests for this are: how many, if any, licensed products are in the company's line; and does the company have an inventor relations department or system for outside submissions? Study product. Get catalogues. Surf the Web.

➤ You want to sell to a company that would be classified by the U.S. Navy as a *friendly port*. The best way to find out is by meeting other inventors who have licensed to the company. I have found that while companies in the same industry do not talk to each other, inventors discuss contract terms, share impressions, and otherwise spill their guts to each other at the drop of a hat. After all, it is us against them.

Every September, a group of us toy inventors and our spouses get together and spend a three-day working weekend at a beautiful country inn in Vermont. Some folks travel to Vermont from as far away as California and England. What do we do while walking through the woods, biking, antiquing, and eating? We share experiences we have had with our licensees. "Roger is a terrific guy." "I was ripped-off by so and so." "I got a $10,000 advance from David, what did you get?" "How did you have that clause removed?" And on and on it goes.

WACKY PATENTS

Fork with Timer
Patented June 6, 1995
United States Patent 5,421,089

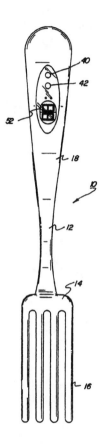

After the weekend, attendees' phones typically ring with executives wanting to know if their names came up in conversation, and if so, in what context. As for the executives, they reap what they sow.

A key question to ask other inventors is if they have had an audit conducted of a specific company's books and if so, what were the results. The answer could tell volumes about the company.

Another way to meet inventors is through national, regional, or local inventor groups and/or organizations. See Chapter 21, "Inventor Organizations," for details on how to hook up. Here, again, there tends to be great camaraderie among the inventors.

Attend Trade Shows

The butchers, the bakers, and the candlestick makers—every enterprise takes part in trade fairs.

National, regional, and local events promote the sale of almost anything you can imagine. There are trade shows for everything from hardware, consumer electronics, apparel, and aircraft to nuclear medicine, dental equipment, comic books, and musical instruments. If it is manufactured and sold, you can be sure that it has been marketed at a trade show somewhere, sometime.

Bright Ideas

The first safety pins were used in Europe some 4,000 years ago. But people jabbed themselves with their sharp, open tips. It wasn't until 1849, in New York City, that Walter Hunt invented a pin that was, indeed, safe. He put a clasp over the dangerous tip. Actually, had he not been in debt, he might never have invented the safety pin. A guy whom he had tapped for $15.00 said he would forgive the debt and pay Hunt $400 if he could make something useful from a piece of wire. He bent and twisted the wire for a few hours and came up with the safety pin design. Hunt's creditor made the fortune.

One-Stop Shopping

Trade shows are not the best venues to present inventions to potential licensees. They are a must for getting the beat on a particular market and its dynamics. It is all there for you to peruse, at your leisure. Competitors line up side-by-side allowing you to compare products and pricing and to look for industry innovations and trends. There is no better or more cost-effective way to acquire product literature than at a trade show. Manufacturers publish product sheets and info kits just for trade show distribution. And many come with a price list!

Note: Some shows have closed booths. To gain entry—not an impossible task—you may have to be particularly inventive!

Please remember that companies pay to exhibit. Depending upon the show and city, costs can run from a few thousand dollars to the millions. Their primary reason for being there is to ring up sales and get leads. They are not there to meet inventors. So you want to blend into the background and white noise, observing and picking up flyers, news releases, and so on.

The sales force does not review new concepts. It is responsible for selling, not developing product. It is a waste of time and dangerous to expose inventions to salespeople at trade shows or anywhere for that matter. Sales types can be, however, excellent sources of information about companies and the industry and normally love to chat about their products, the state of the market, and so on.

Meet 'n Greet

Trade shows are also an excellent place to meet and network with executives to whom you otherwise would not have access. They rarely take their *bodyguards* to shows; it is too expensive and, after all, they are there to meet new people. They even make it easier by wearing nametags. I have made super contacts in hotel elevators, lobby queues, and shared taxi rides to and from the exhibition centers.

The best kinds of shows at which to meet senior executives are national or international. The smaller regional or local trade shows are typically not frequented by heavyweights. Nonetheless, such shows provide a less hectic atmosphere and many of the same resource materials.

Worth the Price of Admission

For most trade shows, admission is free to the trade. All you usually need is a business card to enter the exhibition area. Whenever possible, register in advance by mail and you may not even have to present a card at the door. Advance registration forms are typically found in trade magazines a few months before the event. Allowing people to do this takes the pressure off the registration process onsite at the event. The organizers and the trade want people to be inside buying, not in the lobby waiting for nametags.

How to Locate the Right Trade Show

There are a few methods for discovering where and when trade shows for any particular industry will be taking place.

Notable Quotables

"Difficulties exist to be surmounted."

—Ralph Waldo Emerson

Fast Facts

The Patent and Trademark Depository Library Program began in 1871 when a federal statute provided for the distribution of printed patents to libraries for use by the public. During the program's early years, twenty-two libraries, mostly public and all but a few located east of the Mississippi River, elected to participate. Since 1977, the PTDL network has grown to four times its original size.

1. Ask a manufacturer or distributor in your field of invention. The sales and marketing people will have such information at their fingertips.

2. Contact the trade association that covers your field of invention. More than 3,600 trade associations operate on the national level in the United States. A great way to start is to peruse the *Encyclopedia of Associations,* available at most libraries.

3. Through the Internet you can get information on some 15,000 trade shows worldwide. Go to www.showtrans.com.

Conferences and Meetings: Networking Meccas

The biggest difference between trade shows and conferences is that you almost always pay to attend conferences. This is because the primary reasons for attending conferences include hearing experts speak, picking their brains, sharing your ideas, and networking.

Conferences are excellent places to get to know the people behind the products. Socializing is encouraged and the atmosphere is calmer than at trade shows. There is no pressure to buy. There is no pressure to sell. The object is to make friends, brainstorm, and exchange ideas. Participants can increase their *know how* and *know who* at the same time.

Many conferences offer simultaneous resource fairs. Many trade fairs have conferences or seminars scheduled.

Take My Words for It

Split Royalty: Situation when two or more inventors/licensors divide a royalty.

Finding Conferences in Your Area

Several methods are available for finding out where and when conferences for a particular industry will take place.

1. Ask a manufacturer or distributor in your field of invention. Many larger manufacturers have training departments that can provide helpful information. Cold calls work if you are polite in the way you make your request.

2. As with trade shows, contact the trade association that covers your field of invention. Once again, check *Encyclopedia of Associations.*

3. Ask department heads and professors at nearby universities where your field of interest is taught. Universities, particularly those teaching engineering and kindred technical fields, will have a current schedule of conferences on hand.

4. Using Internet search engines, such as google.com and dogpile.com, you will find all kinds of specialized conferences.

Big Companies vs. Small Companies

The reality is that 80 percent of any business is done by 20 percent of the companies in a particular market. And given a choice, you want to be with the larger company. Unfortunately, you are not usually given a choice. So often it is any port in a storm.

411

Do you have an energy-saving invention that you need money to perfect? If so, the Department of Energy, Office of Industrial Technologies' Inventions and Innovation Program funds up to $200,000 to promising projects demonstrating both energy-saving in-novation and future commercial market potential. The I&I Program emphasizes funding projects that will have significant energy savings on a national level within the following focus industries: Agriculture, Aluminum, Chemicals, Forest Products, Glass, Metal-casting, Mining, Petroleum, and Steel. Visit the OIT Web site at www.oit.doe.gov for details.

Large Companies

Let's look first at large companies vis-à-vis the opportunities they offer you.

➤ Large companies need so much to fill their pipeline that a failure could make you more money than a hit with a small company.

Hasbro and Mattel, for example, would not publish a game that did not launch with at least 250,000 copies, and then have the possibility of increasing in year two and so forth. A smaller publisher might be content with 20,000 copies the first year, and see 50,000 copies as having hit the mother lode.

Hasbro and Mattel would not license a toy that could not do at least $15 to $20 mil-lion in year one and then expand into a line. Their overheads do not allow them to license single items, no matter how clever. A smaller company might launch a toy that sells on a few thousand units per year. This is why larger companies usually see everything first.

➤ Large companies can give you huge advance/guarantee packages. Smaller companies are normally lower in the advance but are willing to give a higher royalty.

➤ Large companies typically have advertising and promotion budgets and departments to spend these dollars on your product. They may have outside agencies, too. Smaller companies sometimes barely get a press release out—unless the president writes and mails it—and have no budget for making noise.

➤ Large companies have clout. I recall years ago asking Mattel how confident it was about securing shelf space for a new, edgy product of mine it had licensed. "If they like that pink aisle, they will give us a shot," quipped a vice president. Of course, he was referring to Barbie. Smaller companies often have trouble getting a buyer on the phone to set up a meeting and show your product, let alone get an order.

➤ Large companies could pay you millions of dollars in royalties and not bat an eyelash. The smaller company might pain over signing a royalty check for $2,000.

➤ Large companies can afford to invest in product. The smaller companies are usually undercapitalized or otherwise unwilling to gamble on large runs without a guarantee in hand. Well, there are no guarantees, just opportunities.

➤ Large companies are typically multinational and get global distribution for your products, and quickly. Small companies do not have sales and distribution offices overseas and usually make their foreign deals through agents.

➤ Large companies have extensive R&D facilities equipped with state-of-the-art equipment. Small companies contract out their development and prototyping.

➤ Large companies have strong front lines and benches deep in talent: engineers, programmers, model-makers, sculptors, quality control experts, designers, copy writers, packaging people, et al. Smaller companies farm most work out to freelancers, which can be problematic when the crunch is on.

➤ Large companies benefit from economies of scale. Small companies are not able to hammer vendors for lower prices because their MOQs (minimum order quantity) are less.

➤ Large companies carry higher product liability insurance than small companies and usually add inventors to it if this is requested by the licensor.

➤ Large companies can power product in ways small companies cannot is perhaps the best way to sum it up.

Notable Quotables

"Embrace rejection. Sometimes it's the only thing you have going for you."

—Barbara Slate, creator of "Angel Love" and other comic characters

WACKY PATENTS

Combination Beverage Tray and Sun Visor
Patented March 10, 1992
United States Patent 5,094,343

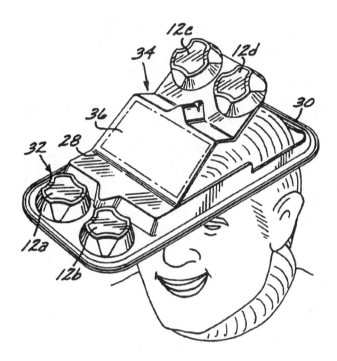

Small Companies

On the other hand, smaller companies do have their positive attributes.

If you cannot convince a large company to sign on, the smaller company may be your only alternative. And lightning can strike. It happens all the time. Here is an example of an experience of mine in this regard.

In 1993, we were awarded a U.S. patent for a dramatic departure on baby bottle designs. Inspired by the spiral pattern on the Nerf Turbo football, our spiral grip was seen by most companies as being too far out. No one wanted it.

One day during the summer of 2000, the phone rang and it was my old friend, Harvey Lepselter, to tell me that he had landed a job as senior vice president for R&D/Marketing at a start-up Long Island company, Babies 'n Things.

"What do you have for infants?" he asked. I thought for a moment, mentioned a couple of items, and sent them up for him to review. They did not meet the bill. After

Bright Ideas

James Fergason holds over 100 U.S. patents, among them a series that is the foundation of the multibillion dollar LCD industry. The Wakenda, Missouri, native invented the first practical uses of liquid crystals. A former associate director of the Liquid Crystal Institute at Kent State University in Ohio, today he is an independent inventor.

411

The Office of Independent Inventor Programs was established at the USPTO in 1999. Reporting directly to the Commissioner of Patents and Trademarks, the office provides independent inventors and entrepreneurs a direct channel to the highest levels of the USPTO. Your feedback and input relative to USPTO issues of concern will be heard. For information, call (703) 306-5568; fax (703) 306-5570; e-mail: independentinventor@uspto.gov.

explaining why the submissions were not appropriate, he asked if there was anything else. "No," I responded. Not one to take no for an answer, Harvey asked me to look around in my prototype closet, again. Because he's such a close friend, I took the time. Then I remembered the baby bottle.

A year after his call, we have makers in the Far East ready to go into production, samples of the bottle have been shown to the trade, and purchase orders are being sent. There have thus far been no negatives. If you find my bottle in a store, under the trademark *Spirals*, you will know that we made it, albeit a few years later than planned. And that's just fine with us. Timing is everything.

Harvey is expanding the line into spiral-grip juice bottles, spill-proof cups, fork and spoon sets, comb and brush sets, and so forth. This is what happens when a great product concept meets a great product champion and marketer like Harvey.

Here are some of the most salient issues to consider when you are looking at a small company.

➤ Small companies may give your baby tender loving care as it is likely more important there than at the large company. Multinational companies eat like elephants and, to put it politely, evacuate like sparrows. They always have back-up product in development, and if a snag is hit on one product, rather than solve it, someone may kill it and pick up a new one that is easier to develop *vis-à-vis* milestones that must be met.

➤ Small companies frequently need the inventor and tend to embrace his or her assistance. Large companies sometimes look at the inventor like a hitchhiker with pets.

➤ Small companies with aggressive leadership are decisive. There's less molasses of process and *administrivia*. I have seen them move like a raven on road kill while the large company misses the meal.

➤ Small companies mold opinion while the large companies are busy measuring it.

So, What's the Answer?

The aforementioned notwithstanding, when all is said and done, there is no correct answer. Even if a company does everything right, and the stars line up properly, products fail. Therefore, what I look for in companies—whatever their size—is that they apply their best efforts to develop, market, and sell my product, in commercial quantities, and under terms and conditions that are fair and equitable to both sides.

Both large and small companies can be all drop back, and no pass; or as they say in Texas, all hat, no cattle. Both types of companies have disappointed me, as I've been surprised and delighted, too.

Public Companies vs. Private Companies

When it comes to public vs. private, I have no preference. Your decision should be based upon what is best for your product. Maintain the frame of mind that you are evaluating the company, not the inferior position that the company is considering you.

You can learn a lot about publicly held companies by perusing a copy of their annual reports. Form 10-K, the most useful of all reports filed with the Securities and Exchange Commission, reveals the following important tidbits:

➤ When the company was organized and incorporated.

➤ What the company produces and percentages of sales any one item may be.

➤ How the company markets: via independent sales reps or its own regional staff offices.

➤ Whether or not it pays royalties, and how much per year.

➤ How much money is spent to advertise and promote its products.

➤ Details on design and development.

411

Athena, the Greek goddess of warfare, wisdom, and arts and crafts, was skilled at weaving, embroidery, and spinning. The Ancient Greeks credited her with the invention of the earthenware pot, plough, flute, rake, chariot, ship, ox-yoke, bridle, and the trumpet. The aim of Inventive Women.com is to feature female inventors who embody the spirit of Athena. This Web site from Canada offers inspirational stories about Canadian women inventors. Check out www.inventive.com.

Notable Quotables

"The secret of genius is to carry the spirit of the child into old age, which means never losing your enthusiasm."

—Aldous Huxley

➤ Significant background on production capabilities.

➤ If the company is involved in any legal proceedings.

➤ An accurate picture of the competition.

➤ And much more.

Finding Information on Public Companies

The best place to obtain deep, detailed information on a publicly traded company is at the Securities and Exchange Commission (SEC), Washington, D.C. The independent, bipartisan, quasi-judicial federal agency was created on July 2, 1934 by act of Congress. It requires a public disclosure of financial and other data about companies whose securities are offered for public sale.

The SEC requires all public companies (except foreign companies and companies with less than $10 million in assets and 500 shareholders) to file registration statements, periodic reports, and other forms electronically. Anyone can access and download this information for free. On the Internet, go to www.sec.gov to find links to and instructions for searching the EDGAR database.

The SEC will, upon written request, send you copies of any document or information. In your request, state the documents or information needed, and indicate a willingness to pay the copying and shipping charges. Also include a daytime telephone number. Address all correspondence to: Securities and Exchange Commission, Public Reference Branch, Stop 1-2, 450 Fifth Street NW, Washington, D.C. 20549.

The SEC operates public reference rooms in Washington, D.C., Chicago, and New York City. They provide, for your inspection, all publicly available records.

Take My Words for It

Gee Whiz Factor: That element in or about an invention that makes people take notice.

Annual Reports: Corporate annual reports are on file with the SEC or can be obtained directly from the company. There is no charge for annual reports that are ordered from a company; if you get annual reports from the SEC, it will require copying, which costs money. Contact the executive in charge of Investor Relations or the Senior Vice President and Chief Financial Officer at the particular company that you are researching.

I think the 10-K is the most useful of all SEC filings. It will tell you, among other things, the registrant's state of business. This form is filed within 90 days after the end of the company's fiscal year. The SEC retains 10-Ks for 10 years.

411

These Web sites are among the best about inventors and invention.

memory.loc.gov/ammem/hhhtml/hhhome.html

www.nps.gov/edis/home.htm

www.cbc4kids.ca/general/the-lab/history-of-invention/default.html

web.mit.edu/invent/

mustang.coled.umn.edu/inventing/Inventing.html

www.nationalgeographic.com/features/96/inventions/

www.inventornet.com/

www.uspto.gov/go/kids/

colitz.com/site/wacky.htm

Part one of the 10-K reveals, among other things ...

1. How long the company has been in business. What you would expect from an established company may vary from what you would tolerate at a start-up firm.

2. What the company produces, percentages of sales any one item constitutes, seasonal/nonseasonal, etc. It is critical to have a complete picture of the company's products, their strengths and markets, and any seasonality or other restrictions.

3. How the company markets, e.g., via independent representatives or regional staff offices. It is important to know how a company gets something on the market and where sales staff loyalty is. For example, company employees typically have more loyalty than independent sales reps that handle more than one company's line.

4. Whether or not it pays royalties and how much per year. You can often see how much work is done with outside developers and whether it licenses anything. An example of such wording is this from a 10-K: "We review several thousand

ideas from professionals outside the Company each year." Another read, "The Company is actively planning to expand its business base as a licenser of its products." Such statements show that doors are open!

5. How much the company spends to advertise and promote product. If yours will require heavy promotion and the company does not promote, you may be at the wrong place. It is counterproductive to take promotional products to companies that do not promote.

6. Details on design and development. You should know before approaching a company whether an internal design and development group exists and its strength. I found one 10-K in which a company stated, "Management believes that expansion of its R&D department will reduce expenses associated with the use of independent designers and engineers and enable the Company to exert greater control over the design and quality of its products." It could not be more obvious that outside inventors were not wanted.

7. Significant background on production capabilities. It is valuable to know in advance the company's in-house production capabilities and what its outsourcing experiences are in your field of invention. It is no use taking a technology to a company that does not have experience making it.

8. If the company is involved in any lawsuits. You may not want to go with a manufacturer that is being sued. Maybe it has just risen from a bankruptcy. All this kind of information is an excellent indicator of corporate health.

9. The ownership of certain beneficial owners and management. This gives you the pecking order and power structure. You will see who owns how much stock (including family members), and what percentage this represents. Age and years with the company are also shown.

10. Competition. This will give you a frank assessment of the company's competition and its ability to compete. One 10-K I read admitted, "The Company competes with many larger, better-capitalized companies in design and development ..." It is unlawful to paint a rosy

Notable Quotables

"Good companies respond quickly to change; great companies create change."

—Robert Kriegel, David Brandt, co-authors, *Sacred Cows Make the Best Burgers*

Fast Facts

In Fiscal Year 2000, the USPTO received 296,490 trademark applications. During this period, it issued 106,383 registrations. 64,700 filings were received via the Internet (e-TEAS, Trademark Electronic Application System).

picture when it doesn't exist. The 10-K is one of the few places you can get an accurate picture of the company's competitiveness. Would you want to license a product to a company that states, for example, "Most of the Company competitors have financial resources, manufacturing capability, volume, and marketing expertise which the Company does not have." This signals you to check out the competition.

Bright Ideas

Do you recognize these mothers of invention?

➤ Mary Anderson patented windshield wipers in 1903.

➤ Melita Bentz invented the Melita Automatic Drip Coffee Maker in 1908.

➤ Josephine Cochrane patented a dishwasher in 1914.

➤ Hattie Alexander found the cure for meningitis in the 1930s.

➤ Lise Meitner discovered and named nuclear fission in 1939.

➤ Marion Donovan patented the first disposable diaper in 1951.

➤ Helen G. Gonet invented an electronic Bible in 1984.

Private Companies

There are no regulations requiring that private companies fill out the kinds of revealing reports public companies do. You will not have details at your fingertips about private companies like you do with public ones. But, by digging, you can come up with some useful stuff. Here are some questions I try to get answers to before talking to a private company. Answers come to me from a combination of sources ranging from state incorporation records to interviews with competition, suppliers, stores (as appropriate), Internet sources, and the owners themselves. Finding the answers requires digging, but this background information may be critical to your long-term success. Here are some questions you'll want answered.

1. A corporation, partnership, or sole proprietorship? This can have legal ramifications from the standpoint of liabilities the licensee assumes. A lawyer can advise you on the pluses and minuses of each situation.

2. When was it organized or incorporated? If a corporation, in which state is it registered? When a company was organized will give you some idea as to its experience. The more years in business, the more tracks in the sand. The state in which it is registered will tell you where you may have to go to sue it.

3. Owners, partners, and officers? Always know with whom you are going into business. In the end, companies are people—not just faceless institutions.

Take My Words for It

Wooden stake letter: A rejection letter from a manufacturer.

4. What are the bank and credit references? How a company pays its bills is important for obvious reasons, and its capital base is worth assessing.

5. Is the manufacturer the source for raw material? Does it fabricate? This will help estimate a company's capabilities for bringing your invention to the marketplace.

6. How many plants does the company own (lease) and total square footage? Warehouses? This kind of information will help complete the corporate picture.

7. What products are currently manufactured or distributed? Do not waste time pitching companies that do not manufacture your type of invention. Maybe a company you thought to be a manufacturer is really only a distributor.

Bright Ideas

The telescope was accidentally discovered in 1698 when Dutch eyeglass maker Hans Lippershey held one lens in front another and realized that the image was magnified.

8. How does the company distribute? Find out about the direct sales force. Make inquiries concerning outside sales reps and jobbers. Does the company use mail order, house-to-house, mass marketing, or another form of distribution? This will quickly reveal how a company delivers product and whether its system is appropriate for your concept. With a mass-market item, it would be foolish to approach a door-to-door marketer regardless of its success.

Where to Find Product and Corporate Profiles

There are many ways to get background information on a company and its product. Here are two of them.

The Thomas Register

One of the best and most comprehensive sources for product and corporate profiles is the *Thomas Register*. Available in most public library reference rooms, *Thomcat*, as it is known, contains information on more than 168,000 U.S. and Canadian companies in alphabetical order, including addresses and phone numbers, asset ratings, company executives, the location of sales offices, distributors, plants, and service and engineering offices. If you know a brand name, you can locate it in the *Thomcat*, too. There are 135,415 brand names included in the database. *Thomas Register* also contains 63,669 product headings. And, at this writing, there are 7,782 online supplier catalogs and Web links on *Thomas Register* on the Internet.

You can access this information in print for free at most major libraries, on the Internet (www.thomasregister.com), and by CD-ROM. Should you wish to purchase a *Thomas Register,* for the most current price information, call: 1-800-222-7900.

Standard & Poor's

If your focus is on the financial condition of a public company, through the S&P Web site, you can gain access, free of charge, to approximately 6,000 corporate profiles. These snapshots provide a great deal of information, including names of top corporate officers. The Web site for Standard & Poor's, a division of The McGraw-Hill Companies, is www.standardandpoors.com

Does the Shoe Fit?

After you have read all the literature and investigated the company inside and out, you must ask yourself: Can the company deliver? And will you be comfortable working with its people?

The abbreviation "Inc." after a company name is not significant. Nice offices, a few secretaries, a fax machine, a copier, and computers do not a successful relationship or product make.

The Least You Need to Know

➤ When assessing potential licensees, remember that just because a company gives a successful image doesn't mean there is steak under the sizzle.

➤ Get business references, especially from inventors who have licensed products to your prospects.

➤ Attend trade shows, and conferences, as a way to better understand your industry, its products, and technologies and meet potential licensees. Information is power!

➤ Make sure the companies you select to approach are really worth the effort.

➤ In the end, default to the company with which you are most comfortable working.

Chapter 5

Knock. Knock. Buy My Invention, Please!

In This Chapter

➤ Open Sesame—getting inside

➤ Only fools rush in

➤ Pick your targets—do your G2

➤ The corporate culture

"For every entrepreneur-inventor like Aaron Lapin and his Reddi-Wip, there are hundreds of thousands of engineers working away daily at institutionalized inventing, and countless pauper-inventors twisting pieces of wire into shapes that will never see a merchant's shelf … But the free-enterprise system holds out the opportunity for those who wish to take it."

—Henry Petroski for *The Wall Street Journal*

Well, have you decided yet whether you want to go with my modus operandi and license your concept to a manufacturer or start your own company to develop, produce, and bring it to market?

If you want to raise venture capital (a.k.a. vulture capital), skip to Part Four on how to protect your intellectual property, and find a nearby university or adult education center where how to raise venture capital is taught. To learn about state and federal programs, call the Small Business Administration's toll-free information line: 1-800-827-5722.

On the other hand, if you want to license product, stay where you are and read on. This chapter focuses on the process of licensing product that can throw off royalty income to you.

First Impressions

You cannot present your invention until you get through the door. And this action, by its high visibility, becomes an integral part of your presentation.

You are a stranger if you have never dealt with the company before and, as such, untested. You will stand out. First impressions are lasting impressions. So, do it right, and you will always be welcome. Mess it up, and it could haunt you into the future.

Fast Facts

Here are the top 10 companies awarded U.S. patents in 2000 and the number of patents by each.

1.	International Business Machines	2886
2.	NEC	2021
3.	Canon	1890
4.	Samsung Electronics	1441
5.	Lucent Technologies	1411
6.	Sony	1385
7.	Micron Technology	1304
8.	Toshiba	1232
9.	Motorola	1196
10.	Fujitsu	1147

While your mission is, of course, to sell your invention, you are always selling yourself first. Don't ever lose sight of this fact. Your credibility can be more critical than the efficacy of your invention. Why? Because no one will put their career and money on the line for a person they do not trust or feel is capable of delivering the goods.

Your first concern must be how you will be perceived. Even if you are capable of dreaming up umpteen different innovative products for a company, without a delivery system, nothing will happen. If you cannot command respect from company management, your inventions will never be taken seriously—if at all. You cannot put a dollar value on your ability to make an encore presentation. The pitch doesn't begin until Act II.

Stop! Look! Listen! How to get through the door deserves considerable thought and reflection. Do not take it lightly because it is in this initial stage that you'll set the tone for future discussion. Images will be engraved into psyches. To do this right requires imagination, experience, and the ability to think out the ramifications of future moves before making them. Like a game of chess, this process resembles war in that it consists of attack and defense and has as its object making the king surrender.

Anyone can get a company's attention if he or she is willing to pay the price. If it's not done right, the price can be steep as in the bum's rush out. It takes a very talented person with a unique concept to gain access and then be invited for lunch, dinner, and if you're really good, an overnight stay, so to speak. Getting inside is one thing, but the amount of time you hold your position is what separates the men from the boys, the women from the girls.

By the time you finish this book, it is my hope that you'll possess all the knowledge required to not only be invited to show product, but to become part of the corporate family of trusted outside creative resources.

Notable Quotables

"There ain't no rules around here! We're just trying to accomplish something."

—Thomas Edison

N.I.H. Syndrome

Not every company welcomes outside submissions. Many do not want to see anything from independent inventors. The Not Invented Here syndrome is very much alive and well in American industry. There are many reasons for it. Here are a couple of them.

A lot of the resistance comes from selfish self-interests. "If you have a 100-person R&D department spending millions of dollars a year and a lone inventor comes along with a better idea, it makes it harder to justify your department to your boss," Michael Odza, publisher of Technology Access Report, told *The Wall Street Journal* in an interview.

Woody Freelander, a former director of marketing and licensing at Union Carbide Corporation, has another take on the problem. He feels if a corporation reviews and then rejects a submission it opens itself for potential lawsuits should they ever do something akin to it, even if what they do is not influenced by the inventor submission.

He adds that being so careful, "may insulate corporations from lawsuits, but it also insulates them from great ideas."

Some companies are N.I.H. only in select areas and open to ideas in others. Here is a July 2001 e-mail response from Microsoft to a query about how to make a submission.

Bright Ideas

Lincoln Logs celebrated its 85th birthday in 2001. They were designed and developed in 1916 by John Lloyd Wright, son of celebrated American architect, Frank Lloyd Wright. The younger Wright conceived his idea for Lincoln Logs while traveling in Japan with his father. Construction techniques used in the foundation of the earthquake-proof Imperial Hotel, which his dad designed, were his inspiration.

"Thank you for contacting Microsoft.

We have received your e-mail and would like to inform you of Microsoft's policy with regard to receiving ideas. Please first review Microsoft's unsolicited submission policy found on the following Web site:

http://microsoft.com/info/cpyright.htm

While Microsoft does accept suggestions for existing products and services, we do not accept suggestions for new products, technologies, processes, etc. We hope that you will understand our intention to avoid any potential misunderstandings or disputes that may arise from submissions of information not related to current Microsoft products. Thus, we are returning your information without review. Microsoft does value your feedback. We would like to encourage you to continue to send us suggestions on the products and services you use today.

If you have any additional questions, please let us know by replying to this message.

Thank you."

If I come up against an N.I.H. atmosphere, candidly, I go elsewhere. There are too many opportunities out there for me to waste my time on people who don't see my value or that of the inventions in my bag.

WACKY PATENTS

Electric Extraction of Poisons
Patented July 5, 1898
United States Patent 606,887

Choosing Your Target and Making Your Mark

Once you have decided which companies to approach, pick out a target and a point of entry. Depending upon how the company is organized, it could be via senior management, legal, research and development, marketing, an outside consultant, or anywhere in between. You'll find that every company is different. Hit the wrong target and it could result in wasted time, review and comment by the wrong people, rejection, or worse.

What remains the same in each company is that you have to approach it as if planning a military operation the first time.

To sell an idea is to engage in warfare; hence my military metaphors. It is a battle of wits and nerves to convince a stranger to open the door and invite you inside. It is a battle to get the stranger to listen, invite colleagues to listen, and then invite you back for a reprise. It is a battle to get anyone—friend or stranger—to take on the challenge of a new and untested invention, make a financial commitment, work like the devil to overcome growing pains inherent in any development cycle, and then manufacture, test, market, and sell your item.

Jobs are at stake. Careers are on the line. The harder the challenge, the more commitment is required. The natural tendency of people is to take the easy way out, which may mean to deep-six your product before it can be called a failure. No one likes to fail, but especially corporate types if their company has no tolerance for it, and they will not be rewarded for the success. Unless the executive has something to gain, such as a bonus, raise, or other benefit, then why rock the boat? Those experienced in corporate culture know that one *gotcha* cancels out 100 *ataboys*.

Notable Quotables

"Be open to share. The professional inventor might add something to the product—half of something sold is better than all of something in your closet."

—Joe Wetherall, Floam

Fast Facts

National Science Foundation studies consistently show that small companies introduce, on average, $2\frac{1}{2}$ times as many innovations per employee as large companies.

There are three basic approaches to warfare: direct attack, compromise, and retreat. Anything less than direct attack isn't worth the energy. No one has ever won a battle that was willing to compromise before a shot had been fired.

The best advice I can give you is to try and deal with people who have responsibility and decision-making power over product acquisition. You'll not know who this is within any particular company until you do your intelligence gathering.

This person may not be the company's CEO. It usually is not because great leaders allow their people to do their jobs. This is why they were hired. If the idea survives the internal review process, sooner or later it will reach the front office. Now, once you have built relationships, if you feel a decision has been made that's wrong, you may consider taking it to a higher authority. I have frequently done this. Sometimes I am successful; more often I am not able to turn a negative decision around. But I am appealing to friends and do it in a very professional manner. I begin every pitch with something like—"in matters controversial, my position's well-defined, I always see both points of view, the one that's wrong and mine."

Experience does dictate, however, that you should not put too much faith in people who just ferry product submissions back and forth between points in a building. These folks, while perhaps very nice people—some may even have vice presidential stripes—are tossed into the fray by their bosses as cannon fodder. They are typically so far removed from the main theatre of operation that they need a road map to find the president's office. And even if they can find it, they do not have his or her ear.

Be polite, respectful, and friendly to the supporting cast. But you need to know upon whom to spend your personal capital and energies. Screen actors learn not to waste their energy on wide shots but to conserve their most emotional performances for close-ups, and extreme close-ups. It's no different when you are presenting product.

The Corporate Culture

The people most successful at getting through the door and building relationships are those with previous corporate experience. This is because they can totally relate to and empathize with executives at large companies. The corporate culture is quite different than any-thing most independent inventors have ever experienced. It is rife with dynamic inaction, and optimization of the status quo. As James Boren put it, people in bureaucracies can devitalize ideas with deft thrusts of yesbuttisms and forthright avoidisms.

If an executive does not return your calls, don't take it personally. He or she is on overload. Your time will come. Many amateur inventors take this to heart. If someone who has become a close friend tries to hammer you in a deal, don't take it personally. He or she is just following orders. Time and time again those with whom I am closest are sent in to do battle. Often they cannot afford to let their bosses see a twinkle in their eyes.

People who have not worked in executive manage-ment usually do not have a clue what these people have to deal with on a day-by-day basis. It isn't easy, and the last thing they want is some inventor who thinks there is a troll under every bridge, or worse, the kind of person who sleeps with one eye open and a gun under the pillow.

411

An awesome Web site from which to access all corners of the federal government is FirstGov, the first-ever government Web site to provide the public with easy, one-stop access to all on-line U.S. federal government re-sources. This cutting-edge site allows users to browse a wealth of information—everything from researching ip at the Library of Congress to tracking R&D at the national laboratories.

Just click on www.firstgov.gov and away you go.

Lookin' to Hook 'Em

You need a hook, one beyond the appropriateness of the invention you are hawking. I like to look at an executive's background for some connection to me, e.g., where he or she grew up, went to school, spent summer holidays, common interests, and so on. And if I can find this out before our first meeting, all the better. It just might help me get the meeting.

I have lost count of how many times I have been able to break the ice through some external connection. At one company, I actually found a distant cousin through marriage. To this day, we call each other cuz.

I use a variety of sources:

> ➤ **Internet search engines.** Three of my favorites are Google.com, AltaVista.com, and Dogpile.com.

> ➤ **Who's Who.** There are many versions of this directory, e.g., *Marquis Who's Who In America, Who's Who In Manufacturing, Who's Who In Entertainment, Who's Who In The East,* and so on. In addition to detailed biographical and career information such as schools, birthplace, names of spouses and children, government service, awards, and so forth, I have even found home addresses.

WACKY PATENTS

Fire-Escape
Patented November 18, 1879
United States Patent 221,855

➤ **Annual reports.** Public companies frequently run bio sketches of senior management. These can be acquired from the companies themselves, stockbrokers, the SEC, select business library reference rooms, and so on.

➤ **Industry organizations.** If the executive is an officer of his or her industry group, it will likely have background information.

➤ **Media archives.** I love to run names through Lexus/Nexus or another full text legal, business, medical, and news information service.

➤ **Trade publications.** Often magazines specific to an industry will interview and/or otherwise profile a person. While not heavy with personal information, I can get great insights into a person for a good interview.

Take My Words for It

Guarantee: Minimum sum of money that a manufacturer assures an inventor he will earn on a product even if it is dropped or performs poorly.

You need the company or you would not be there. So, while it's important that you show yourself as independently creative, take the *"we"* approach not the *"I"* approach. There is no "i" in team, and companies function through teamwork. The faster the invention goes from *my concept* to *our concept* the better.

Sign on the Dotted Line

Many companies will ask that an agreement be signed before they will accept the submission of outside ideas. This may surface when you first approach the company or on the day you make the formal presentation. I have never had a problem with such requests. I always know with whom I am dealing and feel confident in the relationship. If I did not, I wouldn't be there in the first place.

I recall my presentation of Star Bird, our electronic toy spaceship, at Milton Bradley in 1978. I was asked to sign a nonconfidentiality form and replied, "OK. I'll do it because you're too big a company to rip me off, and I am too little to worry about it." We went on to build a relationship that still exists today with current management.

The best way to handle this is to have the document faxed to you in advance of your pitch. I cannot imagine this as an inconvenience to the company. At the same time, you should always verify what you are asked to sign, and modifications can be made. If you are uncertain, consult an intellectual property attorney.

Even if you sign such a document, it does not give the company *carte blanche* to steal your idea. In some states, the law of torts affords limited protection to the owner of a trade secret for the misappropriation of his or her ideas. Not all ideas are trade secrets.

In fact, most of what you may be sharing in your meeting would be covered by the submission agreement.

Some inventors go for a *quid pro quo*, i.e., if they sign the company's nondisclosure agreement (NDA), they expect theirs to be signed. Do what makes you comfortable. Many companies have no problem reciprocating in this way.

Fast Facts

The Web site for the U.S. Patent and Trademark Office is the MOST visited U.S. government URL. In fact, it is one of the world's most visited Web sites. According to its Webmaster, the USPTO Web site gets between 1,100,000 and 1,300,000 hits per day.

A trade secret is a plan or process, tool, mechanism, or compound known only to its owner and people to whom it is necessary to confide it.

To establish a cause of action for misappropriation, you must show that you had a confidential relationship, shared a trade secret, and the company made use of the information in a breach of confidence. I am not an attorney, but there is an implied confidentiality of trade secrets, where there isn't for general ideas, when you share them in spite of the fact that you signed a nondisclosure document.

A suspicious attitude may seriously inhibit your progress. Put your time and energies into creating concepts versus overprotecting them. Become paranoid over this, i.e., beyond what is reasonable caution, and no one will ever see your ideas.

See Chapter 16, "Securing Your Copy Rights," for greater detail about trade secrets.

The Least You Need to Know

➤ First impressions are lasting impressions.

➤ Plan your approach and entry very carefully.

➤ If you don't understand the corporate culture, team with someone who does. Rookie moves can get you thrown out at first.

➤ Look out for Number 1, but don't step in Number 2.

➤ Don't get freaked out over signing nondisclosure agreements.

Chapter 6

How to Turn a Proposal into a Marriage

In This Chapter

➤ Nothing astonishes like the truth—flaunt it

➤ The more the opposition knows about you, the better for your relationship

➤ How to present your ideas

➤ Elements of a great proposal

➤ Multiple submissions—sometimes it pays to shotgun a proposal to various companies

➤ Start strong, and end stronger—as the popular Chinese proverb goes, you never want to see the head of a tiger and the tail of a snake

"Independent inventors are the lifeblood of the toy industry. This important, elite group of (mostly) brilliant, hard working, creative individuals are unsung heroes, inventing, discovering, and building some of the most exciting, innovative, inventive toys, games, and learning aids for the real winners of their efforts, consumers. They are most often unknown people and companies in the shadows getting their rewards and inspirations from seeing their product ideas succeed with people all over the globe. Toy inventors have been one of the most important groups in our success over the years and I am indebted to them all for their dedication, support and brilliance."

—Roger A. Shiffman, President, Worldwide Marketing and Brand Development, Hasbro Inc.

Life's a pitch! And nowhere does a pitch need more energy than when it comes to new product concepts. The pitch not only has to be powerful and efficacious, but it needs post-pitch propulsion (PPP)—the ability to survive long after you have departed. But, above all, it must be honest.

Honesty Is the Only Policy

A little B.S. is OK. After all, fertilizer makes beautiful flowers. And it's part of the entertainment. Seasoned execs have B.S. meters and will let you know if you start to pin their needles or redline. But this is a business and there is a lot riding on decisions, so make it the truth, the whole truth, and nothing but the truth, please.

When you were a child you heard the old saw, *honesty is the best policy*. I'd make these words by Cervantes stronger: Honesty is the *only* policy. It does not pay to be less than totally up front with potential licensees and those with whom you are co-inventing or in business. If you think that by hiding or fudging a flaw or fact about the invention's origin, ownership, technology, and so forth, you are avoiding a problem that might queer the deal, you are so wrong. If you are not honest up front, you are asking for trouble down line.

Full and honest disclosure makes for smoother sailing. No one likes surprises, especially licensees after they have made an investment. On the other hand, no one expects your product to be perfect. Every rose has its thorn. I cannot guarantee that your candor will be met by the same level of honesty from the other side, but in the end, your reputation will be all the stronger for it. Your reputation, by the way, will have more to do with your success than your concepts. You can take this fact to the bank!

You Should Hear a Pin Drop

When you are pitching, and doing it well, you should have the rapt attention of everyone within your cry and gaze. If you do, telephones will not be answered, people will not interrupt, and eyes will not glaze over with ennui. You will have them in the proverbial palm of your hand.

To that end, here are some pointers:

➤ Get an appointment to show your idea. Never send in a model or prototype unless there is no other way to do it. Products are best demonstrated by their inventors and questions can be quickly answered.

➤ Get as high up the corporate product review food chain as possible. If possible, do it one-on-one. This way attention is focused on the product, and there are fewer chances for distractions.

➤ Unless the reviewer knows you well, start out the meeting by briefing him or her (or the group) on your most significant accomplishments and any other personal choice morsels that might help set the scene and make them more receptive.

WACKY PATENTS

Portable Self-Powered Band Saw
Patented February 10, 1987
United States Patent 4,641,560

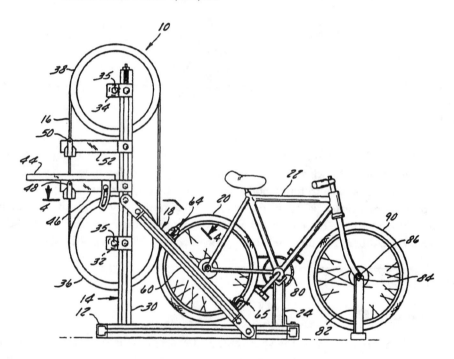

➤ While every inventor is passionate about his or her brainchild, offer up some objective information about it. This might include the results of focus group testing, for example.

➤ Make the presentation professional. If you want to operate in today's marketplace, you need to exhibit to your audience that you are in step with it.

➤ If you hit a snag, think fast. Many times a manufacturer will say to me, just as I am getting into a presentation, that the product is not for his or her company. This is when you need to be even more inventive and see if through some modification the item can be made to fit.

➤ If the potential licensee is on the fence after you have completed your dog-and-pony show, offer to continue to work on spec. This can have the affect of keeping the product alive and getting the manufacturer invested. It increases the likelihood of the product getting a curtain call.

➤ Always have a plan of action when you wrap up the meeting. Everyone needs to know what needs to happen next, who does what. Chances for a sale at the pitch session are rare (though not impossible!). Typically, manufacturers like to bring good ideas back for different people within the company to comment. As you will learn, if you do not know it already, falling in love and getting to the altar are quite different things.

Bright Ideas

In 1989, Tomima Edmark, a 36-year-old marketing rep for IBM, saw a woman in a movie theater sporting a French twist hair-do. Hmm. She turned to her mom and wondered aloud if it was possible to turn a ponytail inside out. Soon after that epiphany she made a prototype from circular knitting needles and started testing it with friends. The results were beyond positive. Women loved it. Topsy Tail, one of the most successful hairstyling products, was born and ultimately brought in over $80 million in global sales.

The Three Ps

Once you are no longer in the spotlight, and everyone has returned to their desks, all kinds of disparate forces come into play. The idea you presented may not even be remembered shortly thereafter, prototypes notwithstanding. When it is time to show your submission to a wider audience—a day, five days, or even a few weeks hence—to people who did not have the benefit to feel your passion, this is when products frequently start circling the drain, or worse, get sucked down it. This is where the product needs PPP (Post-Pitch-Propulsion)!

Charlie Brower, a 1981 inductee to the Advertising Hall of Fame, explains the fragility of a new idea. "A new idea is delicate," he says. "It can be killed by a sneer or a yawn; it can be stabbed to death by a quip and worried to death by a frown on the right man's brow."

I was the new product acquisition consultant to a public company a few years ago. My assignment: to sweep across the country, accompanied by the vice president for R&D, meet with inventors, and bring back appropriate product for the company's marketing department to consider. I recall how, on more than one occasion, when it came time to present a particular product, we would look at each other in hopes that the other guy remembered how to operate it. If the inventor had provided a background binder, or video, we were off to the races. But when we had nothing to refresh our memories, the product was not shown. We would reschedule the internal review to give the inventor time to supply us with a video and instructional information, but it was never so advantageous the second time around. Therefore, when you make that first pitch, cover every base.

Written material should be presented in three-ring binders or folders, the kind which have cover and spine pockets. Design a cover page and use tabs to separate sections. These notebooks become one-stop information sources for you and the executives. Binders are available at any office supply store. There is a large selection of colors and sizes.

Make sure that every product submission is accompanied by its own background package. This can take many forms, but typically I favor a written proposal—the components of which are outlined below—plus marker renderings, if appropriate, and a video.

Notable Quotables

"Don't blame manufacturers for not wanting your invention. They have their own needs; learn what they are."

—Israel Gamzo, inventor

Elements of a Proposal

Every proposal I write begins with an executive summary, a paragraph that allows corporate executives to get a quick read on the product, and do a gut check. This is a simple paragraph, nothing elaborate, one that paints an image of the invention and your objectives.

Here are some examples:

➤ *Oops & Downs: The Firehouse Full of Fun* plays like a 3-dimensional Chutes & Ladders. The multilevel board game is designed around a toyetic environment that features playing piece figures with internal reeds or other air-activated sound-making devices. The levels are interconnected by vertical or near vertical tubes of various lengths (depending upon the levels connected). Each playing piece figure has a different sound signature when dropped down a tube. Alternatively, the reed/sound-making device may be located in the base of the tube, or connected to the tube in such a way that the air drives not only sound, but also elements, such as a randomizer. The playing pieces can be used as whistles. U.S. Patented.

Bright Ideas

"Be it known that I, Harry Houdini, a citizen of the United States, and a resident of New York City, borough of Brooklyn, in the county of Kings, in the State of New York, have invented a new and improved diver's suit ...." So began the specification of Patent No. 1,370,316, that issued on March 1, 1921 to the American magician who won fame as an escape artist. Houdini was born in Budapest, Hungary, in 1874.

Fast Facts

The first patent awarded in North America was in 1641. The Massachusetts General Court granted it to Samuel Winslow, a colonist, for a method to extract salt. Many North American patents that issued prior to independence and the formation of the United States were concerned with the manufacture of salt because it was so important in the preservation of foodstuffs.

➤ *Insecta GigANTica* is an anthropomorphic ant habitat designed inside a three-dimensional, injection-molded, plastic representation of a prehistoric beast or other creature.

➤ *Switchblade* is a pair of training skates that transforms from four-wheel quad (standard configuration) into four-wheel in-line. It is based upon a variable geometry chassis, i.e., a collapsing parallelogram. U.S. Patented.

Between the Covers

Here are the categories (as appropriate) that I like to include in a presentation binder:

1. *Operating Instructions*: Take nothing for granted. Nothing! The worst thing that can happen is an executive's inability to use a product after you depart. Don't let the simplicity of your item draw you into a false sense of security. If I were to submit something as simple as a ballpoint pen, I would prepare written, illustrated, and video instructions. No item is fail-safe when you are not there to operate it. It's hard enough to guarantee successful operation when you are there.

2. *Marketing Plan*: Highlight and detail your item's unique features and advantages over existing products. Define its appeal and target audience. Suggest follow-ups, including second generations and line extensions, if appropriate. Manufacturers like products that have a future, especially if they are looking at beaucoup start-up dollars in the development and launch phases.

You do not need a graduate degree in marketing to work up this kind of information. The more you can do to define the market and positioning of your concept, the better.

3. *Trademark*: Offer possible trademarks and taglines. I like to suggest everything from word marks to logotypes. If you have conducted a trademark search, include its results or the status of any applications you may have in play. The right mark or slogan can go a long way toward securing a sale. For information on trademark searches, see Chapter 15, "Mark Your Words."

4. *Patents*: Before you submit any concept to a manufacturer (or investor), a patent search should be conducted. Include the results of any search, USPTO actions, and so on. If a patent has been issued to you already, submit a copy. For information on patent searches, see Part Three, "Goin' for the Gold."

5. *Advertising/Publicity*: I like to suggest advertising and publicity hooks. This information, like a good trademark, helps make presentations more persuasive and polished. It is also available to the manufacturer for focus groups.

6. *Video*: If a still picture is worth a thousand words, moving images are worth a million. We do not let anything out of our studio without a demo video. Playback machines are found in every company. Other than a face-to-face presentation, nothing beats a motion picture. By the way, you can purchase varying lengths of tape from wholesale jobbers. Most of our tapes are precut to 10 minutes. These are less expensive to purchase, and lighter for mailing purposes, than the standard 120 minute VHS tapes you find everywhere from drugstores to gas stations.

Notable Quotables

"There's no such thing as a crackpot inventor. Edison might have been the crackpot of the century ... but his stuff clicked."

—U.S. Patent Commissioner Coe (1940)

Don't worry if the camerawork is a bit rough. This can work to your benefit. There is a warm and sincere feel and tone to homebrew video presentations. If they are too slick, the potential licensee may think you are covering up something. Put it all out there and let the product do its stuff.

In addition to using video as a medium for instructions, we also use them to do technical briefings and also to show people testing prototypes. There is nothing like showing satisfied consumers. If we have a technical briefing and ideas for a focus group, we might consider submitting two separate tapes so that two departments do not have to share one tape.

We are just starting to get into video streaming and burning CDs as other vehicles of communication for presenting the features and operations of our inventions.

Lots of companies are using videos with consumers in a similar style. My wife's new car came with a video and a CD-ROM as did a camera of mine. In both cases, the moving images complimented what was written in the instruction booklets.

Your worst nightmare is a breakdown in communications. Such full motion audio-visual components added to a presentation help avoid it.

WACKY PATENTS

Fly Deterrent Apparatus
Patented April 2, 1991
United States Patent 5,003,721

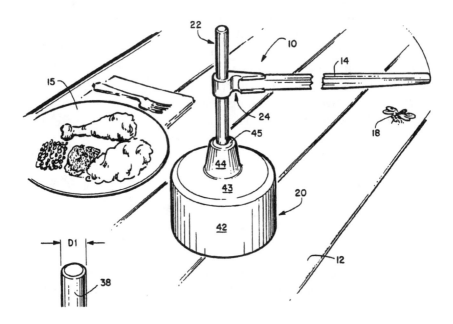

7. *Technical*: In writing and on video/CD-ROM, you should address everything from design, engineering, and manufacturing issues to component sourcing and costing. Include exploded views, part lists, and anything else that will help a corporate research and development designer or designer understand your item's technical and manufacturing profile.

8. *Personal Resumé*: If you are unknown to the company, provide a background sheet on your capabilities. Depending upon the nature of the submission, a green light may depend upon a manufacturer's confidence in your ability to make the product happen, albeit under the company's guidance.

Pitching Isn't Enough. Pitch In, Too.

Approach every product submission in such a way that you could, if contracted by the manufacturer, take the item outside and do it for them. More and more manufacturers are relying on inventors to take products to tooling. This was not the case years ago, but with personnel cutbacks and increased workloads, often the only way a product gets done is through the inventor's being able to manage a development program. And don't expect to be paid for everything you do in this regard. Frequently, other than out-of-pocket expenses, I don't ask for payment. This is always a judgement call.

When possible, include with your proposal (in the "Technical" section) …

➤ A sheet listing all components with respective prices from various sources. Pricing from three different sources is a good bet. When possible, a mix of domestic and offshore sources for pricing is best. Do not forget to include the volume the quotes are based upon, plus vendor contacts.

➤ Note the type of material(s) desirable, for example, polyethylene, wood, board, and so on. Provide substitutions and options for consideration.

➤ When you calculate the item's cost, do not forget to consider the price of assembly (if any). The quoting vendors will be helpful here.

➤ If your item requires retail packaging, add an extra 15–30 percent.

➤ Add an extra 20 percent for modifications and losses. At this point, you have the item's hard cost.

➤ To arrive at the manufacturer's selling price, add in your royalty, an amount of money for promotion (if appropriate), and a gross profit margin for the manufacturer (65 percent). You may wish to estimate the mark-up at the retail end (if appropriate). A good estimate is the hard cost multiplied by three or four: five for a T.V. promoted item.

➤ Important: Don't be misguided and cost components and quote work-for-hire fees based upon the size of a company. Recently, I was working on a new game and puzzle line and a provider of artwork put an outrageous fee on reproduction rights. When I tried to get the price down for my licensee, the executive gating authority for the artwork said that he was holding firm because the licensee "could afford it."

Notwithstanding the fact that our licensee was a multibillion dollar, multinational company, each product it manufacturers and sells has its own budget, price points, and so on. and must stand on its own. So, make your decisions according to the specific product and, even then, sometimes it pays in the long run to give a bit. It's worth repeating: Pigs get fat, hogs get slaughtered.

Fast Facts

To patent, or not to patent, that is the question. A patent can be a double-edged sword. While it allows the inventor the right to exclude others—for twenty years from the date the application was first filed—from making, using, and selling his or her innovation, it also makes it public for everyone to see. To get a patent, one must reveal invention. Thus, not every inventor seeks patent protection. For example, the Coca-Cola Company prefers to keep its formula secret, receiving some protection under trade secret laws.

Multiple Submissions

If you have more than one prototype, and the situation is appropriate, you may wish to consider making submissions to more than one manufacturer at the same time. I have no set rule about this. I go case by case, guided by experience. The decision is made easier for me if I have patent and/or trademark protection.

If a company asks you to hold off further presentations until it has an opportunity to review the item at greater length, try to set guidelines. In all fairness, some products require a reasonable number of days to be properly considered. However, if you feel the company is asking for an unreasonable period of time, seek some earnest money to hold the product out of circulation. The amount of time and money is negotiable. Also insist that the product not be shown to anyone outside the company.

Take My Words for It

Multiple submission: Submission by an inventor of the same concept simultaneously to several potential licensees.

The value of the *multiple submission* is not only to have it reviewed by more companies at a faster pace, but it may also set up for a bidding war. I have done this from time to time and it is an understood tactic of negotiation. Do not be timid about suggesting it, just know when and where to do it—and only for special products.

Unfavorable Odds

The odds you are up against are staggering. For example, in the business of selling television entertainment story lines, each network may see between 1,000 and 1,500 ideas per year. Each commissions between 50 and 60 scripts. Pilots are shot for between 25 and 30. Then the networks will order, on average, between 8 and 10. Few make it to 13 episodes.

Other industries are not that heavily bombarded. Once we designed a neat water faucet and found no competition to distract those to whom I pitched, save for the in-house development department. In such instances, companies tend to be all the more conservative. Since their market is steady and loyal, they do not want to do anything that could upset their market share.

Fast Facts

The world's first patent was granted to architect Filippo Brunelleschi in Florence, Italy. The year was 1421. It was for a barge crane to transport marble.

Your Champion

In order for your product to sustain itself through the review and development process, it will need a champion, a white knight. Typically this standard-bearer will come from among those attending your first meeting. This is the person who will be representing your product as it passes from review to review. This is a process that can resemble a ride through the Danzig Corridor at night being tracked by enemy radar and dodging occasional triple-A fire.

It will be the responsibility of this executive to keep you up to date on the progress of review. Try and get a schedule. No manufacturer should be allowed an open-ended time frame. There need to be parameters set before you take leave of the meeting.

Schedules slip, however, and things may not fire off on time. Each case is different, of course. You will have to use your judgment to determine when it is time to pull the plug, if things start dragging. I am typically guided by how the product is moving along through the internal system. If I get a sense that it is sitting in a closet, I'll ask for it. One thing you can be assured is that no manufacturer will send something back that it is sold on. If your product comes back, it means there is no constituency for it.

The Least You Need to Know

➤ There is nothing so powerful as truth—be honest when it comes to your invention and business.

➤ Don't play the Big Room like a lounge act—if you get an executive's attention, strive for the heights of quality and professionalism.

➤ Speed doesn't kill, stopping fast does—people appreciate presentations that move apace, but abrupt stops can spook your audience.

➤ Scratch the place that itches—if there is a problem, fix it before things get out of hand.

➤ If you're not goin' to kiss 'em, don't make 'em stand on their tip toes—don't tease people with concepts you cannot deliver.

➤ Invention reviews, like trains, run on a schedule. Unlike trains, they are frequently late—you be on time even if the executives are not.

Chapter 7

How to Negotiate Your Deal

In This Chapter

➤ Negotiate yourself or have a partner do it—do not rely 100 percent on lawyers

➤ Disclosure forms do not bite—sign whatever is fair

➤ Everything has its price, including winning

➤ Agreeing to agree is the best first step in negotiation

➤ Levy's 10 Commandments of Negotiation

"For years we tried to get by with only product conceived internally. It didn't work. Our outlook was too insular. We now get ideas from the outside inventor community. We insist they stay involved with implementation. The concepts are better. The end product is better. It has an edge that we would not get from the inside. These guys—the outside guys—think differently than normal people. We are looking straight ahead. They are looking forward but sideways, at the same time."

—Barry Tunick, President & CEO, Centuri Corp.

Negotiating contracts is a skill that can be learned. People tend to make it complex. It ain't. But sooner or later in the process, you may come face to face with lawyers—those on the side of your opposition, and your own. So let's discuss the lawyers first.

On Lawyering—One Man's Opinion

Lawyering, once a respected profession, has evolved into just another business, one involving self-promotion, boredom, greed, and billable hours.

"I call it the Twilight Zone factor," said a lawyer interviewed by *Philadelphia* magazine. "Nothing we do as lawyers is rooted in reality. The fees we charge have no economic basis in the work actually done. It's whatever the market will bear. The issues we dispute are increasingly not real world issues but artificial conflicts that we created and that we prolong. And the worst part is that the expectations we have of ourselves all call for Superman in a three-piece suit. What I hate about being a lawyer is always reaching out to touch something—but it's never there."

Now that I have put lawyering into perspective, let me add that there are many very good lawyers. However, while a lawyer may know more than you do about the fine points of law, few practicing attorneys have proven themselves to be sharp in business, especially when it comes to making tough decisions, those that make deals sing. Law school is, after all, just a trade school. Nothing beats empirical business experience. And many lawyers with marketplace experience no longer practice law but join the ranks of management and entrepreneurism.

Notable Quotables

"If a man can write a better book, preach a better sermon, or make a better mousetrap than his neighbor, though he builds his house in the woods the world will make a beaten path to his door."

—Ralph Waldo Emerson

Should You Use a Lawyer to Approach the Company?

Absolutely not! This sends the wrong message. It may set off all types of bells and whistles at the company and likely trigger a response from the legal department, fighting fire with fire. This is not what you want. If at all possible, you want to go one-on-one with a senior executive or several representatives from marketing or research and development, depending upon which department drives product selection. A lawyer will send the wrong message, one that you are distrustful. There is more than enough time for legal advice during the ritual dance of license negotiations.

Lawyers intimidate most people. If you let them, they'll confound you with facts, blind you with Latin, and plague you with precedents. Corporate attorneys love ambiguity, complexity, and advancement of only their side of the issues. The last thing they want is candor, clarity, or compromise. Frequently business executives have to rein them in and apply sound business principles.

Fast Facts

On August 25, 1814, the British burned Washington. Dr. William Thornton, Superintendent of Patents, saved the Patent Office from destruction by pleading with the British commander not to *"burn what would be useful to all mankind."* The Patent Office was saved.

Then on December 15, 1836, the Patent Office was completely destroyed by fire. The loss is estimated at 7,000 models, 9,000 drawings, and 230 books. More serious is the loss of all records of patent applications and grants.

Of course, if you are asked to sign a product disclosure form and you feel uncomfortable with the language it contains, then by all means run it by counsel. But do not take a lawyer to your pitch meeting or subsequent technical reviews. You need to be perceived as an athlete, not a spectator.

Do You Need a Lawyer for Contracts?

Perhaps. Maybe no. This decision will depend upon your own experience in the art of negotiation and crafting intellectual property deals. I used a law firm for my first intellectual property licensing agreement, got the feel for it, and then went it alone, for the most part. This experience was invaluable also for what it taught me about how lawyers bill. I now know how to direct my lawyers and avoid all kinds of unnecessary expenses. Frankly, this could be the topic of a *Complete Idiot's Guide* because that is what I felt like after getting that first bill, a complete idiot. Take advantage of me once, shame on you; do it again, shame on me. Nonetheless, even today, after having done hundreds of deals for my own ip and helping friends negotiate their packages, I still call in a business lawyer, from time to time, if faced with an extremely complex deal with a major licensee, especially if it involves important third party partners.

Bright Ideas

Four days after the United States detonated an atomic bomb on Bikini Atoll, French designer Louis Reard presented his new design for a bathing suit for the first time. He called it the bikini.

Though, even if I engage the services of my business attorney, I still remain very much involved—and he likes it. If an ip issue arises, I do not hesitate to involve my patent attorney. If a trademark issue arises, I have a different attorney. I do not hire my patent attorney to negotiate business deals, or my business attorney to work patent deals, and so forth.

The most efficacious way to find yourself a business attorney skilled in your field of enterprise is through personal recommendations. In my case, I considered all the chief legal officers at the toy companies with whom I had negotiated over the years. I looked for the one who had been most fair to me, who took my side if it was right, and did not stonewall for his company just to grandstand and look like a hero to his or her bosses. Then the day this person resigned to open a private practice, I was the second inventor to sign up.

WACKY PATENTS

Apparatus for Converting Aircraft Exhaust into Useful Energy
Patented December 7, 1999
United States Patent 5,998,882

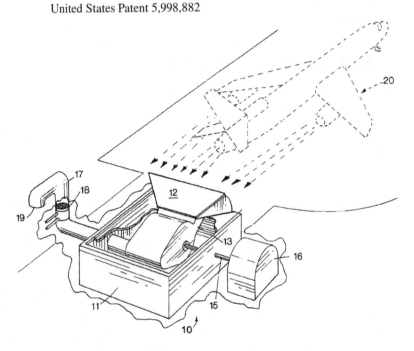

Do You Need a Lawyer for Patents?

Yes! Yes! Yes! Please see Part Three for in-depth information on this topic.

Conducting Business

The most basic rule is to conduct your business in your style. Set the pace. Do not get caught up in your prospective licensee's timetables and priorities. Things tend to get worse under pressure during a negotiation.

Before you head into the boardroom to negotiate a contract, put these pearls of wisdom into your briefcase.

➤ Stop. Look. And listen.

➤ Say no, then negotiate.

➤ Trust everybody, but cut the cards.

➤ Don't wish for luck; prepare for luck.

➤ If it looks like a duck and quacks like a duck, expect a duck.

➤ Don't get mad; don't get even; get ahead.

➤ Never murder a person who is committing suicide.

➤ Bite the bullet only if you can stand the taste of gunpowder.

Fast Facts

How much should you ask for as an advance? I normally ask the company what it typically pays and justification for the figure. Whatever it offers, try for more. At the same time, double-check with others who may have licensed products to the manufacturer. Inventors tend to share information with each other quite freely.

Winning at What Cost?

Getting what you want does not always have to be at another person's expense. It is possible to get what you want and still let your opponent have something. After all, you are entering into what you both hope will be a long and mutually beneficial relationship. As our political process demonstrates, societies thrive best not on triumph in domestic debates, but on reconciliation. Nothing would ever be accomplished if every technical disagreement turned into a civil war.

A good deal is one in which all sides meet their needs. Needs can be reconciled. Compromise is okay. Unfortunately, not every person you meet at the bargaining table believes in this theory. Some people will give off signals that they are not trustworthy from the start. Then there are the slick ones, who never appear to be the killers that they are.

Notable Quotables

"Every new invention, every triumph of engineering skill, is the embodiment of some scientific idea; and experience has proven that discoveries in science, however remote from the interests of everyday life they may at first appear, ultimately confer unforeseen and incalculable benefits on mankind."

—Robert Routledge, editor

105

Terms aside, my own rule of thumb is that unless I am totally comfortable with the executives and the company, I don't even sit down to deal. I have always been guided by the feeling that a bad deal isn't worth it under any circumstances.

Agreeing to Agree

Prior to discussing the nuts and bolts of a specific licensing contract, I want to know three things up front:

1. *Does the company license from outside inventors?* If it does, I will want to know which products and from whom they were licensed. I will definitely call the inventors if I have no experience with the company. If they tell me that there is no inventor product in their line, then I need to find out why. I have seen some companies that welcome inventors just to get a look at what's being shown. They never license anything.

2. *Is the company willing to pay me a fair royalty on the net sales of each unit sold?* Executives should have no problem telling you which products have inventor royalty loads. If they don't, you're outta there.

3. *Is the company willing to pay me an advance against future royalties, and possibly a guarantee?* No strings attached. There should be no problem telling you the levels of advances, and guarantees the company pays. Some companies do not pay guarantees.

Once I establish a basis for negotiation, contractual terms typically do not stand in the way. And they should not so long as I want to sell and the manufacturer is serious to license. Everything usually shakes out.

Many inventors suffer from a disease I call "sellitus." These folks will license their inventions to anyone who shows interest and for just about anything. Their feeling is that if they can get an advance, take it. Some money is better than nothing. Not true! No amount of scratch or level of royalty/guarantee is worth a bad deal. No amount of money or level of royalty/guarantee is worth taking unless you are 100 percent confident in the company, its honesty, stability, and ability to deliver on the specific performance required by the contract. Contracts are only as good as the people that sign them.

I have experienced situations when I could not get companies to honor their contracts on a product that bombed. I have experienced situations when I could not get companies to honor their contracts on so-so products. I have experienced situations when I could not get companies to honor their contracts on hit products. Nothing is worse than a revenue-generating product, at any level of performance, that is not filling your coffers with royalties when due and payable. This is an inventor's worst nightmare. You must *always* be able to walk away from an uncomfortable situation.

Advances

The advance is important because it can help you recoup a portion of your outlay for research and development, and it serves as a barometer for gauging the amount of interest at the company. It is not always possible to earn an advance that will cover all of your expenses.

A good way to calculate an advance is to base it on a quarter or a third of the royalties the manufacturer would have to pay you during the first year of projected sales. For example, if the company tells you it estimates 100,000 units in year one, and that it will sell at an average net wholesale price of $10, your royalty, if five percent, would amount to $50,000. Twenty-five percent of $50,000 is $12,500. At a third the number works out to an advance of $16,667.

This advance could be paid as a lump sum upon signing or in stages during the first year of the agreement. This is all open to negotiation, but the more you can get up front the better.

Royalties

Most industries that license concepts from outside inventors have royalty structures worked out. In publishing, there is a sliding scale that climbs from 10 percent to 12.5 percent and, after a certain number of copies sold, levels off at 15 percent of the cover price. In character licensing and toy invention, the royalty rate ranges from four percent to 15 percent, although E.T. in its heyday captured 20 percent. Most character and toy invention licenses hit somewhere between five and eight percent. An honest company will tell you what is fair and equitable within its industry. There is nothing to be gained in the long run by lying because sooner or later you'll know if you have been treated fairly.

Fast Facts

A mere listing of recipe ingredients is not protected under copyright law. However, where a recipe or formula is accompanied by substantial literary expression in the form of an explanation or directions or when there is a collection of recipes as in a cookbook, there may be a basis for copyright protection.

Guarantees

Guaranteed minimum royalties can also be negotiated. In this case, the licensee of your item would guarantee you no less than a certain amount of money within a predetermined time frame. Again, this amount would be based upon what the licensee projects your item will earn on an annual basis.

Many agreements have clauses for both earned royalties and minimum guaranteed royalties.

The Option Agreement

There are times when a manufacturer is not quite ready to do a licensing agreement but wants exclusive rights to study or research your invention for a limited period of time. In this case, an option agreement is appropriate.

The amount of money a manufacturer is willing to pay for an option is open to negotiation. I have received options as high as $20,000 for a thirty-day hold. The money is usually against future royalties should a deal materialize. If no deal is struck, you keep the money. If you can get the money and not have it repayable against future royalties, go for it. This would be like a signing bonus.

I do not know a formula for negotiating option money. The fact that a manufacturer is willing to pay an option does show a certain level of interest and commitment. From there, it follows that the greater the interest and commitment, the greater the amount of money the manufacturer is willing to risk.

I have received options and then seen products sit in a closet until the option period expired.

Options are not always desired. You may not want to do an option if it will throw off your timing in terms of opportunities to present the same product to other potential licensees. Further, you must be sure that the option is not offered as a ploy to take your invention out of play for a period of time.

I put an option agreement in Appendix A. You may wish to use it as drafted or as the basis for something you are stylizing.

Fast Facts

Copyright does not protect names, titles, slogans, or short phrases. In some cases, these things may be protected as trademarks. Contact the U.S. Patent and Trademark Office at (800) 786-9199 for further information. However, copyright protection may be available for logo artwork that contains sufficient authorship. In some circumstances, an artistic logo may also be protected as a trademark.

Bright Ideas

Atlanta pharmacist John Pemberton was trying to mix up a remedy for headaches when he discovered what would become Coca-Cola.

Levy's 10 Commandments of Contract Negotiation

Here is a list of guidelines I have developed in over a quarter century on the front lines of contract negotiation.

1. *Negotiate yourself.* In choppy seas, the captain should be on the deck. No one will do it better than you. No one has more to gain or lose. If you need a lawyer, just be sure to play good guy–bad guy.

2. *Thou shalt not committee.* Any simple problem can be made insoluble if enough people discuss it.

3. *Try to avoid corporate lawyers.* It is always best to negotiate with an executive who is in a decision-making position. Lawyers are paid not to make executive decisions but to set rules and follow them. They see themselves as protectors, saving the executives from themselves. Yet I have found that the most successful executives break rules all the time.

WACKY PATENTS

Animal Track Footwear Soles
Patented September 24, 1968
United States Patent 3,402,485

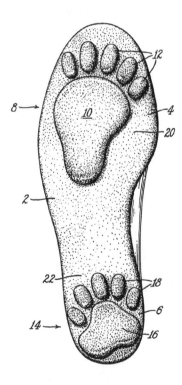

4. *Never respond to pygmies chewing at your toenails.* Don't roll over just because someone says that without x, y, or z the project will not be approved. The company wants to do the deal or you would not be in negotiation. Executives—not lawyers—are responsible for profits. If your invention can boost revenues, executives will shine. You'll know when you've hit an immovable object.

5. *Two plus two is never four.* Exceptions always outnumber rules. Established exceptions have their exceptions. By the time one learns the exceptions, no one remembers the rules to which they correspond.

6. *If it ain't on the page, it ain't on the stage.* Written words live. Spoken words die. During negotiations, confirm every conversation with a memorandum to eliminate any misunderstanding about who agreed to what.

7. *When in doubt, ask.* Asking dumb questions is far easier than correcting dumb mistakes.

8. *Keep it short and to the point.* The length of a business contract is inversely proportional to the amount of business.

9. *Do not accept standard contracts.* In any so-called standard contract, boilerplate terms should be treated as variables. Not until a contract has been in force for six months will its most harmful terms be discovered. Nothing is as temporary as that which is called permanent.

10. *Have fun!* The moment I stop enjoying a negotiation, I pick up my marbles and go home. An agreement is a form of marriage and both parties must be compatible for it to succeed. But, falling in love and reaching the altar are two different things.

Notable Quotables

"The most pleasure we get from life is sweating."

—Chester Carlson, inventor, Xerography

Terms of Endearment

If you get to the point that a company wishes to cut a licensing deal, the licensing agreement in Appendix A will be invaluable. These sample agreements are worth many thousands of dollars in terms of the time and effort put into crafting them.

You or your lawyer may wish to use them as the basis for your agreements or go through them cherry-picking clauses and terms that you find appropriate to your situation.

It is my hope that these agreements serve to alert you and your legal counsel to many points that are either omitted entirely from a manufacturer boilerplate contract or are written entirely from the manufacturer perspective.

Some manufacturers have standard licensing agreements which they prefer to use. Others will ask you to submit your own. In either case, you will find that most issues are negotiable.

My dad taught me that contracts are only as good as the people who sign them. Remember this. Do not make a deal with people you do not trust, no matter how much you feel the agreement is in your favor.

He also instructed me that every contract has its own spirit and that I should always be clear about the spirit of any agreement I execute. Often I will articulate such an understanding and put it on record through letters to my prospective licensee. While not part of the formal agreement, should push ever come to shove in a court of law, a judge and jury would probably not disregard the letters.

Patents. Trademarks. Who Pays?

I have never accepted one red cent from a manufacturer for use in filing USPTO applications. Some inventors believe in allowing their licensees to finance or control their applications. I do not. This is because should there ever be a meltdown between us, I do not want my licensee to be able to claim having contributed to the patent, and thereby seek a claim of partial ownership. I simply make sure that I get enough money in the advance to cover the patent work. Even if I have to use the entire amount of the advance, I will.

This also allows me to control the patent from the standpoint of how it's sliced up. For example, if I control it, then I may be able to license the same technology to various companies whose products are in different categories.

I also try to own the trademarks for similar reasons. It's all about control of the ip, after all.

Fast Facts

Secretary of State James Madison gave the Patent Office the status of a distinct unit or division within the Department of States in 1802 by appointing Dr. William Thornton, at a salary of $1,400 per year, "to have charge of issuing patents." The salary was later increased to $1,500.

The Least You Need to Know

➤ Negotiate for yourself. Don't let others characterize your positions unless you like to play that game. It just makes lawyers wealthy.

➤ Never fear to negotiate. Never negotiate out of fear.

➤ Thou shalt not committee.

➤ Try not to deal only with lawyers.

➤ Written words live, spoken words die.

➤ When in doubt, ask.

➤ Keep it short and to the point.

Chapter 8

Key Deal Points

In This Chapter

➤ Corporate boilerplate can contain goodies

➤ Relationships vs. transactions

➤ Fairness and flexibility

➤ Management by objectives

➤ What you want in an agreement

"Nobody eats until someone sells something. And you can't sell something until it's been created. The independent creator and the marketer must behave as if they thoroughly depend on one another, because they do. That means that as tensions in the creative process emerge, as conflicts between making and selling arise, everything is on the table except the relationship itself. The relationship must survive. True partners in the creative process must focus on meeting the needs of the relationship as well as the terms of an agreement."

—Michael Ross, Executive Vice President and Publisher, World Book, Inc.

If you get to the point that a company wishes to negotiate a license for your invention, congratulations. This is a major accomplishment and a credit to you and your invention. But your work is far from over. In a sense, it is just beginning. Now you need to forge a licensing agreement. This will take experience, patience, thick skin, stamina, common sense, a diplomat's ear, and a good sense of humor. And frequently you may have to be able to jump into troubled waters without making a splash, to borrow an appropriate metaphor from Art Linkletter.

In Chapter 7, "How to Negotiate Your Deal," we discussed how to negotiate. In this chapter I shall comment on, in broad strokes, select issues from the sample licensing agreement found in Appendix A. By the way, if you are not quite ready to negotiate a license, I have provided a sample option agreement, too, in Appendix A.

I Do Not Have All the Answers

I could never possibly address all the issues you may face and how they relate to your invention and industry. Every case is different. Contracts are crafted by the winds of change and the waters of time. No contract is 100 percent bullet-proof. But there are common denominators to agreements, and I have attempted to break out a few of them for you. If I am missing something, hopefully you'll find it addressed in the sample agreement in Appendix A. If I missed an issue, please drop me a line care of my publisher. I am always open to suggestions and new ways to approach licensing.

I have never seen a perfect contract from either the licensor's or licensee's point of view. The smartest and most experienced business people and lawyers let things slip. Contracts are ultimately only as good as the people that sign them. Some people see a contract negotiation as a fight. I prefer to view it as a ritual dance. And I am most happy when my dance card is full. (Wow! Does this metaphor date me.)

Notable Quotables

"If a contract is good, it gathers dust on the shelf. If you need to keep looking at it, you're in trouble."

—Jason Smolen, Esq., Smolen and Plevy, P.C.

Show Me Yours, I'll Show You Mine

Many manufacturers have standard license agreements that they prefer to use with inventors. This assures them that everything they want is included. It's like a landlord's lease. And it is easy for their lawyers to follow. It is more time-consuming for lawyers to work with an unfamiliar document and to figure if all their issues are covered. On the other hand, smaller companies that do not have legal departments and/or do not want to spend money on outside counsel may ask you to submit a proposed agreement. In either case, you will find that most issues are negotiable, if the manufacturer is really serious about wanting to license your invention and work with you—and conversely, you want the deal to materialize. The more the company wants your ip, the greater its willingness to be fair and flexible.

I like to see what a company uses for its standard agreement, even if I plan on suggesting my language as the basis for the deal. In the first place, it allows me to see the negotiation from the opposition's point of view. It is to your advantage to take a moment and consider your licensee's position. You will see what the future may hold for you, e.g., the licensee's exit strategy, ways to avoid payments to you, and so on. And, frequently, I find in a corporate contract terms that play to my benefit and that were not in my agreement. This is a real Eureka Moment. So, if you can see the company's proposed agreement, by all means do it. In fact, ask for it.

Inspection of the corporate agreement will show you quickly how fair a company is with inventors. Companies send a message through their boilerplate. A few years ago, I was hired as a product acquisition consultant to a public company. Part of my charge was to negotiate license agreements on its behalf. I looked at the company's standard license agreement and found numerous issues missing. When I asked the CEO if he would agree to include them he said, of course, if someone asks. I recommended that we take a proactive stance and put the clauses in before I started negotiating. I wanted to send a comforting message to the inventors. Further, I was being paid by the hour and it was not worth my time to hassle over issues that were givens. The CEO, an enlightened fellow, wanted to reach out to the inventing community and send the right message, so he agreed to my recommendation. I must have negotiated over 20 licenses for the company, and all went through without a hitch.

Fairness and Flexibility Rule

Two important attributes of a win/win licensee are fairness and flexibility as it relates to both the market and to the license agreement. It is critical, of course, to have a written agreement that clearly spells out the terms of the deal. "But once that contract has been signed, the licensor and licensee must focus on meeting the needs of their relationship rather than the terms of the agreement," says Michael Ross, Executive Vice President and Publisher, World Book, Inc. "It's the relationship that will sustain the partnership, not the contract.

"If as things move along, the original terms of the agreement no longer make sense, if the signed contract puts either party at a disadvantage or threatens their business model, then both parties must be willing to modify the agreement," Ross adds. "I have seen many partnerships fail because of an agreement that started out fine for both parties but, due to changes in the market, became unsustainable for one of the parties. You have to decide what you want more: a strong, long-term relationship or strict, principled adherence to a contract. This is fundamental to a win-win partnership. Many people say they want a relationship, but they behave as if they want a transaction."

Fast Facts

Try not to conduct negotiations before 9:00 A.M. or after 4:00 P.M. Before 9:00 A.M., you appear too anxious, and after 4:00 P.M. corporate attorneys may have their minds on cashing in their chips at the end of the day and not on the agreement.

115

Years ago I noticed quarter after quarter that I was not making any money from a certain product, but sales were strong. So I looked carefully at the royalty statement and then I saw the problem, a three percent royalty. Ouch! It should have been six percent. I called the vice president of marketing and asked why I was receiving half of what I deserved. "Because that's what you evidently agreed to in the contract," he replied. This man was not at the company when I made the deal. In any event, I checked and he was correct. I had made a serious error. I must have been asleep when I cut the deal. I asked him what he could do to cure my dilemma, and he said, "It's easy. We'll just change it to six percent." He even went back a couple of quarters and made up the loss to me. This executive knew how to build a relationship. To this day we still work together. And I'll never forget the gesture.

I have been blessed to have had the opportunity to do business with many wonderful people who have not sought to take unfair advantage of my associates and me.

I have also been exposed to executives to whom the only win/win is when they win twice. They are uncomfortable without having the advantage. These guys handle nickels like manhole covers. They are Loophole Louies who cannot be trusted no matter what they agree to on paper. They are the portent and epitome of moral and spiritual disorder. "Some rob you with a six gun, and some with a fountain pen," wrote Woody Guthrie. Be alert. Lerts survive.

Contracts are a two-way street. I have had companies request that I change an agreement long after it has been in force or that I take an unreasonably low advance or royalty. If I feel it is a fair request, I'll do my best to make it work. There is nothing greater for both sides or more enviable than a deal in which the inventor and the manufacturer feel victorious and share in the rewards.

I would much rather negotiate with an executive who is well rewarded, someone who has something to gain by my success. These are the kinds of people who negotiate the fairest deals. The problems arise when companies do not give their people a strong incentive package. This is when relationships suffer from shortsightedness.

Management by Objectives

I was chatting recently about licensing agreements with Bob Jones, partner in the accounting firm Harriton, Mancuso, and Jones, P.C., North Bethesda, Maryland, and an indispensable member of our team at Richard C. Levy & Associates. I was wondering aloud why certain companies play hardball with an inventor when the win seems insignificant vis-à-vis the potential loss to a company's relationship with the goose that lays the golden eggs, the inventor. He called it Management by Objectives. "It was popular in many businesses in the 1980s and early 1990s. Many people still are in love with it, but in my opinion it is the reason that many companies do stupid things when it comes to routine common-sense decision-making. The basic concept of Management by Objectives is to 1) set goals for employees; 2) measure their progress in achieving their goals; and 3) compensate them based on their achievements," Bob said. "The problem is that the most important goals of the company (things like customer satisfaction and inventor relations) are the most difficult to measure. So management sets goals that can be quantified rather than goals that are important. Typically the goals focus on short-term profit rather than long-term success. Thus, the employees focus their efforts in the wrong place and, frequently, such effort is counterproductive."

The Spirit of Agreement

The licensing agreement provided in Appendix A, as written, or a form thereof, can be an extremely important document to you as an inventor faced with the opportunity to license an invention. In terms of the time and effort that was put into crafting it, the document is worth many thousands of dollars in legal fees.

Twenty-some years ago when I cut my first deal, many points might have been handled informally between an executive and myself, and not reduced to writing. But, because of the way executives play musical chairs these days, jumping from job to job, company to company, it's best not to depend on informality but memorialize as much as possible in writing.

Every agreement has its own spirit. Therefore, you should always be clear about the spirit of every one you execute. Corporate lawyers like things vague. It works to their favor should push come to shove. Lack of specificity and haziness leads to more than one interpretation. The corporate lawyer can use this situation to muddy the waters. It will put you into a defensive position; one that likely forces you to spend money on legal counsel and a court for interpretation.

Sometimes I cannot get the spirit and specificity into an agreement. Then I will articulate my understanding and put it on record through letters and e-mails to the manufacturer. While not part of the formal agreement, should I ever get into a court of law, a judge and jury may take these into account.

Disclaimer: I am not an attorney-at-law. I am not giving legal advice. The agreements in this book are composites of many I have negotiated. They are provided as a quick-access reference only. Each deal you make, as each industry, will have its own esoteric requirements.

WACKY PATENTS

Hot Weather Hat
Patented November 12, 1985
United States Patent 4,551,857

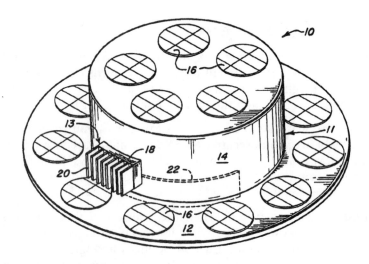

Setting the Scene and the Mind

Yea, though you may walk through the alley of the shadow of debt, show no hunger. You need to think like a person who can walk away from a deal. Prepare yourself to postpone immediate gratification for long-term goals. Too many amateur negotiators suffer from "sellitus," i.e., an affliction that forces them to make a deal at any cost.

Avoid the temptation to overwhelm. You must not be perceived as either an egomaniac or a victim. The image you want to portray is that of a person who is modest, honest, generous, hospitable, though a bit eccentric. Show yourself as a down home fellow (or gal) with a penthouse personality.

Now let's look at some points that I feel deserve explanation. These are in no order of priority once you get past the section on indemnifications. I put this first because it needs to be uppermost in your mind, even ahead of advances and royalties.

➤ **Indemnification of Licensee.** This is, in my opinion, the most important part of any agreement from the inventor's standpoint. It can be a minefield in terms of personal risk. The last thing you want is to have to reimburse a licensee for losses and expenses. In some agreements, mere *claims* of wrongdoing can trigger all kinds of nightmares for inventors. I have seen agreements that allow a licensee to hold up inventor royalties if someone simply *claims*, through a letter to the licensee, that a licensed invention infringes someone's patent. Adding insult to injury, this agreement did not even require the licensee to pay interest to the inventor on held funds. Nor did it have a time limit on how long funds could be held. By the way, nothing stopped the licensee from continuing to manufacture and market the guy's invention.

Licensees have insurance, e.g., product liability, errors and omissions, and so on, to protect themselves against all kinds of problems. Inventors typically do not. This is such a critical part of any license agreement that I highly recommend that you have competent legal counsel review requests for indemnification that you are asked to sign. The last thing you want to do is lose personal assets, such as a home or a car, because you get entangled in a liability fight.

You cannot indemnify against future damage from submarine patents. No one can do this. You can search prior art until the cows come home and never gain access to pending patents. The good news is that until and unless another patent appears that reads on your invention, you would not owe that inventor or patent holder any money for past royalties. If a patent issued that conflicted with your patent or product, you'd have to deal with it from that point forward.

➤ **Indemnification of Licensor.** Your licensee should not balk at covering you under appropriate insurance policy(s). It usually only takes a letter from a licensee to its insurance company. It's as easy as adding another driver to a car policy. It should not increase the cost of the policy(s) to the licensee, nor require any expense.

Bright Ideas

The first scientific lie detector was reportedly invented circa 1895 by an Italian criminologist, Cesare Lombroso. He modified a small, water-filled container, called a hydrosphygmograph. A person shoved their hand through a rubber seal into the water. Changes in the suspect's pulse or blood pressure would make the water level rise, in turn causing a drum to turn when air was pushed through a tube by the pressure. Lombroso modified this instrument to record physical changes in pulse and blood pressure.

➤ **Description of Invention.** You'll want to describe your invention as broadly as possible. Start extreme. Cut it large and kick it into place. You'll be able to edit the definition and work it to everyone's satisfaction. But if you open with too narrow a definition, it becomes difficult to introduce new ideas at a later time.

➤ **Claim Limited Knowledge.** If you cannot make an unqualified statement as to certain warrants and representations, insert the words "to the best of my knowledge." For example, "WHEREAS, LICENSOR hereby warrants and represents that, **to the best of its knowledge**, it is the sole and exclusive owner of all rights in the ITEM, that it has the sole and exclusive right to grant the license herein … "

➤ **Exclusivity.** Only license to a company those rights it is capable of exploiting, which are typically those rights it is willing to breakout and pay for on an individual basis. Don't allow the company to cast a wide net. Part of every agreement should be the following stipulation: "All rights and licenses not herein specifically granted to LICENSEE are reserved by LICENSOR and, as between the parties, are the sole and exclusive property of LICENSOR and may be used or exercised solely by LICENSOR."

➤ **In on the Take-Off, In on the Landing.** You want the agreement to continue for as long as the product upon which royalties are payable to you, under provisions of the agreement, shall continue to be manufactured or sold by the Licensee.

Notable Quotables

"… we said 'What is it that makes the United States such a great nation?' And we investigated and found that it was patents, and we will have patents."

—Korekiyo Takahashi, later to be first Japanese Commissioner of Patents, 1886

Notable Quotables

"An independent inventor rarely has a product that merits multiple licensees in the same geographical and product areas—though it does happen. Exclusivity is generally the expected thing, and it is better for you."

—Calvin D. MacCracken, inventor, holder of more than 300 U.S. and foreign patents

Many companies may try to tie your royalty term to the life of your patent. This is nuts. Why should you suddenly be cut out of the action just because a patent expires? It is easy to handle if the license is not dependent upon your being issued a patent. If it is, then the manufacturer will claim that without patent protection, competition will cut into its profits. This is a sound argument. As a compromise, agree that if—after the patent turns into a pumpkin—there is solid evidence of market erosion from competitive product, you will take a reduced royalty based upon a sound mathematical formula.

➤ **Advance.** The size of the advance is usually in direct proportion to the kind of support the company will give your product. For example, if you are paid $1,000, it is much easier for a licensee to deep-six your project, say in the face of a manufacturing problem, than if it had paid $100,000. The greater the financial commitment, the more reason the company has to make the product go.

Frequently advances are based upon a third or a quarter of first year sales. This is a starting point, but there are always exceptions. Advances should always be non-refundable. In other words, if you deliver an acceptable prototype, you keep the money no matter what happens downstream.

➤ **Royalty.** Every industry has its own royalty scale. Whatever that number is, the key to your agreement is how sales upon which the royalty is based are defined. Never sign an agreement that does not define in detail exactly how your royalty is to be calculated. To make a sweeping generality like "Net Sales," and not define it, is unacceptable. This can easily become a mine field.

Do not be timid about suggesting a sliding royalty scale. For example, if the industry standard is five percent, ask for an increased royalty if the product performs past a certain level. There is a magic number that can trigger a higher royalty. Find it.

By the way, in some industries, product that is manufactured and delivered to the buyer overseas earns a higher royalty for the inventor. Why? This is because the licensee does not incur costs, such as shipping product across from Asia and warehousing it. Many large retailers, for example, buy product in Hong Kong and have it consolidated and shipped across at its own expense as a way of getting a better price from the manufacturer.

411

Camp Invention inspires creativity and inventiveness through engaging, relevant, and meaningful activities that allow child-sized imaginations to run wild. Held in 47 major metropolitan areas, this weeklong summer day camp for children in grades two through six incorporates science, math, history, art, invention, creativity, and problem solving. With 19 different curriculum modules that have been piloted and tested by certified educators, campers are guaranteed to have a new experience every year. There is a staff-to-student ratio of one to eight.

For information, call the National Inventor's Hall of Fame at (330) 762-4463.

➤ **Guarantees.** This is negotiable and should be based upon what the company forecasts in sales over the term of your pact.

➤ **Best Efforts.** You need to be sure your agreement requires the licensee to use its best efforts. I recall once when a lawyer tried to change the language in a contract of mine from "Licensee's best efforts" to "Licensee's reasonable efforts." I responded with the following example. I asked how he would feel if a surgeon promised to use his or her reasonable efforts when operating on him instead of his or her best efforts. I won the point, but even so, not without a struggle. Obviously, there is a significant difference in the legal meanings of these terms.

➤ **Specific Performance.** There needs to be milestones. Every right you license requires its own performance parameters. In this way, should the licensee fail to perform some function, you will have an escape route. Every agreement you sign needs a way out in the case a licensor isn't getting the job done. Licensees can fail to meet product introduction dates, miss payment and/or reporting deadlines, and so forth.

WACKY PATENTS

Desk Attachment
Patented October 28, 1975
United States Patent 3,915,528

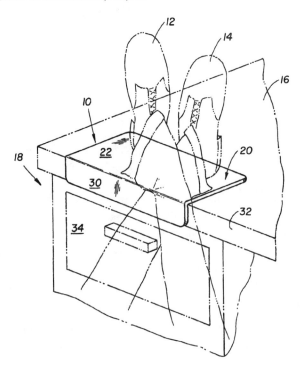

➤ **Foreign Rights.** If you are asked for foreign rights, make each country a separate deal in terms of specific performance and, if possible, advances and guarantees. In this way, the licensee will not take anything for granted. The company will know that it needs to pay attention to your product everywhere, not just at home.

➤ **IP Searches.** Demand that your licensee conduct its own patent, copyright, and trademark searches and satisfy itself that your invention does not infringe anything in any of these fields. Make this fact a part of your agreement, for example, that the licensee did its own search.

➤ **Right to Audit.** Always require the right to audit your licensee's books of account. Never sign an agreement without this clause. I do not recall how many times I have opted to audit licensees, but except for once, we have always found money owed. In these cases, it was either human error or, if done intentionally—for example, to show increased income for a certain quarter—no one tried to hide anything. As my auditor likes to say, "they don't hide their omissions, they just don't give me a road map to find them."

Take My Words for It

Indemnification: An assurance by which one person or entity engages to secure another against anticipated losses or to prevent the other from being harmed by certain legal consequences of an act or forbearance on the part of one of the parties or a third person.

Once I was negotiating with a corporate lawyer who did not want to allow me to audit. After I explained why I had to have the right, he agreed. When I asked why the company simply didn't add the audit clause to its boilerplate, he answered, "Then everyone might want to audit and we don't have the time to deal with it." What a stupid answer, and how shortsighted. In the end, I did not sign with this company.

➤ **Take an Interest in Late Payments.** Try to get interest plus extra points applied to late royalty payments. Here's why. Some corporate financial types like to play games with royalties. They hold them up to get the benefit of some extra float from your money. If the licensee has no obligation to pay interest on late payments, there is no incentive to pay on time. And if all the licensee has to pay is interest, you are essentially giving the company a free loan, and without the hassle of making

Notable Quotables

"Business has only two basic functions—marketing and innovation."

—Peter F. Drucker, author/expert on management and organization

application to a lender. But if the licensee has to pay you interest plus a couple of points over prime, for example, then this will cost the company money, and it is more likely to pay you on time.

➤ **Three Strikes and You're Out.** Whenever possible, I like to write my agreements in such a way that if I put the licensee on notice for the same problem three times, then I can break the agreement. This is only fair. Further, if there are conditions beyond the licensee's control, I'll allow a certain amount of time for the cure and then it's over.

The Least You Need to Know

➤ There are two sides to every deal—yours and theirs. Don't be selfish and overreaching in your demands.

➤ Set the tone and volume for easy listening. The atmosphere needs to be friendly and nonconfrontational.

➤ Necessity has no law.

➤ It's all about relationships, not transactions. Your deal should contain the kinds of terms that make both parties desire a long-term relationship.

Part 3

Goin' for the Gold

On April 10, 1790, President George Washington signed the bill that laid the foundation of the modern patent system. In the 212 years since the ink on that bill dried, the patent system has encouraged and nurtured the genius of many hundreds of thousands of inventors.

This part covers how you and society-at-large benefit from patents, trademarks, trade secrets, and copyrights. This information is not meant to take the place of advice from competent patent counsel, but rather to familiarize you with methods of protecting your intellectual property. It will also hopefully save you headaches and money.

It is designed to give you instant erudition. You will be better equipped to defend yourself when discussing your inventions with prospective licensees and dazzle them a bit, too, with esoteric trivia and convincing repartee. Conversational expertise is a high art that can be learned.

Last, but far from least, this section seeks to impress upon you the importance of patent attorneys. If you can't tell a good one from a bad one, some guidance is also provided.

Pay the tolls required to protect your ip, and follow the advice. It will bring down your cost per mile.

Chapter 9

The United States Patent and Trademark Office

In This Chapter

➤ Uncle Sam offers protection for your ideas

➤ If it ain't on the page, it may not be on the stage

➤ The USPTO works for you

➤ Disclosure Documents—A bargain at $10.00

➤ Coming Attractions—Patents, TMs, Copyrights

"The United States of America is the greatest country on earth and chiefly among the things we have good reason to boast about are these: (1) America's unique natural resource—the independent inventor, and (2) our similarly unique intellectual property protection system which helps keep our inventors inventing and our economy booming."

—Q. Todd Dickinson, Former Under Secretary of Commerce for Intellectual Property and Director of the United States Patent and Trademark Office, 1998–2001

The United States government gives you several ways to protect your ideas, including patents, trademarks, and copyrights. If your ideas have physical form, it's the patent you want as your first line of defense.

Most companies will not license an invention unless it has been or can be patented. The stronger the patent, the better the deal you can negotiate. The stronger the patent, the better the chances are for keeping competition away for a limited time.

Fast Facts

Patent applications are received at the rate of over 300,000 per year. The Patent and Trademark Office receives over five million pieces of mail each year.

IMPORTANT: The chapters in this book on the protection of your intellectual property are provided only as a general reference primer about ip and the operations of the Patent and Trademark Office. They attempt to answer many of the questions commonly asked by inventors but are not intended as a comprehensive textbook on ip law and complex issues. Intellectual property laws, regulations, filing fees, and so forth are in a constant state of change, pushed and pulled by technologies, marketplaces, and special interests. These chapters are not designed to take the place of competent legal counsel, which I encourage you to seek.

In these chapters, whenever I refer to "you," the assumption is that you, the reader, are the inventor or a co-inventor of record.

The Big Three in IP

Here is a short introduction to the basic types of patent protection available to you. Utility patents are granted to the inventor or discoverer of any new and useful process, machine, manufacture, composition of matter, or any new and useful improvement thereof. Examples of inventions protected by utility patents are ...

➤ The Wright brothers' airplane. Pat. No. 821,393

➤ Thomas Edison's electric lamp. Pat. No. 223,898

➤ Nintendo's Game Boy. Pat. No. 5,184,830

Plant patents are granted on any distinct and new variety of asexually reproduced plants. Examples of inventions protected by plant patents are ...

➤ Bosenberg's climbing or trailing rose. PP 1

➤ Method of Growing Plants in Soil. PP 4,067,712

➤ Kalanchoe plant named Veracruz. PP 5,927

Design patents are granted on any new, original, and ornamental design for an article of manufacture. Examples of inventions protected by design patents are ...

➤ The Statue of Liberty. Des. No. 11,023

➤ A Dispensing Container for Tablets. Des. No. 200,000

➤ The Spirals baby bottle. Des. No. 340,771

Utility and plant patents are granted for a term which begins on the date of the grant and ends 20 years from the date the patent application was first filed, subject to the payment of maintenance fees.

Design patents are granted for a term of 14 years from the date of grant. There are no maintenance fees.

Patents may be extended only by special act of Congress, except for some pharmaceutical patents whose terms may be extended to make up for lost time due to government-required testing.

Keepin' a List and Checkin' It Twice

This book is not about the process of invention *per se*; however, it is, in part, about protection of inventions. And in that regard, it is very important that you keep records throughout each project in an Inventor's Notebook. Here are six dates that need to be memorialized in writing. Co-inventors, colleagues, or friends who have a grasp of your invention should witness each entry. Store your Inventor's Notebook in a safe place.

1. The date you conceived the invention.
2. The date you reduced the invention to practice.
3. The date you first show your invention to others.
4. The date your invention is first published.
5. The date you first offer the invention for sale.
6. The date you license the invention.

> **Notable Quotables**
>
> "A country without a patent office and good patent laws is just a crab, and can't travel any way but sideways and backwards."
>
> —Mark Twain, humorist

Why are these dates important?

➤ If you and one or more inventors file for a patent on the same invention, at the same time, dates of conception and reduction to practice can give you the edge.

Conception: A notebook entry, for example, showing the time and date you had the brainstorm. If you can make a simple sketch, this would make the entry even more efficacious. Sign and date the sketch, too.

➤ Reduction to Practice: This is when you built a breadboard or prototype or filed a patent application.

➤ The law states that you must file a patent application within one year of the date you first use the invention for commercial purposes, or put it up for sale or licensing at, let's say, an inventor expo. If you show it to others who are under a confidentiality agreement, this is not deemed to have been placed in "public use." A notebook entry of such activity can establish your position should the need arise.

➤ If you are challenged, this date can be critical. You lose the right to apply for a patent within one year after you offer an invention for sale. So, knowing this date may provide invaluable proof that you fall within the limit.

➤ Sold does not mean that money changes hands. You could do a trade, for example. Whichever it is, should you ever need proof of this date, you will have it in the notebook.

WACKY PATENTS

Vehicle and Deformable Wheel Therefor
Patented December 28, 1965
United States Patent 3,226,129

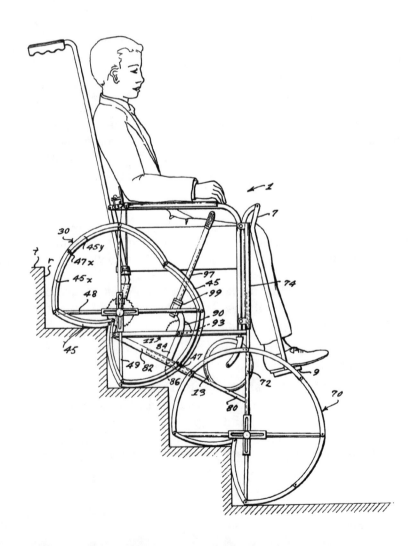

Bright Ideas

Dutch inventor Cornelius Van Drebbel is credited with constructing the first compound microscope using two sets of convex lenses. During the early 1620s, he designed and built his most famous invention, the submarine. Although a similar design had been described 50 years earlier, his is the first known submarine to have been tested. Greased leather stretched over a wooden frame, the U-boat was propelled by oars projecting through the sides and sealed with leather flaps. It was capable of traveling twelve to fifteen feet below the surface. Tubes running to the surface with floats at the top supplied fresh air.

Drebbel also invented the first thermostat, which used a column of mercury and a system of floats and levers to hold a steady temperature within a furnace. He later invented an incubator for hatching eggs that used his principle for temperature regulation.

Definition of a Patent

A patent for an invention is the grant of a property right to the inventor, issued by the Patent and Trademark Office. The term of a new patent is 20 years from the date on which the application for the patent was filed in the United States or, in special cases, from the date an earlier related application was filed, subject to the payment of maintenance fees. U.S. patent grants are effective only within the U.S., U.S. territories, and U.S. possessions.

The right conferred by the patent grant is, in the language of the statute and of the grant itself, "the right to exclude others from making, using, offering for sale, or selling" the invention in the United States or "importing" the invention into the United States. What is granted is not the right to make, use, offer for sale, sell or import, but the right to exclude others from making, using, offering for sale, selling, or importing the invention.

The Patent Law

The patent law specifies the subject matter for which a patent may be obtained and conditions for patentability. The law establishes the Patent and Trademark Office to administer the law relating to the granting of patents and contains various other provisions relating to patents.

411

General Trademark Information:
(800)–USPTO-9199

Automated Line/Status of TM
Applications: (703) 305-8747

Trademark Assistance Center:
(703) 308-9000

Correcting Mistakes on
Registrations: (703) 308-9500

Trademark Trial and Appeal
Board: (703) 308-9300

Assistant Commissioner for
Trademarks: (703) 308-8900

Notable Quotables

"Inventing is easy! Doing hardware and software is easy; building models ... a snap, if you
know how. Selling the damn
stuff ... that's the hard part! ...
And by the way, when you've
finally got a licensee, get smart,
get legal help with the Agreement because they'll try to screw
you every time!"

—Ralph H. Baer, creator, the
home video game industry

The American Inventors Protection Act was enacted
November 29, 1999 as Public Law 106-113. For its
text, please visit the USPTO Web site or request a
copy of it by calling the USPTO Information Line at
(800)-USPTO-9199 or local (703)-308-4357.

What Is Patentable?

In order for an invention to be patentable, it must be
new as defined in the patent law, which provides that
an invention cannot be patented if: "(a) the invention
was known or used by others in this country, or
patented or described in a printed publication in this
or a foreign country, before the invention thereof by
the applicant for patent," or "(b) the invention was
patented or described in a printed publication in this
or a foreign country or in public use or on sale in this
country more than one year prior to the application
for patent in the United States."

If your invention has been described in a printed publication anywhere, or posted on the Internet, has been
in public use or on sale in this country more than one
year before the date your patent applications is filed
in this country, a patent cannot be obtained. In this
connection it is immaterial when the invention was
made, or whether the printed publication or public
use was by you or by someone else. If you describe the
invention in a printed publication or use the invention publicly, or place it on sale, you must apply for a
patent before one year has gone by, otherwise any
right to a patent will be lost.

Even if the subject matter sought to be patented is not
exactly shown by the prior art, and involves one or
more differences over the most nearly similar thing already known, a patent may still be refused if the differences would have been obvious. The subject matter
sought to be patented must be sufficiently different
from what has been used or described before that it
may be said to be obscured to a person having ordinary skill in the area of technology related to the invention. For example, the substitution of one material
for another, e.g., ABS to tin, or changes in size, are
typically not patentable.

The Examiners (Say Ah!)

The work of examining applications for patents is divided among a number of examining groups, each group having jurisdiction over assigned fields of technology. Each group is headed by a group director and staffed by examiners. The examiners review applications and determine whether patents can be granted. Appeals can be made to the Board of Patent Appeals and Interferences from decisions refusing to grant a patent, and a review by the Commissioner of Patents and Trademarks may be requested by petition. The examiners also identify applications that claim the same invention and start proceedings, known as interferences, to determine who was the first inventor.

In addition to the examining groups, other offices perform various services, such as receiving and distributing mail, receiving new applications, handling sales of printed copies of patents, making copies of records, inspecting drawings, and recording assignments.

Established by Law, Built by Innovation—The USPTO

Congress established the USPTO to issue patents on behalf of the government. The Office as a distinct bureau may be said to date from 1802 when a separate official in the Department of State who became known as the Superintendent of Patents was placed in charge of patents. The revision of patent laws in 1836 reorganized the Patent and Trademark Office and designated the official in charge as Commissioner of Patent and Trademarks. The Patent and Trademark Office remained in the Department of State until 1849, when it was transferred to the Department of Interior. In 1925, it was transferred to the Department of Commerce where it is today. Today the head of the USPTO is designated the Under Secretary of Commerce for Intellectual Property and Director of the United States Patent and Trademark Office.

The U.S. Patent and Trademark Office has about 5,700 employees, of whom about half are examiners and others with technical and legal training. Patent applications are received at the rate of over 300,000 per year. The Patent and Trademark Office receives over five million pieces of mail each year.

411

All your business with the USPTO should be transacted in writing and all correspondence relating to patent matters should be addressed: ASSISTANT COMMISSIONER FOR PATENTS, WASHINGTON, D.C. 20231. Be sure to include your full return address, including zip code. The principal location of the USPTO is Crystal Plaza 3, 2021 Jefferson Davis Highway, Arlington, Virginia. Your personal presence there is unnecessary.

Through the issuance of patents, providing incentives to invent, invest in, and disclose new technology worldwide encourages technological advancement. Under this system of protection, American industry has flourished. New products have been invented, new uses for old ones discovered, and employment opportunities created for millions of Americans.

You must write a separate letter (but not necessarily in separate envelopes) for each distinct subject of inquiry, such as assignments, payments, orders for printed copies of patents, orders for copies of records, and requests for other services. Do not include inquiries with letters responding to Office actions in applications.

Bright Ideas

Clara Barton, founder of the American Red Cross, served as the first female clerk in the United States Patent Office (now the U.S. Patent and Trademark Office). Thomas Jefferson was its first patent examiner.

If your letter concerns a patent application, be sure to include the application number, filing date, and Group Art Unit number. If your letter concerns a patent, it must include your full name, the title of the invention, the patent number, and the date of issue.

An order for a copy of an assignment must give the book and page, or reel and frame, of the record as well as the inventor's name; otherwise, the USPTO will hit you with an additional charge for the time consumed in making the search for the assignment.

Patent applications are not open to the public, and no information concerning them is released except on written authority from you, a co-applicant, your assignee, your attorney, or when necessary to the conduct of the business of the USPTO.

However, with certain exceptions, utility and plant applications filed on or after November 29, 2000, including international applications which are filed under 35 USC 363 on or after November 29, 2000 and are in compliance with 35 USC 371, shall be published promptly after the expiration of a period of 18 months from the earliest domestic or foreign filing date of the application. Publication of utility and plant applications is required by the American Inventors Protection Act of 1999, Public Law 106-113.

It is noted that an application shall not be published if an applicant makes a request *upon filing*, certifying that the invention disclosed in the application has not and will not be the subject of an application filed in another country, or under a multilateral international agreement, that requires 18-month publication. An applicant who has made a nonpublication request but who subsequently files an application directed to the invention disclosed in the application filed in the Office in a foreign country must notify the USPTO of such filing within 45 days after the date of such foreign filing. An applicant's failure to timely provide such a notice will result in the abandonment of the application (subject to revival if it is shown that the delay in submitting the notice was unintentional). Patents and related records, including records of any decisions, the records of assignments other than those relating to assignments of patent applications, books, and other records and papers in the Office, are open to the public. They may be inspected in the Patent and Trademark Office Search Room or copies may be ordered.

The Office cannot respond to queries concerning the novelty and patentability of an invention before you file your application; give advice as to possible infringement; advise on the propriety of filing an application; respond to queries as to whether, or to whom, any alleged invention has been patented; and act as an advisor on patent law or as your counselor, except in deciding questions arising before it in regularly filed cases. Examiners will gladly furnish information of a general nature either directly or by supplying or calling your attention to an appropriate publication.

Only Inventors Need Apply

According to the law, only the inventor may apply for a patent, with certain exceptions. If a person who is not the inventor should apply for a patent, the patent, if it were obtained, would be invalid. The person applying in such a case who falsely states that he/she is the inventor would also be subject to criminal penalties. If the inventor has died, the application may be made by legal representatives, that is, the administrator or executor of the estate. If the inventor is mentally unstable, the application for patent may be made by a guardian. If an inventor refuses to apply for a patent or cannot be found, a joint inventor or a person having a proprietary interest in the invention may apply on behalf of the nonsigning inventor. If two or more persons make an invention jointly, they apply for a patent as joint inventors. A person who makes a financial contribution is not a joint inventor and cannot be joined in the application as an inventor. It is possible to correct an innocent mistake in erroneously omitting an inventor or in erroneously naming a person as an inventor.

Officers and employees of the Patent and Trademark Office are prohibited by law from applying for a patent or acquiring, directly or indirectly— except by inheritance or bequest—any patent or any right or interest in any patent.

Notable Quotables

"Great spirits have always encountered violent opposition from mediocre minds."

—Albert Einstein

Fast Facts

You do not need an attorney to file for a trademark, but you are responsible for observing and complying with all substantive and procedural issues and requirements. The Patent and Trademark Office cannot select an attorney for you. The names of attorneys who specialize in trademark law may be found in the telephone yellow pages or by contacting a local bar association.

Copy Documents, Not Ideas, Please!

Printed copies of any patent, identified by its patent number, may be purchased from the USPTO. The current fee schedule is available by calling (800) 786-9199 or (703) 308-4357 or by accessing the USPTO's Web site at www.uspto.gov.

The USPTO Web site will allow you to search and print out copies of patents for free. There are numerous nongovernment patent search engines that you can find on the Internet. I prefer not to recommend them by name because I do not know anything about them, and they may not be there by the time you take a look.

Meet Your U.S. Patent Office

This book is all about taking risks, so I'll take one. As we prepare to publish, former two-term U.S. Congressman James E. Rogan (R–CA) has been nominated by President Bush to become Undersecretary of Commerce for Intellectual Property and Director of the U.S. Patent and Trademark Office. The drums say he faces little opposition and will likely make it. Therefore, I have decided to take a chance and include his bio sketch.

Coming from a hardscrabble background and pulling himself up by his proverbial boot-straps, in 1996 Jim won the first of two consecutive terms to the United States Congress. He was selected to be one of only two members to serve on the House Commerce and Judiciary Committees, two of the most powerful committees. Jim was a House prosecutor in the historic U.S. Senate impeachment trial of President Clinton. This brought him recognition for his prosecutorial skills. But his attacks against President Clinton backfired on him, and he lost his seat in his heavily Democratic district. Jim's unsuccessful reelection battle became the most expensive House race in American history.

Before running for Congress, Jim won a special election to the California State Assembly, where he was unanimously elected during his freshman term to serve as the first Republican Majority Leader in almost 30 years. The respected *California Journal* magazine named him the Assembly's most effective legislator and also ranked him "number one in integrity."

Disclosure Documents

The USPTO accepts and preserves for a two-year period papers disclosing an invention pending the filing of an application for patent. This disclosure is accepted as evidence of the dates of conception of the invention, but provides you no patent protection nor should it be considered a "grace period" during which you can wait to file your application without a possible loss of benefits.

Although there are no stipulations to content, and claims are not required, the benefits afforded by the Disclosure Document Program will depend directly upon the adequacy of your disclosure. Therefore, it is strongly recommended that the document contain a clear and complete explanation of the manner and process of making and using the invention in sufficient detail to enable a person having ordinary knowledge in the field of the invention to make and use the invention. When the nature of the invention permits, a drawing or sketch should be included. The use or utility of the invention should be described, especially in chemical inventions. This disclosure is limited to written matter or drawings on heavy paper, such as linen or plastic drafting material, having dimensions or being folded to dimensions not to exceed $8^1/_2$ x 13 inches (21.6 by 33 cm.). Photographs are also acceptable. Number each page, and make sure that the text and drawings are of such quality as to permit reproduction.

WACKY PATENTS

Spherical Rolling Hull Marine Vessel
Patented January 20, 1976
United States Patent 3,933,115

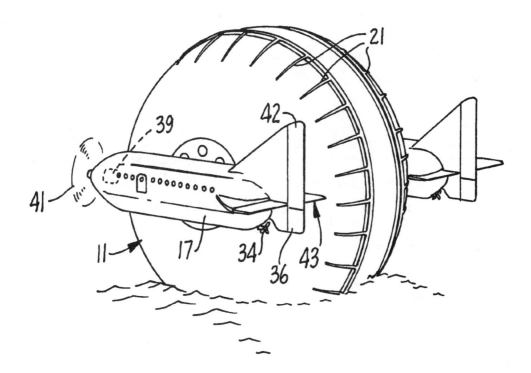

Fast Facts

The first inventions have been traced to the Paleolithic Period which ran from circa 2¹/₂ million years ago to 8,000 B.C.E. Old Stone Age people created axes, chisels, and other hand tools by chipping bone, flint, horn, and ivory into myriad shapes. The bow and arrow and the spear were invented to hunt. It was also discovered during this period that striking flint on metal ore could cause fire.

In addition to the fee, the Disclosure Document must be accompanied by a stamped, self-addressed envelope (SASE) and a separate paper in duplicate, signed by you as the inventor. The USPTO upon receipt will stamp these papers, and the duplicate request will be returned in the SASE together with a notice indicating that the Disclosure Document does not provide patent protection and that a patent application should be diligently filed if patent protection is desired.

The $10 fee must accompany the Disclosure Document when it is submitted to the USPTO. A check or money order must be made payable to "Commissioner of Patents and Trademarks." Mail with the Disclosure Document to: Commissioner of Patents and Trademarks, Box DD, Washington, D.C. 20231.

Fees are subject to change annually. Fees may be confirmed by calling the Public Service Branch at (703) 308-4357.

Your request may take the following form:

Date: _____, 200_

To: Commissioner of Patents and Trademarks

From: Jane Q. Inventor

Dear Commissioner:

The undersigned being the inventor of the disclosed invention request that the enclosed papers be accepted under the Disclosure Document Program, and that they be preserved for a period of two years. A check in the sum of $10 is attached hereto.

My invention is (insert description).

There are (insert number) different approaches I intend to take. They are illustrated on the enclosed (insert number) sheets.

Thank you very much,

Jane Q. Inventor

123 Street Name

City, State, Zip

Tel: (123) 456-7890

If you opt to file a Disclosure Document, be aware that ...

➤ The two-year retention period should not be considered to be a "grace period" during which you can wait to file a patent application without possible loss of benefits. It must be recognized that in establishing priority of invention an affidavit or testimony referring to the Disclosure Document must usually also establish diligence in completing the invention or in filing the patent application since the filing of the Disclosure Document.

➤ Any public use or sale in the U.S. or publication of the invention anywhere in the world more than one year prior to the filing of your patent application on the invention disclosed will prohibit the granting of a patent on it.

➤ The Disclosure Document is not a patent application, and the date of its receipt in the Patent and Trademark Office will not become the effective filing date of any patent application subsequently filed. It will be retained for two years and then be destroyed unless referred to in a separate letter in a related application within two years.

➤ The program does not diminish the value of the conventional witnessed and notarized records as evidence of conception of your invention, but it should provide a more credible form of evidence than that provided by the popular practice of mailing a disclosure to oneself or another person by registered mail.

Notable Quotables

"Just keep working hard, test models well ... keep in contact with potential customers to find out what types of products they want."

—Ray Lohr, inventor, the Big Wheel

Submarine Patents (Periscope Up!)

In the United States, patents remain secret until they are granted. In other words, once you file your application, no one other than select USPTO officials, such as examiners, know what you have invented. The process to get a patent can be a drawn-out affair, so it is possible for competitors to unknowingly develop and market a technology or mechanism, for example, for which others have already filed patents.

The term submarine patent applies to the situation where a company or inventor surfaces with a patent to an invention that a competitor has been using for some time and asks for royalties. Further, the inventor who has the submarine patent may never have proven the invention as it is not required anymore that inventors build proving models of their ideas.

The most celebrated of such cases involved Jerome H. Lemelson, the nation's most prolific contemporary inventor, who held over 550 patents, including some on the bar code scanner. According to *Fortune*, May 14, 2001, his theoretical patents earned him $1.5 billion in licensing fees. Lemelson died in 1997 at age 74.

Between 1992 and 1995, he licensed his bar code scanning technology used in electronics and automobile manufacturing to more than 70 companies, including Sony, Apple Computer, and Daimler-Benz, but not before having to engage in huge legal battles.

In the April 9, 1997 edition of *The Wall Street Journal*, staff reporter Bernard Wysocki, Jr. explained it like this. "It was as if the 1954 and 1956 filings were roots of a vast tree. One branch 'surfaced' in 1963, another in 1969, and more in the late 1970s, the mid 1980s, and the early 1990s. All direct descendants of the mid 1950s filings, they have up-to-date claims covering more recent technology, such as that for bar-code scanning."

One of Lemelson's former attorneys, Arthur Lieberman, told *Fortune*, "In many cases he didn't patent inventions. He invented patents. … He would look at the magazines and determine the direction of industry." Lieberman said that Lemelson would use his knowledge, get to the Patent Office first, and thus lay the foundation for future claims should there be breakthroughs by inventors in a particular field.

While Lemelson technically played by the rules to amass a $500 million fortune, recently the loopholes that allowed this were closed through the lobbying efforts of big industry. P.S.: Lemelson's contingency attorney is reported to have earned over $150 million in fees!

Bright Ideas

Men have been shaving off their beards with sharp implements since ancient times. Cave paintings show shells, sharks's teeth, and sharpened flint used as razors. But there is an American inventor who changed the face of mankind by revolutionizing shaving habits.

King Camp Gillette invented the first disposable blade in 1901. Gillette created a thin, double-edged blade that was fastened to a special guarded holder and could be thrown away when it got dull. An entire generation was converted to the safety razor when the U.S. government issued Gillette razors to its troops during World War I.

Office of Independent Inventor Programs

In November 1999, Congress passed the American Inventors Protection Act. This act, among other things, laid the foundation for the establishment of the Office of Independent Inventor Programs (OIIP). The principal mission of this office is to ensure USPTO-based support and encouragement of independent inventors and small business concerns. Through innovative educational outreach programs and a nationwide network of contacts, OIIP offers a variety of resources to assist inventors with patent and trademark application processes. In addition, the Office has taken aggressive measures to protect inventors from the growing menace of fraudulent invention marketing firms.

Meet Your U.S. Patent Office

Richard J. Apley was appointed the Director of the Office of Independent Inventor Programs in March 2000. Through Mr. Apley's efforts, the Independent Inventor Resources page on the USPTO Web site continues to provide award-winning information to the independent inventor.

Mr. Apley has recently been appointed to the Consumer Protection Initiatives Committee. This Committee is part of the United States Attorney General's Council on White Collar Crime. Mr. Apley's presence on this Committee is intended to raise the enforcement aspects of his war against the invention promotion scam companies.

A native of Brooklyn, New York, Mr. Apley received a Bachelor's degree in Civil Engineering from Rensselaer Polytechnic Institute in 1966 and began his career at the Patent and Trademark Office immediately thereafter. In 1974, Mr. Apley received a Juris Doctor Degree from the University of Baltimore.

USPTO independent inventors make up a substantial segment of the USPTO's customer base. OIIP has established a variety of outreach efforts to provide educational services designed for the independent inventor. Outreach teams travel across the country holding inventor workshops on intellectual property. A list of upcoming workshops is available on the Independent Inventors Resource page at the USPTO's Web site at www.uspto.gov. The range of topics covered at these workshops include ...

➤ Basic facts about patents and trademarks—types of intellectual property protection.

➤ Avoiding scam promotion and marketing firms—what to look out for when getting advice.

➤ Tips on preparing patent and trademark applications.

➤ Writing patent claims—the do's and don'ts of claim construction.

➤ Updates on new rule changes affecting independent inventors.

➤ Hands-on computer search training—check to see if a patent or trademark already exists on a discovery.

➤ Hot technology discussions on Internet business methods, software, and biotechnology patents.

This personal approach brings the United States Patent and Trademark Office to you. These specialized services are designed to help you with specific questions relating to your invention. OIIP also works closely with the nationwide network of Patent and Trademark Depository Libraries (PTDLs). PTDLs are public, state, and academic libraries that, like OIIP, disseminate patent and trademark information and support the diverse intellectual property needs of the public. PTDLs are a good place to find out if someone else has already patented your invention or obtained a federal registration for a trademark on goods or services similar to that you are seeking to use. Listed below are some more of OIIPs ongoing nationwide outreach programs:

➤ Annual Independent Inventor Conferences providing comprehensive programs dedicated to serving and educating the independent inventor.

➤ On-campus workshops at universities throughout the country.

➤ Saturday seminars on introducing the independent inventor to intellectual property.

➤ Workshops run in partnership with Small Business Development Centers across the nation.

➤ Participating in conferences run by professional organizations groups, such as the American Society for Engineering Education.

➤ Outreach teams meeting with regional inventor and entrepreneurial organizations, such as the National Collegiate Inventors and Innovators Alliance.

For information on any of these initiatives, please consult the USPTO Web site or call (703) 306-5568.

Best of all, many of the resources available through the Office of Independent Inventor Programs and PTDLs are free of charge.

Coming Attractions

In the following chapters, you will find details about each of the methods of protection made available to you by the government. They are, in order of presentation ...

➤ Utility Patent: A utility patent covers any new and useful process, machine, manufacture, or composition of matter, or any new and useful improvement thereof, subject to the conditions and requirements of the law. A patent cannot be obtained upon a mere idea or suggestion. Examples of utility patents include fiber optics, computer hardware, and medications.

Notable Quotables

"Life is an adventure, not a guided tour."

—Anonymous

➤ Plant Patent: The plant patent protects any asexually reproduced distinct and new variety of plant, including cultivated sports, mutants, hybrids, and newly found seedlings, other than a tuber-propagated plant or a plant found in an uncultivated state. Hybrid tea roses, Silver Queen corn, Better Boy tomatoes are all types of plant patents.

➤ Design Patent: The design patent protects only the appearance of an article, not its structural or functional features. Proceedings relating to granting of design patents are the same as those relating to other patents with a few differences. The look of an athletic shoe, a bicycle helmet, and the *Star Wars* characters are all protected by design patents.

➤ Trademark: A trademark is a word, name, symbol, or device that is used in trade with goods to indicate the source of the goods and to distinguish them from the goods of others. A servicemark is the same as a trademark except that it identifies and distinguishes the source of a service rather than a product. The terms "trademark" and "mark" are commonly used to refer to both trademarks and servicemarks. The roar of the MGM lion, the pink of the insulation made by Owens-Corning (who uses the Pink Panther in advertising by permission from its owner), and the shape of a Coca-Cola bottle are familiar trademarks.

➤ Trade Secret: The trade secret is, as its name implies, information that companies keep secret to give them an advantage over their competitors. The formula for Coca-Cola is the most famous trade secret.

➤ Copyright: Copyright is a form of protection provided to authors of "original works of authorship," including literary, dramatic, musical, artistic, and certain other intellectual works, both published and unpublished. The copyright protects the form of expression rather than the subject matter of the writing. The Copyright Office of the Library of Congress registers copyrights. *Gone with the Wind* (the book and film), Destiny's Child recordings, and video games are all works that are copyrighted.

143

Fast Facts

In 1994, one of America's most prolific inventors, the late Jerome H. Lemelson and his wife, Dorothy, established the Lemelson-MIT Program at the Massachusetts Institute of Technology. Administered solely by MIT and based at the Sloan School of Management, the Program is chaired by internationally recognized economist Professor Lester C. Thurow. The mission of the program is to inspire new generations of American scientists, engineers, and entrepreneurs by celebrating, through awards and educational activities, living role models in these fields.

The national Lemelson-MIT Awards consist of the world's largest single prize for invention and innovation, the annual half-million dollar Lemelson-MIT Prize as well as the annual Lemelson-MIT Lifetime Achievement Award.

The Least You Need to Know

➤ Uncle Sam provides ways to protect your inventions.

➤ Consult competent intellectual property counsel.

➤ Keep an Inventor's Notebook and have it witnessed.

➤ The American Inventors Protection Act was enacted in 1999.

➤ Document Disclosure—the cost of a movie ticket.

➤ Patents and trademarks can be money in the bank.

Chapter 10

It All Begins with a Patent Search

In This Chapter

➤ You have the Mother of All Ideas—here's what to do next

➤ Three ways to search (patents)

➤ Steps to the manual search (patents)

➤ How to search trademarks *for free*

➤ How to make money as a bounty hunter

There you sit eating dinner when, without warning, the *Mother of All Ideas* flashes through your mind at the speed of light. You leap up and write it down. Visions follow. A larger home. A sports car—perhaps two. Vacations. Private jet travel. Expensive watches. Jewelry. American Express Platinum. Fashion. Then just as you reapproach Alpha Level, you ask yourself the sobering question that always follows the *Mother of All Ideas: Has the concept already been done by someone else?*

You are not alone. This is the same question every inventor, gadgeteer, tinkerer, and daydreamer asks after feeling the kind of exhilaration that only the *Mother of All Ideas* can cause.

Fast Facts

The USPTO's research collection is immense. More than 30 million documents are on hand, including over six and a half million U.S. patents, nine million cross-references, and 16 million foreign patents. The Scientific Library has a collection of 120,000 volumes and provides access to commercial databases. The USPTO Public Search Room has 21 linear miles of shelving, with about 65,000 new pages of documents added weekly to an estimated 250 million pages on file.

Looking for a Green Light

The answer to this question may be found through a patent search. The search will tell you if your idea has been patented already, and if so, if the patent is still in force.

The USPTO's patent cataloging system is pretty complex, and the amount of prior art (read: patents previously issued) you may need to look through can be staggering. The Office has issued over 6.5 million patents to date, and the number grows daily. At its Public Search Room in Crystal City, Virginia, there are 30 million references on file, according to Edith Wilkness, Manager, USPTO Public Search Room.

You cannot avoid doing a search if you wish to know if your idea is novel. You will need the results of a search if you wish to protect your idea with a patent.

When you make application for a patent, an examiner will do a search, and if your application is rejected based upon prior art, you will have lost the application fee, not to mention significant time and energy. But, even if none of the earlier patents shows all the details of your idea, they may point out important features or better ways of doing the invention.

411

Would you like to learn how to search from the pros? The USPTO offers monthly training for its EAST, WEST, and X-Search systems. A prepaid fee of $25 reserves you a seat in a class and includes one set of training materials. Extra materials or manuals may be purchased for $25 each. Off-schedule, three-hour personal training sessions are available at the USPTO for a fee of $120. Classes take place at the USPTO Public Training Facility, Arlington, Virginia, with hands-on workstation access.

For information, call (703) 308-3040

In the event nothing is found to prevent or delay your application, the information gathered by a search will prove helpful, acquainting you with the details of patents related to your invention.

By the way, since not all inventions are patented, it's also a good idea to research your particular market for evidence of your idea. You might do this through a combination of library research, Web surfing, and one-on-one interviews with experts in your field of invention or trade.

Note: See Part Four for information on how to search trademarks.

How to Conduct a Patent Search

You may approach a search in three ways:

1. Hire a patent attorney.

2. Hire a patent searcher.

3. Do it yourself.

Let's look at all these options.

Patent Attorney Directed Search

Going through a lawyer to search patents will cost the least amount of time and the most money. Attorneys do not conduct their own searches; they do not have the time, or skills, in most cases. They are too busy drafting claims, prosecuting patents, going to court in some cases, and fulfilling other duties. This is no different than dentists who no longer find it cost-effective to clean teeth, or physicians who do not give vaccinations because their time is better spent on services that can generate greater income.

Patent attorneys employ professional researchers. You hire the attorney—the attorney gets someone to conduct the search. Then the attorney adds a mark-up to the search bill, sometimes as much as several hundred percent. Many lawyers cloak this in the term "handling fee." To save this extra expense, some inventors hire their own researcher or do the search themselves.

Most patent attorneys will not render an opinion based upon a search conducted by anyone other than their own searcher. I have always told my lawyers that if they would not accept the work of my search firm, or searches done by myself, I would go elsewhere where such work would be acceptable. I figure I am paying the bills and if I am willing to take the risk, the lawyer should not have a problem. My lawyer agrees to this system.

I do not go through a patent attorney because I see no reason to pay for a legal opinion. If the search results show no prior art in my field of invention, I do not need an attorney to tell me that the coast is clear. Conversely, if a search reveals prior art that is spot on my invention, I do not need an attorney to tell me that my idea has been done before. I might, on the other hand, hire an attorney to help me end run an existing patent through the use of language in the application.

If you hire a lawyer, get a quote in advance. The fee will be based on how all-encompassing you want the search to be.

Direct Hire Professional Search

If you want to save lawyer fees and mark-ups, consider going directly to a patent search firm. Searchers are best found through inventor grapevines, inventor associations, or university intellectual property departments. In larger cities, you can also check the yellow pages under "Patent Searchers." But be careful not to fall into a trap set by some disreputable invention marketing organizations. They list themselves in the phone book under "Patent Searchers" with a toll-free number. This is another way they hook unsuspecting inventors into service contracts. Get all the facts upfront. See Chapter 2, "Beware of Invention Marketing Flimflam Artists," for how to identify disreputable organizations and avoid being ripped-off. Some reputable searchers ask for money up front if you are not known to them. This is understandable. Just make sure you are told the cost of the search beforehand, and get references.

Ask for a rate sheet, then get on the phone and discuss the exact services you need. Costs vary depending on the complexity of the search. Electronic, chemical, biological, botanical, and medical searches are often more expensive than a mechanical search. In most cases, there will be incidental charges for copies, phone and fax, online fees, and shipping and handling of your materials. This is all standard.

Most important, ask if the searcher is experienced in your field of invention. If you are searching a chemical patent, don't hire someone skilled in mechanical devices.

Unless you have a history with a search firm, ask for a letter of nondisclosure before you sign on.

The cost to search a utility patent in the Washington, D.C., area runs between $200 and $300. Once the search has been completed, if you want to obtain an opinion as to the patentability of your invention, add the cost of your lawyer. If you need to show a prospective licensee that your invention has a good shot at a patent, or that it is unlikely to infringe existing product, a letter from competent patent counsel may do the trick.

We use Greentree Information Services (GIS), a patent search boutique, located in Bethesda, Maryland. The telephone number is (301) 469-0902; E-mail: g.greentreeinform@verizon.net. George Harvill, founder of GIS, has been doing our work for over 10 years. You may wish to contact GIS as part of your comparative shopping. There is no one better or more honest in the business than the Greentree team. The average patent search by GIS costs between $250 and $300.

The Do-It-Yourself Patent Search

Several methods are available should you decide to do the patent search yourself.

1. **The USPTO Patent Public Search Room**. The USPTO operates a Patent Public Search Room located in Arlington, Virginia. Here, every U.S. patent granted since 1836 may be searched and examined. Many inventors like to make at least one pilgrimage to the Patent Public Search Room. It is located less than five minutes from National Airport by taxi. Metro Rail serves it off the Blue and Yellow Lines, Crystal City Station. There are several hotels within walking distance.

Upon your arrival, the USPTO will issue to you, at no cost, a nontransferable user pass. It is wise to double-check the hours of operation by calling toll-free (800) 786-9199 or locally (703) 305-4463. Depending where in the facility you want to search, the Patent Public Search Room is typically open from 8:00 A.M. to 8:00 P.M.

The Patent Public Search Room (PSR) is really something to behold. Every inventor should treat himself/herself to a visit. You can touch and feel some original documents, including everything from Abraham Lincoln's 1849 patent (No.6,469) for a device to buoy vessels over shoals, to Auguste Bartholdi's design patent on a statue entitled "Liberty Enlightening the World," better known as the Statue of Liberty.

Today the PSR provides 40 workstations for the automated searching of patents using the examiner systems Web-based Examiner Search Tool (WEST)

Bright Ideas

In the 1920s, Francis W. Davis was chief engineer at the truck division of the Pierce Arrow Motor Car Company. Seeing how hard it was to steer heavy vehicles, Davis quit his job, rented a small engineering shop in Waltham, Massachusetts, and began experimenting to find a solution.

He developed a hydraulic power steering system that led to power steering. Power steering was commercially available by 1951.

Take My Words for It

Prior art: Previously issued patents that are discovered through a patent search.

and Examiner Automated Search Tool (EAST). Pre-Grant Published Applications became available in March of 2001 (see following). Full document text is searched on patents issued since 1971 and images and from 1790 to the present may be retrieved. Some foreign documents are available. Use of these workstations is free as of this writing (summer of 2001). There is a nominal charge for copies of what you print out.

On March 15, 2001, the USPTO published its first set of patent applications under the American Inventors Protection Act, a 1999 law making far-reaching changes to the U.S. patent system.

"Publication of patent applications before a patent is granted is one of the most fundamentally significant changes to the U.S. patent system in over 100 years," said Nicholas Godici, acting Under Secretary of Commerce and acting Director of the USPTO. "Published applications will become an important reservoir of reference materials for patent examiners and a valuable resource to the public as the volume of published applications increases."

Forty-seven applications were published in a variety of technical fields, including surgical devices, chemical processes, and business methods. The published patent applications may be viewed as images or text searched at www.USPTO.gov/patft/index.html. New applications are published every Thursday. The number of patent applications published by Office is anticipated to increase over the next 18 months until roughly 3500 applications are published weekly.

Publication of patent applications is now required for the vast majority of filings made on or after November 29, 2000. Publication occurs after expiration of an 18-month period following the earliest effective filing date. The earliest effective filing date may be influenced by a number of factors, including foreign filing. Previously U.S. patent applications were held in confidence until a patent was granted, while other major patent offices around the world have a history of publishing patent applications.

If you are going to file for foreign patents, you need to advise the USPTO of this when you make application for a U.S. patent. If you have no intention of going for foreign patents, the USPTO will keep your application under wraps until a patent is awarded, if this happens.

Fast Facts

Copyright, a form of intellectual property law, protects original works of authorship, including literary, dramatic, musical, and artistic works such as poetry, novels, movies, songs, computer software, and architecture. Copyright does not protect facts, ideas, systems, or methods of operation although it may protect the way these things are expressed.

WACKY PATENTS

**Target in a Bowl or Urinal to Attract
the Attention of Urinating Human Males**
Patented August 30, 1977
United States Patent 4,044,405

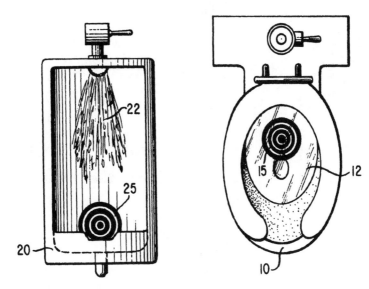

2. **The Scientific Library of the Patent and Trademark Office.** Nearby the Patent Public Search Room is the Scientific Library of the Patent and Trademark Office. The Scientific Library makes publicly available over 120,000 volumes of scientific and technical books in various languages, about 90,000 bound volumes of periodicals devoted to science and technology, the official journals of 77 foreign patent organizations, and over 12 million foreign patents. The hours are from 8:45 a.m. to 4:45 p.m.

Whether you do a manual or a computer search, make sure to look through every possible class and subclass that the patent office personnel suggest or that you feel are pertinent, and then add some for good measure.

3. **Internet Search.** If you have Internet access from home or office, you can conduct searches *pro se.* Go to www.USPTO.gov and have at it. IBM also hosts a search site: www.ibm.patent.com

To search foreign patents, there is only one free site. It is run by the World Intellectual Property Office (WIPO) at http://pctgazette.wipo.int/eng. The WIPO Web site provides access to various intellectual property data collections hosted by the WIPO. These include Madrid, PCT, and JOPAL (nonpatent reference) data and support fully searchable information retrieval and display by users on demand. Access to the

151

Digital Library is available to the general public free-of-charge. The services are operational and are updated on a daily, weekly, and monthly basis respectively.

Be aware that these databases are intended for use by the general public. Due to limitations of equipment and bandwidth, they are not intended to be a source for bulk downloads of USPTO data. Bulk data can be purchased from the Office at cost. The USPTO monitors who uses these databases. If someone generates an unusually high number of daily database accesses (e.g. searches, pages, or hits), whether generated manually or in an automated fashion, the USPTO may deny access to these servers without notice, according to Pamela Rinehart, Manager, Research & Administration and Patents Webmaster

Fast Facts

Characteristics of an Effective Logo

➤ Reflective of brand identification

➤ Reflective of brand improvement

➤ Novel

➤ Simple

➤ Telegenic

➤ Charismatic

➤ Promotable on multiple levels

Patent and Trademark Depository Libraries

Every inventor should conduct, or at least watch, at least one hands-on patent search to fully understand and appreciate the process. Obviously, not everyone can visit the Patent and Trademark Office's Patent Search Room in Arlington, Virginia. If you cannot make the trip, you may inspect copies of patents at a Patent and Trademark Depository Library (PTDL), a nationwide network of prestigious academic, research, and public libraries. "In 1996 we achieved our goal of having one PTDL in each state," says Amanda Putnam, manager of Patent and Trademark Depository Library programs. "Our next goal is to provide coverage in large metropolitan areas not already covered," she adds.

"Because the USPTO does not have regional offices, they have the PTDLs," explains Ms. Putnam, a 12^{1}/$_{2}$-year Office veteran. In addition to being research centers, the USPTO uses these as sites for outreach programs. For example, when the American Inventor Protection Act passed, officials put on seminars at the PTDLs to explain it to the intellectual property community. The USPTO's Office of Independent Inventor Programs uses the PTDLs for its seminars.

PTDLs are the best deal in town. They provide the public with a local link to the USPTO, expert reference assistance, patent and trademark databases, seminars and workshops, and USPTO searching resources. Most of the services are offered at no or a very low cost.

PTDLs continue to be one of the USPTO's most effective mechanisms for publicly disseminating patent information. PTDLs receive current issues of U.S. patents and maintain collections of patents issued earlier. The scope of these collections varies from library to library, ranging from patents of only recent years to all or most of the patents issued since 1790.

The patent collections in the PTDLs are open to the general public, and I have always found the librarians very willing to take the time to help newcomers gain effective access to the information contained in patents. In addition to the patents, PTDLs usually have all the publications of the U.S. Patent Classification System, including the *Manual of Classification, Index to the U.S. Patent Classification, Classifications Definitions, Official Gazette of the United States Patent and Trademark Office.*

At each PTDL, you can conduct a manual search using the computerized database, CASSIS. This permits access to the weekly USPTO publication, *The Official Gazette.* CASSIS is limited in its range and capabilities. If you do find relevant prior art through CASSIS, which is not always easy, the PTDL should be able to make you copies off microfilm.

The complete list of Patent and Trademark Depository Libraries is in Appendix B. There is no charge for you to search their patent collections. Because of variations among the PTDLs in their hours of service and the scope of their patent collections, you should contact the library in advance about its collection and hours, to avoid possible inconveniences.

Meet Your U.S. Patent Office

Mande Putnam is the Manager of the USPTO's PTDL Program that oversees a national network of 88 libraries located in all 50 states, the District of Columbia, and Puerto Rico. Mande conducts seminars, briefings, and training classes locally and nationally. In 1997, she was awarded the U.S. Department of Commerce Bronze Medal for her consistently exceptional service to the nationwide network of Patent and Trademark Depository Libraries.

Prior to coming to the USPTO, Mande was the PTDL Representative and Science Reference Librarian at the University of Delaware in Newark for three years. She also served as a library technical assistant at the Mathematics, Engineering, and Computer Science Branch Library at the University of New Hampshire in Durham for nearly 10 years.

Mande received her BS from the University of New Hampshire and Masters in Library Science from the University of Rhode Island. She is a member of the Special Libraries Association, the DC Library Association, the Patent Documentation Society, and the Patent and Trademark Office Society.

As mentioned above, a PTDL branch may have a specialized collection. To see the inventory of what's available, go to www.USPTO.gov and look under PTDLs.

Even though I live near enough to the Alexandria, Virginia, Public Search Room, I often opt to do my work at the University of Maryland's PTDL, located within its Engineering and Physical Sciences Library. Crowded with books and not much larger than a small meeting room, the library offers only a couple of chairs. However, here I can do my search work and have access to a very extensive collection of technical publications outside the PTDL that I enjoy browsing through for ideas and technologies. Such "extras" are not available at the main government facility, and I consider them a bonus.

Notable Quotables

"A good catchword can obscure analysis for fifty years."

—Wendell L. Willkie, politician

Bright Ideas

A workman left a soap-mixing machine on too long.

He was so embarrassed by his mistake that he ran outside and tossed the residue into a stream so his boss would not see it. Imagine his surprise when the incriminating evidence of his mistake floated to the surface. Ivory, the soap that floats, was born.

Electronic Databases

Basic patent and trademark electronic search products are provided to all PTDLs by the USPTO. Many PTDLs also subscribe to WEST (Web Examiner's Search Tool). Partnership PTDLs in Sunnyvale, California, Detroit, Michigan, and Houston, Texas, offer both text and image retrieval of patents and trademarks. Note: The databases available from the USPTO's Web site outlined following may not be available for general access at all PTDLs.

➤ Optical Disk Products at PTDLs—Describes USPTO electronic search products regularly provide to PTDLs

➤ Trademark Search System (X-Search)—Trademark text and image searching is available at PTDL Partnership sites in Sunnyvale, California, Detroit, Michigan, and Houston, Texas.

➤ USPTO Internet Search Systems—Search the U.S. Patent Database and Trademark Acceptable Identification of Goods and Services Manual.

➤ Trademark Electronic Search System (TESS)—TESS provides access to the same text and image database of trademarks as currently provided to examining attorneys at the USPTO via the X-Search system.

➤ USPTO Web Patent Database—Full text of all U.S. patents issued since January 1, 1976 and full-page images of each page of every U.S. patent issued since 1790.

PTDL Publications

Here is an inventory of what publications and documents you will typically find at a Patent and Trademark Depository Library.

➤ Patent and Trademark Depository Library Program—Describes the mission, history, and operation and services of the PTDLs

➤ List of PTDL Libraries—List includes the address and telephone number of all current PTDLs

➤ Optical Disk Products at PTDLs—Lists optical disk products available for public used at all PTDLs

➤ Patents: The Collection for All Reasons—Describes the ways in which this unique resource can be used

➤ The Seven-Step Strategy—Outlines a suggested procedure for patent searching

➤ Conducting a Trademark Search at a PTDL—Outlines a suggested procedure for trademark searching

➤ Examples and descriptions of patent and trademark document types

➤ Patent Document Kind Codes

➤ Patent Document Kind Codes (PDF Document)

➤ USPTO Search Facilities Hours and Location

➤ Document Disclosure Program

➤ International Schedule of Classes of Goods and Services

➤ International Schedule of Classes of Goods and Services (PDF Document)

If you live in a city with a PTDL, a librarian there can usually assist you in finding a list of those who make a living searching patents.

Don't be put off if a librarian is reluctant to give a specific recommendation; they are not permitted to provide legal advice nor personally recommend any patent professionals or search organizations.

Take My Words for It

Intellectual property:
Anything that can be patented, trademarked, or copyrighted—any idea.

Fast Facts

In May of 2001, the USPTO opened the U.S. Patent and Trademark Museum at 2121 Crystal Drive, Suite 0100, Arlington, Virginia. It contains a permanent exhibit plus one exhibit that rotates every three months. Open to the public Monday through Friday, 10:00 A.M. to 4:00 P.M. For information, call (301) 306-0455.

411

You may be able to take advantage of cutting-edge technologies and facilities that Sandia National Laboratories has to offer.

Contact: Corporate Business Development and Partnerships Center Organization 1300, Mail Stop 0185, Sandia National Laboratories, P.O. Box 5800, Albuquerque, New Mexico 87185

Phone: (505) 845-7730

Fax: (505) 844-3513

E-mail: net_admin@giss.tt. sandia.gov

URL: www.sandia.gov

Notable Quotables

"Inventing is a combination of brains and materials. The more brains you use, the less material you need."

—Charles F. Kettering, inventor, electric cash register

Patent Search Steps

Here is a brief guide to manual searches at the PSR and PTDLs for U.S. patents. No matter where you decide to conduct a search, certain steps must be taken in any patent search.

Step 1: If you know the patent number, go to the *Official Gazette* to read a summary of the patent. This publication is available at any of the above-mentioned patent search facilities and in many public library reference rooms.

Step 2: If you know the patentee or assignee, look at the *Patent/Assignee Index* to locate the patent number. This is available at any of the patent search facilities. In Crystal City, it is on microfiche and in card catalogues.

Step 3: If you know the subject, start with the *Index to the U.S. Patent Classification*.

Step 4: Once you have jotted down the class(es) and subclass(es) out of the *Index*, refer to the *Manual of Classification* and check this information in relation to the hierarchy to see if it is close to what you need. The *Manual of Classification* is available at all patent search facilities.

Step 5: Using the class/subclass numbers you have found, look at the U.S. Patent Classification Subclass and Numeric Listing and copy the patent numbers of patents assigned to the selected class/subclass. If you are at the Crystal City facility, take the class/subclass numbers into the stacks of patents and begin "pulling shoes." To pull shoes is to physically remove patent groupings from the open shelves.

Step 6: Then, using the *Official Gazette* again, look at the summaries of those patents.

At the Crystal City facility, you will not have to go back to this publication since the actual patents are there.

Step 7:   Upon locating the relevant patents, examine the complete patent in person or on microfilm, depending upon where you conduct the search.

Step 8:   Print copies of all relevant prior art. Your patent attorney will want to cite some of it in your application.

WACKY PATENTS

Combination Toy Dog and Vacuum Cleaner
Patented November 13, 1973
United States Patent 3,771,192

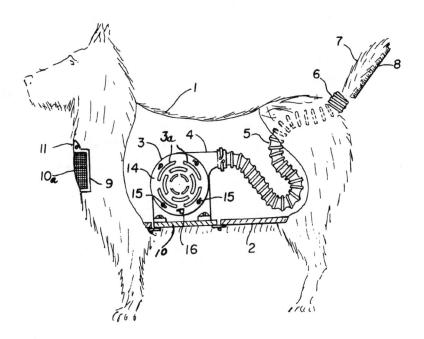

Patent Classification System

Patents are arranged according to a classification system of more than 465 classes and over 200,000 subclasses. The *Index to the U.S. Patent Classifications* is an alphabetical list of the subject headings referring to specific classes and subclasses of the U.S. patent classification system. The classifications are intended as an initial means of entry into the USPTO's classification system and should be particularly useful to those who lack experience in using the classification system or who are unfamiliar with the technology under consideration.

The classifications are to searching a patent what the card catalog is to looking for a library book. It is the only way to discover what exists in the field of prior art. The classifications are a star to steer by, without which no meaningful patent search can be completed. Before you begin your search, use the classifications to plot your direction. First, look for the term that you feel best represents your invention. If a match cannot be found, look for terms of approximately the same meaning, for example, describing a similar function, effect, or application. By doing some homework before you begin searching, such as familiarizing yourself with the *Index* and locating the class and subclass numbers for terms that pertain to your invention, you'll save time.

Bright Ideas

Allured by photography, music teachers Leopold Godowsky and Leopold Mannes co-invented an easy-to-use, practical color film. Supporting themselves by teaching music and putting on concerts, in their spare time they would mix up concoctions in Mannes's kitchen. Their work caught the attention of Kodak, and the company offered them full-time, well-paid jobs. In 1935, Kodak introduced Kodachrome film, the result of their work.

Once you have recorded the identifying numbers of possibly pertinent classes and subclasses, refer to the *Manual of Classification*, a loose-leaf USPTO volume listing the numbers and descriptive titles of more than 300 classes and 95,000 subclasses used in the subject classification of patents, with an index to classifications. This manual is also available at the Patent and Trademark Depository Libraries.

The classifications are arranged with subheadings that can extend to several levels of indentation. A complete reading of a subheading includes the title of the most adjacent higher heading and so on until there are no higher headings. Some headings will reference other related or preferred entries.

New classes and subclasses are continuously based upon breaking developments in science and technology. Old classes and subclasses are rendered obsolete by technological advance. In fact, if you have suggestions for future revisions of the classifications or if you find omissions or errors, you are encouraged to alert the USPTO. Send your suggestions to Editor, U.S. Patent Classification, Office of Documentation, U.S. Patent and Trademark Office, Washington, D.C. 20231.

How to Order Copies of Prior Art

If you cannot get a copy of a specific patent(s) through a PTDL or the Internet site www.usUSPTO.gov, you may order from the Patent and Trademark Office copies of original patents or cross-referenced patents contained in subclasses comprising the field of search. Mail your request to Patent and Trademark Office, Box 9, Washington, D.C. 20231.

Payment may be made by check, coupons, or money. Expect a wait of up to four weeks when ordering copies of patents by mail from the USPTO.

For the convenience of attorneys, agents, and the general public in paying any fees due, deposit accounts may be established in the USPTO with a minimum deposit of $50. For information on this service, call (703) 308-0902.

What to Do with Your Search Results

Study the results of the patent research. You may be out of luck if a previously patented invention is very similar to yours; your invention may even be infringing on another invention. On the other hand, one or more patents may describe inventions that are intended for the same purpose as yours but are significantly different in various ways. Look these over and decide whether it is worthwhile to proceed. Consult a patent attorney if you have any doubt.

If the features that make your invention different from the prior art provide important advantages, you should discuss the situation with your attorney to determine whether a fair chance exists of obtaining a patent covering these features.

I have found from experience that a good patent attorney can often get some claim to issue, albeit not always a strong one. A patent for patent's sake is usually possible. Whether it will be worth the paper it is printed on is another matter. Do not make this decision lightly because the patent process is not cheap. The average utility patent will cost about $2,500.

Searching Trademarks

Trademark searching is so streamlined and foolproof today that it can all be done from your personal computer via the Internet. There is no need to hire a search firm. In fact, Greentree Information Services, my searcher of choice, no longer accepts

411

BountyQuest is an Internet destination where companies post large cash rewards for vital information. I saw one this morning for $10,000. The rapidly growing, high-stakes patent arena is the source of BountyQuest's first rewards, where access to fugitive information helps resolve today's raging patent controversies.

BountyQuest opened for business in 2000 and is privately held. I have no experience with the company and list it as a piece of intellectual candy. For more information, visit www. bountyquest.com.

Take My Words for It

Infringer: One who misappropriates another person's intellectual property.

assignments to search trademarks because it's now something people can do for themselves.

For details on trademark searches, see Chapter 15, "Mark Your Words."

The Last Word ...

When determining which search method is best for you, consider the following: How much money can you spare, how much time can you spare, and how well could you do the job yourself? Finding out early that the *Mother of All Ideas* is old news can save you a lot in developmental and legal costs, not to mention time. Conversely, you just might find out that your idea is the next sliced bread.

The Least You Need to Know

➤ When you search for gold, sometimes you get the gold, sometimes you get the shaft. Don't be surprised if your search reveals a crowded field of invention.

➤ Patent searching—there's no need to pay retail.

➤ PTDLs are user-friendly.

➤ There's no need to pay for a federal trademark search.

Chapter 11

How to Hire a Patent Attorney

In This Chapter

➤ Yes, you need a patent attorney

➤ No, you shouldn't do it yourself

➤ It's a buyer's market

➤ What to look for under the hood

➤ Where you can save major dollars

"America's creative genius is truly an invaluable national asset which in my view arises from our independent spirit. An important part of this great resource continues to reside in the independent inventor community. Clearly these entrepreneurial innovators are helping ensure that American industry remains competitive in the global marketplace."

—John K. Williamson, Assistant General Counsel, Intellectual Property, PPG Industries

The art of drafting a patent is not brain surgery, but it does take an expertise that most inventors do not possess. Even those skilled in the arcane language of the patent may not be up to date on patent regulations with regard to the prosecution of a patent application, the handling of office actions, etc. This process is not without red tape, and as with any bureaucracy, things are always in transition.

411

Intellectual Property Owners (IPO) is a nonprofit association that serves the owners of patents, trademarks, copyrights, and trade secrets. Founded in 1972 and based in Washington, D.C., its membership is diverse. There are more than a hundred Fortune 500 member companies including General Electric, 3M, IBM, AT&T, and PPG Industries as well as several hundred independent inventors and patent attorneys and a few universities. IPO's National Inventor of the Year Award recognizes America's most outstanding inventors. Winners epitomize the American tradition of technological leadership and "Yankee ingenuity."

For information and a membership application, call: (202)-466-2396, e-mail: info@ipo.org, or visit IPO's Web site (www.ipo.org)

Executive Director: Herbert C. Wamsley.

Do You Need a Patent Attorney?

Yes. Count on it. If you think it is expensive to use a patent attorney, see what it costs you if you do not hire one. While it is perfectly legal for you to draft and prosecute your own patents (i.e., working *pro se*), I strongly recommend that you hire patent counsel for all patent work except for design patents.

Without equivocation, time after time, the value of my patents has been enhanced by the contribution of a savvy patent attorney, someone who knows how to define invention and navigate the waters of prior art. The fact is, anyone can get a patent on almost anything. What good patent counsel will do is increase the odds that a patent awarded adequately protects your invention.

"Patent writing should be done by those specifically skilled in the art," says Tomima Edmark, inventor of Topsy Tail, the invention that turned a ponytail inside out and made over $80 million in worldwide sales. "Writing your own patent application is a big mistake."

Calvin D. MacCracken, who holds 80 U.S. patents and 250 foreign ones, advises in his *Handbook for Inventors*, "Writing your own patent is long, hard work ... If you can somehow afford a good patent attorney to do the whole job, that may well produce a better patent ... "

Note: This chapter concerns utility patents. For my advice on design patents, please refer to Chapter 14, "How to Apply for a Design Patent." I do not recommend patent counsel for design patents, nor spending money on a search of prior art. Plant patents are covered in Chapter 13, "Flower Power: How to Apply for Plant Patents."

You should not go the do-it-yourself, *pro se* route. Only use step-by-step, do-it-yourself books or computer programs as primers. These books have a wonderful tutorial benefit, but it is reckless and foolhardy for those not skilled in patent specification preparation, particularly claim drafting, to do it for themselves.

A patent is a form of lottery ticket. It's the Big Spin. The invention it covers may hit pay dirt. Therefore, you want to make every effort to assure a patent has teeth and cannot be easily attacked. While patent attorneys are not perfect, working together with the inventor it is more likely that stronger claims will be written.

Take My Words for It

Customer: The most important person to your business. This can be your licensee or the end user of your invention.

You can do your own income tax. For people who do not make a lot of money, this may be the most cost-effective way to deal with the IRS. But those who have substantial earnings or estates hire CPAs. They do not do their income tax with a self-help book. There is too much at stake. Wealthy people use CPAs to level the playing field and give themselves every benefit of the law. Inventors should do the same through the counsel of a patent attorney.

Here's another way to look at it. If you bought a state lottery ticket and hit the big prize, say a multi-state purse, would you purchase a do-it-yourself book on income tax, or hire the best CPA to assure you keep as much of the money as possible under the law?

Bright Ideas

As a visitor to Labrador in the early 1900s, Clarence Birdseye was impressed by the quality of the fish and game frozen by the Eskimos. In 1924, he started the Freezing Company and this kicked off the frozen fruit and vegetable industry. Birdseye was granted a patent in 1930 for his method of packaging frozen food.

Patents are invaluable should a product hit the mother lode and, therefore, must be afforded every advantage. So, even if you really know your stuff, it is recommend that you have competent counsel review your work. There is no guarantee that a licensed practitioner will not make a mistake, but if he or she does, they will know how to correct it, and they carry malpractice insurance. Do you?

Bottom line: Smart inventors use experienced advisors to assure they obtain the strongest protection available on their inventions.

Is That Your Final Answer?

Here are some questions to ask the lawyers you interview.

➤ Do you draft the patent or is it done by an assistant?

WACKY PATENTS

TV Control Device
Patented June 15, 1976
United States Patent 3,962,748

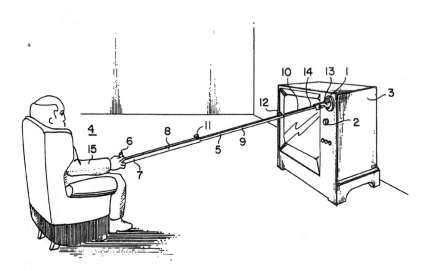

➤ How long will it take you to complete the job, i.e., write the initial application and have it filed?

➤ Are you up-to-speed on The American Inventors Protection Act that was enacted November 29, 1999, as Public Law 106-113?

➤ Are there any hidden charges in addition to service fees and disbursements, including government fees, etc.? Lawyers like clients to pick up their overhead plus fees. Some lawyers charge for incoming faxes. Refuse to pay for fax traffic between you and your patent firm if you are located in the same city.

➤ What is the charge for photocopies? This can be a profit center for some patent lawyers. This is not as bad as it used to be, though. Some state legal ethic codes, e.g., Virginia, only allow lawyers to recover their costs.

If the price is too high, cut a better deal. If there are co-inventors, get one copy and have one of the inventors copy and distribute the material.

Services that specialize in copying patent files for law firms charge as much as $1.00 per page, which is then marked-up by the patent attorney.

You can buy black-and-white copy service less expensively at Kinko's or Staples, for example, at five to seven cents per page, less for higher volumes. How much mark-up, if any, is fair?

➤ How are telephone consults billed? Are you going to be charged every time you ask a question? I set these ground rules early in any relationship with counsel.

➤ May I have a list of references, and their phone numbers? You'll want to talk to other independent inventors and see if they were satisfied.

➤ What kind of guarantee comes with the work? In other words, you want to be sure you do not get eaten alive by fee creep, which can be caused by interferences and appeals at the USPTO. Richard G. Besha, Esq., a patent attorney at Nixon & Vanderhye, Arlington, Virginia, points out that it may take two or three years to prosecute a patent, depending upon the amount of office action involved. He advises that inventors nail down the price up front because a lawyer's hourly rate is most likely to be more by the time the work has been completed.

If your lawyer directs your search and drawing initiatives and mistakes are made, he or she will stand behind the work. The lawyer simply points out the mistakes to their subcontractors and takes it out of their hides.

Notable Quotables

"Don't get on the stage when it's leaving town."

—Greg Hyman, co-inventor, Tickle Me Elmo!

Notable Quotables

"When patterns are broken, new worlds can emerge."

—Tuli Kupferberg, poet, free-formist

Levy's Rules for Hiring a Patent Attorney

Consider the following points when retaining counsel. Read them carefully. They could save you time and money.

1. Make sure your patent attorney is registered by the Patent & Trademark Office.
   The USPTO keeps a register of over 25,700 attorneys and agents. To be listed, a
   person must comply with the regulations prescribed by the USPTO, which requires proof that the person is of good moral character and of good repute and
   that he or she has the legal, scientific, and technical qualifications necessary to
   give inventors valuable service. Certain qualifications must be demonstrated by
   passing an exam. Those admitted must have a college degree in engineering or
   science or the equivalent of such a degree.

A listing of patent lawyers and agents registered by the USPTO, organized state-by-
state, city-by-city, may be found at any Patent and Trademark Depository Library nationwide in the publication, *Patent Attorneys and Agents Registered to Practice before the
U.S. Patent and Trademark Office.* If you wish to purchase a current copy at $50.00
(Stock #003-004-00693-5), contact the U.S. Government Printing Office, Superintendent of Documents, Washington, D.C. 20402. For information, call
(202) 512-1800; fax (202) 512-2250.

A faster way to run a name check is via the Internet. Simply go to www.uspto.gov
and click on Patent Attorneys & Agents.

The drums say that in actuality there are far fewer people practicing patent law than
it would seem from the list. The USPTO list may contain lawyers and patent agents
who have gone to the other side of the grass, or are no longer in business. The
USPTO plans to begin weeding this garden soon.

2. Hire a patent attorney who is a specialist in your technology. You would not
   want a dermatologist to do your heart surgery. Neither would you want an electronic patent specification written by an attorney whose specialty is mechanical
   engineering. Satisfy yourself of the lawyer's expertise. Interview more than one
   candidate. Patent counsel should be able to help you broaden your claims by
   probing your mind to make sure that you have considered all possible embodiments and improvements. Only those versed in your field of invention will be
   able to do this effectively.

   Be wary of lawyers who pitch themselves as agents to help sell your invention.
   You're hiring patent counsel, not a salesman.

3. Only hire patent counsel who understands the ins and outs of The American
   Inventors Protection Act that was enacted November 29, 1999, as Public Law
   106-113. This is complicated stuff for the brightest of them.

4. Shop around. It's a buyer's market. If the lawyer is inflexible, go elsewhere.

5. Request an estimate. Patent attorneys are able to give close estimates once they
   understand the scope of work. Once you have an acceptable price, ask your

attorney to agree in writing and cap it off. Otherwise, you may find your budget busted. Make a package deal whenever you can. You are selling money, not buying services.

6. Do not embarrass yourself by insisting that the lawyer sign a confidentiality agreement before you'll disclose your invention. Patent lawyers do not steal ideas. If you are preoccupied about this, get over it. As Dick Besha says, "It's unethical for a patent lawyer to steal ideas, and it's a great way to get disbarred."

7. It is especially important at a large firm that you know who will do your work. The big firms need litigation and hefty retainers to make money. They do not make enough to pay the light bills drafting claims and prosecuting patents for independent inventors.

You want to be important to the attorney. Years ago I found one lawyer putting our work on hold while he took care of business for a more senior attorney at the firm.

You do not want your work rushed. Thought must be given to going for as wide a set of claims as possible.

WACKY PATENTS

Leash with Sound
Patented April 23, 1996
United States Patent 5,509,859

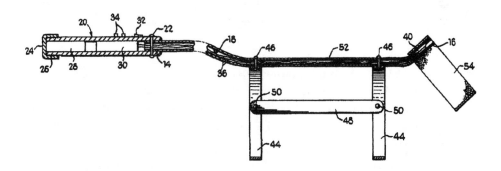

Make sure that you work will not be farmed out to a less experienced attorney in the firm.

8. If possible, hire your own patent searcher. Lawyers do not search patents. They hire specialists and then mark up the bills. Large firms typically have people on

staff who go every day to the USPTO, others use freelancers. You will save a lot of money making a direct hire. See Chapter 9, "The United States Patent and Trademark Office," on the hire of patent searchers.

Note: If the attorney allows you to handle this process, he or she may ask that they be indemnified from problems that could arise from a less than satisfactory search. For example, your searcher could miss a key piece of prior art. They will also not render a written opinion on it unless you pay extra for it.

I look at it this way. If I hire a highly qualified searcher, someone who also does work for the law firms, then I am willing to take that risk in return for the savings. I do not need a written opinion to figure out if the prior art precludes me from getting protection. The search results will show this.

9. If possible, hire your own patent draftsman, too. Lawyers don't draw. They hire specialists and then mark up their bills. Larger firms frequently have draftsmen on staff, others use freelancers. Here, again, you'll save money if you make the call.

10. If several lawyers show up for a meeting, ask who they are, what is their purpose, and if you are paying for them. If you are, be very sure they are needed. "One guy should be able to handle a patent," says Richard G. Besha, Esq.

Bright Ideas

In the early 1920s, R. A. Watkins, owner of a small printing plant in Illinois, was approached by a man who wanted to sell him the rights to a homemade device made of waxed cardboard and tissue on which messages could be printed and then easily erased by lifting up the tissue. Watkins wanted to think about the proposition overnight and told the man to return the next day.

In the middle of the night, Watkins's phone rang; it was the inventor calling from jail. The man said that if Watkins would bail him out, he could have the device. Watkins agreed and went on to acquire the U.S. patent rights as well as the foreign rights to the device, which he called the Magic Slate.

Another Money Saver

The more groundwork you lay for the patent attorney, the better shape you will be in on a couple fronts.

➤ It will take the attorney less time to work up the specifications and claims if he or she does not start with a blank paper.

➤ The practitioner will have the benefit of your ideas when drafting claims. One of the greatest contributions an inventor can make to the drafting of claims is to point out to the attorney how the competition might end-run them and get around their patent.

No one knows an invention better than its inventor. Develop an in-depth description of your invention and draft all the claims you can think of. Don't worry about how to justify them. It's important that the patent attorney have an idea of the invention's scope and reach.

411

If you wish to file a formal complaint against a patent lawyer or agent registered to practice before the USPTO, contact the Office of Enrollment and Discipline. Phone: 703-306-4097 Fax: 703-306-4134 Address: Director of the United States Patent and Trademark Office, Box OED, Washington, DC 20231.

The Least You Need to Know

➤ Patent attorneys are required.

➤ Do it yourself and you may do yourself in.

➤ Shop around—it's a buyer's market.

➤ Steer clear of large law firms.

➤ You can hire searchers and draftsman and, thereby, save money.

Part 4

Uncle Sam Wants (to Help) You!

The United States of America has had over two hundred years of Patent and Copyright laws on its books. Is it possible that early lawmakers James Madison, George Read, Rufus King, Benjamin Franklin, Alexander Hamilton, George Washington, and Thomas Jefferson could have foreseen the importance of their hard work as it advances America's sciences and useful arts into the twenty-first century?

Imagine how brilliant and omniscient the drafters of the U.S. Constitution and successive statutes were when they thought to write, in Article 1, Section 8, that Congress shall have the power to "promote the Progress of Science and useful Arts, by securing for limited Times to Authors and Inventors the exclusive Right to their respective Writings and Discoveries."

The golden eggs laid by the inventors, gadgeteers, cranks, tinkerers, thinkers, imagineers, and entrepreneurs that continue to hatch American industry have been protected and nurtured by a vital—albeit imperfect—system of intellectual property laws that has stood the test of time.

The chapters in this section focus on the methods of protection available to you thanks to our forefathers. Patents. Trademarks. Copyrights. Trade Secrets. The information is not meant to take the place of competent legal advice, merely to familiarize you with the terrain as you continue on your quest for success.

Chapter 12

How to Apply for a Utility Patent

In This Chapter

➤ Economy version—the provisional patent

➤ The real thing, the nonprovisional patent

➤ Staking your claims on invention

➤ Prototypes generally are not required

➤ Now you can patent computer programs

"We need to thank our creative inventors for not only our good life, but a healthy one in a great land of opportunity. When I look back at the thousands of inventors that I have helped, I see not only the successful companies, but all the lives that they have touched for the better."

—Lawrence J. Udell, Executive Director, California Invention Center, Center for New Venture Alliance, Intellectual Property International, Ltd.

If you have invented an elevator winding device, an apparatus for attaching tag pins, a tape drive mechanism, a three-dimensional digitizer, a preschool toy, a U-joint mount, or simply a better mousetrap, you may wish to consider the kind of protection that a nonprovisional utility patent can provide. It is the strongest position you can take, for the following reasons:

➤ Document Disclosures buy you nothing in the eyes of a prospective licensee. It is only a way of establishing a date of conception. Hey, what do you expect for $10?

➤ The provisional patent is used to grab a first-to-file date while you pull together the doh-re-me to finance the next phase, which is the most important, a non-provisional patent. This could run into the many thousands, depending upon the complexity of your invention, and how many office actions it will require before (or if) it issues.

➤ Design patents are simply too easy to get around.

Manufacturers get a warm and fuzzy feeling from broad utility patents. A utility patent on an invention will really pump up your concept's shine and get everyone's attention. The more bullet-proof you can make your invention, the better. A strong utility patent can give your licensee a monopoly on making, using, and selling the invention. This is what it's all about.

Before deciding whether to proceed with the filing of any patent application, you have to consider a patent search. This is discussed in detail in Chapter 10, "It All Begins with a Search." Once you have made that decision, dive into this chapter to see the options available to you.

Provisional Application for a Patent

Since June 8, 1995, the USPTO has offered the option of filing a provisional application, which was designed to provide a lower cost first patent filing in the United States and to give you parity with foreign applicants. Claims and oath or declaration are not required for a provisional application. Provisional application provides the means to establish an early effective filing date in a patent application and permits the term "Patent Pending" to be applied in connection with the invention. Provisional applications may not be filed for design inventions.

Filing Date

The filing date of a provisional application is the date on which a written description of the invention—and drawings, if necessary—are received in the USPTO. To be complete, a provisional application must also include the filing fee and a cover sheet specifying the application is a provisional application for patent. You would then have up to 12 months to file a non-provisional application as described following.

The claimed subject matter in the later filed nonprovisional application is entitled to the benefit of the filing date of the provisional application if it has support in the provisional application.

Provisional applications are not examined on their merits. A provisional application will become abandoned by the operation of law 12 months from its filing date. The 12-month pendency is not counted toward the 20-year term of a patent granted on a subsequently filed nonprovisional application, which relies on the filing date of the provisional application.

The cost of provisional application preparation by a patent attorney will vary depending on the length of disclosure and the complexity of the invention. I have heard stories about inventors paying the same for a provisional as a nonprovisional because the provisional application must meet the enablement requirements of the patent statue (see 35 USC 112, first paragraph). It must instruct those of ordinary skill in the art how to make and use the invention. So, to help keep the cost down, provide as much information as possible to your patent counsel on how to make and use your proposed invention, to control expenses for preparing the application.

A surcharge is required for filing the basic filing fee or the cover sheet on a date later than the filing of the provisional application. For up-to-date fees, call (703) 308-4357 or (800) 786-9199. At the same time, you can also ask for a brochure on the Provisional Patent. Or check the USPTO's Web site at www.uspto.gov for fees and explanations.

Nonprovisional Application for a Utility Patent

A nonprovisional application for a patent is made to the Assistant Commissioner for Patents and includes, in the following order of presentation:

1. **A letter of transmittal.** A transmittal letter should be filed with every patent application to instruct the USPTO on the services you desire in the processing of your application. In this cover letter, inform the director of your

Notable Quotables

"It is not important what you cover in school ... It is important what you uncover."

—Anonymous

Bright Ideas

Jacob Schick, a retired U.S. Army colonel and inventor, was inspired to develop a razor that worked without soap or water. After World War I, Schick devoted himself to inventing an electric razor. His wife mortgaged their Connecticut home to finance the venture. The patented design that resulted used a series of slots to hold the hairs while a series of moving blades cut the hair off.

name, address, telephone number, the type of application, the title of your invention, and the contents of the application.

2. **Specification.** The specification must include a written description of the invention and of the manner and process of making and using it. The specification is required to be in such full, clear, concise, and exact terms as to enable any person skilled in the art or science to which the invention pertains, or with which it is most nearly connected, to make and use it.

The specification must set forth the precise invention for which you are seeking patent protection, in such a way as to distinguish it from other inventions and from what is old. It must describe completely a specific embodiment of the process, machine, manufacture, composition of matter, or improvement invented and must explain the method of operation or principle whenever applicable. Write up the best embodiment you contemplate for your invention.

Fast Facts

During the last century, inventors were prolific. Here are some important twentieth-century inventions and their approximate dates of conception, according to *The World Book*:

Safety razor: 1901	Modern plastics: 1930s
Air-conditioning: 1902	Xerography: 1938
Airplane: 1903	Transistor: 1947
Helicopter: 1907	Compact disc: 1982
Television: 1920s	

In the case of an improvement to an invention, the specification must particularly point out the part(s) of the process, machine, manufacture, or composition of matter to which your improvement relates. The description should be confined to the specific improvement and to such parts that cooperate with it or as may be necessary to complete understanding or description of it. The pages of the specification, including claims and abstract, should be numbered consecutively, starting with page one. The page numbers should be centrally located above, or preferably, below the text.

➤ Title. The title of the invention, which should be as short and specific as possible (best if it does not exceed 280 typewritten spaces), should appear as the heading on the first page of the specification, if it does not otherwise appear at the beginning of the application.

➤ Cross-reference to related applications, if any.

➤ Reference to a microfiche appendix, for computer program listings, if any. The total number of microfiche and total number of frames should be specified.

411

Since October 27, 2000, the USPTO has been accepting electronic patent filings. The required software is available, free of charge, for download from the USPTO's Patent Electronic Business Center (EBC) on the Web site www.uspto.gov. Electronic Filing System (EFS) software assembles application components (including drawings), calculates fees, validates content; and compresses, encrypts, and transmits the application to the USPTO.

EFS is a work in progress. At this writing, it does not accept patent applications for designs, new plants, provisionals, PCT, and reissues. It does not take requests for reexamination. Keep checking on it, though. It's only a matter of time until it does all this and more.

➤ Background of the Invention. The specification should set forth the background of the invention in two parts:

1. **Field of the Invention:** This section should include a statement of the field of endeavor to which the invention pertains. This section may also include a paraphrasing of the applicable U.S. patent classification definitions or the subject matter of the claimed invention. This section may also be titled "Technical Field."

2. **Description of the related art (or prior art):** This section should contain a description of information known to you, including references to specific documents, which are related to your invention. This section should also contain, if applicable, references to specific art-related problems involved in the prior art that are solved by your invention.

➤ Summary of the Invention. This section should present the substance or general idea of the claimed invention in summarized form. The summary may point out the advantages of the invention or how it solves previously existing problems, preferably those problems identified in the Background of the Invention. A statement of the object of the invention may also be included.
The summary should precede the detailed description.

➤ Abstract of the Disclosure. The purpose of the abstract is to enable the USPTO and the public to determine quickly from a cursory inspection the nature and gist of the technical disclosures of the invention. The abstract points out what is new in the art to which the invention pertains. It should be in narrative form and generally limited to a single paragraph on a separate page.

➤ Claims. The specification must conclude with a claim particularly pointing out and distinctly claiming the subject matter that you regard as your invention.

WACKY PATENTS

Calvary Equipment
Patented November 7, 1899
United States Patent 636,430

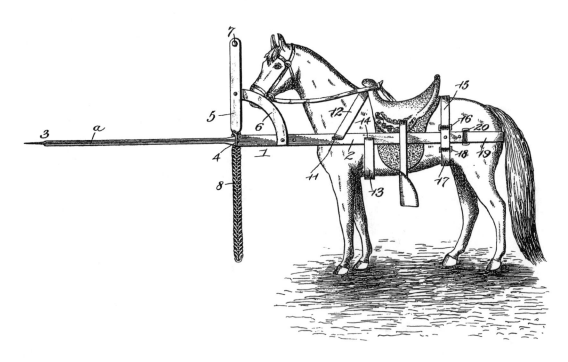

More than one claim may be presented provided the claims differ substantially from each other and are not unduly multiplied.

One or more claims may be presented in dependent form, referring back to and further limiting another claim or claims in the same application. Any dependent claim that refers to more than one other claim ("multiple dependent claim") shall refer to such other claims in the alternative only. A multiple dependent claim shall not serve as a basis for any other multiple dependent claim. For fee calculation purposes under $1.16, a multiple dependent claim will be considered to be that number of claims to which direct reference is made therein. For fee calculation purposes, also, any claim depending from a multiple dependent claim will be considered that number of claims to which direct reference is made in that multiple dependent claim.

The claim or claims must conform to the invention as set forth in the remainder of the specification. The terms and phrases used in the claims must find clear support or antecedent basis in the description so that the meaning of the terms in the claims may be ascertainable for reference to the description.

3. **Drawings.** A patent application is required to contain drawings if drawings are needed for the understanding of the subject matter sought to be patented. The drawings must show every feature of the invention as specified in the claims. Omission of drawings will cause an application to be considered incomplete. An application for a design patent must contain at least one drawing.

Notable Quotables

"To understand is to invent."

—Jean Piaget, Swiss developmentalist

When there are drawings, there must be a brief description of the several views of the drawings, and the detailed description of the invention must refer to the different views by specifying the numbers of the figures. It also must refer to the different parts by use of reference letters or numerals (preferably the latter). For specific guidelines to drawings, refer to Chapter 14, "How to Apply for a Design Patent."

4. **Oath or Declaration.** This document must be signed by all the actual inventors. An oath may be administered by any person within the United States, or by a diplomatic or consular officer of a foreign country, who is authorized by the United States to administer oaths. A declaration does not require any witness or person to administer or verify its signing. Thus, use of a declaration is preferable.

Notable Quotables

"Don't quit your day job!"

—Norman and Arlene Fabricant, co-inventors, Dr. Drill 'n Fill

179

The document must identify the application to which it is directed. It must give the name, city, either state or country of residence, country of citizenship, and post office address of each inventor, and it must state whether the inventor is a sole or joint inventor of the invention claimed. Additionally, designation of a correspondence address is needed on the oath or declaration. Providing a correspondence address will help to ensure prompt delivery of all notices, official letters, and other communications.

➤ Fee payment. And last but not least, don't forget to put in your check. Fees for patent applications are subject to change and should always be double-checked before filing. Having made improper payments in the past, which caused delays and penalties, I now call several times before writing a check to the USPTO. For up-to-date fees, call (703) 308-4357. Please remember that two sets of fees exist— one for a small entity and one for other than a small entity. If you qualify as a small entity for patent fee purposes, you should complete one of the forms verifying small entity status in order to receive the benefit of reduced fees. If you find that you need additional guidance filing your application, hire a patent attorney, or call the USPTO's Special Processing Branch at (703) 308-1202.

Bright Ideas

Charles Goodyear had no formal education. When his family hardware business failed and he could not clean up the mess, he was put in debtors's prison. Ironically, it was there that he started experimenting to find a more stable rubber.

On June 15, 1844, Goodyear was awarded Patent No. 3,633 for "Improvement In India–Rubber Fabric." He combined sulfur and white lead with India–rubber and heated the compound. This created a soft, pliable substance unaffected by temperature. His invention never made him any money. In 1860, he died in poverty. Twenty–eight years later, tires emblazoned with his name rolled out of Frank Seiberling's factory, named for the man who invented the process of vulcanizing.

Models Not Generally Required

Now that you know what *is* required for your utility patent application, here is something that generally is *not* required. Models were once required in all cases admitting a model, as part of the application, and these models became part of the record of the patent. Such models are no longer generally required (the description of the invention in the specification, and the drawings, must be sufficiently full and complete and capable of being understood to disclose the invention without the aid of a model) and will not be accepted unless specifically called for by the examiner.

If the invention relates to a composition of matter, you may be asked to furnish specimens of the composition or of its ingredients or intermediates for the purpose of inspection or experiment.

But if you want to license your invention, you better have a "looks like/works like" prototype to show. Companies do not license ideas. They need to see prototypes, or at the very least an operational breadboard.

Solamente Ingles, Por Favor

All application papers must be in the English language or a translation into the English language will be required along with the required fee. All application papers must be legibly written on only one side either by a typewriter or mechanical printer in permanent dark ink or its equivalent in portrait orientation on flexible, strong, smooth, nonshiny, durable, and white paper.

Fast Facts

Since the early 1980s, the U.S. Patent and Trademark Office has been working in concert with other federal agencies, corporations, and associations to bring into national focus a number of grassroots school programs promoting thinking skills instruction. As a result of that effort, Project XL was initiated in 1985 as a national partnership designed to encourage proliferation of such programs and to develop new programs and materials which will promote critical and creative thinking and problem-solving skills for all children in our Nation's schools.

To get the book, *The Inventive Thinking Curriculum Project*, Third Edition, call (800) USPTO-9199 or (703) 308-4357. This is free of charge.

The Rules of the Game

The papers must be presented in a form having sufficient clarity and contrast between the paper and the writing to permit electronic reproduction. The application papers must all be the same size—either 21.0 cm by 29.7 cm (DIN size A4) or 8½ by 11 inches (21.6 cm by 27.9 cm), with a top margins of at least ¾ inch (2.0 cm), a left side margin of at least 1 inch (2.5 cm), a right side margin of at least (¾ inch (2.0 cm) and a bottom margin of at least ¾ inch (2.0 cm) with no holes made in the submitted papers. It is also required that the spacing on all papers be 1½ or double spaced and the application papers must be numbered consecutively (centrally located above or below the text) starting with page one. The application for patent is not forwarded for examination until all required parts, complying with the rules related thereto, are received. If any application is filed without all the required parts for obtaining a filing date (incomplete or defective), you will be notified of the deficiencies and given a time period to complete the application filing (a surcharge may be required)—at which time a filing date as of the new date of such a completed submission will be given to you. If you do not correct the omission within a specified time period, the application will be returned or otherwise disposed of; the filing fee, if submitted, will be refunded less a handling fee as set forth in the fee schedule.

411

There are opportunities to pick up technologies and sell or license your patents via the Internet. I cannot vouch personally for the following services, but include them for their interest and potential.

➤ PatentAuction.com is an auction site for patents, trademarks, and copyrights from all over the world.

➤ Yet2.com claims a database of more than $2.5 billion in licensable technology. Its funding comes from a stellar cast of world class companies, including AGFA, 3M, BASF, P&G, Dupont, General Mills, and Ciba.

➤ NewIdeaTrade.com invites companies, individuals, universities, and government agencies to promote, buy, sell, and license new ideas and inventions, patents, copyrighted works, trademarks, and other intellectual property.

Now that you have all the parts of the application ready to go, keep the following in mind.

➤ It is desirable that all parts of the complete application be deposited in the Office together; otherwise, each part must be signed and a letter must accompany each part, accurately and clearly connecting it with the other parts of the application.

➤ All applications received in the USPTO are numbered in serial order, and you will be informed of the application serial number and filing date by a filing receipt.

➤ The filing date of an application for patent is the date on which a specification (including at least one claim), and any drawings necessary to understand the subject matter sought to be patented are received in the USPTO. Or, it's the date on which the last part completing the application is received in the case of a previously incomplete or defective application.

Notable Quotables

"Creativity is intelligence having fun."

—Anonymous

I Do Solemnly Swear ...

Your oath or declaration is required by law for a non-provisional application. You must swear that you believe yourself to be the original and first inventor of the subject matter of the application and must make various other statements required by law and various statements required by Patent and Trademark Office rules. The oath must be sworn by you before a notary public or other officer authorized to administer oaths. A declaration may be used in lieu of an oath. Oaths or declarations are required for applications involving designs, plants, and utility inventions and for reissue applications. A declaration does not need to be notarized. When filing a continuation, or divisional application, a copy of an oath or declaration may be used; or a continued prosecution application may be filed that requires neither a new oath nor declaration, not a copy of an oath or declaration from a prior application.

The oath or declaration must be signed in person by you or by the person entitled by law to make application on your behalf. The full first and last name with middle initial or name, if any, of each inventor is required. The post office address and citizenship of each inventor are also required.

Sample forms are available by calling the USPTO General Information Services at (800) 786-9199 or (703) 308-4357 or by accessing USPTO Web site at www.uspto.gov under the section titled "USPTO Forms." The paperwork in a complete application will not be returned for any purpose whatsoever nor will the filing fee be returned. If you have not kept copies of the papers, the Office will furnish copies for a fee.

183

WACKY PATENTS

Automatic Hair-Cutting Machine
Patented March 22, 1966
United States Patent 3,241,562

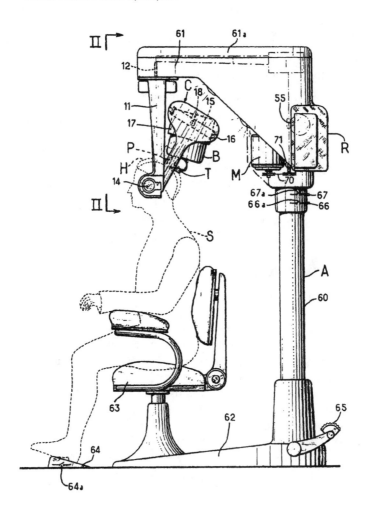

Bright Ideas

Sylvan N. Goldman, son of Jewish immigrants, was born in 1898. He grew up in the Oklahoma Territory. After some ups and downs, by the mid-'30s he owned half of the Piggly-Wiggly grocery chain.

In 1936, Goldman wondered how to help his customers carry more groceries. Goldman had an idea. He and mechanic, Fred Young, started to tinker. Their first shopping cart was a metal frame that held two wire baskets. The frame was designed to be folded to nest the baskets.

By 1940, shopping carts were engrained in American life. Supermarket checkouts were re-designed and the layout of aisles changed. In 1947, the folding cart gave way to the single basket carts we use today.

Patentability of Computer Programs

Can computer programs be patented? The answer is not simple. Under certain tests the USPTO will award patent protection to a piece of software. The former Court of Customs and Patent Appeals (CCPA), known today as the Court of Appeals for the Federal Circuit, has held that computer processes are statutory unless they fall within a judicially determined exception.

The original cases that went to the U.S. Supreme Court from the CCPA provided guidance to the USPTO as to patentability of computer-related inventions and software. However, there is disagreement between the USPTO and some patent attorneys on the interpretation of the cited court cases.

As if this situation was not murky enough, in recent years, there have been a spate of cases that are prompting the USPTO to review its guidelines.

411

Here is another interesting Web site. In April of 2001, www. PatentValuePredictor.com was launched. It provides patent valuation services. The automated service allows you to select a patent and then obtain valuation reports on it. The report provides the nominal size of the patent protected market and the valuation of the patent. Multiple patents can be selected.

I have no experience in the area of patenting computer software. But since the topic is of interest to many of you, you may wish to contact patent examiner Joseph J. Rolla. His telephone number at the USPTO is (703) 305-9700; fax: (703) 308-5355. E-mail: joseph.rolla@uspto.gov. He is up-to-date on all the issues.

As a stand-alone invention, a software program *per se* may not be patentable, but in view of new court decisions, the USPTO interpretation of existing case law may change.

If you have a computer software program that you wish to patent, it just may be possible. Consult a patent lawyer who stays current with the case law. Or watch for news about this in the *Official Gazette* or the *Manual of Patent Examining Procedure*.

Just the Fax, Please

Among those documents that the USPTO **will not** accept by fax are ...

➤ New or continuing patent applications of any type.

➤ Assignments.

➤ Issue fee payments.

➤ Maintenance fee payments.

➤ Declarations or oaths under 37 CFR 1.63 or 1.67.

➤ Formal drawings.

➤ All papers relating to international patent applications.

➤ Papers to be filed in applications subject to a secrecy order under 37 CFR 5.1-5.8 and directly related to the secrecy order content of the application.

Fast Facts

You do not have to obtain a Federal registration to establish rights in a trademark. By using the mark in commerce, you'll have what are called common law rights. Generally, the first to either use a mark in commerce or file an intent to use application with the U.S. Patent and Trademark Office has the ultimate right to use and registration. However, there are many benefits of federal trademark registration.

Your facsimile submissions may include a certificate for each paper stating the date of transmission. A copy of the facsimile submission with a certificate faxed therewith will be evidence of transmission of the paper should the original be misplaced. The person signing the certificate should have a reasonable basis to expect that the paper would be transmitted on the date indicated. An example of a preferred certificate is the following:

Certification of Facsimile Transmission

I hereby certify that this paper is being facsimile transmitted to the Patent and Trademark Office on the date shown below.

_____

Type or print name of person signing certifying

_____ Signature

Date: _____

When possible, the certification should appear on a portion of the paper being transmitted. If the certification is presented on a separate paper, it must identify the application to which it relates and the type of paper being transmitted (e.g., amendment, notice of appeal, etc.).

In the event that the facsimile submission is misplaced or lost in the USPTO, the submission will be considered filed on date of the transmission, if the party who transmitted the paper ...

1. Informs the USPTO of the previous facsimile transmission promptly after becoming aware that the submission has been misplaced or lost.

2. Supplies another copy of the previously transmitted submission with the Certification of the Transmission.

3. Supplies a copy of the sending unit's report confirming transmission of the submission. In the event that a copy of the report is not available, the party who transmitted the paper may file a declaration under 37 CFR 1.68, which attests on a personal knowledge basis or to the satisfaction of the Commissioner to the previous timely transmission.

If all criteria above cannot be met, the USPTO will require you to submit a verified showing of facts. Such a showing must indicate to the satisfaction of the Commissioner the date the USPTO received the submission.

The Least You Need to Know

➤ A provisional patent costs less and does less to protect your invention.

➤ A nonprovisional patent has teeth that grip. This patent is what you ultimately want for the greatest protection of your invention.

➤ It's important to keep your application in the proper order.

➤ Claims, done wrong, can turn steak into dog food.

➤ If you opt not to build prototypes, I hope you like to eat patents because no one pays for paper.

➤ You can now patent computer programs, but the USPTO and the courts are still developing the guidelines and controlling authority.

Chapter 13

Flower Power: How to Apply for a Plant Patent

In This Chapter

➤ Patented plants can grow into money trees and other greenery

➤ What you can protect

➤ How to make application

➤ Where to get the answers

➤ Helpful hints

"There is a demand for an expanding plant pallet and American inventors are meeting it. Innovative and unique flora that bloom profusely all year, free of pests or slow growing, no prune plants that offer flowers, fragrance, berries and fall color, the plant inventor has found a way to create it, often resulting in a vastly improved, aesthetically pleasing landscape with lower maintenance costs and the need for fewer pesticides."

—Joel M. Lerner, landscape columnist, *The Washington Post*

Question: What do the following plants have in common: a hybrid tea rose named "Ruiyel," a lantana named "Mongen," an azalea named "Panfilia, a chrysanthemum named "Golden State," and nectarine tree named "Western Pride"?

Answer: They were all awarded United States patents.

The USPTO has issued over 11,800 plant patents to date. Henry Bosenberg received Plant Patent No. 1 in 1931 for a climbing rose. Plant patent 10,000 was awarded to breeder David Lemon in a ceremony at the U.S. Botanical Garden in Washington, D.C., in 1997 for his Regal geranium named Lois. Today Art Unit 1661 averages circa 750 patents a year.

Interest in Plant Patents, a Growing Business

Plant patents can bring financial gains to their inventors and the companies that commercialize such intellectual property.

Seed companies and plant breeders sell patented "designer plants" through catalogues and in nurseries to homeowners and landscapers. Yoder Brothers, Incorporated shows 72 patents on chrysanthemums. Ball Horticultural Company has more than 20 patents. Mikkelsens, Incorporated has 14 plant patents. There are 16 patents on Kentucky Blue Grass by OMS Investments, Incorporated. And even the Queen of England has two patents for ash trees, applied for through the Canadian Department of Agriculture.

There are about 3,400 species of trees, shrubs, and bushes in the rose family. A USPTO search reveals over 2,000 patents on roses. Here is how a patent abstract reads, in part, for a bush in the rose family (not an actual rose!) invented by David Austin. It is Plant Patent 11211, *Physocarpus opulifolius* CV "monlo,"—a new and distinct selection of Ninebark that offers a unique combination of an outstanding cold-hardy shrub with intense foliage color throughout the seasons peaking in summer to a maroon red and contrasting to the creamy-white flowers.

Spring Meadow Nursery, in its 2001 catalog, actually shows the royalty payments on a per-plant basis, near the price. Under the write-up for *Physocarpus opulifolius* "Monlo" (PP11211), it states that 57 cents of the price is royalty. This plant was developed by Kordes Nursery and introduced by Monrovia Nursery. The same catalog lists a 30 cent royalty on each sale of "Abelia confetti" (PP8472), and so forth. It is the first time I have ever seen an inventor royalty broken out and shown as part of the price.

Forgene, Incorporated received a patent on a white spruce tree that can grow at twice the normal rate. Neil Nelson, inventor of the Super Tree, said the patent marks the first time in U.S. patent history that the USPTO has awarded a general patent for a tree.

Other trees have been given patent protection as plant patents, but until the Nelson patent, the USPTO had never issued a general patent on a tree. "This patent was issued in recognition of the milestone genetic improvement incorporated in these hybrid trees," said Nelson.

Bright Ideas

This may be a first! Plant patent 11616 was awarded for an azalea that was named after USPTO examiner Jim Ron Feyrer. It seems that Robert Edward Lee, its *pro se* inventor, of Independence, LA, liked Jim and honored him by designating his azalea by the name Jim Ron Feyrer.

Fast Facts

The most crowded subclass in plant patents is 139. It shows 322 patents issued for hybrid tea roses (light to medium red).

Beyond the Garden Walls

In 2000, the U.S. Patent Office issued three new plant-related utility patents to Portland-based Exelixis Plant Sciences, Incorporated. Utility plant patents are handled by Art Unit 1638. Some plants can qualify for both plant and utility patents.

The patents were awarded for a promoter to regulate the expression of genes in plants, a novel protein to detect a new strain of grapevine leaf-roll virus infection in grape plants and a strain of bacillus that has been effective in combating plant fungal and bacterial infections. Exelixis, formerly Agritope, has had 15 United States and seven foreign patents issued. Applications for 39 other patents are pending.

Floyd Zaiger and Family (Zaiger Genetics) have achieved international prominence for their fruit and rootstock hybridizing program. Known around Art Unit 1661 as very nice people, the Zaigers have introduced several hundred varieties over the past five decades and hold over 100 U.S. plant patents, varieties developed for home orchard as well as commercial use.

Notable Quotables

"Life is a garden, dig it!"

—Anonymous

411

Six videos are now available from the U.S. Patent and Trademark Office at $20.00 apiece.

➤ Conducting a Search (13 minutes, color)

➤ The USPTO Today (13 minutes, color)

➤ Project XL (10 minutes, color)

➤ From Dreams to Reality: A Tribute to Minority Inventors (15 minutes 17 seconds, color)

➤ Trademarks: The Fingerprints of Commerce (9 minutes, color)

➤ Dreams and Discovery—National Inventors Hall of Fame (15 minutes 17 seconds, color)

A RealPlayer® clip of each video can be viewed at the USPTO Web site: www.uspto.gov.

To order, call (800) PTO-9199.

Driscoll's, known for berries, has 198 patents in subclasses 208 and 209. The earliest date back to 1976. In 2000, six patents issued. Stark Brothers, known for the Red Delicious apple, has 34 plant patents assigned to it. By the way, since Stark started selling rights to the Red Delicious plant in 1893, it has sold over 15 million "copies" of it to orchards.

Most of the aforementioned companies own patents because they were assigned to them by others who invented the plants. Stark and Driscoll, for example, do not have the inventors on staff.

Multinational corporations (such as Georgia-Pacific, International Paper, Boise Cascade, and Union Camp) are actively looking for ways to increase the density of trees whose wood is destined for use as paper pulp and in construction. There are genetic engineering efforts to reduce branching in trees grown specifically to make furniture, increase growth rates in wood burned for fuel, change fruit trees for modified taste, vary the ripening characteristics of fruit, and so on. There is even a company trying to develop a caffeine-free coffee plant. If this could be done there would be no need for the expensive process required to produce decaf coffee. To this end, if plants are your "field" of invention, so to speak, this challenge could bring you lots of "beans" if you are able to do it.

Who Can Apply for a Plant Patent?

If you have invented or discovered and asexually reproduced a distinct and new variety of plant, other than an edible tuber propagated plant or a plant found in an uncultivated state, the government makes it possible for you to patent it. The grant, which lasts for 20 years from the date of filing the application, protects your right to exclude others from asexually reproducing, selling, or using the plant so reproduced.

Bright Ideas

Luther Burbank, a horticulturist and plant breeder, developed, discovered, or improved some 800 varieties of trees, vegetables, fruits, and flowers. His most successful "invention" was the Burbank potato, developed in 1872. He is also known for the Santa Rosa plum and the Shasta daisy.

No Trespassing— Patent-Protected Grounds

Your protection is limited to …

➤ A living plant organism which expresses a set of characteristics determined by its single genetic makeup or genotype, which can be duplicated through asexual reproduction, but which can not otherwise be "made" or "manufactured."

➤ Sports, mutants, hybrids, and transformed plants are comprehended; sports or mutants may be spontaneous or induced. Hybrids may be natural, from a planned breeding program, or somatic in source. While natural plant mutants might have naturally occurred, they must have been discovered in a cultivated area.

➤ Algae and macro fungi are regarded as plants, but bacteria are not.

Note: While the United States Patent and Trademark Office does accept utility applications having claims to plants, seeds, genes, and so on, the topic is well beyond the scope of this book. To obtain information, contact the USPTO Information Services Division at 1-800-786-9199 or a registered patent attorney who specializes in plants.

Infringement

It has been very difficult to prove infringement because so much has depended upon coloration. However, today patent applicants are including the molecular biology of their plants to make future identification in infringement cases easier to prove.

WACKY PATENTS

Motorized Ice Cream Cone
Patented October 26, 1999
United States Patent 5,971,829

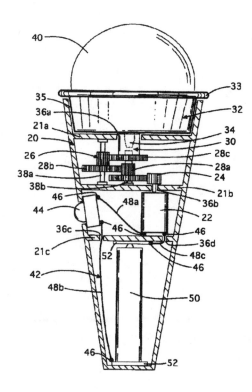

The infringers are people who take cuttings from original plants, perhaps bought legally at a nursery, and replicate them to their own benefit. For example, someone could buy one patented apple tree, take it back to his or her orchard, and then breed acres of them over time, thereby robbing the inventor of royalties.

Turning to Trademarks

Breeders are starting to use trademark protection more and more to cover themselves when their patents expire. Here is a case in point. There is a very popular apple coming in from Australia. It is called the Pink Lady Apple. And it is extremely popular these days. The technical name is Kripps Pink. The patent is halfway through its term of 20 years. The patent owner (assignee) is working hard now to establish the trademark Pink Lady so that when the patent "turns into a pumpkin," he will be able to fend off the competition through brand equity. People will want the Pink Lady Apple brand, just as label-conscience consumers buy watches, cars, clothing, and so on.

The Cost of Doing Business

Approximately 50 percent of all plant patents are filed *pro se*, i.e., by their inventors without the assistance of patent counsel. This is because there is only one claim, and it is as illustrated and described. In other words, what you see is what you get. It is not unlike the design patent in that regard. If inventors want to get into the molecular biology of their plants, they typically hire a botanist to draft the description and may have an attorney check it for format.

Figure the price of photography and printing of two images of the plant. Pictures or watercolor drawings are required if color is a distinguishing characteristic of the new variety. If you do not submit color photographs or drawings, the examiner may require them.

In 2001, an issue fee of $300 ($600 for inventive entities having 500 or more employees) was payable to the U.S. Patent and Trademark Office upon allowance of the patent. This fee changes each October or soon thereafter.

If you are going for a plant utility patent this could cost some serious "green." These applications run between $1,800 and $3,700. This is a rough and tough estimate that does not include the price of photos or drawings. Add to this the price of prosecution, usually from $800 to $1,700. Then there are the issue fees, as just stated.

Fast Facts

Composite family: About 20,000 species.

Orchid family: More than 20,000 species.

Pea family: About 17,000 species.

Lily family: About 4,000 species.

Mustard family: About 3,000 species.

Morning-glory family: 1,800 species.

For the most current fees, check the USPTO Web site at www.uspto.gov, call (703) 308-4357 or (800) 786-9199, or by fax at (703) 305-7786. Fees change annually around October.

Making Application

An application for a plant patent consists of the same parts as other applications, with the addition of a plant color-coding sheet. Like the utility patent, the term of a plant patent is 20 years from the date the application was filed in the United States, or if the application contains a specific reference to an earlier filed application under 35 U.S.C. 120, 121, or 365(c), from the date the earliest such application was filed.

The Application

Your application for a plant patent and any responsive papers pursuant to the prosecution duplicate copies are no longer required. The original should be signed.

Specification

The specification should include a complete detailed description of the plant and the characteristics that distinguish it over related known varieties. It should also include its antecedents, expressed in botanical terms in the general form followed in standard botanical text books or publications dealing with the varieties of the kind of plant involved (evergreen tree, dahlia plant, rose plant, apple tree, and so forth) rather than a mere broad nonbotanical characterization, such as is commonly found in nursery or seed catalogs.

Among the factors which must be ascertained for a reasonably complete botanical description for the claimed plant are ...

➤ Genus and species.

➤ Habit of growth.

➤ Cultivar name.

Fast Facts

A proponent of the legislation that would make plants patentable, inventor Thomas Alva Edison, sent a telegram to Congress which read, in part: "Nothing that Congress could do to help farming would be of greater value and permanence than to give to the plant breeder the same status as the mechanical and chemical inventors now have through patent law. There are but a few plant breeders. This will, I feel sure, give us many Burbanks."

Notable Quotables

"All mankind is divided into three classes: those who are immovable, those who are moveable, and those who move."

—Benjamin Franklin

➤ Vigor.

➤ Productivity.

➤ Precocity (if applicable).

➤ Botanical characteristics of plant structures (i.e., buds, bark, foliage, flowers, fruit, and so on).

➤ Fertility (Fecundity).

➤ Other characteristics which distinguish the plant, such as resistance(s) to disease, drought, cold, dampness, fragrance, coloration, regularity and time of bearing, quantity or quality of extracts, rooting ability, timing or duration of flowering season, etc.

The amount of detail required in a plant patent application is determined on a case-by-case basis and is determined by the similarity of the prior art plants to the plant being claimed. The examiner will evaluate the completeness of the application. The examiner's judgment may be tempered by the level of activity in a specific market class. The botanical description of a plant in a market class with a high level of commercial activity may require greater detail, substance, and specificity than that for a plant in a market class of little activity.

Here is how to frame your Specification for submission to the USPTO.

Fast Facts

If a plant label has a patent number written on it, you need permission to propagate it even for your own use. Most hybridizers will give you permission to propagate a rose for your own use, but not for profit. Asexual propagation without the written permission of the patent holder is against federal patent laws.

➤ Title of the Invention. The title of the invention must include the name of the claimed plant.

➤ Cross-Reference to Related Applications (if any). Related applications include …

1. A utility application from which the claimed plant is the subject of a divisional application.

2. A continuation (co-pending, newly filed application) or CPA to the same plant filed when a parent application has not been allowed to a sibling cultivar.

3. An application not co-pending with an original application that was not allowed.

4. Co-pending applications to siblings or similar plants developed by the same breeding program, and so forth.

The Claim

A plant patent is granted on the entire plant. It therefore follows that only one claim is necessary and only one is permitted.

The Oath: I Do Solemnly Swear ...

Together with the required oath or declaration, you must include a statement that you (and your co-inventors, if any) have asexually reproduced the new plant variety. If the plant is a newly found plant, the oath or declaration must also state that the plant was found in a cultivated area.

Drawings

While you are permitted to submit watercolor drawings, the USPTO basically gets photographs from everyone these days. So, if you go that route, send them in duplicate, not mounted on chip board or any other subsurface. They should be printed on a full-sized piece of paper. The sizes required are 8½ x 11 or A4 (relates to European size).

Specimens—Send Me No Flowers

Specimens of the plant variety, its flower, or fruit should not be submitted unless specifically called for by the examiner.

411

The Plant Variety Protection Act (Public Law 91577), passed December 24, 1970, provides for a system of protection for sexually reproduced varieties, for which protection was not previously provided, under the administration of a Plant Variety Protection Office within the Department of Agriculture. If you have any questions about the protection of sexually reproduced varieties, you should address them to Commissioner, Plant Variety Protection Office, Agricultural Marketing Service, National Agricultural Library Bldg., Room 0, 10301 Baltimore Blvd., Beltsville, Md. 20705-2351.

Cost: Green Fees

Fees change annually, so be sure to call the USPTO or visit the USPTO Web site and double-check the prices before taking any action. Telephone: 1-800-786-9199 or (703) 308-4357. URL: www.uspto.gov. If you qualify as a small entity, the USPTO reduces the filing and issue fees by half.

Inquiries

If you have any questions relating to plant patents and pending plant patent applications, please contact the Patent and Trademark Office. I interviewed nine-year USPTO veteran Supervisory Patent Examiner Bruce Campell, who holds a Ph.D. in botany from UC-Davis. He was extremely patient and helpful to me in the writing of this chapter.

Give him a call at (703) 308-4205. In Plant Patent Unit 1661, he supervises Primary Examiner Howard J. Locker at (703) 308-2924, and Primary Examiner Kent Bell at (703) 306-3224. This unit has a total of eight examiners.

Provisions and Limitations

Patents to plants which are stable and reproduced by asexual reproduction, and not a potato or other edible tuber-reproduced plant, are provided for by Title 35 United States Code, Section 161 which states:

> Whoever invents or discovers and asexually reproduces any distinct and new variety of plant, including cultivated sports, mutants, hybrids, and newly found seedlings, other than a tuber propagated plant or a plant found in an uncultivated state, may obtain a patent therefor, subject to the conditions and requirements of title. (Amended September 3, 1954, 68 Stat. 1190).

The provisions of this title relating to patents for inventions shall apply to patents for plants, except as otherwise provided.

Plant patents must also satisfy the general requirements of patentability. The subject matter of the application would be a plant that you developed or discovered and which has been found stable by asexual reproduction.

To be patentable, it would also be required ...

➤ That the plant was invented or discovered and, if discovered, that the discovery was made in a cultivated area.

➤ That the plant is not a plant excluded by statute, where the part of the plant used for asexual reproduction is not a tuber food part, as with potato or Jerusalem artichoke.

➤ That the person or persons filing the application are those who actually invented the claimed plant, i.e., discovered or developed and identified or isolated the plant, and asexually reproduced the plant.

➤ That the plant has not been sold or released in the United States of America more than one year prior to the date of the application.

➤ That the plant has not been shown to the public, i.e., by description in a printed publication more than one year before the application for patent with an offer to sale; or by release—even as a gift—or sale of the plant more than one year prior to application for patent.

➤ That the plant be shown to differ from known, related plants by at least one distinguishing characteristic, which is more than a difference caused by growing conditions, fertility levels, and so on.

➤ The invention would not have been obvious to one skilled in the art at the time of invention by applicant.

If you have any doubt as to the patentability of a specific plant, consult a qualified legal authority prior to making application to assure that the plant satisfies statutory requirements and is not exempted from plant patent protection.

Inventorship

An inventor is any person who contributed to either step of invention. For example, if you discover a new and distinct plant and asexually reproduce it, you would be a sole inventor. If you discovered or selected a new and distinct plant and a second person asexually reproduced the plant and ascertained that the clone(s) of the plant were identical to the original plant in every distinguishing characteristic, the second person would properly be considered your co-inventor. If either step is performed by a staff, every member of the staff who performed or contributed to the performance of either step could properly be considered a co-inventor. Thus, a plant patent may have a plurality of inventors.

However, if you direct that the asexual reproduction be performed by a custom propagation service or tissue culture enterprise, those performing the service for you would not be considered co-inventors.

Asexual Reproduction

Asexual reproduction is the propagation of a plant to multiply the plant without the use of fusion of gametes to assure an exact genetic copy of the plant being reproduced. Any known method of asexual reproduction which renders a true genetic copy of the plant may be used. Acceptable modes of asexual reproduction would include but may not be limited to …

➤ Rooting cuttings.

➤ Grafting and budding.

➤ Apomictic seeds.

➤ Bulbs.

➤ Division.

➤ Slips.

➤ Layering.

➤ Rhizomes.

➤ Runners.

➤ Corms.

➤ Tissue culture.

➤ Nucellar embryos.

The purpose of asexual reproduction is to establish the stability of the plant. This second step of the invention must be performed with sufficient time prior to application for patent rights to allow the thorough evaluation of propagules or clones of the claimed plant for stability, thus assuring that such specimens retain the identical distinguishing characteristics of the original plant.

WACKY PATENTS

Air Conditioned Shoe
Patented September 20, 1966
United States Patent 3,273,264

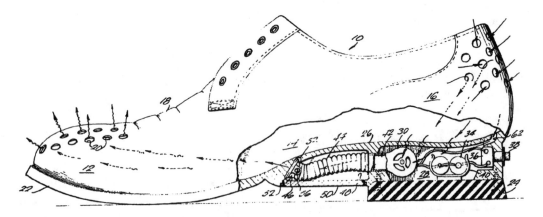

Helpful Hints

When you are making application for a plant patent, please ...

➤ Make every attempt not to present a name for the plant which has already been used or is confusingly similar to a plant of the same market or botanical class. Search old catalogs and available international register listings before assigning a name to a plant.

➤ File all drawings (and photos) in duplicate. Be sure that two sets of drawings (PTO no longer accepts mounted drawings) accompany the application when filed, and that these are of reasonable fidelity to the specified colors of the plant. Be sure that the scale and clarity of the drawings are appropriate to allow for adequate reproduction even if reduced in scale upon publishing.

➤ Include a transmittal sheet that itemizes the contents of the application as filed.

➤ File each individual application in a separate envelope, and be sure to include all the parts of each application in the same envelope. Request that a filing receipt bearing the serial number of the application be returned to you.

➤ Model the application after a recent patent of acceptable format and content that describes a plant which is related to or in the same market class as the claimed plant, if one is available.

➤ Check that the oath or declaration is that required for a plant patent application. Ensure that you have signed the oath or declaration in permanent ink. Check that your mailing address is correct and complete.

➤ Where color is a distinguishing characteristic of the plant, specify the color of the plant as defined by reference to an established color dictionary (e.g., Pantone) that is recognized in this country. The color reference most commonly used is the Royal Horticulture Society of England Colour Chart (RHS Colour Chart).

➤ Be sure that drawings filed are complete, correctly mounted, and reasonably correspond with the colors of the plant that are specified and to the true and characteristic plant coloration.

➤ Include the appropriate filing fee with your application to avoid processing delays.

Fast Facts

➤ In subclass 307, there are 131 patents on red poinsettias.

➤ In subclass 330, there are 112 patents on red geraniums.

➤ In subclass 198, there are 213 patents on yellow flesh, freestone, standard-size peaches.

➤ Direct pre-examination questions concerning the application to the Examiner, by telephone, to expedite prosecution.

➤ Include your current telephone number with all correspondence.

New patent applications should be mailed to—

The Honorable Commissioner for Patents of Patents and Trademarks
Box: Patent Application
Washington, D.C. 22031

The Least You Need to Know

➤ Money grows on trees and flowers, too.

➤ You can get a utility patent on plants.

➤ Fifty percent of plant patents are filed *pro se.*

➤ To be patentable, a plant must be found stable by asexual reproduction.

➤ Any known method of asexual reproduction which renders a true genetic copy of the plant may be used.

➤ The USPTO no longer accepts mounted drawings of plants for which application is made.

Chapter 14

How to Apply for a Design Patent

In This Chapter

➤ A design patent is inexpensive ip insurance

➤ It's all about form over function

➤ You don't need a lawyer to apply

➤ The Crest Fluorider story

➤ Design patents vs. utility patents

➤ Elements of a design patent

"If it weren't for the long series of both basic and 'minor' inventions—and I put 'minor' in quotes because many minor inventions had great impact on the human race ... man would be walking around with a stone in one hand and a stick in the other looking for something to eat."

—Jacob Rabinow, inventor, holder of 225 U.S. patents

Design patents are a method to protect ornamental and cosmetic aspects of your inventions—*not* their function. Perhaps the most celebrated design patent ever granted is Number 11,023, issued on February 18, 1879, to Auguste Bartholdi on his design for a statue, "Liberty Enlightening the World," one that we call the Statue of Liberty.

So, if your product has a unique appearance, and this is important to its success, a design patent can be a worthwhile investment. And it is not an expensive one.

Think of the distinctive designs of a Mazda Miata, an iMac computer monitor, a bottle of Classic Coke, Casio's G-Shock watch, to mention a few such products. Without a doubt the look of these products contributes to their popularity. Design patents are taken out on such products to foil knock-off artists who, though not necessarily pretending to market the authentic item, trade on the good will and dress of the leadership product by causing confusion in the consumer's mind.

Fast Facts

Each year, approximately $25 billion of federally funded research and development takes place at more than 700 federal laboratories and centers. More than 100,000 scientists and engineers work at federal laboratories and centers and address virtually every area of science and technology.

Insurance Against Me-Too Competitors

It does not have the teeth of a utility patent, but if you want an inexpensive way to legally place a "Patent Pending" or "Patented" on your product, or add protection to an invention covered by a utility patent, maybe a design patent is for you.

The range of ornamental appearances that have been patented during the more than 150 years design patents have existed is very impressive. Over 400,000 designs have received design patent protection since the first one was granted to George Bruce for "Printing Type" on November 9, 1842.

Form over Function

You can get design patents on just about anything: baby bibs, sweatbands, tissue box holders, rearview mirrors, dishes, toys, vending machines, telephones, pencils and pens, and even internal combustion engines.

Volkswagen licensed Infogrames, the French entertainment conglomerate, to do the computer game *Beetle Buggin'*. The legal copy reads: "Trademarks, design patents, and copyrights are used with the approval of the owner Volkswagen AG." In this case, the German automobile manufacturer appears to be using the design patent to keep people away from its intellectual property.

Rubbermaid has design patents on containers. Totes protects umbrella handle designs. Parker Pen takes them out on writing instruments. Ford has design patents on quarter panels and other car parts. Patenting the design of car door panels and the like can prevent competitors from selling replacement parts modeled after the factory parts.

An industry that relies very heavily on design patents is cosmetics. The appearance of a perfume bottle, for example, is critical to a brand's success. Design is what attracts the consumer long before he or she has experienced the scent.

"The chances to get a design patent are high," says Richard G. Besha, Esq., a patent attorney with Nixon & Vanderhye, Arlington, Virginia, who has been working in the field for 40 years. "It's just a matter of comparing drawings. If the examiner finds something different, he awards a patent. The level of obviousness is fairly low."

Bright Ideas

Gertrude B. Elion, 1988 Nobel Laureate in Medicine and Scientist Emeritus with Burroughs-Wellcome Company, is credited with the synthesis of two of the first successful drugs for leukemia, as well as Imuron, an agent to prevent the rejection of kidney transplants, and Zovirax, the first selective antiviral agent against herpes virus infections. Researchers who discovered AZT, a breakthrough treatment for AIDS, used Elion's protocols. In 1991, she was the first female inductee into the National Inventors Hall of Fame.

Besha says that design patents are so easy to obtain that he does not even conduct searches of prior art for his clients. "Rejections are that rare," he says confidently. "Ninety-nine percent of them issue."

411

You can gain access to $25 billion worth of federally funded research and development that annually takes place at more than 700 federal laboratories and centers. Uncle Sam wants to transfer federal technologies and expertise into commercial applications that will improve the U.S. economy.

Your key to this wealth of information is available on the Internet. Visit: http://flc2.federallabs. org/index.html

Putting the Competition on Notice

For little expense and effort, a design patent is another way to stake out an ip claim. It permits you to legally post a no trespass sign in the form of a notice that reads "Patent Pending," "Patent Applied For," or "Patented." By the way, you do not have to notify with the words: "Design Patent Pending," "Design Patent Applied For," or even give the design patent number when it issues. It is best to keep 'em guessin'. If your competitors know it is a design patent, their decision to end-run you will be much easier to make and carry out.

Design patents are intended to protect the ornamental and cosmetic aspects of products—but not their function. The disclosure and description of the invention in a design application is entirely in the drawing and not in the words. The single claim in a design patent is for "the appearance of a (whatever the product is usually called) as shown (in the drawing)."

Lawyers Need Not Apply

Whether to use or not use a patent attorney is a personal decision. I, however, do not use patent counsel to prepare and file design patent applications. Unlike complicated utility and plant patents, where patent lawyers are invaluable, the drafting and processing of design applications are very easy and uncomplicated. Paying a lawyer to handle design patents is tossing money out the window. The application form is simple, esoteric language is not required to draft claims, and searches are unnecessary. A design patent search doesn't even require reading. It's all in the line drawings, or photographs, as the case may be. The visual element is your biggest expense (plus USPTO fees). If you do the application and filing yourself, it will cost you (at the date of this writing) $160 as a Small Entity, plus $220 if it issues. This totals $380. Then you have the formal drawings which will be required whether you apply *pro se* or through a law firm. This can cost you some serious dollars if many drawings are required.

Fast Facts

➤ Samuel Mulikin, in 1791, became the first inventor to hold multiple patents.

➤ Thomas Jennings, believed to have been the first African-American patentee, received a patent in 1821 for "dry scouring of clothes."

➤ Mary Kies invented a device for "weaving straw with silk or thread." She was the first woman to obtain a U.S. patent. The year was 1809.

If you retain a law firm, a good guesstimate is between $650 and $1,000. You can be sure the lawyer will markup the drafting prices by a minimum of 100 percent.

A design patent is good for 14 years, and there are no maintenance fees.

How to Find a Draftsman

The best way to find draftsmen is through recommendations by other inventors. If this is not possible, ask around a Patent and Trademark Depository Library if there is one in your area. See Appendix B, "Resources," for a complete listing of PTDLs. Other options include references from engineering schools and, when all else fails, the yellow pages. Years ago the USPTO had a list of bonded patent draftsmen. In those days, it was easy to find someone through this qualified roster. These draftsmen were bonded because they frequently had to make modifications to original drawings. But since January 1, 1991, no one has been allowed to alter original drawings. If you want to make a change to a drawing on an application today, a new drawing must be submitted.

"But they accept copies today," says Robert MacCollum, a draftsman from Silver Springs, Maryland, whose career spans 36 years. "In fact, they encourage it," he adds. They also allow submissions via the Internet. Bob thinks allowing drawings to be submitted through the Internet was done to cut down on paper. He hastens to point out, however, that for foreign filings original drawings are still necessary. "The reason for this is that they may have to print them out for 20 countries," he says.

Depending upon the complexity of the invention, MacCollum charges between $50 and $150 per sheet, the high end being rare. Design drawings can typically be done with one or two sheets. Utility drawings can require many more. The most sheets he has ever needed for an application was 20.

If you opt to submit photographs, you may well be able to shoot them yourself.

To make the drawings, draftsmen need reference art or models of the invention. "Some inventors have sent me videotapes of product which I drew off a television monitor. I recall once having to run outside my home and sketch a loading device attached to a flatbed truck. It took me all afternoon to do this and get it to scale." But his most unusual memory was the time a Taiwanese furniture maker actually sent him three outdoor benches as reference art. When asked what he did with them afterwards, he responded, "They came and got them."

Design Patents Can Be Valuable

In the early 1980s, we spent $500 to learn that lawyers were not necessary in such matters. At the time, I had been using a large law firm for utility patents and, naturally, released our first design patent to them. I did not know any better.

The lawyer said he would "write it up." I was asked to provide the draftsman with a prototype of the design. It was a tricycle with a mainframe shaped like a toothpaste tube. It ultimately became Proctor & Gamble's Crest Fluorider, a premium offering.

When Design Patent 273,774 issued, I saw the claim for the first time. I had been used to reading complicated claims on our mechanical patents. Many were so arcane that I had trouble comprehending them. Not this time. In the case of our "Child's Riding Vehicle," the claim was one line. It read: "The ornamental design for a child's riding vehicle, as shown and described."

The Crest Fluorider program was very successful for us, so the $500 legal expense was a wash. But the

Fast Facts

Design patents are an important method for protecting games. Inventors cannot protect "game play," but they can seek design patent protection for their board layouts. In other words, no one can stop a game publisher from selling a path game, but how that path and its squares are designed and laid out on the board, from an ornamental standpoint, is protectable.

design patent was soon to become very important, and not vis-à-vis a competitive premium, but between us inventors and P&G.

There was little chance that the trike would be knocked off. No other toothpaste brand had $12 million to invest in the production and promotion of such a product. P&G ordered 30,000 units just to put up on displays in supermarkets nationwide. The design patent benefited us when P&G used our proprietary design throughout the pages of a juvenile coloring book that it distributed to dental offices. The Cincinnati consumer goods manufacturer did not want to pay us for the use of our design on the cover and inside this book. The P&G lawyers saw it as fair use. But when we presented our design patent award, they immediately changed their tune. We agreed on a one-time payment for the right to emblazon our design on the one million books the company had already published and distributed. By the way, we owned the mark Fluorider, too.

WACKY PATENTS

**Toy Figures with Rupturable
Microcapsules for Simulated Bleeding**
Patented February 27, 1996
United States Patent 5,494,472

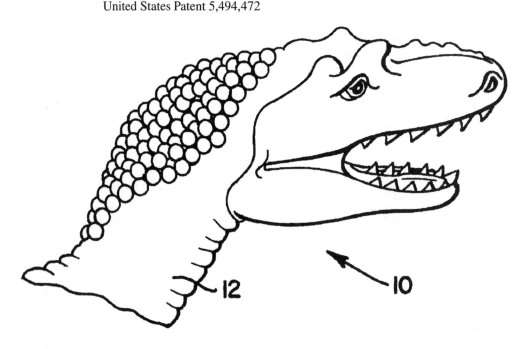

Defining Design

The USPTO defines a design as the visual ornamental characteristics embodied in, or applied to, an article of manufacture. Since a design is manifested in appearance, the subject matter of a design patent application may relate to the configuration or shape of an article (e.g., the Black & Decker Snake Light, a Bose Wave radio, and so on), to the surface ornamentation applied to an article (e.g., swirls on a Coke bottle, and so on), or to the combination of configuration and surface ornamentation (e.g., Jean-Paul Gaultier eau de toilette, and so on). A design for surface ornamentation is inseparable from the article to which it is applied, and cannot exist alone. It must be a definite pattern of surface ornamentation, applied to an article of manufacture. Patent law provides for the granting of design patents to anyone who has invented a new, original, and ornamental design for a manufactured product. A design patent protects only the appearance of the article and not its structural or utilitarian features.

Types of Designs and Modified Forms

An ornamental design may be embodied in an entire article or only a portion of an article or may be ornamentation applied to an article. If your design is directed to just surface ornamentation, it must be shown applied to an article in the drawings, and the article must be shown in broken lines, as it forms no part of the claimed design. Draftsmen skilled in the art will know the regulations.

Claims

A design patent application may only have a single claim. If you have designs that are independent and distinct, they must be filed in separate applications since they cannot be supported by a single claim. Designs are independent if there is no apparent relationship between two or more articles. For example, a pair of sunglasses and a car side mirror are independent articles and must be claimed in separate applications.

411

The principal statutes of the United States Code that govern design patents are available on the USPTO Web site www.uspto.gov and set forth in chapter 1500 of the Manual of Examining Procedure. To purchase the manual, contact the Superintendent of Documents, U.S. Government Printing Office, Washington, D.C. 20402. Tel: (202) 512-1800.

Notable Quotables

"Handling rejection must be part of your regular diet, and success your occasional dessert."

—Roger Lehmann, co-inventor, P.J. Sparkles

Designs are considered distinct if they have different shapes and appearances even though they are related articles. For example, two vases having different surface ornamentation creating distinct appearances must be claimed in separate applications. However, modified forms, or embodiments of a single design concept, may be filed in one application. For example, vases with only minimal configuration differences may be deemed a single design concept and both embodiments may be included in a single application.

Fast Facts

The U.S. Patent Office had already granted more than 500 automotive patents by 1895, only a couple years after Charles and Frank Duryea demonstrated the first practical American car. By the 1920s, there were thousands of patents covering a wide range of automobile innovations, and the industry employed almost five million workers.

Improper Subject Matter for Design Patents

A design for an article of manufacture that is dictated primarily by function lacks ornamentality and is not proper statutory subject matter, e.g., a mechanism.

Similarly, a design for an article of manufacture that is hidden in its end use and whose ornamental appearance is of no commercial concern prior to reaching its end use lacks ornamentality and is not proper statutory subject matter, for example, the inside of an exhaust muffler.

In addition, for a design to be patentable it must be "original." Clearly a design that simulates a well-known or naturally occurring object or person is not original as required by statute. Furthermore, subject matter that could be considered offensive to any race, religion, sex, ethnic group, or nationality is not proper subject matter for a design patent application.

The Difference Between Design and Utility Patents

In general terms, a "utility patent" protects the way an article is used and works while a "design patent" protects the way an article looks. Both design and utility patents may be obtained on an article if invention resides both in its utility and ornamental appearance.

While utility and design patents afford legally separate protection, the utility and ornamentality of an article are not easily separable. Articles of manufacture may possess both functional and ornamental characteristics.

Invention marketing services exist to help inventors license and commercialize their inventions, or to otherwise profit from their ideas. While some organizations are legitimate, most are not (see Chapter 2). The dishonest types are often fast to recommend that you pursue a patent for your idea because this is a profit center for them. To put the odds in their favor that a patent will issue, they'll have you go for a design patent and may not tell you the difference between a design patent and a utility patent. They will, however, charge you as if it was a utility patent, and then make you think that what issues is invaluable. Dishonest brokers will automatically recommend patent protection for your idea with little regard for the value of any patent that may ultimately issue.

Be wary of any agent who is willing to promote your invention or product without making a detailed inquiry into the merits of your idea and giving you a full range of options that may or may not include the pursuit of patent protection.

411

Under the best of conditions, trying to identify and reach people within a huge bureaucracy like the USPTO can be a challenge. To reduce frustration and increase your chances for success, you need the Information Directory. This useful 140+-page resource contains the complete Office telephone directory, divided into organizational and alphabetical sections. It is a must in every serious inventor's resource library.

If you wish to receive a copy of the Information Directory, call (800) 786-9199 or (703) 308-4357, or fax (703) 305-7786. Copies may be picked up at the Patent Search Room (Walk-in Counter), 2021 S. Clark Pl., Crystal Plaza 3, Lobby, Arlington, VA 22202.

Elements of a Design Patent Application

The elements of a design patent application should include the following:

1. Preamble, stating your name, title of the design, and a brief description of the nature and intended use of the article in which the design is embodied.
2. Description of the figure(s) of the drawing.
3. Feature description.
4. A single claim.
5. Drawings or photographs.
6. Executed oath or declaration.

The filing fee is also required. A contact the USPTO by phone (703-308-4357) or go on the Internet to be sure the fees have not changed. Small entities (an independent inventor, a small business concern, or a nonprofit organization) get the filing fee reduced by half if the small entity files a Statement Claiming Small Entity Status.

The Preamble

The Preamble should state your name, the title of your design, and a brief description of the nature and intended use of the article in which the design is embodied. All information contained in the preamble will be printed on the patent, should the claimed design be deemed patentable.

Bright Ideas

Herb Schaper, a letter carrier for the U.S. Postal Service, would whittle wooden fishing lures while walking his route. He discovered that one in the form of a flea captivated the interest of children. He named it Cootie and in 1948 built, by hand, 40,000 wooden Cootie games. Three years later, more than 1,200,000 were produced with the aid of machinery. By 1978, Cootie's thirtieth birthday, more than 30 million games had entertained children worldwide. The number today is over 36 million Cootie games since its introduction. Herb was one mailman who knew how to deliver!

The title of the design must identify the article in which the design is embodied by the name generally known and used by the public. Marketing designations are improper as titles and should not be used. Examples of such improper designations would be: Air Trigger, Spirals, Furby, and so forth. A title must be descriptive of the actual article (e.g., wristwatch, baby bottle, toy car). This aids the examiner in developing a complete field of search of the prior art and further aids in the proper assignment of new applications to the appropriate class, subclass, and patent examiner as well as the proper classification of the patent upon allowance of the application. It also helps the public in understanding the nature and use of the article embodying the design after the patent has been published. Thus, you are encouraged to provide a specific and descriptive title.

The Figure Descriptions

These indicate what each view of the drawings represents, i.e., front elevation, top plan, perspective view. Any description of the design in the specification, other than a brief description of the drawing, is generally not necessary since, as a general rule, the drawing is the design's best description. However, while not required, a special description is not prohibited.

In addition to the figure descriptions, the following types of statements are permissible in the specification:

1. Description of the appearance of portions of the claimed design that are not illustrated in the drawing disclosure (i.e., "the right side elevational view is a mirror image of the left side").

2. Description disclaiming portions of the article not shown, that form no part of the claimed design.

3. Statement indicating that any broken line illustration of environmental structure in the drawing is not part of the design sought to be patented.

4. Description denoting the nature and environmental use of the claimed design if not included in the preamble.

Notable Quotables

"There are no secrets to success. It is the result of preparation, hard work, and learning from failure."

—U.S. Secretary of State Collin L. Powell

A Single Claim

A design patent application may only include a single claim.

The claim defines the design that you wish to patent, in terms of the article in which it is embodied or applied. The claim must be in formal terms to "the ornamental design for (the article which embodies the design or to which it is applied) as shown." The description of the article in the claim should be consistent in terminology with the title of the invention.

When there is a properly included special description of the design in the specification, or a proper showing of modified forms of the design, or other descriptive matter has been included in the specification, the words "and described" should be added to the claim following the term "shown," and the claim should read: "The ornamental design for (the article which embodies the design or to which it is applied) as shown and described."

WACKY PATENTS

Unicycle Roller Skate
Patented April 21, 1992
United States Patent 5,106,110

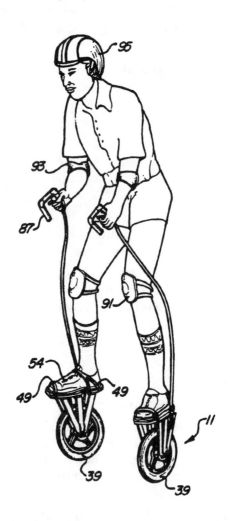

Drawings or Photographs

The drawing disclosure is the most important element of the application. Every design patent application must include either a drawing or a photograph of the claimed design. As the drawing or photograph constitutes the entire visual disclosure of the claim, it is of utmost importance that the drawing or photograph be clear and complete, that nothing regarding the design sought to be patented is left to conjecture.

The design drawing or photograph must comply with the disclosure requirements. To meet the disclosure requirements, the drawings or photographs must include a sufficient number of views to constitute a complete disclosure of the appearance of the design claimed.

Drawings are normally required to be in black ink on white paper. Photographs, in lieu of drawings, are permitted subject to the requirements.

The Views

The drawings or photographs should contain a sufficient number of views to completely disclose the appearance of the claimed design: i.e., front, rear, right and left sides, top and bottom. While not required, it is suggested that perspective views be submitted to clearly show the appearance and shape of three-dimensional designs. If a perspective view is submitted, the surfaces shown would normally not be required to be illustrated in other views if these surfaces are clearly understood and fully disclosed in the perspective.

Bright Ideas

Margaret Knight has been called the female Edison. Her 26 patents cover inventions as diverse as a window frame and sash, machinery for cutting shoe soles, and improvements to internal combustion engines. Her most significant patent was for machinery that would automatically fold and glue paper bags to create square bottoms, an invention that dramatically changed shopping habits.

Fast Facts

It is important to remember that *any* public use or sale in the United States or publication of your invention anywhere in the world more than one year prior to the filing of a patent application on that invention will prohibit the granting of a U.S. patent on it. Foreign patent laws in this regard may be much more restrictive than U.S. laws.

Keep this in mind when you consider the efficacy of showing nonpatented inventions at inventor expos, to the news media, and so forth. The premature exposure of an invention may cut its chances to be eligible for patent protection.

Views that are merely duplicates of other views of the design or that are merely flat and include no ornamentality may be omitted from the drawing if the specification makes this explicitly clear. For example, if the left and right sides of a design are identical or symmetrical, a view should be provided of one side and a statement made in the drawing description that the other side is identical/symmetrical. If the bottom of the design is flat, a view of the bottom may be omitted if the figure descriptions include a statement that the bottom is flat and unornamented.

The term "unornamented" should not be used to describe visible surfaces that include structure that is clearly not flat. In some cases, the claim may be directed to an entire article, but because all sides of the article may not be visible during normal use, it is not necessary to disclose them. A sectional view that more clearly brings out elements of the design is permissible; however, a sectional view presented to show functional features, or interior structure not forming part of the claimed design, is neither required nor permitted.

Surface Shading and Drafting Symbols

The drawing should be provided with appropriate surface shading which shows clearly the character and contour of all surfaces of any three-dimensional aspects of the design. Surface shading is also necessary to distinguish between any open and solid areas of the design. Solid black surface shading is not permitted except when used to represent the black color as well as color contrast. Lack of appropriate surface shading in the drawing as filed may render the design non-enabling under 35 U.S.C. 112, first paragraph. Additionally, if the shape of the design is not evident from the disclosure as filed, the addition of surface shading after filing may be viewed as new matter. New matter is anything that is added to or deleted from the claim, drawings, or specification, that was neither shown nor suggested in the original application.

Broken Lines

A broken line disclosure is understood to be for illustrative purposes only and forms no part of the claimed design. Structure that is not part of the claimed design, but is considered necessary to show the environment in which the design is used, may be represented in the drawing by broken lines. This includes any portion of an article in which the design is embodied or applied to that is not considered part of the claimed design. When the claim is directed to just surface ornamentation for an article, the article in which it is embodied must be shown in broken lines.

In general, when broken lines are used, they should not intrude upon or cross the showing of the claimed design and should not be of heavier weight than the lines used in depicting the claimed design. Where a broken line showing environmental structure must necessarily cross or intrude upon the representation of the claimed design and obscures a clear understanding of the design, such an illustration should be included as a separate figure, in addition to the other figures which fully disclose the subject matter of the design.

Photographs

The Office will accept high-quality black-and-white photographs in design patent applications.

➤ Photographs submitted on double-weight photographic paper must have the drawing figure number entered on the face of the photograph. Photographs mounted on Bristol board may have the figure number shown in black ink on the Bristol board proximate the corresponding photograph.

➤ Photographs and ink drawings must not be combined in a formal submission of the visual disclosure of the claimed design in one application. The introduction of both photographs and ink drawings in a design application would result in a high probability of inconsistencies between corresponding elements on the ink drawings as compared with the photographs. Photographs submitted in lieu of ink drawings must not disclose environmental structure but must be limited to the claimed design itself.

➤ Color drawings and color photographs will be accepted as formal drawings in design applications as long as they meet the requirements set forth in 37 CFR 1.84 (a) (2) and (b) (1). These can be found through the USPTO Web site. It is www.uspto.gov.

Fast Facts

On April 10, 1790, President George Washington signed the bill that laid the foundation of the modern American patent system. Three years earlier, in Philadelphia, the Constitutional Convention had given Congress the power "to promote the progress of science and useful arts by securing for limited times to authors and inventors the exclusive right to their respective writings and discoveries."

For over 210 years, the patent system has encouraged the genius of hundreds of thousands of inventors.

➤ If color photographs are submitted as informal drawings and you do not consider the color to be part of the claimed design, a disclaimer must be added to the specification as follows: "The color shown on the claimed design forms no part thereof." Color will be considered an integral part of the disclosed and claimed design in the absence of a disclaimer filed with the original application. If no disclaimer has been included, the omission of color in the later filed formal drawings will be treated as introducing new matter into the claim. A disclaimer may only be used when filing informal drawings. The law requires that the disclosure in formal photographs be limited to the design for the article claimed.

The Least You Need to Know

➤ Design patents are an inexpensive form of protection.

➤ They do not have the teeth of a utility patent.

➤ You don't need legal counsel to apply.

➤ The forms are as easy as A B C to complete.

➤ Design patents are used by many agents as a profit center.

Chapter 15

Mark Your Words

In This Chapter

➤ The name game

➤ Licensing trademarks—$141 billion business

➤ Funny foreign faux pas

➤ How to apply for federal trademarks

"Swiss watches. Chinese tea. Australian outback. Egyptian pyramids. Yankee Ingenuity."

"Only one of these captures the dreams and possibilities of tomorrow. Yankee ingenuity is the substance upon which America's rich enterprise history is built, and there is no better definition of that substance than the American Inventor. Inventing is more than the "American Dream." Combined with hard work, inventing is the future of America—and it belongs to anyone who will chase their dreams."

—Andy Gibbs, CEO PatentCafe.com, Inc., Member Inaugural Patent Advisory Committee, U.S. Patent and Trademark Office

What do Kleenex®, Ford®, Furby®, IBM®, Barbie®, Mr. Clean®, Poppin' Fresh®, and the Gerber Baby have in common with the distinctive buildings that house McDonald's®, and Fotomat®, as well as the Campbell's soup can? They are all registered trademarks and are very important to their owners as tools to sell their products and services.

There Is Nothing Like a Brand, Nothing in the World

Do not underestimate the contribution a good trademark can make to your licensing effort. It always creates fast product identification and can help communicate the item's story. I, therefore, spend time coming up with the most appropriate trademark for every product we develop.

For example, my pitch to Proctor & Gamble that it license our unique big wheel trike design would not have had the same impact without our trademark, Fluorider®. Proctor & Gamble placed our unique ride-on in 33,000 supermarkets under this trademark.

When we invented and patented a toy truck that transformed from a conventional wheel configuration to an in-line configuration, via a variable geometry chassis, the trademark Switchblade® was licensed by Remco as part of the deal.

And our line of Micro Machines® that was built around authentic state police cruisers, motorcycles, and aircraft was contingent upon our licensing to the manufacturer our trademark, Troopers®.

Trademarks can also be very important as a source of additional income should the trademark on the principal invention become valuable. For example, if your invention hits pay dirt under a trademark you control, you may have opportunities to license collateral merchandise, an arena that your licensee may or may not participate in with you.

For example, Caterpillar® is more than earth-moving equipment today. It is also a line of rugged footwear. Furby® had its trademark licensed for much more than toys. It was on everything from pencils to popcorn. The licensing business today is over $140 billion.

"The right licensing deal with the right company can bring in meaningful royalty income with no cost of sales," says Michael Ross, executive vice president and publisher of *The World Book*. "This revenue goes right to the bottom line. Accountants and CEOs love this kind of revenue."

Trademarks Can Take Many Forms

A trademark includes any word, name, symbol, device, or any combination—used, or intended to be used—in commerce to identify and distinguish the goods of one manufacturer or seller from goods manufactured or sold by others and to indicate the source of the goods. In short, a trademark is a brand name. A trademark can be …

➤ A coined word (Trix®, Acura®).

➤ An everyday word with no connection to the product it promotes (Ivory®, Apple®).

➤ A phrase (All the News That's Fit to Print®, Catch the Wave®).

➤ A word that describes a quality or product function (Blockbuster®, Marks-a-Lot®).

➤ A coined word that suggests product performance (Timex®, Jell-O®).

➤ A foreign word with or without significance to the item (Volkswagen®, Dos Equis®).

➤ The names of a product's inventor or company founder (Ford®, Piaget®).

➤ The name of a celebrated person selected for a positive image (Lincoln®, Raleigh®).

➤ A name from literature (Peter Pan®, Atlas®).

➤ Initials (CVS®, MCA®).

➤ Numbers (7-11®, 66®).

➤ A combination of letters and numbers (WD-40®, S-500).

➤ A pictorial mark (Gerber Baby, Playboy Bunny).

➤ A distinct color (John Deere green, Toro red).

➤ A sound (NBC chimes).

➤ A scent (since 1990).

Fast Facts

The first 10 trademarks issued in the U.S. were, in order:

Averill Chemical-Paint Company, Liquid paint; J.B. Baldy & Co., Mustard; Ellis Branson, Retail coal; Tracy Coit, Fish; William Lanfair Ellis & Co., Oyster packing; Evans, Clow, Dalzell & Co., Wrought-iron pipe; W.E. Garrett & Sons, Snuff; William G. Hamilton, Cartwheel; John K. Hogg, Soap; Abraham P. Olzendam, Woollen hose. All were registered on the same day, October 25, 1870.

Dollars & Scents

Clark's Oh-Sew-Easy Needles of Goleta, California (invented by Clark Osewez) was awarded the first fragrance trademark registration for its line of sewing threads perfumed with "a high impact fresh floral fragrance reminiscent of plumeria blossoms."

Explaining the decision, J. David Sams, Chief Administrative Law Judge of the USPTO's Trademark Trial and Appeal Board, offered, "If it looks like a trademark and quacks like a trademark, it is a trademark."

In reviewing the Oh-Sew-Easy application, the Board found that no one else was using "high impact … plumeria blossoms" fragrance or any fragrance whatsoever in the marketing of sewing thread. That made the use of a fragrance distinctive.

Supreme Court Makes a Colorful Decision

Since the 1950s, Qualitex Company has used a distinctive green-gold color on the pads it makes and sells to dry-cleaning firms for use on dry-cleaning presses. In 1989, Jacobson Products, a Qualitex rival, began to sell its own press pads to dry-cleaning firms; its pads were a similar green-gold color.

Bright Ideas

Sanka derives its name from a contraction of the French phrase *sans caffeine.*

In 1991, Qualitex registered the special green-gold on press pads with the USPTO as a trademark (Registration No. 1,633,711). Further, it brought a trademark infringement suit challenging Jacobson's use of the green-gold color.

The case made it all the way to the U.S. Supreme Court which, in a unanimous opinion delivered by Justice Breyer on March 28, 1995, determined that a color may sometimes meet the basic legal requirements for use as a trademark.

Notable Quotables

"Colors fade, temples crumble, empires fall, but wise words endure."

—Edward Thorndike, psychologist

Lost in the Translation

Since your item may one day be marketed overseas, when selecting a trademark, do your best to see what it means in other languages, and how it will translate. Why is this important? Here are some of my favorite bloopers.

➤ Nova in Spanish means "It does not go." This caused a major *problema* for Chevy south of the border, down Mexico way.

➤ Coors put its slogan "Turn It Loose" into Spanish where it read: "Suffer from Diarrhea." Shares of Dos Equis went up!

➤ Scandinavian vacuum manufacturer Electrolux used the following in an American campaign: "Nothing sucks like an Electrolux®." Nuf said.

➤ Clairol introduced its "Mist Stick®," a curling iron, into Germany only to find out that "mist" is slang for cow manure. Not too many people had a use for a "Manure Stick."

➤ Coca-Cola® was brought into China as "Kekoukela." To their surprise it meant "Bite the wax tadpole," or "female horse stuffed with wax," depending upon the dialect.

After researching 40,000 characters, Coke® decided upon "kokou kole"—"Happiness in the mouth."

Take My Words for It

Logotype: an identifying symbol (as in advertising), sometimes called a logo.

The Morton® Umbrella Girl trademark, first used in 1914, was registered in 1946. The logo seen on the container today was introduced in 1968. Also trademark protected is the slogan, "When it rains, it pours."

➤ Coke® was not the only Chinese trademark gaffe. Pepsi's "Come Alive With the Pepsi Generation" was translated to read "Pepsi Brings Your Ancestors Back from the Grave."

➤ Frank Perdue's slogan, "It takes a strong man to make a tender chicken," was translated into Spanish as "It takes an aroused man to make a chicken affectionate." Ouch!

➤ Parker had a ball-point pen introduced in Mexico; the ads were supposed to have read: "It won't leak in your pocket and embarrass you." Instead, the company thought the word for embarrass was *embarazar* (to impregnate), so the ad read: "It won't leak in your pocket and make you pregnant."

➤ When American Airlines wanted to advertise its new leather first-class seats in the Latin American markets, it translated "Fly In Leather" literally, which meant *en Espanol* "Fly Naked" (*Vuela en cuero*).

These are good for a laugh, within the context of this book, but these mistakes cost their companies lots of money, not to mention embarrassment.

Even though your licensee will probably do diligence on any trademark you recommend or assign to it, you should also take care to avoid potential problems by considering everything from federal and common law searches to how the mark may translate into foreign languages. Your conclusions should be shared with your licensee.

United States Patent and Trademark Office

Federal registration of trademarks falls under the jurisdiction of the Trademark Office, a division of the United States Patent and Trademark Office. In fiscal year 2000, the USPTO received 296,490 applications from which it issued a record 106,383 trademark registrations. This is a 27.2 percent increase in registrations from fiscal year 1999 and is primarily due to the number of applications filed following enactment of the Intent-to-Use legislation.

The average time between filing an application and its disposition (in other words, registration, abandonment, or issuance of notice of allowance) was 5.9 months at the end of FY2000, and the trend to date is toward even quicker turnaround times.

411

For a comprehensive overview of U.S. trademark law, go to the Web site of Cornell Law School. No subscription fees. The pages are not cluttered with commercial messages or banner advertising. It is a nonprofit activity of the Cornell Law School. http://www.law.cornell.edu/topics/trademark.html

For information regarding prosecution of trademark applications before the USPTO, go to the USPTO's Web site at www.uspto.gov. From this Web site, it is possible to search pending and registered trademarks, track the status of a trademark application or registration, and to file a trademark application.

The current team is one of the most experienced ever in the Trademark Office. I call the examiners often and have never once been disappointed or frustrated. You would never know it is a bureaucracy.

Correspondence and Information

All correspondence about trademark matters should be addressed to Director of Patents and Trademarks, Washington, D.C. 20231, unless you have the name of a particular examiner or other official.

Here are some phone numbers you may find useful:

➤ General Trademark or Patent Information: (703) 308-HELP.

➤ Automated (Recorded) General Trademark or Patent Information: (703) 557-INFO.

➤ Automated Line for Status Information on Trademark Applications: (703) 305-8747.

➤ Additional Status Information: (703) 308-9400.

➤ Assignment Branch: (703) 308-9711.

➤ Certified Copies of Registrations (703) 308-9726.

➤ Information Regarding Renewals [Sec. 9], Affidavits of Use [Sec. 8], Incontestability [Sec. 15], or Correcting a Mistake on a Registration: (703) 308-9500.

➤ Information Regarding Applications Based on International Agreements or for Certification, Collective, or Collective Membership Marks: (703) 308-9400.

➤ Trademark Trial and Appeal Board: (703) 308-9300.

Bright Ideas

John S. Pemberton, a druggist in Atlanta, brewed up the first kettle of Coca-Cola in 1886. Its main ingredients were coca, the dried leaves of a South American shrub, and cola, extracted from the kola nut. The American public coined the abbreviated name, Coke. Coke was registered as a federal trademark in 1920.

What Kinds of Marks Are Available?

Besides the trademark, there are other kinds of marks you can apply for from the Office. Let's look at them.

➤ **Trademark.** A "trademark," as defined in section 45 of the 1946 Trademark Act (Lanham Act) "includes any word, name, symbol, or device, or any combination thereof adopted and used by a manufacturer or merchant to identify his goods and distinguish them from those manufactured or sold by others." Examples of trademarks include Coca-Cola, Barbie, Ford, and Men Are from Mars, Women Are from Venus.

WACKY PATENTS

Pantyhose Garment with Spare Leg Portion
Patented February 3, 1998
United States Patent 5,713,081

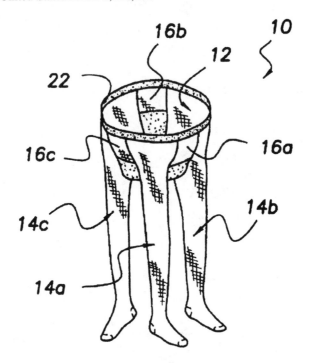

➤ **Service Mark.** A mark used in the sale or advertising of services to identify the services of one person and distinguish them from the services of others. Titles, character names, and other distinctive features of radio or television programs may be registered as service marks notwithstanding that they, or the programs, may advertise the goods of the sponsor. Examples of service marks include American Express and Mr. Goodwrench.

➤ **Certification Mark.** A mark used upon or in connection with the products or services of one or more persons other than the owner of the mark to certify regional or other origin, material, mode of manufacture, quality, accuracy, or other characteristics of such goods or services. Or that the work or labor on the goods or services was performed by members of a union or other organization.

Examples of certification marks of quality include the UL symbol of Under-writers Laboratories and 100 percent Pure Florida's Seal of Approval. Examples of certification marks of service include the Automobile Association of America's Approved Auto Repair and the Motion Picture Association of America's movie ratings.

➤ **Collective Mark.** A trademark or service mark used by the members of a cooper-ative, an association, or other collective group or organization. Marks used to in-dicate membership in a union, an association, or other organization may be registered as collective membership marks. Examples of collective marks include the National Collegiate Athletic Association, the National Rifle Association of American Member, the Automobile Association of America, and Sigma Delta Chi.

➤ **Trade and Commercial Name.** Marks differ from trade and commercial names used by manufacturers, industrialists, merchants, agri-culturists, and others to identify their busi-nesses, vocations, occupations, or other names or titles lawfully adopted by persons, firms, associations, companies, unions, and other organizations. The latter are not subject to registration unless actually used as trade-marks. Examples of trade and commercial names include Coca-Cola Company, HY-Grade Auto Supply, and Sony Corporation of America.

Notable Quotables

"Advertising may be described as the science of arresting the human intelligence long enough to get money from it."

—Stephen Leacock, humorist, es-sayist, teacher

Function of Trademarks

The primary function of a trademark is to indicate the origin of a product or service; however, trademarks also serve to guarantee the quality of the goods bearing the mark and, through advertising, create and maintain a demand for the product. Trademark rights are acquired only through use of the trademark; this use must con-tinue if the rights you can acquire are to be preserved. Registration of a trademark in the USPTO does not in itself create or establish any exclusive rights, but it is recogni-tion by the government of your rights to use the mark in commerce to distinguish your goods from those of others.

Do You Need a Federal Trademark Registration?

While federal registration is not necessary for trademark protection, registration on the Principal Register does provide certain advantages:

1. A constructive date of first use of the mark in commerce. This gives you nation-wide priority as of that date, except as to certain prior users or prior applicants.

2. The right to sue in federal court for trademark infringement.

3. Recovery of profits, damages, and costs in a federal court infringement action and the possibility of treble damages and attorneys' fees.

4. Constructive notice of a claim of ownership. This eliminates a good faith defense for a party adopting the trademark subsequent to your date of registration.

5. The right to deposit the registration with U.S. Customs in order to stop the importation of goods bearing an infringing mark.

Take My Words for It

Trademark: a word or design used on an article of merchandise or service to identify it as the product of a particular manufacturer; also called a brand name.

6. *Prima facie* evidence of the validity of registration, your ownership of the mark, and your exclusive right to use the mark in commerce in connection with the use of goods or services specified in the certificate.

7. The possibility of incontestability, in which case the registration constitutes conclusive evidence of your exclusive right, with certain limited exceptions, to use the registered mark in commerce.

8. Limited grounds for attacking a registration once it is five years old.

9. Availability of criminal penalties and treble damages in an action for counterfeiting a registered trademark.

10. A basis for filing trademark applications in foreign countries.

Marks Not Subject to Registration

A trademark cannot be registered if it …

1. Consists of or comprises immoral, deceptive, or scandalous matter or matter that may disparage or falsely suggest a connection with persons, living or dead, institutions, beliefs, or national symbols, or bring them into contempt or disrepute.

2. Consists of or comprises the flag or coat of arms or other insignia of the United States, of any state or municipality, of any foreign nation, or any simulation thereof.

3. Consists of or comprises a name, portrait, or signature identifying a particular living individual except by his written consent or the name, signature, or

portrait of a deceased president of the United States during the life of his widow, if any, except by the written consent of the widow.

4. Consists of or comprises a mark which so resembles a mark registered in the Patent and Trademark Office or a mark or trade name previously used in the United States by another and not abandoned, as to be likely when applied to the goods of another person, to cause confusion, to cause mistake, or to deceive.

Registerable Marks

The trademark, if otherwise eligible, may be registered on the Principal Register unless it consists of a mark which ...

1. When applied to your goods/services is merely descriptive or deceptively misdescriptive of them, except as indications of regional origin, or

2. Is primarily merely a surname

Such marks, however, may be registered on the Principal Register, provided they have become distinctive as applied to your goods in commerce. The Commissioner may accept as *prima facie* evidence that the mark has become distinctive as applied to your goods/services in commerce, proof of substantially exclusive and continuous use thereof as a mark by you in commerce for the five years preceding the date you filed the application for registration.

All marks capable of distinguishing your goods and not registerable on the Principal Register, which have been in lawful use in commerce for the year preceding your filing for registration, may be registered on the Supplemental Register. A mark on this register may consist of any trademark, symbol, label, package, configuration of goods, name, word, slogan, phrase, surname, geographical name, numeral, device, or any combination of the foregoing.

Fast Facts

People are more prone to purchase goods that have an associated brand they are familiar with. Because of this, the licensing of trademarks worldwide is a $140-plus billion business. Remember years ago how airports, for example, had all local restaurants. Today most food services in airports are branded.

Bright Ideas

B.V.D. underwear takes its name from the men who started the company in 1876—Bradley, Voorhees, and Day.

Searches for Conflicting Marks

You are not required to conduct a search for conflicting marks prior to applying with the USPTO. However, some people find it useful. *I highly recommend it.* The application fee, which covers processing and search costs, will not be refunded even if a conflict is found and the mark cannot be registered. In evaluating your application, an examining attorney will conduct a search and notify you if a conflicting mark is found.

411

To keep up with the business of brand licensing, subscribe to *The Licensing Book*, a magazine published monthly by Adventure Publishing Group, Inc., 1501 Broadway, Suite 500, NYC, NY 10036. Tel: (212) 575-4510. It is a controlled circulation magazine sent free to those who qualify.

To determine if there is a conflict between two marks, the examiner determines whether there would be likelihood of confusion—that is, whether relevant consumers would be likely to associate the goods or services of one party with those of the other party as a result of the use of the marks at issue by both parties. The principal factors to be considered in reaching this decision are the similarity of the marks and the commercial relationship between the goods and services identified by the marks. To find a conflict, the marks need not be identical, and the goods and services do not have to be the same.

There are several ways to do a search. You could hire a patent attorney, engage the services of a professional trademark search firm, or do it yourself.

Law Firm Trademark Search

Your patent attorney will gladly handle a trademark search. Lawyers rely on the services of a professional trademark search firms and then add a premium of 40 percent to 100 percent or more, depending on what the market will bear and the firm's overhead.

If you decide to hire counsel, get an estimate first. Also find out how much the law firm charges for copies. Avoid surprises.

A lawyer will most likely give you a search that goes much wider than the USPTO. If on the ball, he or she would typically purchase a search by Thomson & Thomson, the world leader in trademark services. For information, call toll free: 1-800-356-8630. For an understanding of T&T, visit its Web site: http://www.thomson-thomson.com.

Professional Trademark Search

You could hire your own searcher, but such work has, for the most part, been overtaken by TESS, the Trademark Electronic Search System, established by the USPTO.

Through the Internet you can access and review more than three million pending, registered and dead federal trademarks.

"I do not accept trademark searches anymore unless they involve logos," said George Harvill, president of Greentree Information Service, Bethesda, Maryland. "I cannot take money for something people can do free for themselves via the Internet."

While trademark logos (as differentiated from names) can also be searched via the USPTO's Internet site, there is a learning curve, and I have better things to do with my time. Further, I want to be very sure that I get correct results. Even the pros have to be careful.

Meet Your U.S. Patent Office

Anne H. Chasser, the Commissioner for Trademarks, is responsible for a budget of $65 million and more than 700 employees. She oversees the examination and registration of trademarks and is responsible for proposing policy and programmatic changes in the trademark system and for advocating increased protection for the trademark property rights of U.S. citizens throughout the world.

Ms. Chasser has been involved in collegiate licensing since the late 1970's and was a founder of the Association of Collegiate Licensing Administrators, an association of 300 U.S. and international collegiate trademark administrators, licensees and affiliated organizations. She served as its president in 1990.

Ms. Chasser received her Bachelor's degree at the University of Dayton and a Master's degree in Public Policy and Management from Ohio State University.

"Although I could do the logo searches via the Internet from my office, I conduct them at the USPTO because the system is much easier to use there, thus increasing the odds that I will not miss anything," adds Harvill.

I use Greentree Information Service for all my trademark work. GIS may be reached by calling (301) 469-0902. Ask for a current rate sheet and always compare its prices with those of other services available to you.

Making Application

If you find the mark available, go to TEAS, the Trademark Electronic Application System, at http://teas.uspto.gov/V1.22/. TEAS allows you to fill out a form and check it for completeness over the Internet. Using e-TEAS you can then submit the form directly to the USPTO over the Internet, making an official filing online. Or using PrinTEAS, you can print out the completed form for mailing to the USPTO. It's your choice!

Do-It-Yourself Trademark Search

There are a number of ways you could approach your search if you decide to go it alone:

You may visit the Trademark Office's Public Search Room, located on the second floor of the South Tower Building, 2900 Crystal Drive, Arlington, Virginia 22202. The staff up there is very helpful, and once you learn the layout, you can breeze through the search process by hand or computer terminal.

Trademark information on CD-ROM has been distributed to the Patent and Trademark Depository Libraries (PTDLs). These products include T®ADEMARKS Registrations, which contains all currently registered U.S. trademarks, TRADEMARKS Pending Applications, and T®ADEMARKS Assignment File, which contains ownership information.

By the way, these products are available for sale to the public and may be ordered from the USPTO's Office of Information Products Development, Crystal Plaza 2, Room 9D30, Washington, D.C. 20231. The telephone number is (703) 308-0322.

Searching the USPTO via the Internet

See above section: Professional Trademark Search.

By the way, if you want to be as thorough as possible, back up the USPTO search with Thomson & Thomson. Do this yourself and avoid the lawyer's mark-up.

For good measure, I always take my proposed trademarks and run them through several Internet search engines (e.g., dogpile.com, altavista.com, yahoo.com, etc.) to see if something turns up that might cause interference for me.

Establishing Trademark Rights

Trademark rights arise from either (1) actual use of the mark or (2) the filing of a proper application to register a mark in the USPTO stating that you have a bona fide intention to use the mark in commerce regulated by the U.S. Congress. (See below, under Types of Applications, for a discussion of what is meant by the terms "commerce" and "use in commerce.") Federal registration is not required to establish rights in a mark, nor is it required to begin use of a mark. However, federal registration can secure benefits beyond the rights acquired by merely using a mark. For example, the owner of a federal registration is presumed to be the owner of the mark for the goods and services specified in the registration and to be entitled to use the mark nationwide.

There are two related but distinct types of rights in a mark: the right to register and the right to use. Generally, the first party who either uses a mark in commerce or files an application in the USPTO has the ultimate right to register that mark. The USPTO's authority is limited to determining the right to register. The right to use a mark can be more complicated to determine. This is particularly true when two parties have begun use of the same or similar marks without knowledge of one another and neither has a federal registration. Only a court can render a decision about the right to use, such as issuing an injunction or awarding damages for infringement. It should be noted that a federal registration can provide significant advantages to a party involved in a court proceeding. The USPTO cannot provide advice concerning rights in a mark. Only a private attorney can provide such advice.

WACKY PATENTS

Dust Cover for Dog
Patented September 4, 1963
United States Patent 3,150,641

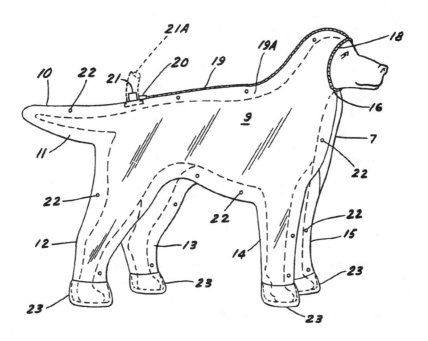

Terms of a Trademark

Unlike copyrights or patents, trademark rights can last indefinitely if the owner continues to use the mark to identify its goods or services. The term of a federal trademark registration is 10 years, with 10-year renewal terms. However, between the fifth and sixth year after the date of initial registration, the registrant must file an affidavit setting forth certain information to keep the registration alive. If no affidavit is filed, the registration is cancelled.

Types of Applications for Federal Registration

You may apply for federal registration in three principal ways.

1. Anyone who has already commenced using a mark in commerce may file based on that use (a "use" application).

2. Anyone who has not yet used the mark may apply based on a bona fide intention to use the mark in commerce (an "intent-to-use" application). For the purpose of obtaining federal registration, commerce means all commerce which may lawfully be regulated by the U.S. Congress, for example, interstate commerce or commerce between the United States and another country. The use in commerce must be a bona fide use in the ordinary course of trade, and not made merely to reserve a right in a mark. Use of a mark in promotion or advertising before the product or service is actually provided under the mark on a normal commercial scale does not qualify as use in commerce. If you file based on a bona fide intention to use in commerce, you should note that you will have to use the mark in commerce and submit an allegation of use to the USPTO before the USPTO will register the mark.

3. Additionally, under certain international agreements, anyone may file in the United States based on an application or registration in another country. For information regarding applications based on international agreements, please call the information number listed above (under the heading Information Numbers).

Bright Ideas

"The Uncola" was registered as a trademark by the Seven-Up Company over the objections of the Coca-Cola Company, which made the case that no entity should be permitted exclusive rights to a term that was the equivalent of noncola.

Who May File an Application?

The application must be filed in the name of the owner of the mark: usually an individual, corporation, or partnership. The owner of a mark controls the nature and quality of the goods or services identified by the mark.

The owner may submit and prosecute its own application for registration or may be represented by an attorney. The USPTO cannot help select an attorney.

Foreign Applicants

If you do not live in the United States, you must designate in writing the name and address of a domestic representative—a person residing in the United States "upon whom notices of process may be served for proceedings affecting the mark." This person will receive all communications from the USPTO unless you are represented by an attorney in the United States.

Where to Send the Application and Correspondence

The application and all other correspondence should be addressed to The Commissioner of Patents and Trademarks, Washington, D.C., 20231.

411

Li©ense magazine is another trade publication that provides up-to-date information on the licensing industry and features on brands and the movers and groovers behind them.

It is a controlled circulation magazine, free to those who qualify. Contact: *Li©ence*, One Park Avenue, NYC, NY 10016. (888) 527-7008.

Use of the "TM," "SM," and "®" Symbols

Anyone who claims rights in a mark may use the TM (trademark) or SM (service mark) designation with the mark to alert the public to the claim. *It is not necessary to have a registration, or even a pending application, to use these designations.* The claim may or may not be valid. The registration symbol, ®, may only be used when the mark is registered in the USPTO. It is improper to use this symbol at any point before the registration issues. Please omit all symbols from the mark in the drawing you submit with your application; the symbols are not considered part of the mark.

Examination

About five months after filing, an examining attorney at the USPTO reviews the application and determines whether the mark may be registered. If the examining attorney determines that the mark cannot be registered, the examining attorney will issue a letter listing any grounds for refusal and any corrections required in the application. The examining attorney may also contact you by telephone if only minor corrections are required. If a correction or modification can be done by phone, that's how the examiners prefer to handle it. I have always found trademark examiners to be most helpful and professional. Unlike many bureaucrats, they tend to favor less paper.

You must respond to any objections within six months of the mailing date of the letter, or the application will be abandoned. If your response does not overcome all objections, the examining attorney will issue a final refusal. You may then appeal to the Trademark Trial and Appeal Board, an administrative tribunal within the USPTO.

A common ground for refusal is likelihood of confusion between your mark and a registered mark. Marks that are merely descriptive in relation to your goods or services, or a feature of the goods or services, may also be refused. Marks consisting of geographic terms or surnames may also be refused. Marks may be refused for other reasons as well.

411

Copies of the *Trademark Official Gazette* may be obtained from the Superintendent of Documents, Government Printing Office, Washington, D.C. 20402. For more information, call (202) 783-3238.

Publication for Opposition

If there are no objections or if you overcome all objections, the examining attorney will approve the mark for publication in the *Official Gazette*, a weekly publication of the USPTO. The USPTO will send a Notice of Publication to you indicating the date of publication. In the case of two or more applications for similar marks, the USPTO will publish the application with the earliest effective filing date first. Any party who believes it may be damaged by the registration of the mark has 30 days from the date of publication to file an opposition to registration. An opposition is similar to a formal proceeding in the federal courts but is held before the Trademark Trial and Appeal Board. If no opposition is filed, the application enters the next stage of the registration process.

Issuance of Certificate of Registration or Notice of Allowance

If your application was based upon the actual use of the mark in commerce prior to approval for publication, the USPTO will register the mark and issue a registration certificate about 12 weeks after the date the mark was published, if no opposition was filed.

If, instead, the mark was published based upon your statement of having a bona fide intention to use the mark in commerce, the USPTO will issue a Notice of Allowance about 12 weeks after the date the mark was published, again provided no opposition was filed. You then have six months from the date of the Notice of Allowance to either (1) use the mark in commerce and submit a Statement of Use, or (2) request a six-month Extension of Time to File a Statement of Use. You may request additional extensions of time only as noted in the instructions. If the Statement of Use is filed and approved, the USPTO will issue the registration certificate.

Bright Ideas

It all began when the Ideal Toy Company produced the "Teddy Bear," named for President Teddy Roosevelt. Permission was granted on a royalty-free basis. The art of merchandising hasn't been the same since. Today trademark licensing is a $62 billion business.

The Least You Need to Know

➤ Trademarks can be more important than patents.

➤ You don't need a federal TM registration, but it adds to your punch.

➤ Save money. Do the search and application yourself, on line. Try it. You'll like it.

➤ Get a jump on things with an Intent-To-Use application.

Chapter 16

Securing Your Copy Rights

In This Chapter

➤ Copyright is a no-brainer to obtain

➤ What can and cannot be protected

➤ See what © means

➤ How long does copyright protection last?

➤ Striking the right CORDS—Electronic filing

➤ Forms and their functions

"The vitality of thought is in adventure. Ideas won't keep. Something must be done about them. When the idea is new, its custodians have fervor, live for it, and, if need be, die for it."

—Alfred North Whitehead, British mathematician, logician, and philosopher

What do Hal David's hit song "Do You Know the Way to San Jose?" John Gray's best-seller *Men Are from Mars, Women Are from Venus*, the film *The Graduate*, the printed matter on a can of Diet Coke, and this book have in common? If you said they are all protected by copyright, you would be correct.

Copyrights—They're Different

Copyrights are very different from patents and trademarks. A patent primarily prevents inventions, discoveries, or advancements of useful processes from being manufactured, used, or marketed by anyone other than the patentee. A trademark is a word, name, or symbol to indicate origin and, in so doing, distinguish the products and services of one company from those of another. Copyright protects "original works of authorship" that are fixed in a tangible form of expression. The fixation need not be directly perceptible so long as it may be communicated with the aid of a machine or device. Copyrightable works include the following categories:

➤ Literary works

➤ Musical works, including any accompanying words

➤ Dramatic works, including any accompanying music

➤ Pantomimes and choreographic works

➤ Pictorial, graphic, and sculptural works

➤ Motion pictures and other audiovisual works

➤ Sound recordings

➤ Architectural works

These categories should be viewed broadly. For example, computer programs and most "compilations" may be registered as "literary works;" maps and architectural plans may be registered as "pictorial, graphic, and sculptural works." Barbie and Ken, Mattel dolls, are copyrighted as sculptural works.

Copyright does not protect ideas, concepts, systems, or methods of doing something. Copyrights protect the form of expression rather than the subject matter of the writing. You may express your ideas in writing or drawings and claim copyright in your description, but be aware that copyright will not protect the idea itself as revealed in your written or artistic work.

Notable Quotables

"It doesn't matter if you try and try and try again, and fail. It does matter if you try and fail, and fail to try again."

—Charles F. Kettering, inventor, car ignition system

The Copyright Office

Copyrights are not handled by the Patent and Trademark Office. For this discussion we move across the Potomac River from the USPTO's Crystal City, Virginia, headquarters to Washington, D.C., up Independence Avenue, and onto Capitol Hill. This is where the Library of Congress is located. This august institution is primarily responsible for administering copyright law.

In fiscal year 1999, the Copyright Office transferred over 950,000 copyright deposit copies, valued at more than $36 million, to the Library of Congress for its collections.

The Library of Congress, of which the Copyright Office is a part, was established in 1800. It has circa 115 million items in its collections, including over 25 million books and other printed matter. The special collections include over 35 million charts, maps, photos, etc. There are also about 5,700 incunabula (books printed before 1501).

You may visit the Copyright Public Information Office at 101 Independence Avenue SE, Washington, D.C., or call (202) 707-3000. Recorded information on copyright is available 24 hours a day, 7 days a week. Information specialists are on duty to answer queries by phone or in person from 8:30 A.M. to 5:00 P.M., Monday through Friday, except holidays. Mail should be sent to Register of Copyrights, Copyright Office, Library of Congress, Washington, D.C. 20559-6000.

What Would an Inventor Copyright?

Copyright protection is available to you for both published and unpublished works. I slap copyright notices on many things that I create, e.g., proposals, instruction sheets, game content, game boards, package copy, video presentations, sculptures, drawings, photographs, etc. I do not go through the formal process of registering everything, but I typically place the copyright notice on appropriate product, which is legal.

If a licensee opts to utilize my copyrighted material, I insist that my copyright notice appear on the package or the elements to which it pertains. I typically make it a part of the license agreement. Few object. A couple times I was told that a product could only have one copyright notice and that it had to be the company's ©. A call to the Library of Congress settled it. Products can list as many copyrights as are appropriate. For example, there can be one on the artwork, another on the package text and trade dress, yet another on the instructions, etc.

Take My Words for It

KISS: Keep It Simple, Stupid. Used to describe tightly designed, easy-to-understand products.

How Do You Secure a Copyright?

The way in which copyright protection is secured under the present law is frequently misunderstood. In years past, it was required that you fill out forms and send them to the Library of Congress together with a check and a number of copies of the original work. Today, no publication or registration or other action in the Copyright Office is required to secure copyright under the new law.

241

Under present law, copyright is secured "automatically" when the work is created, and the work is "created" when it is fixed in a copy or phonographically recorded for the first time. In general, "copies" are material objects from which a work can be read or visually perceived either directly or with the aid of a machine or device, such as books, manuscripts, sheet music, film, videotape, or microfilm.

However, it is still prudent to make a formal application with the Library of Congress for certain products. This serves to establish a "public record" of your claim and gets you a certificate of registration, which is required if you ever have to go into a court of competent jurisdiction over infringement. If you receive a copyright within five years of publication, it will be considered to be *prima facie* evidence in such a court.

Registration is recommended for a number of reasons. You may wish to register your work to have the facts of your copyright on the public record and have a certificate of registration. Registered works may be eligible for statutory damages and attorney's fees in successful litigation. Finally, if registration occurs within five years of publication, it is considered *prima facie* evidence in a court of law.

Copyright does not protect names, titles, slogans, or short phrases. In some cases, these things may be protected as trademarks. Contact the U.S. Patent and Trademark Office at (800) 786-9199 for further information. However, copyright protection may be available for logo artwork that contains sufficient authorship. In some circumstances, an artistic logo may also be protected as a trademark.

Fast Facts

➤ August 18, 1787: James Madison submitted to the framers of the Constitution a provision "to secure to literary authors their copyrights for a limited time."

➤ May 31, 1790: The first copyright law was enacted under the new U.S. Constitution. A term of 14 years with privilege of renewal for an additional 14 years was offered.

➤ June 9, 1790: The first copyright entry, *The Philadelphia Spelling Book* by John Barry, was registered in the U.S. District Court of Pennsylvania.

Who May File an Application?

The following persons are legally entitled to submit an application form:

➤ *The author.* This is either the person who actually created the work or, if the work was made for hire, the employer or other person for whom the work was prepared.

➤ *The copyright claimant.* The copyright claimant is defined in Copyright Office regulations as either the author of the work or a person or organization that has obtained ownership of all the rights under the copyright initially belonging to the author. This category includes a person or organization that has obtained by contract the right to claim legal title to the copyright in an application for copyright registration.

➤ *The owner of exclusive right(s).* Under the law, any of the exclusive rights that make up a copyright and any subdivision of them can be transferred and owned separately, even though the transfer may be limited in time or place of effect. The term "copyright owner" with respect to any one of the exclusive rights contained in a copyright refers to the owner of that particular right. Any owner of an exclusive right may apply for registration of a claim in the work.

➤ *The duly authorized agent of such author, other copyright claimant, or owner of exclusive right(s).* Any person authorized to act on behalf of the author, other copyright claimant, or owner of exclusive rights may apply for registration.

➤ *There is no requirement that applications be prepared or filed by an attorney.* Therefore, don't throw your money away.

Mary Berghaus Levering, Associate Registrar for National Copyright Programs, says it is taking between six to eight months now to process copyright applications.

Notice of Copyright

Before you publicly show or distribute your work, notice of copyright is required. The use of the copyright notice is your responsibility and does not need any special advance permission from, or registration with, the Copyright Office.

Bright Ideas

Play-Doh originated as a wallpaper-cleaning compound at a Cincinnati-based company that made soap and cleaning solutions. Instead of manufacturing it as a cleaning product, the company realized its toy potential, removed the chemical element naptha, and thus Play-Doh, the original reusable modeling compound, was born. More than two billion containers of Play-Doh have been sold since 1956.

The notice for visually perceptible copies should contain the following three elements:

1. The symbol © or the word "Copyright," or the abbreviation "Copr."

2. The year of first publication of said work. In the case of complications or derivative works incorporating previously published material, the year of first publication of the compilation or derivative work is enough. The year may be omitted where a pictorial, graphic, or sculptural work, with accompanying text (if any), is reproduced in or on greeting cards, postcards, stationary, jewelry, dolls, toys, or any useful article.

WACKY PATENTS

Sexual Armor
Patented January 7, 1908
United States Patent 875,845

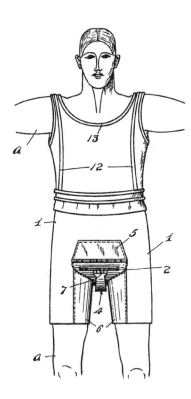

3. The name of the owner of copyright in the work, an abbreviation by which the name can be recognized, or a generally known alternative of the owner.

Example: © 2001 Barbara J. Slate (You should affix the notice in such a way as to give it reasonable notice of the claim of copyright.)

How Long Does Copyright Last?

The Sonny Bono Copyright Term Extension Act, signed into law on October 27, 1998, amends the provisions concerning duration of copyright protection. Effective immediately, the terms of copyright are generally extended for an additional 20 years. Specific provisions are as follows:

➤ For works created after January 1, 1978, copyright protection will endure for the life of the author plus an additional 70 years. In the case of a joint work, the term lasts for 70 years after the last surviving author's death. For anonymous and pseudonymous works and works made for hire, the term will be 95 years from the year of first publication or 120 years from the year of creation, whichever expires first.

➤ For works created but not published or registered before January 1, 1978, the term endures for life of the author plus 70 years, but in no case will expire earlier than December 31, 2002. If the work is published before December 31, 2002, the term will not expire before December 31, 2047.

➤ For pre-1978 works still in their original or renewal term of copyright, the total term is extended to 95 years from the date that copyright was originally secured. For further information see Circular 15a or the Copyright Office's Web site www.loc.gov/copyright/.

What Is Not Protected by Copyright?

Several categories of material are generally not eligible for federal copyright protection. These include among others …

➤ Works that have not been fixed in a tangible form of expression (for example, choreographic works that have not been notated or recorded, improvisational speeches or performances that have not been written or recorded).

➤ Titles, names, short phrases, and slogans; familiar symbols or designs; mere variations of typographic ornamentation, lettering, or coloring; mere listings of ingredients or contents.

➤ Ideas, procedures, methods, systems, processes, concepts, principles, discoveries, or devices, as distinguished from a description, explanation, or illustration.

➤ Works consisting entirely of information that is common property and containing no original authorship (for example: standard calendars, height and weight charts, tape measures and rulers, and lists or tables taken from public documents or other common sources).

Fast Facts

If you ever have trouble getting information from a federal agency, remember these four letters: FOIA. The Freedom of Information Act (FOIA), which can be found in Title 5 of the United States Code, section 552, was enacted in 1966 and provides that any person has the right to request access to federal agency records or information. This right of access is enforceable in court. All agencies of the United States government are required to disclose records upon receiving a written request for them, except for those records that are protected from disclosure by the nine exemptions and three exclusions found in the FOIA.

Striking the Right CORDS

The Copyright Office began developing CORDS (Copyright Office Electronic Registration, Recordation, and Deposit System) in 1993, as its fully automated, innovative system to receive and process digital applications and digital deposits of copyrighted works for electronic registration via the Internet. Through CORDS, copyright applications can be filed electronically by sending applications and deposits in digital form. The CORDS system facilitates full electronic processing, both initial preparation by applicants on the "front end" and completely automated processing on the "back end" by the Copyright Office. CORDS is an efficient vehicle for registering and depositing "born digital" works with the Copyright Office and a vital link between the producers of such works and the digital collections of the Library of Congress as the ultimate beneficiary.

The overall goal of the CORDS system is to provide to all creators and distributors the ability to submit their applications and works electronically for copyright registration over the Internet and to have their copyright-related documents, such as assignments and transfers of copyright, recorded in the public records of the U.S. Copyright Office.

The Copyright Office has four major objectives in implementing CORDS:

Fast Facts

In 1783, Connecticut became the first state to pass a copyright statute. "An Act for the Encouragement of Literature and Genius" was enacted because of the advocacy of Dr. Noah Webster.

1. To make it much easier, faster, and more efficient for copyright applicants to submit their applications and deposits of works for copyright registration.

2. To enhance the Office's services for its customers by speeding up registration processing time, improving communications with users, and increasing the security of deposits since registration proceeds more quickly through electronic submissions that avoid the cumbersome limitations of the Office's current hard copy-based procedures.

3. To control costs and operate more efficiently through the effective use of technology.

4. To facilitate acquisition of "born digital" works for the collections of the Library of Congress.

Mary Berghaus Levering, Associate Registrar for National Copyright Programs, explains that CORDS is not yet available to the public, but it will be one day. For the time being, it is reserved for companies that are seeking to protect their electronic works.

Bright Ideas

➤ The country's first feature film, D.W. Griffith's *Birth of a Nation*, was registered for copyright protection in 1915.

➤ *God Bless America* by Irving Berlin was registered in 1939.

➤ Mattel's Barbie doll was registered in 1958. Registration of the Ken doll follows in 1960.

How to Submit Registrations

To register a work, send the following elements in the same envelope or package to:

Library of Congress
Copyright Office
101 Independence Avenue, S.E.
Washington, D.C. 20559-6000

1. A properly completed application form.

2. A nonrefundable filing fee of $30 (effective through June 30, 2002) for each application.

NOTE: Copyright Office fees are subject to change. For current fees, please check the Copyright Office Web site at www.loc.gov/copyright, write the Copyright Office, or call (202) 707-3000.

In Search of Copyright Records

The records of the Copyright Office are open for inspection and for searching by you. Moreover, on request, the Copyright Office will search its records for you at the statutory hourly rate of $65 for each

Notable Quotables

"It takes courage to be creative; just as soon as you have a new idea, you're in the minority of one."

—E. Paul Torrance, author, "The Creativity Passion."

hour or fraction of an hour. For information on searching the Office records concerning the copyright status or ownership of a work, request Circular 22, "How to Investigate the Copyright Status of a Work," and Circular 23, "The Copyright Card Catalog and the Online Files of the Copyright Office."

Copyright Office records in machine-readable form cataloged from January 1, 1978, to the present, including registration and renewal information and recorded documents, are now available for searching on the Internet. These files may be examined through LOCIS (Library of Congress Information System). You may connect to LOCIS through the World Wide Web at www.loc.gov/copyright/rb.html.

Take My Words for It

SWAG: Sophisticated Wild Ass Guess.

Bright Ideas

Isaac Singer introduced the in-stallment plan, an innovation that may have changed American life even more profoundly than the sewing machine. Beginning in 1856, a machine could be bought for $5 down and $5 per month. The plan was an immediate success. In only a few months, sales tripled.

For Further Information

Circulars, announcements, regulations, other related materials, and all copyright application forms are available from the Copyright Office Web site at www.loc.gov/copyright.

Circulars and other information (but not application forms) are available from Fax-on-Demand at (202) 707-2600.

For general information about copyright, call the Copyright Public Information Office at (202) 707-3000. The TTY number is (202) 707-6737. Information specialists are on duty from 8:30 A.M. to 5:00 P.M. Monday through Friday, eastern time except federal holidays. Recorded information is available 24 hours a day. Or, if you know which application forms and circulars you want, request them from the Forms and Publications Hotline at (202) 707-9100 24 hours a day. Leave a recorded message.

For information by regular mail, write to:

Library of Congress
Copyright Office
Publications Section, LM-455
101 Independence Avenue, S.E.
Washington, D.C. 20559-6000

How to Investigate the Copyright Status of a Work

There are several ways to investigate whether a work is under copyright protection and, if so, the facts of the copyright.

1. Examine a copy of the work (or, if the work is a sound recording, examine the disk, tape cartridge, or cassette in which the recorded sound is fixed, or the album cover, sleeve, or container in which the recording is sold) for such elements as a copyright notice, place and date of publication, author and publisher.

2. Make a personal search of the Copyright Office catalogs and other records.

3. Have the Copyright Office make a search for you.

Individual Searches of Copyright Records

The Copyright Office is located in the Library of Congress, James Madison Memorial Building, 101 Independence Avenue SE, Washington, D.C.

Most records in the Copyright Office are open to public inspection and searching from 8:30 A.M. to 5 P.M., Monday through Friday (except legal holidays). The various records freely available to the public include an extensive card catalog, an automated catalog containing records from 1978 on, record books, and microfilm records of assignments and related documents. Other records, including correspondence files and deposit copies, are not open to the public for searching. However, they may be inspected upon request and payment of a $20 per hour search fee.

If you wish to do your own searching in the Copyright Office's public files, you will be given assistance in locating the records you need and in learning searching procedures. If the Copyright Office staff actually makes the search for you, a search fee of $20 per hour will be charged. The search will not be done while you wait.

The Copyright Office is not permitted to give legal advice. If you need information or guidance on matters, such as disputes over the ownership of a copyright, suits against possible infringers, the procedure for getting a work published, or the method of obtaining royalty payments, it may be necessary to consult an attorney.

Application Forms

All forms are now available to you via the Internet. These are the forms you will most likely require: Form TX (Text), Form VA (Visual Arts). On the Web site you will find additional forms: Form CA (Supplementary) and Form RE (Renewal). The cost is $30 per registration of copyright at this writing

Fast Facts

Protection was given to dramatic works in 1856.

> **Form TX:** For published and unpublished nondramatic literary works. This comprises the broadest category, covering everything from novels to computer programs, game instructions, and invention proposals.

WACKY PATENTS

Animal Trap
Patented December 26, 1882
United States Patent 269,766

Form VA: For published and unpublished works of the visual arts. This would be for artwork you may have developed as an adjunct to your invention, charts, technical drawings, diagrams, models, and works of artistic craftsmanship.

Form CA: For application for supplementary copyright registration. Use when an earlier registration has been made in the Copyright Office and some of the facts given in that registration are incorrect or incomplete. Form CA allows you to place the correct or complete fact on record.

Form RE: Renewal registration. Use when you wish to renew a copyright.

The Least You Need to Know

➤ Copyright protection is free.

➤ You don't need a lawyer to file.

➤ It's all on the Library of Congress Web site.

Chapter 17

I've Got a Secret

In This Chapter

➤ Open the Coke but don't "pop" its secret

➤ How to tell if you have a trade secret

➤ Trade secrets can last indefinitely

➤ How to expose a trade secret without liability

➤ Uniform Trade Secrets Act

"A sekret ceases tew be a sekret if it iz once confided it iz like a dollar bill, once broken, it iz never a dollar again."

—Josh Billings, *Affurisms* (1865)

Your invention may have a trade secret associated with it, i.e a plan or process, tool, mechanism, or compound known only to you and your partners and/or employees to whom it is necessary to confide it.

The trade secrets of a company are its crown jewels. Trade secrets are not patented because through doing so they would no longer be secret and the owner would lose any competitive business advantage the secret afforded. This is why Coke has never taken out a patent on its formula.

Arguably the most celebrated and legendary trade secret is the Coca-Cola formula. When people refer to it, they mean the ingredient called "7X," a mixture of fruit-oils and spices that gives the syrup its signature flavor. It is very important to the Coca-Cola Company to keep its formula secret. In 1977, the Indian government demanded

Notable Quotables

"Everybody steals in commerce and industry. I've stolen a lot myself. But I know how to steal. They don't—and that's what's the matter with them."

—Thomas Alva Edison

Coca-Cola reveal the formula if it wanted to market its product in the subcontinent. The Atlanta, Georgia–based company said rather than reveal its secret, it would sacrifice this huge market opportunity.

Trade secrets are potentially unlimited in duration.

The protection provided by a trade secret is lost if someone else discovers the information either independently or by analyzing or dissecting a product through what is called "reverse engineering."

Trade secrets do not need to be registered with or granted by any government agencies. If you want to keep something as a trade secret just take reasonable steps to keep your secret, well, secret.

Fast Facts

Talking about secrets, here's a great story. On August 1, 2000, the Patent Office issued U.S. Patent 6,097,812 on a crytographic system. The patent application was filed on July 25, 1933 and assigned to the United States of America as represented by the National Security Agency, Washington, D.C.

The system was used to crack enemy codes during WWII. The government has kept the lid on it all these years. Of course, today it is overtaken by modern technology.

In the Court

Trade secret protection is a state right under the Uniform Trade Secret Act or similar state laws, and it mainly provides relief should information be leaked to your competitors.

In order to warrant such relief through a court of law, the trade secret must be shown to be both commercially valuable and far enough removed from general knowledge that it is reasonably difficult to discover, e.g., in a vault or protected by like measure. Also, a company must show that it has been diligent in keeping its information secret. Since patented inventions are made publicly available upon granting of the patent, patent protection and trade secret protection are mutually exclusive; however, since patent applications are kept confidential until and unless they are approved, save for the new 18-month publication rule, an invention can remain a trade secret if the patent application is rejected.

The most common kinds of trade secrets include chemical formulas or recipes and manufacturing processes or techniques.

WACKY PATENTS

Annunciator for the Supposed Dead
Patented December 22, 1891
United States Patent 465,548

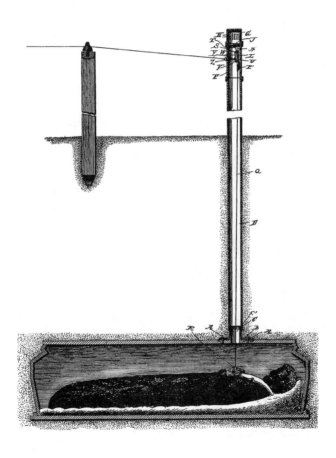

Can Independent Inventors Have Trade Secrets?

Sure you can, but simply classifying product development information as a trade secret is not enough. Further, and for example, information known to the public or that can be easily gathered from reading trade publications, scientific journals, and so forth is not considered a trade secret.

The biggest problem you have is how to keep your trade secrets under wraps. The most frequent disclosure of trade secret information is by current and former employees.

May 23, 2001, *The Los Angeles Times* reported that software company Avant Corporation agreed to pay $27 million in fines with the possibility of more to come after its CEO and six other current and former executives pleaded *no lo contendere* to criminal charges in the theft of computer code from a competitor where Avant's founders had worked.

At the annual conference of the Risk & Insurance Management Society on May 14, 2001, Bradford C. Lewis of Fenwick & West L.L.P. told a panel in reference to trade secrets: "It's a much more informal process, but you do have to take specific steps within your organization in order to qualify for trade secrecy protection."

It can also take place when you are pitching a product concept and you share trade secrets as part of your sale's strategy. If you have not taken careful and deliberate steps to protect the trade secret, then you may have compromised your secret. In this case, you'd want the potential licensee to sign a hold confidential document.

If the document you sign with the prospective licensee acknowledges your trade secret and promises (on behalf of the company and its employees) to hold your information confidential, then the use or sharing of same could be interpreted as willful and malicious misappropriation.

Bright Ideas

➤ The first rickshaw was invented in 1869 by an American Baptist minister, the Rev. E. Jonathan Scobie, to transport his invalid wife around the streets of Yokohama.

➤ Benjamin Franklin, at age 83, invented bifocals because he hated wearing two pairs of glasses.

Notable Quotables

"We must look forward to the future as that is where most of us will be spending the rest of our lives."

—Charles F. Kettering, inventor, spark plug

WACKY PATENTS

Flood Protection Container for Vechicles
Patented February 16, 1982
United States Patent 4,315,535

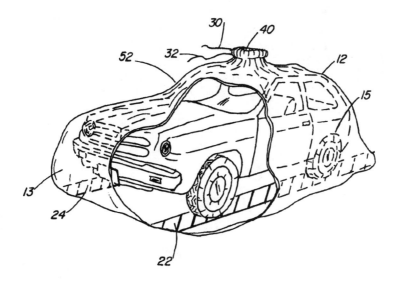

Uniform Trade Secrets Act

The Uniform Trade Secrets Act (UTSA) is legislation drafted by the National Conference of Commissioners on Uniform State Laws. Copies of the UTSA can be ordered from the National Conference of Commissioners on Uniforms State Laws, 676 North St. Clair Street, Suite 1700 Chicago, Il 60611.

Forty states have enacted various statutes modeled after the UTSA and therefore the UTSA should not be relied upon without consulting with intellectual property counsel.

Keep a Tight Lip

The best advice is not to reveal anything of a trade secret nature until and unless you have appropriate documentation agreed to and signed off on by an officer of the reviewing entity. Your nondisclosure document should be drafted by an attorney who specializes in trade secrets. Don't just assume that a patent counsel can handle it.

Fast Facts

The formulas for Coca-Cola, Silly Putty, and Sea Monkeys have never been patented. They are protected through trade secrets.

255

The Least You Need to Know

➤ Trade secrets are not filed with the government.

➤ Loose lips sink ships.

➤ There is no statute of limitations.

➤ If you have to reveal a trade secret to make the sale, think twice about it. Then if you still want to do it, make sure that everyone to whom it is shown signs on the dotted line.

➤ Get competent legal advice.

Chapter 18

Say, Ah! The Patent Examination Process at the USPTO

In This Chapter

➤ Follow your patent application behind the scenes inside the USPTO

➤ How not to slip on appeal

➤ How to identify patent infringement

➤ Patent enforcement insurance

➤ Abandonment of a patent

"The stories of America's inventors abound in genius, insight, and ambition—along with frustration and heartbreak. But they tell much more ... they sketch the development of a Nation."

—National Geographic Society

If your patent application passes initial muster, it will be assigned to the appropriate examining group and then to an examiner. Patent applications are handled in the order received.

The application examination inspects for compliance with the legal requirements and includes a search through U.S. patents, prior foreign patent documents which are available in the USPTO, and available literature—e.g., magazines, newspapers, doctoral dissertations, and so on—to ensure that your invention is new. A decision is reached by the examiner in light of the study and the result of the search.

Don Coster of the Nevada Inventor Association, after a visit to the USPTO, says: "Our patent applications go through a process that is so thorough and so efficient that it is hard to believe unless you see it in action. The application does not go directly to an examiner. It must first be examined for content and completeness. The drawings are checked and screened for things like military sensitivity or unlawful usage. Once accepted as legal and complete, (the application) is classified for the proper art group. This is very critical. If the wrong examiner ends up with it on his or her table, it might be months before he or she even gets a first look at it because applications are taken in the order that they're received ... Those people are so conscientious that it rarely ever happens."

First Office Action

You, if you applied *pro se*, or your attorney will be notified of the examiner's decision through what the USPTO refers to as an "action." An action is actually a letter that gives the reasons for any adverse response or any objection or requirement. The examiner will cite any appropriate references or information that you will find useful in making the decision to continue the prosecution of the application or to drop it.

If the invention is not considered patentable subject matter, the claims will be rejected. If the examiner finds that the invention is not new, the claims will be rejected; but the claims may also be rejected if they depict an object that is found to be obvious. It is not uncommon for some or all the claims to be rejected on the examiner's first action; very few applications sail through as first submitted.

411

The Rothschild Petersen Patent Model Museum is reportedly the largest privately owned collection of United States patent models in the world. Containing nearly 4,000 patent models and related documents, it spans America's Industrial Revolution. Alan Rothschild is working to establish a National Patent Model Museum. In the meantime, his collection is housed in a private residence in Cazenovia, New York. Visits are by appointment only. If you are interested in helping, call Alan at (315) 655-9367, or e-mail to maxertaxer@aol.com.

To see the background on his initiative, visit Web site: www.patentmodel.org.

Your First Response

Let's say the examiner gives you the thumbs down on all or some of your claims. Your next move if you wish to continue pursuing the patent is to respond, specifically pointing out the supposed errors in the examiner's action. Patent examiners have a lot on their plates and their units are typically understaffed for the amount of work they handle. When you respond to an examiner, keep the following in mind.

➤ Examiners must process a specific number of patents to be considered productive by their superiors for periodic job performance ratings. The bottom line is that as careful as they try to be, they make mistakes that can be reversed with careful and cogent argument by you as a *pro se* inventor, or together with your attorney.

➤ Your response should address every ground of the objection and/or rejection. Show where the examiner is wrong. The mere allegation that the examiner has erred is not enough. Do not be timid about it if you feel he or she has made a mistake.

➤ Your response will cause the examiner to reconsider, and you will be notified if the claims are rejected, or objections or requirements made, in the same manner as after the first office action examination. This second action usually will be the final one.

➤ If you are a *pro se* inventor, feel free to call your examiner on the telephone to discuss your case. His name and number will be on the office action. I have always found examiners to be most hospitable and helpful.

➤ If you are represented by patent counsel, typically the examiners will not entertain your calls or visits without counsel. This is the way it is. I know that there are good reasons for it, but I am a bit cynical and feel the rule not to see inventors without their lawyers was done to keep the lawyers's revenue stream coming in.

Over the years, I have gone more than a few times to meet with an examiner. My lawyer typically sits there while we make our points. No one is more passionate than the inventor, and who knows the product best? The inventor, of course. But this is the way it is.

➤ Once an examiner refused to allow us to come in alone unless we dismissed our patent attorney. So, I called him up, explained the

Bright Ideas

➤ In 1989, Englishman Tim Berners-Lee invented the World Wide Web, an internet-based hypermedia initiative for global information sharing. He never made money on his invention.

➤ Galileo invented the thermometer in 1593.

problem, and took him off the case. In this instance, we felt confident that we had the argument and saw no reason to pay patent counsel more money for unnecessary meetings. We went. We saw the examiner. And we won the point. Our patent issued. Then we rehired the attorney.

➤ Whether you go alone or with your attorney, don't drop in unannounced. It is to your benefit that the examiner has the time to prepare for your visit and get up to speed on the case. Remember that personal interviews do not remove the necessity for response to USPTO actions within the required time, and the action of the USPTO is based solely on the written record.

Final Rejection

On the second or latter consideration, the rejection of claims may be made final. Your response is then limited to appeal and further amendment is restricted. You may petition the director in the case of objections or requirements not involved in the rejection of any claim. Response to a final rejection must include cancellation of, or appeal from, the rejection of each claim so rejected and, if any claim stands allowed, compliance with any requirement or objection as to its form.

In determining such final rejection, your examiner will repeat or state all grounds of rejection then considered applicable to your claims as stated in the application.

The odds? As in the case of the examination by the USPTO, patents are granted in about two of every three applications filed.

Notable Quotables

"There are certain things that our age needs. It needs, above all, courageous hope and the impulse to creativeness."

—Bertrand Russell, philosopher and mathematician

Amending Your Application

The preceding section referred to amendments to an application. Following are some details concerning amendments:

1. You may amend before or after the first examination and action as specified in the rules, or when and as specifically required by the examiner.

2. After final rejection or action, amendments may be made canceling claims or complying with any requirement of form that has been made, but the admission of any such amendment or its refusal, and any proceedings relative thereto, shall not operate to relieve the application from its condition as subject to appeal or to save it from abandonment.

3. If amendments touching the merits of the application are presented after final rejection, or after appeal has been taken, or when such amendment might not otherwise be proper, they may be admitted upon a showing of good and sufficient reasons why they are necessary and were not earlier presented.

4. No amendment can be made as a matter of right in appealed cases. After decision on appeal, amendments can only be made as provided in the rules.

WACKY PATENTS

Cigarette Ring
Patented February 20, 1936
United States Patent 2,109,609

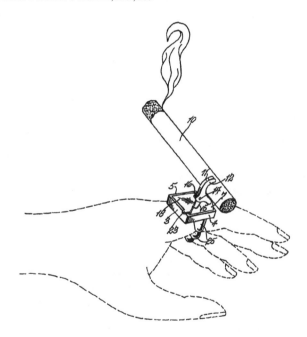

5. The specifications, claims, and drawings must be amended and revised when required to correct inaccuracies of description and definition of unnecessary words and to secure correspondence between the claims, the description, and the drawing.

All amendments of the drawings or specifications, and all additions thereto, must conform to at least one of them as it was at the time of the filing of the application. Matter not found in either, involving a departure from or an addition to the original disclosure, cannot be added to the application even though supported by a supplemental oath or declaration and can be shown or claimed only in a separate application.

Fast Facts

In a patent application, erasures, additions, insertions, or alterations of the papers and records must not be made by you. Amendments are made by filing a paper directing or requesting that specified changes or additions be made. The exact word or words to be stricken from or inserted in the application must be specified and the precise point indicated where the deletion or insertion is to be made. Effective March 1, 2001, there is a new method for making amendments by use of clean replacement paragraphs or sections for amending the specification and clean replacement claims for amending the claims (see 37 CFR 1.121). Now applicants may simply create a clean new version, which can be supplied as the amendment, and use a word processing compare function to create a separate marked up version to indicate the changes being made. The marked up version of the changes to the specification and/or claims must be submitted along with the clean copy of the amendment.

Amendments are "entered" by the patent examiner through the making of proposed deletions by drawing a line in red ink through the word or words canceled and by making the proposed substitutions or insertions in red ink, small insertions being written in at the designated place and larger insertions being indicated by reference.

The claims may be amended by canceling particular claims, by presenting new claims, or by amending the language of particular claims (such amended claims being in effect new claims). In presenting new or amended claims, you must point out how they avoid any reference or ground rejection of record that may be pertinent.

No change in the drawing may be made except by permission of the examiner. Permissible changes in the construction shown in any drawing may be made only by your draftsman or you if you did the drawings. A sketch in permanent ink showing proposed changes to become part of the record, must be filed for approval by the USPTO before the corrections are made. The paper requesting amendments to the drawing should be separate from other papers.

The original numbering of the claims must be preserved throughout the prosecution. When claims are canceled, the remaining claims must not be renumbered. When claims are added by amendment or substituted for canceled claims, they must be numbered consecutively beginning with the number next following the highest numbered claim previously presented. When the application is ready for allowance, the examiner, if necessary, will renumber the claims consecutively in the order in which they appear or in such order as may have been requested by you.

411

The National Institute of Standards and Technology (NIST) conducts and supports scientific and engineering research in disciplines ranging from chemistry and physics to information technology. In carrying out this research, NIST works collaboratively with industry, academia, and government. Research tools developed at NIST—including measurement methods, standards, data, and various technologies—assist industrial, academic, and government scientists worldwide. To help you find the information you need, contact our Public Inquiries office at (301) 975-NIST or inquiries@nist.gov.

Time for Response and Abandonment

The maximum period given for response is six months, but the Director of the Office has the right to shorten the period to no fewer than thirty days. The typical response time allowed to a USPTO action is three months. If you want a longer time, you usually have to pay extra money for an extension. The amount of the fee depends upon the response time desired. If you miss any target date, your application will be abandoned and made no longer pending. However, if you can show whereby your failure to prosecute was unavoidable or unintentional, the application can be revived by filing a petition to the Office of Petitions and including the appropriate fee. The proper response must also accompany the petition if it has not yet been filed.

How to Make Appeals

If the examiner circles his or her wagons and begins to stonewall, there is a higher court. Rejections that have been made final may be appealed to the Board of Patent Appeals and Interferences. This august body is headed by the Chief Administrative Patent Judge and the Vice Chief Administrative Patent Judge. Typically each appeal is heard by only three Administrative Patent Judges. An appeal fee is required, and you must file a brief in support of your position. You can even get an oral hearing if you pay enough.

If the board goes against you, there is yet a higher court, the Court of Appeals for the Federal Circuit. Or you might file a civil action against the Director in the U.S. District Court for the District of Columbia. He won't take it personally; it goes with the territory. The Court of Appeals for the Federal Circuit will review the record made in the USPTO and may affirm or reverse the USPTO's action. In a civil action, you may present testimony in the court, and the court will make a decision.

Bright Ideas

In 1929, David Sarnoff, founder of RCA, asked Russian emigre Vladimir Zworykin, born in Murom, 200 miles east of Moscow, what it would take to develop television for commercial use. "A year and a half and $100,000," he reportedly responded. In reality, it took 20 years and $50 million. Before his death in 1982 at age 92, Zworykin said of his invention: "The technique is wonderful. It is beyond my expectations. But the programs—I would never let my children even come close to this thing."

What Are Interference Proceedings?

Parallel development is a phenomenon that should not be discounted. On numerous occasions a company executive has said to me, "I've seen that concept twice in the last month," or something to this effect. At times, two or more applications may be filed by different inventors claiming substantially the same patentable invention. A patent can only be granted to one of them, and a proceeding known as an "interference" is instituted by the USPTO to determine who the original inventor is, and who is entitled to the patent. About one percent of all applications filed become engaged in an interference proceeding.

Interference proceedings may also be instituted between an application and a patent already issued if the patent has not been issued for more than one year prior to the filing of the conflicting application and if the conflicting application is not barred from being patentable for some other reason.

The priority question is determined by a board of three Administrative Patent Judges on the evidence submitted. From the decision of the Board of Patent Appeals and Interferences, the losing party may appeal to the Court of Appeals for the Federal Circuit or file a civil action against the winning party in the appropriate U.S. district court.

The terms "conception of the invention" and "reduction to practice" are encountered in connection with priority questions. "Conception of the invention" refers to the completion of the devising of the means for accomplishing the result. "Reduction to practice" refers to the actual construction of the invention in physical form. In the case of a machine, it includes the actual building of the machine. In the case of an article or composition, it includes the actual carrying out of the steps in the process; actual operation, demonstration, or testing for the intended use is usually required. The filing of a regular application for patent completely disclosing the invention is treated as equivalent to reduction to practice. The inventor who proves to be the first to conceive the invention and the first to reduce it to practice will be held to be the prior inventor, but more complicated situations cannot be stated this simply.

This is why it is important to have evidence that proves when you first had an idea and when the prototype was made. It is critical that you keep careful and accurate records throughout the development of an idea. The Disclosure Document Program was established by the USPTO for this purpose.

If your utility patent is found to be allowable, a notice of allowance will be sent to you or your attorney. Within three months from the date of the notice you must pay an issue fee.

411

The requirements at the USPTO are subject to change on a frequent basis. It is impossible for most inventors to keep up. Filing an application without sufficient fees may result in the loss of your filing date and/or having to pay a surcharge to reactivate the application. Therefore, before filing any application, to ensure new requirements have not been put into place, and that you are enclosing the proper fee, call (800) 786-9199 or (703) 308-4357 for assistance from Customer Service Representatives or visit the USPTO Web site: www.uspto.gov.

What Rights Does a Patent Give You?

It's a pretty exciting moment when you get your first patent. It comes bound inside a beautiful oyster-white folder that has the U.S. Constitution screened in blue as its background. The large official gold seal of the Patent and Trademark Office is embossed thereon.

Between the covers of that folder is your patent, a grant that gives you, the inventor(s), "the right to exclude others from making, using, or selling the invention throughout the United States" and its territories and possessions for a designated period of time (17 or 20 years, depending on the actions of Congress), subject to the payment of maintenance fees as provided by law. Having a patent does not guarantee your ability nor does it explicitly give you the right to make, use, or sell the invention. Any person is ordinarily free to make, use, or sell anything he or she pleases, and a grant from Uncle Sam is not required. Others may not do so without authorization. You may assign your rights in the invention to another person or company. If you receive a patent for a new concept and the marketing of said concept is prohibited by law, the patent will not help you. Nor may you market said concept if by doing so you infringe on the prior rights of others.

Maintenance Fees

All utility patents that issued from applications filed on or after December 12, 1980, are subject to the payment of maintenance fees that must be paid to keep the patent in force. These fees are due at $3^1/_2$, $7^1/_2$, and $11^1/_2$ years from the date the patent is granted and can be paid without a surcharge during the six-month period preceding each due date. The amounts of the maintenance fees are subject to change every three years.

Be advised that the USPTO does not mail notices to patent owners advising them that a maintenance fee is due. If you have a patent attorney tracking your business, he or she will let you know when the money is due. An attorney gets paid every time your business moves across his or her desk. But if you are doing it by yourself and you miss a payment, it may result in the expiration of the patent. A six-month grace period is provided, during which the maintenance fee may be paid with a surcharge.

Notable Quotables

"Necessity is the mother of invention."

—Roman saying

Can Two People Own a Patent?

Yes. Two or more people may jointly own patents as inventors, investors, or licensees. Most of my patents are joint ownership. Anyone who shares in the ownership of a patent, no matter how small a part they might own, has the right to make, use, or sell it for his or her own profit unless prohibited from doing so by prior agreement. It is accordingly dangerous to assign part interest in a patent of yours without having a definite agreement hammered out vis-à-vis respective rights and obligations to each other.

Can a Patent Be Sold?

Yes. The patent law provides for the transfer or sale of a patent, or of an application for patent, by a contract. When assigned the patent, the assignee becomes the owner of the patent and has rights identical to those of the original patentee.

Assignment of Patent Applications

Should you wish to assign your patent or patent application to a third party (manufacturer, investor, university, employer, etc.), this is possible by filing the appropriate form, Assignment of Patent, or Assignment of Patent Application.

You can sell all or part of the interest in a patent. If you prefer, you could even sell it by geographic region. I consider patents valuable properties, personal assets. Never assume that because you have been unsuccessful in selling a patent, it has no value. You might sell it eventually or find someone infringing it, thus turning it to positive account.

411

If you have been ripped-off by an invention marketing service, the Federal Trade Commission (FTC) has a way for you to file your complaint online. Go to the FTC's Web site www.ftc.gov, and you'll find it under Consumer Protection. While the FTC does not resolve individual consumer problems, your complaint helps investigate fraud and can lead to law enforcement action.

Or you may wish to call toll-free (877) FTC-HELP (382-4357).

Infringement of Patents

Infringement of a patent consists in the unauthorized making, using, or selling of the patented invention within the territory of the United States during the term of the patent. If your patent is infringed—that is, if someone uses it without your permission—it is your right to seek relief in the appropriate federal court.

When I see an apparent infringement of a patent of ours, as has occurred occasionally over the years, the first thing I do is call the company and set up a meeting. I am not litigious. Things can often be worked out between parties. Thus far, I have always been able to do this. Court battles over patents can be long and expensive affairs. Where elephants fight, grass doesn't grow. And, if you want to continue working in your particular field, it is wise to avoid making too many corporate enemies.

Several years ago, I saw an infringement of a patent we hold. One call to the company's president and a quick fax of our patent brought immediate relief in the form of a royalty on all items made to date and in the future. Not only that, but I was invited to submit ideas for licensing consideration.

If your friendly approach is turned away, and you are sure of your position, then the next step is to get a lawyer and decide if a Temporary Restraining Order (TRO) is appropriate. A TRO is an injunction to prevent the continuation of the infringement. You may also ask the court for an award of damages because of the infringement. In such an infringement suit, the defendant may raise the question of the validity of the patent, which is then decided by the court. The defendant may also claim that what is being done does not constitute infringement.

Infringement is determined primarily by the language of the claims of the patent, and if what the defendant is making does not fall within the language of any of the claims of the patent, there is no infringement.

The USPTO has no jurisdiction over questions relating to infringement of patents. In examining applications for patent, no determination is made as to whether the patent-seeking invention infringes any prior patent.

Bright Ideas

In 1926, Alabama-born Waldo Semon, a research chemist at BFGoodrich, Akron, Ohio, put his assigned work aside and tried dissolving polyvinyl chloride (PVC) to create an adhesive for bonding rubber to metal. "People thought of PVC as worthless back then," Semon said. "They'd throw it in the trash." He never created the adhesive, but heating PVC in a solvent at a high boiling point he discovered a substance that was both flexible and elastic. No one knew what to make of it. Today, however, PVC has become the second-best-selling plastic in the world, generating billions of dollars in sales each year.

To Sue or Not to Sue

If you do catch someone infringing your patent, you may decide to sue for damages. This can be a costly exercise. According to Stephen R. May, former manager of Intellectual Property Services Department at Pacific Northwest Laboratory in Richland, Washington, "a full-blown patent lawsuit that actually goes to trial will probably cost a minimum of $75,000 to $100,000, although a very simple case could cost less." In most instances, May reports, the costs can be $250,000 and up.

His advice to inventors: "If you believe someone is infringing your patent, an attorney can draft a 'cease and desist' letter, possibly for as little as a few hundred dollars. This might resolve the matter if the infringer ceases, but in many cases it does not."

The expensive part of any lawsuit is "discovery," in which you and the infringer exchange documents and take depositions of potential witnesses. The photocopying bill alone could run into the thousands of dollars and the process could last anywhere from six months to several years. Trials tend to run from one to six weeks with decisions rendered in a matter of days in the case of a jury, or as long as several months if the verdict is by a judge. If you lose, appeals take more time and money.

Each time I get involved with a lawyer to defend a patent or trademark, money seems to disappear from my bank account. So, it's best if you can work things out between yourself and the infringer and not hire counsel. Both sides benefit. If you need to hire a lawyer, you may wish to try for a contingency deal, i.e. where the lawyer takes a third of any recovery instead of charging you.

Fast Facts

Rod G. Martin, inventor of the foam helicoid football, offered to license nonexclusive rights to manufacture his proprietary football design to Marvlee, which was found making it without permission. Marvlee declined. So, the inventor took Marvlee to court for patent infringement.

Federal Judge James Ware ruled that Marvlee's grooved foam footballs, Pro Bullet, Mini Pro Bullet, Rock Pro Bullet, and Pocket Rocket, infringed Martin's U.S. patent. The judge awarded damages of $282,183 plus interest. Finding the infringement to have been willful, Ware added Martin's legal fees. The total judgment against Marvlee came to $1.23 million.

The suit to safeguard his intellectual property would never have come to pass had Marvlee agreed to pay Martin a fair royalty. Martin licensed seven different manufacturers.

Patent Enforcement Insurance

The only right a patent gives the inventor is the right to defend it in a court of law. And, as mentioned above, patent infringement litigation can be costly. How much? Ask Diane B. Loisel, a nurse from Bowie, Maryland. After obtaining a patent for a cap she had invented for use in neonatal respiratory therapy, she claimed that a company to whom she had presented the concept had begun to manufacture and market it without her permission.

Loisel was told by her patent attorney that to litigate would cost her $250,000 in legal fees. "If you're going to get a patent, you're going to have to fight," her lawyer had told her previously. "But he never told me it would cost so much money," she said.

To help inventors shoulder the risk and responsibility for enforcing their patents against infringers, there are insurance companies that market policies designed to reimburse the litigation expenses incurred by a patent owner in enforcing his or her U.S. patents.

Patent attorney Robert W. Faris, a partner in Nixon & Venderhye of Arlington, Virginia, says of this kind of policy, "One of the downsides of this type of insurance is that the insurance company is reimbursed for its expenses out of the settlement or judgment. This means that if the recovery is on the order of the legal expenses incurred for the litigation, the patent owner could come away with practically no financial recovery although his patent rights will have been vindicated."

Faris adds that the program seems pretty risky for the insurance company. "I don't know how they are able to predict with any certainty what the risks would be beforehand. They would have to be only taking on patents whose chances for infringement are very remote."

One such company permits its insured to choose patent counsel. However, before the company will open the tap and start paying bills, the policy holder must provide a written opinion from his or her attorney attesting to the fact that the matter is one that can be litigated and the policy holder must show proof that the alleged infringement will cause economic damage.

Would Faris recommend patent infringement insurance? "I might well recommend that certain clients look into it because it is the only way some small businesses might be able to enforce their patent rights," he concludes.

He points out that patent infringement insurance does not cover the inventor should his or her U.S. patent infringe an existing patent. In other words, it could protect you (the inventor) from someone infringing your patent but is of no help to you if your patent infringes the patent of another inventor.

Take My Words for It

X: The spot on a licensing agreement where the inventor signs.

Fast Facts

On March 2, 1861, the fee for obtaining patent protection became $35, of which $15 is to be paid at the time of application, and $20 when the patent issues. Today in 2002, the Basic Filing fee (Utility) is $710, or $355 for the independent inventor. This spans 141 years.

Abandonment of Patents

There are two kinds of abandonment: intentional (you let it lapse) and unintentional (due to circumstances beyond your control). If the reason for abandonment is your fault, for example, you simply lost track of dates and missed a deadline, then you must pay the due fee plus a penalty for your mistake. A costly error! Check the USPTO Web site for the latest fee schedule: www.uspto.gov

If your reason is unintentional, for example, you claim to never have received the notice from the USPTO, then you must pay to have your petition considered plus you still have to pay the required fee. You may wish to add a notarized letter to the form explaining your story in detail.

I was involved once in a case that involved the USPTO putting the wrong zip code on our paperwork, an error that caused a one-month delay, and ultimately resulted in our getting slapped with abandonment papers.

WACKY PATENTS

Bowel Movement Energizer System
Patented October 4, 1977
United States Patent 4,051,560

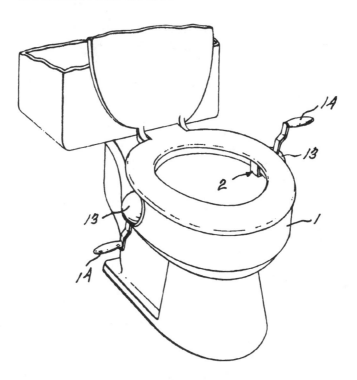

I was able to cure this with a phone call to a senior USPTO official. It was an open-and-shut case, as far as he was concerned. Upon seeing proof of the typo, he personally ordered the abandonment to be withdrawn. We never even had to pay the petition fees; there was just no question about who was wrong.

If you have any questions about how to handle a petition, do not hesitate to call the USPTO at (703) 557-4282 for the latest information. I have had occasion to revive patents and the folks who answer this line are extremely helpful.

Mail petitions for revival to: Director, Patent and Trademark Office, Box DAC, Washington, D.C. 20231. It is a good idea to log all your USPTO correspondence in and out of your office. This will help you keep track of deadlines as well as give you a record of paper flow. Losing paperwork or missing a deadline can be both costly and time-consuming.

The Least You Need to Know

➤ A missed deadline can cause major problems.

➤ If at first you don't succeed, you have options.

➤ Patent examiners are human. They err.

➤ The USPTO is classified as a friendly port.

➤ The written word lives. The spoken word dies.

Part 5

People Who Share, People Who Dare

It has been rumored that at the end of every rainbow there is a pot of gold. Well, it is no different as you approach Part 5. This is your last stop before the appendixes, and it is only fitting that it contains maps to some pots of gold.

In Chapter 19, you'll learn about grants of money you may qualify for if your invention meets certain criteria of the federal government. If you do not qualify for or need such financing, you may be able to benefit from access to Uncle Sam's extensive patent portfolio and/or collaborative R&D opportunities.

One of the last frontiers for the entrepreneurial inventor is the toy industry (including games), and in Chapter 20, you'll learn all about it and what it offers. Cabbage Patch Kids, Candyland, Clue, Etch-a-Sketch, Furby, GI Joe, Micro Machines, Mr. Potato Head, Monopoly, Nerf, Risk, Scrabble, Super Soaker, Teenage Mutant Ninja Turtles, Tickle Me Elmo!, Trivial Pursuit, Twister, and UNO are just a few of the products that were licensed from independent inventors.

It is only appropriate that the final treasure in this book be the friendship of other inventors. To help you meet men and women who share your passion for invention, Chapter 21 opens the world of inventor organizations and associations—local, regional, and national.

I hope you've enjoyed the journey, found it worthwhile, at times entertaining, and even inspirational. Most importantly, I hope you now see that the success you so dearly crave is the by-product of seemingly endless radical factors that must all coalesce within a certain time frame, and with a method madness. There is no easy answer, no easy way. But if you combine what you have learned with a truly innovative concept and add a dash of your own individuality, you will position yourself for cashing in on your inventions.

Chapter 19

Hidden Treasures in Uncle Sam's High-Tech Closets

In This Chapter

➤ NIST—100 years old and going strong

➤ Financial support for enabling technologies

➤ Manufacturing extension partnerships

➤ Federal labs—open for your business

➤ Grants for energy saving inventions: $40,000–$200,000

➤ Grants from SBA: $100,000–$500,000

"The federal government's R&D laboratories, formerly a closed universe of expertise, are aggressively seeking commercial partnerships that further their newly expanded missions. They're out to demonstrate that technology transfer is a two-way street."

—Paul Harris, Founding Publisher, *Technology Business* magazine

There are numerous federal programs available to you, and the NIH (Not Invented Here) Syndrome does not apply. It's amazing how many opportunities exist to blend government resources with your ingenuity.

411

Universities have lots of technology available, too. And here's how to find it: Try the Association of University Technology Managers, a nonprofit organization with membership of more than 2,300 technology managers and business executives who manage intellectual property. AUTM's members represent over 300 universities, research institutions, teaching hospitals, and a similar number of companies and government organizations. Visit AUTM's Web site at http://www.autm.net/index_n4.html.

Notable Quotables

"Creativity often consists of merely turning up what is already there. Did you know that right and left shoes were thought up only a little more than a century ago?"

—Bernice Fitz-Gibbon, inductee, Copywriters' Hall of Fame

The following are those programs that I feel hold the most potential benefit to you as an independent inventor if certain criteria are met. The programs range from financial grants to technology transfer. Let me remind you that government programs involve all kinds of paperwork and red tape. However, if you are able to tolerate working with a large bureaucracy and dealing with its frequent dynamic inaction, one of these programs may hold rewards for you.

National Institute of Standards and Technology

Now celebrating 100 years of service to the nation, the National Institute of Standards and Technology (NIST) is a nonregulatory federal agency within the Commerce Department's Technology Administration. The mission of NIST is to promote economic growth by working with industry to develop and apply technology, measurements, and standards. NIST carries out its mission, in part, through these interwoven programs: NIST Laboratories, Manufacturing Extension Partnership, and Advanced Technology Program.

NIST has an operating budget of about $720 million and is based primarily in two locations: Gaithersburg, Maryland (headquarters—234 hectare/578 acre campus), and Boulder, Colorado (84 hectare/208 acre campus). NIST employs more than 3,200 scientists, engineers, technicians, business specialists, and administrative personnel. About 1,600 guest researchers complement the staff. In addition, NIST partners with 2,000 manufacturing specialists and staff at affiliated centers around the country.

NIST laboratories perform research across a wide range of disciplines, affecting virtually every industry. Primary fields of research include chemical science and technology, physics, material science and engineering, electronics and electrical engineering, manufacturing engineering, computer systems, building technology, fire safety, computing, and applied mathematics.

Reflecting its role as the only federal laboratory exclusively dedicated to serving the needs of U.S. industry, NIST offers more than 300 types of calibrations, 1,000 standard reference materials for calibrating instruments and evaluating test methods, 24 standard reference data centers, laboratory accreditation programs, and free evaluation of energy-related inventions.

To contact NIST with general inquiries about its programs, call: (301) 975-3058; or write via e-mail to inquiries@nist.gov. The NIST Web site is: www.nist.gov.

Grants and awards supporting research at industry, academic, and other institutions are available on a competitive basis through several different Institute offices. For general information on NIST grants programs, contact Joyce Brigham, (301) 975-6329.

Advanced Technology Program (ATP)

NIST's ATP is a competitive program that provides partial ("cost-shared") funding for industrial research that is considered too high-risk for conventional funding (such as from venture capitalists), but that has the potential to spark important economic benefits for the nation. While it does not fund product development, it does support enabling technologies that are essential to the development of new products, processes, and services across diverse application areas. Private industry bears the costs of product development, production, marketing, sales, and distribution.

The Advanced Technology Program provides multiyear co-funding for high-risk, high-payoff civilian technology development by individual companies and industry-led joint ventures. Contact: (800)-ATP-FUND (800-287-3863).

Detailed information is on the Web at www. atp.nist.gov.

Notable Quotables

"Inventing is not a get rich quick business. Many aspiring inventors fail in this business, and most of those who do succeed take five to ten years to make significant income from their invention. The business is a minefield fraught with pitfalls. Knowledge of many fields is necessary to successfully navigate that minefield. For new inventors invention promoters are the biggest risk. For inventors who have created a market, asset thieves then become the biggest risk."

—Ronald J. Riley, Executive Director, InventorEd, Inc.

WACKY PATENTS

Wing Apparatus for Skiers
Patented July 12, 1988
United States Patent 4,756,555

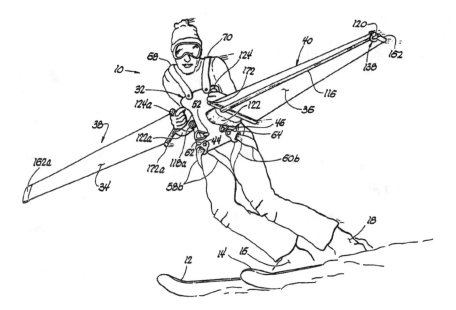

Partnerships

The ATP partners with companies of all sizes, universities and nonprofits, encouraging them to take on greater technical challenges with potentially large benefits that extend well beyond the innovators—challenges they could not or would not do alone. For smaller, start-up firms, early support from the ATP can spell the difference between success and failure. To date, more than half of the ATP awards have gone to individual small businesses or to joint ventures led by a small business. Large firms can work with the ATP, especially in joint ventures, to develop critical, high-risk technologies that would be difficult for any one company to justify because, for example, the benefits spread across the industry as a whole.

Portfolio

The ATP portfolio is highly diversified. The 562 projects to date selected in the first 30 competitions span a broad array of key technologies, with particular concentrations in information technology, biotechnology, electronics, advanced materials, and manufacturing. These awards represent a potential investment of $3.3 billion shared almost equally by industry and ATP. More than 800 companies, universities, independent nonprofit research organizations, and government laboratories have participated in ATP projects. Several hundred additional organizations have participated as subcontractors and strategic partners. Well over half (59 percent) of the awards were made to small businesses or to joint ventures led by a small business.

Proposals

The ATP accepts project proposals only in response to specific, published solicitations. Notices of ATP competitions are published in *Commerce Business Daily*. You may request to be placed on a mailing list (or e-mail list) to receive notification of ATP competitions and other events by calling the ATP automated hotline (1-800-ATP-FUND or 1-800-287-3863) or by sending an e-mail to atp@nist.gov.

The ATP Proposal Preparation Kit may be requested at any time. In addition to the necessary application forms, the kit includes a thorough discussion of ATP goals and procedures as well as useful guidance in the preparation of a proposal. Notices of ongoing competitions, upcoming events, ATP research papers, and descriptions of ongoing and completed ATP projects may be found on the program's Web site.

Here are some Advanced Technology Programs that award grants. Take a look and see if your invention falls within one of these protocols. If it does, pick up the phone and see what's involved by calling one of the contact people listed.

➤ **Critical Infrastructure Protection Grants Program.** This funding is to support research aimed at resolving infrastructure IT security issues relating to civilian, government, and commercial systems. Contact: Donald Marks, (301) 975-5342.

➤ **Fire Research Grants.** These grants pay to sponsor research by academic institutions, nonfederal government agencies, and independent and industrial laboratories that support NIST's fire research laboratory programs. Contact: Sonya Parham, (301) 975-6854.

➤ **Precision Measurement Grants.** This program supports researchers in U.S. colleges and universities for experimental and theoretical studies of fundamental physical phenomena. Contact: Peter Mohr, (301) 975-3217.

➤ **Small Business Innovation Research Program (SBIR).** These NIST grants are for small business research and development efforts that fall within areas recommended yearly by the U.S. Department of Commerce. Contact: Linda Keyes, (301) 975-3085.

➤ **Materials Science and Engineering Grants.** These grants support work in polymers, ceramics, metallurgy, and neutron scattering and spectroscopy research at academic,

Take My Words for It

Mechanical advantage: The ratio of the force exerted by a machine to the force applied to the machine.

industrial, and other nonfederal institutions. Subject to funding availability. Contact: Marlene Taylor, (301) 975-5653.

Manufacturing Extension Partnership (MEP)

Here is another NIST program that may interest you if you want to manufacture and market your invention.

The NIST Manufacturing Extension Partnership is a nationwide network of 400 manufacturing extension centers and field offices providing a wide variety of expertise and services to small manufacturers (under 500 employees) in all 50 states and Puerto Rico. Increasingly, MEP is being viewed as a strategic, long-term partner that can help small manufacturers not only resolve their problems but can also help them transform into high-performance, world-class enterprises.

While part of a national network, each NIST MEP center works directly with area firms to provide expertise and services tailored to their most critical needs, which range from process improvements and worker training to business practices and applications of information technology. Solutions are offered through a combination of direct assistance from center staff and work with outside consultants. NIST MEP centers are staffed by knowledgeable manufacturing engineers and business specialists who typically have years of practical experience gained from working on the manufacturing floor, managing plant operations, or both. NIST MEP center staff also know the local business community and the available local resources and can access additional resources available through the NIST MEP network. As a result, centers help small firms to overcome barriers in locating and obtaining private-sector resources.

NIST MEP centers work with companies that are willing to invest time, money, and/or human resources to improve their businesses. Typical clients include manufacturers who ...

➤ Have been unable to locate the proper resources or technologies they need.

➤ Want expert, impartial advice in helping them evaluate alternative solutions.

➤ Need help solving a specific problem, such as determining the cause of product defects, modifying plant layout to improve workflow, or establishing employee training.

➤ Want assistance in reversing negative business situations—such as sales decreases, loss of market share, or cost increases.

Fast Facts

In calendar year 2000, the U.S. Patent and Trademark Office granted a record number of patent documents, including 157,497 utility, 17,414 design, 548 plant, and 524 reissue patents, and 104 statutory invention registrations, for a total of 176,087 patent documents for the year.

➤ Want to implement new technologies or processes that will help establish them as market leaders.

➤ Seek to improve their ongoing business operations for peak performance.

MEP has proven to be highly effective in helping America's small manufacturers improve their competitiveness. In a recent survey, about 3,000 clients reported that as a result of MEP services, they …

➤ Increased or retained $1.4 billion in sales.

➤ Realized $364 million in cost savings.

➤ Invested $576 million in modernization, including plant facilities and equipment, information systems, and workforce and training.

➤ Created 5,796 jobs and retained 12,357 jobs.

For general inquiries about MEP, call: (301) 975-5020 or (800) MEP-4MFG. The MEP Web site is http://www.mep.nist.gov.

Bright Ideas

J. B. Dunlop, one inventor of the pneumatic tire, was a veterinary surgeon.

In Search of Innovation at USG Labs

I have never applied for R&D funds from the federal government, but I have personally visited many government laboratories in search of new technologies, gizmos, and widgets that I could apply to my concepts. You have heard many of the laboratory names—e.g., Argonne, Fermi, Lawrence Berkeley, Lawrence Livermore, Los Alamos, Oak Ridge, and Sandia.

I recall visiting Los Alamos National Laboratory in New Mexico a few years ago and being told that a team from Hasbro had just been there a day earlier. We were both looking into Nitonol (a.k.a. shape memory alloy).

Open for "Your" Business

Other federally funded research and development centers are open to you as well. Here is a partial list. Each center has its own Web site through which you can pull full details about their programs. A great way to reach them is via Consumer.gov—a "one-stop" Internet link to a broad range of federal information resources available online.

Department of Defense

➤ Institute of Defense Analysis (Alexandria, VA)

➤ Logistics Management Institute (Bethesda, MD)

➤ National Defense Research Institute (Santa Monica, CA)

➤ Software Engineering Institute (Pittsburgh, PA)

➤ Center for Naval Analyses (Alexandria, VA)

➤ Lincoln Laboratory (Lexington, MA)

➤ Aerospace Corporation (El Segundo, CA)

➤ Project Air Force (Santa Monica, CA)

➤ Arroyo Center (Santa Monica, CA)

National Aeronautics and Space Administration

➤ Jet Propulsion Laboratory (Pasadena, CA)

Department of Health and Human Services

➤ NCI Frederick Cancer Research and Development Center, (Frederick, MD)

411

The following Web sites are among the best about inventors and invention:

http://memory.loc.gov/ammem/hhhtml/hhhome.html

http://www.nps.gov/edis/home.htm

http://www.cbc4kids.ca/general/the-lab/history-of-invention/default.html

http://web.mit.edu/invent/

http://mustang.coled.umn.edu/inventing/Inventing.html

http://www.nationalgeographic.com/features/96/inventions/

http://www.inventornet.com/

http://www.uspto.gov/go/kids/

http://colitz.com/site/wacky.htm

National Science Foundation

➤ National Astronomy & Ionosphere Center (Areolbo, PR)

➤ National Center for Atmospheric Research (Boulder, CO)

➤ National Optical Astronomy Observatories (Tucson, AZ)

➤ National Radio Astronomy Observatory (Green Bank, WV)

Knocking around in this chapter, you may find money for your R&D or a home for your invention with the help of an agency or department of the federal government. For example, at the Department of Energy there are people always on the lookout for energy-saving processes and devices. Some concepts in use today might otherwise never have been commercialized had it not been for the assistance of DOE.

Department of Energy

We now move from the NIST campus in Gaithersburg, Maryland, to the Forrestal Building, 1000 Independence Avenue SW, Washington, D.C., home to the Department of Energy (DOE). The U.S government, as represented by DOE, owns title to approximately 1500 active U.S. patented inventions and, in some cases, foreign counterparts; though, according to DOE patent counsel Robert J. Marchick, this number is dwindling as the federal labs seek to control their own ip.

Generally, these patents are available for license to you if you can show a satisfactory plan for commercial use of the invention. Licenses are generally for royalties and other fees and may be nonexclusive or exclusive, with or without field-of-use restriction. Exclusive licenses require a determination, after public notice and opportunity for comment, that the invention is not likely to be commercialized on a nonexclusive basis. Technical assistance from the laboratory where the invention arose may be available.

As I said, a significant number of inventions made at DOE laboratories are owned and licensed directly by the various laboratories. Many of these inventions are included in the DOE patent databases. For further information on possible licensing of these inventions, you may contact the appropriate business contact at the particular DOE laboratory.

If you want to know what's available in patents owned by DOE, contact Robert J. Marchick, patent attorney, USDOE. His mailing address is: U.S. Department of Energy, Washington, D.C. 20585; E-mail. Robert.marchick@hq.doe.gov. Tel: 202-586-4792.

Office of Industrial Technologies (OIT)

DOE's Office of Industrial Technologies (OIT) is mandated to develop and deliver advanced energy efficiency, renewable energy, and pollution prevention technologies for application in the U.S. industrial sector. OIT partners with industry and government, and nongovernmental organizations, including independent inventors, with the goal of significantly improving the resource efficiency and competitiveness of materials and process industries. OIT is part of the Department of Energy's Office of Energy Efficiency and Renewable Energy.

Take My Words for It

Wish List: A list provided by a manufacturer to an inventor that outlines the products the manufacturer would like to consider for licensing.

OIT is helping industry identify and pursue technology needs through public/private sector partnerships. OIT has initiated Industries of the Future, a customer-driven strategy to encourage energy- and resource-intensive industries to work together to …

➤ Create broad, industry-wide goals for the future.

➤ Identify specific needs and priorities through industry-led roadmaps.

➤ Form cooperative alliances to help attain those goals through technology partnerships.

OIT enables nine energy-intensive U.S. industries to determine their collective technology and other needs for tomorrow through its widely acclaimed "Industries of the Future" strategy. This strategy ensures that Federal R&D and other resources are aligned with industry priorities. The industries are …

1. Agriculture.
2. Aluminum.
3. Chemicals.
4. Forest Products.
5. Glass.
6. Metal Casting.
7. Mining.
8. Petroleum.
9. Steel.

OIT Success Stories

I asked the folks at the Office of Industrial Technologies for some examples of success stories and, voilà, here they are. I hope one day your story can be written.

➤ Ken Smedberg, co-inventor of an aerocylinder that prevents air loss common to conventional air cylinders, says without DOE funds "the opportunity would have passed us by." His invention received a grant award of $99,997 from DOE's

Inventions and Innovations Program. DOE reports that the new Areocylinder is helping one large U.S. car manufacturer save approximately $200,000 per year by eliminating compressed air leakage (Hssssssssss) on seven stamping presses.

➤ With the help of nearly $100,000 from DOE's Inventions and Innovations Program, Tom Dinwoodie, CEO and president, PowerLight Corporation, says that the grant enabled the company to perform wind tunnel testing at a critical early period in product validation. "To raise money for testing at this stage might otherwise have been impossible," he says.

"Our WeldComputer TM systems were sold primarily to the aerospace and defense industries. Now, with help from INI program, we have expanded our product line so that half of our sales are to general commercial industries," says inventor Dennis Hull, COO, WeldComputer Corporation.

Be Nice and Maybe You'll Get a Grant

The U.S. Department of Energy also sponsors an innovative, cost-sharing program to promote energy efficiency, clean production, and economic competitiveness in industry. The grant program, known as NICE3, provides funding to state and private industry partnerships (large and small business) for projects that develop and demonstrate advances in energy efficiency and clean production technologies. You are a small business!

Your project proposal application must be submitted through a state energy, pollution prevention, or business development office. State and Industry partnerships are eligible to receive a one-time grant of up to $525,000. The industrial partner may receive a maximum of $500,000 in federal funding. Nonfederal cost share must be at least 50 percent of the total cost of the project.

In total, NICE3 has sponsored 91 projects, with more than half going to small businesses. NICE3 has leveraged $26.3 million in federal funds, with $81.8 million in state and industry funds since 1991.

Fast Facts

Circa 1810, the U.S. Patent Office was located in Washington's Blodgett's Hotel. Patent models were on public display there until 1836, when the hotel and all the models were destroyed by fire.

411

The Intellectual Property Office of Singapore hosts one of the most informative ip Web sites I have seen from any government. It is well worth a visit. http://www.surfip.gov.sg/.

Basic information on financial assistance available through the Office of Industrial Technologies (OIT) Inventions and Innovation (I&I) grant program, the National Industrial.

Competitiveness through Energy, Environment, and Economics (NICE3) grant program, are readily available through the following Web site: www.oit.doe.gov/inventions. This information will also help you determine if these programs are applicable to you or your business.

DOE's Inventions and Innovation (I&I) Program

The Inventions and Innovation (I&I) program provides financial assistance at two levels—up to $40,000 (Category 1) or up to $200,000 (Category 2)—for conducting early development and establishing technical performance of innovative, energy-saving ideas and inventions.

The Category 1 portion of the program will fund up to $40,000 for conceptual ideas. Category 1 applications industrial in nature will be restricted to specific topics considered priorities by DOE. The topic areas for Category 1 industrial applications follow the Office of Industrial Technologies focus industries: Agriculture (bio-based products), Aluminum, Chemicals, Forest Products, Glass, Metalcasting, Mining, Petroleum, and Steel industries.

Specific topic areas accepted under each year's solicitation are listed in the solicitation. To get a current solicitation, go to Web site: www.oit.doe.gov/inventions/grant/apply/apply.shtml or call: 1-202-586-2079.

The Category 2 portion will fund up to $200,000 for more well-developed inventions moving toward prototype development or commercialization. At a minimum, engineering analysis and/or a bench scale model must be complete for an invention to be considered a Category 2 application. The Category 2 competition will be more general in nature, accepting technologies within the areas of industry, power, transportation, or buildings. However, there is a particular interest in projects within the Office of Industrial Technologies focus industries.

To determine the category appropriate for your invention, please refer to the Stages of Development guideline.

Inventions and Innovation grants are open to U.S. citizens—either native-born or naturalized—small businesses that are U.S. owned or institutions of higher learning located in the U.S. Special consideration is given to individual inventors and small businesses. In addition to financial assistance, this program offers technical guidance and commercialization support to successful applicants.

Notable Quotables

"Practice is just as valuable as a sale. The sale will make you a living; the skill will make you a fortune."

—Jim Rohn, business philosopher

Here are the stages in the Inventions and Innovation grant process:

Stage 1—Conceptual: This is the period during which a concept is scientifically proven or is shown to be potentially valid by the application of a test-of-principle model. The objective of this stage is to validate through tests or analyses the performance and implementation potential of a concept.

Stage 2—Technical Feasibility: This is the period during which it is proven possible within the technological state of the art to produce a new product or develop a process from the concept. The objective here is to confirm the target performance of the new product through experimentation and/or accepted engineering analysis and to ascertain that there are no technical or economic barriers to implementation that cannot be overcome by development.

Stage 3—Development: This is the period during which the needed improvements in materials, processes, and design are made and during which the product is tested and proven to be commercially producible. The objective is to make the needed improvements in materials, designs, and processes and to confirm that the product will perform as specified by constructing and testing engineering prototypes or pilot processes.

Stage 4—Commercial Validation: This is the period during which a product or process is prepared for introduction into the marketplace. The objective is to demonstrate the manufacturing techniques and establish test market validity of the new product or introduction of a new process in a system.

Bright Ideas

Twister, the first game that required people to use their bodies as playing pieces, has been played by an estimated 65 million people around the world. Twister actually grew out of a project inventor Reyn Guyer was working on for his father's design company. While trying to develop a promotion for Johnson's shoe polish, it occurred to Guyer that a polka dot paper mat he'd just created might better serve as a game, and Twister was born.

411

NASA Goddard Space Flight Center has expertise in sensors and detectors, guidance, navigation, and control systems and optics. Call its Technology Transfer Office if you have an Earth application for a NASA technology at (301) 286-0561.

Notable Achievements

How successful has DOE's Invention and Innovation Program been? I am confident you'll find the results impressive, too.

➤ More than 500 inventions have received financial support from DOE, with nearly 25 percent reaching the marketplace.

➤ Cumulative sales have reached nearly $710 million.

Small Business Administration

Finally, let us consider the U.S. Small Business Administration (SBA). It was created by Congress in 1953 to help America's entrepreneurs form successful small enterprises. Last year, the SBA offered management and technical assistance to more than one million small business owners.

America's 25 million small businesses, the backbone of our economy, employ more than 50 percent of the private work force, generate more than half of the nation's gross domestic product, and are the principal source of new jobs.

As an independent inventor, you are a small business whether you market your concept or license it to a large manufacturer. As a small business owner and operator, you must know how to manage and finance your enterprises. This is where the SBA may be of assistance, in addition to SBIR (see below).

Through workshops, individual counseling, publications, and videotapes, the SBA helps entrepreneurs understand and meet the challenges of operating businesses— challenges like financing, marketing, and management.

There are two programs that the SBA administers that could be useful to you: SBIR and STTR.

Small Business Innovation Research (SBIR) Program

In 1982, Congress passed the Small Business Innovation Development Act creating the federal Small Business Innovation Research (SBIR) Program. The purpose of the program is to increase the opportunity for small firms to participate in federal research and development. In addition to encouraging the participation of small businesses, the program is designed to stimulate the conversion of research findings into commercial application.

The Act designated the Small Business Administration (SBA) to run the program, govern its policy, monitor its progress, and analyze its results. The SBIR grant program has awarded over $9.5 billion since it began in 1982.

288

WACKY PATENTS

Combined Golf Club and Ball Retriever
Patented December 21, 1965
United States Patent 3,224,781

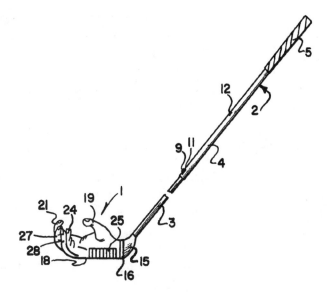

Ten federal agencies with an extramural budget for research or research and development that exceed $100 million annually presently participate in the SBIR Program. They are ...

➤ Department of Agriculture

➤ Department of Commerce

➤ Department of Defense

➤ Department of Education

➤ Department of Energy

➤ Department of Health and Human Services

➤ Department of Transportation

➤ Environmental Protection Agency

➤ National Aeronautics & Space Administration

➤ National Science Foundation

How SBIR Works

Under the SBIR Program, the involved federal agencies request highly competitive proposals from small businesses in response to solicitations outlining their R&D requirements. After evaluating the proposals, each agency awards funding agreements for determining the technical feasibility of the research and development concepts proposed. These awards are as follows …

Phase I. Awards up to $100,000 are made for research projects to evaluate the scientific and technical merit and feasibility of an idea. Time frame: six months. Two-thirds of this work must be done by the small business.

Let's say that you have an idea for a device that could, if successful, solve a problem posed by one of the SBIR agencies. There just might be $100,000 in the agency's budget to help you prove out the concept.

Phase II. The Phase 1 projects with the most potential are funded to further develop the proposed idea for up to two years. Phase II awards can be as high as $750,000. Time frame: two years, and this can be exceeded with justification. One half of this work must be done by the small business. In other words, if you need help from a larger partner, you can seek it.

If you are successful in realizing the first stage of your R&D effort, and the sponsoring agency thinks you are onto something, you just might qualify for Phase II funding.

Phase III. Once you get into the final stage, or the commercialization process, there are no more federal SBIR funds available.

At this point, the federal government encourages you to raise private sector investment or to license your innovation. While the government may extend follow-up production contracts for your technology, it no longer wants to be your partner. Ideally, the federal seed money has been enough to get you off the ground.

Notable Quotables

"Companies that are open to new ideas and are prepared to trade, sell, and buy technology assets from others in a fluid way are in a better position to take advantage of the changing weather and circumstances in their ip gardens."

—Edward Kahn, president, EKMS

State-Supported SBIR Programs

State governments, anxious to build their own industrial bases, have actively supported the SBIR Program by (1) promoting SBIR to small businesses, (2) providing information and technical assistance to SBIR applicants, (3) providing matching funds to SBIR Phase I and II recipients, and (4) helping firms to obtain Phase III funding from both private and state sources.

Why do the states do this? They see independent inventors and small businesses as a good investment because chances are technologies developed in a particular state will stay in the state once commercialized. Innovation leads to hard goods, goods create jobs, jobs employ people, people pay taxes, and so forth.

Bright Ideas

View-Master was the brainchild of William Gruber, a piano tuner by trade and a stereo photographer by hobby. Mr. Gruber's idea was to use color transparency movie film in a hand-held viewing device that contained two eyepieces. This would help the observer combine the images of two photographs, taken from slightly different points of view, into one full-color-three dimensional picture. The type of photography used to shoot such striking images was, and is still, called Stereo Photography.

Each agency listed above has an SBIR office. If you would like to know about SBIR at a particular agency or be put on the mailing lists for SBIR solicitation, contact the appropriate office or go in through the agency Web site. To get on Alert List, go to this Web site: http://sbir.er.doe.gov/sbir/About/about_sbir.htm.

Scoring and Selection Process

Let's take a close look at one SBIR program. DOE uses three evaluation criteria for SBIR grant applications:

1. Strength of the scientific/technical approach.
2. Ability to carry out the project in a cost-effective manner.
3. Impact. Each is defined in the solicitation and carries equal weight.

Your grant application is considered for funding if, based on comments from expert technical reviewers, it …

Notable Quotables

"Mr. Watson, come here, I want you."

—Alexander Graham Bell (to his assistant. These were the first intelligible words transmitted by telephone.)

1. Has no reservations with respect to any of the criteria.

2. Strongly endorses the grant application with respect to at least two of the three criteria.

SBIR Success Stories

We are all inspired by success stories, so here are some from the SBIR program. These are just the tip of the iceberg. SBIR is a very popular and effective federal program.

➤ NASA gave Electronic Imagery, Inc. $486,600 for work on high-definition full-color virtual image processing.

➤ The U.S. Army awarded $48,488 to Coleman Research Corp. for its work on indirect fire weapon simulation.

➤ The Department of Agriculture funded Artificial Intelligence Atlanta, Inc. $49,963 for a system for forest fire detection.

➤ Health and Human Services paid Martek Corp. $49,920 for a new source of arachidonic acid for infant formula.

➤ NSF awarded 3Dgeo Development, Inc. $100,000 to develop its computation of three-dimensional travel times for seismic prospecting via the Fast Marc.

➤ HHS awarded Acacia Biosciences, Inc. $100,000 for the development of a novel antifungal drug discovery tool.

Fast Facts

In 2000, the share of all patents issued to U.S. resident inventors was 55.1 percent, down from the 55.6 percent U.S. share for 1999. California-resident inventors claimed a 20.5 percent share (19,845 patents) of these U.S.-resident inventor patents, followed by resident inventors from New York (7.3 percent, 7,036 patents), Texas (7.0 percent, 6,789 patents), Illinois (4.7 percent, 4,514 patents), and New Jersey (4.5 percent, 4,399 patents). U.S. resident inventors of the following areas had large percentage increases in patent receipts from 1999 to 2000: Nebraska, North Dakota, Idaho, South Dakota, Wyoming, and Vermont.

If you'd like to see more of the award winners, to have a better idea if you would qualify, go to the following Web site: www.sba.gov/sbir/library.html and click on "SBIR/STTR Annual Awards."

For specific information on SBIR programs, call 1-800-827-5722. This number will connect you with the SBA's Small Business Answer Desk.

Small Business Technology Transfer (STTR) Program

There is another competitive SBA program that you may wish to consider: the Small Business Technology Transfer (STTR) program.

The main difference between SBIR and STTR is that all research and development in the STTR pilot program must be conducted jointly by the small business (that's you!) and a nonprofit research institution. Not less than 40 percent of the work conducted under an STTR program award is to be performed by the small business concern and not less than 30 percent of the work is to be performed by the nonprofit research institution.

Phase I. Awards may be as much as $100,000 for up to a one-year effort.

Phase II. Awards may be as high as $500,000 for a two-year effort.

Five federal agencies with an extramural budget for research or research and development presently participate in the STTR Program. They are ...

➤ Department of Defense.

➤ Department of Energy.

➤ Department of Health and Human Services.

➤ National Aeronautics & Space Administration.

➤ National Science Foundation.

Notable Quotables

"There is always an easy solution to every human problem—neat, plausible, and wrong."

—H. L. Mencken, reporter, influential American literary critic.

The FY 2001 budget is expected to be about $5 million.

Federally Funded Research and Development Centers (FFRDC'S)

Each of the following R&D centers is supported primarily by Uncle Sam. To receive STTR solicitations, contact the participating agency and brochures and forms will be sent to you; or make your request via the following Web site: www.sba.gov/sbir/library.html.

➤ Department of Defense

➤ Institute of Defense Analysis (Alexandria, VA)

➤ Logistics Management Institute (Bethesda, MD)

➤ National Defense Research Institute (Santa Monica, CA)

➤ Software Engineering Institute (Pittsburgh, PA)

➤ Center for Naval Analyses (Alexandria, VA)

➤ Lincoln Laboratory (Lexington, MA)

➤ Aerospace Corporation (El Segundo, CA)

➤ Project Air Force (Santa Monica, CA)

➤ Arroyo Center (Santa Monica, CA)

The Least You Need to Know

➤ The spirit of innovation and technology transfer is alive and well in Washington, D.C.

➤ There is no N.I.H. Syndrome.

➤ Uncle Sam may have technological resources and/or funding to help make your dream a reality.

➤ Technology is just a click away—www.fedlabs.org.

➤ Take a patience pill.

Chapter 20

Yes, Inventors, There Is a Santa Claus

In This Chapter

➤ It's a Barnum-and-Bailey, three-ring enterprise

➤ Researching at retail

➤ Success stories

➤ Networking mecca: New York Toy Fair

➤ How to analyze your concept

"The toy industry is fashion/trend-oriented and new product represents its lifeline. The professional independent inventor community is the principle source of the vast majority of new product concepts and without them the toy industry would become stagnated."

—Dale R. Siswick, Senior Vice President of R&D, Hasbro Games Group

The toy industry, although far less entrepreneurial than it was when I got into the business over 20 years ago, is still one of the most potentially lucrative frontiers for the independent inventor. If you want proof of this, ask the inventors of Tickle Me Elmo, Teenage Mutant Ninja Turtles, Cabbage Patch Kids, Pictionary, Trivial Pursuit, Nerf, Twister, K'nex, Bumble Ball, Super Soaker, Koosh, Water Babies, Spin Pops, Hit Clips, Micro Machines, and Connect Four, to name a few.

"The importance of the independent inventor today cannot be overstated. In-house inventing is the equivalent of trying to boil water without using a stove. Top-quality toy concepts are almost impossible to create internally, without an in-house inventor-designer staff; which in today's economy is financially prohibitive and extremely difficult to put together," according to Harvey Lepselter, Senior Vice President for R&D and Marketing at Babies 'n Things.

411

Keep up-to-date on the toy industry, its product, the movers, and the shakers, with the industry's magazine of record, *Playthings*. Subscribe: 345 Hudson Street, New York, NY 10014. Tel: (212) 519-7200. Web site: www.playthings.com. Publisher: Andrea Morris.

Bright Ideas

Hasbro's G.I. Joe, the world's first action figure, was created by toy-inventing dynamo Larry Reiner. The original figure was almost a foot tall and carried authentic equipment from head to toe. It bowed at New York Toy Fair 1964. The first year, Hasbro sold more than $30 million worth of G.I. Joe, "America's Movable Fighting Man." Larry, of blessed memory, was co-inventor of Talking Barney and many other mega-hits throughout the '60s, '70s, '80s, and '90s.

The toy industry is The Greatest Show on Earth. It is a high-wire act without a safety net in which manufacturers walk a financial tightrope that stretches from Christmas to Christmas. Corporate impresarios try their best to top one season's hits the next year, and they rely on the magic of toy inventing gurus to make it happen. In few industries can one find such a blending of creative talents, disciplines, polytechnologies, media, theater, self-interest, circus, idealism, cynicism, masquerade, pomp, exaggeration, and ingenuity as prevails in the toy and game business.

An Industry Overview

The United States/North America is the largest market for toys in the world, followed by Japan, Germany, France, the United Kingdom, Asia, and Western Europe. After experiencing the largest increase in a decade in 1999, toy sales shipments dropped 1.4 percent in 2000, from $16.6 billion to $16.4 billion, according to Patrick Feely, chairman of the Toy Industry Association (TIA)—formerly Toy Manufacturers of America (TMA), the industry trade association. In 2000, this translates to $23 billion in retail sales. Feely predicts that the traditional toy market will grow by six percent in 2001.

In 2000, the U.S. toy industry shipped over 3.36 billion units, comprising an estimated 125,000–150,000 individual products with 7,000 new items introduced at the 2001 American International Toy Fair.

The toy manufacturers spent over $837 million on advertising in 2000, with ninety percent of the total going to television spots, according to the TIA.

Although today's families are having fewer children than the last generation's, with higher education and income levels they are spending more, averaging $350 per child, each year on toys. Add to this that, according to AARP, there are approximately 60 million grandparents in the United States. NPD Group estimates that this demographic segment accounts for 14 percent of toy sales.

The United States leads the world in toy development. According to the book *Inside Santa's Workshop,* a measure of professional independent inventors' productivity is the percentage of new products that come from them. Major toy companies get thousands of unsolicited ideas over the transom, and certain senior executives interviewed for *Inside Santa's Workshop* credit the inventing community with originating 50 to 75 percent of their lines every year.

The 70 professional inventors interviewed for *Inside Santa's Workshop* told the authors that they and/or their groups come up with an average of 100 to 150 original concepts each year.

So, where do you do your product research? Go shopping! Be guided by this information. Wal-Mart sells more toys than Toys " Я " Us. Wal-Mart had 2,624 stores in 2000 and did 19 percent of industry volume. Toys " Я " Us came in second with 16.5 percent through its 710 stores. Then it falls off dramatically to K-Mart at 7.4 percent, Target 6.8 percent, KB 5.11 percent, and so forth.

Some cities have stores that specialize in used toys. These are wonderful places to find older toys and product that we can cannibalize for parts when we are building prototypes.

The Toys Legends Are Made From

There are dozens of inspiring inventor stories that show how timely ideas were used to establish businesses or expand lines dramatically through creativity and imagination.

> ➤ Scrabble was invented in 1931 by Alfred M. Butts, an out-of-work architect who was a lifelong devotee of anagrams and crossword

Fast Facts

Following online book sales, perhaps no industry was affected as immediately as the toy industry by Internet commerce. Online toy sales catapulted from $45 million in 1998 to $425 million in 1999, according to NPD Group, Inc. and Media Metrix.

Notable Quotables

"Aren't we lucky to be creative. I really feel that it is the life energy that keeps us all going. I like to tell newcomers that if they have that creative urge to keep going, it can happen; but to learn to love rejection, there is so much of it."

—A. Eddy Goldfarb, inventor, Chattering Teeth (you remember them!) and 600 other toys and games.

puzzles. The game was originally called "Crisscross Words." Renamed Scrabble in 1948, over 100 million Scrabble games have been sold worldwide to date.

➤ Trivial Pursuit was invented by three young Canadians in 1979. In the game's first year on the market, Selchow & Righter, the game's original U.S. manufacturer, sold 22 million sets at retail prices as high as $40. The next year it sold six million copies, and the next five million. Trivial Pursuit has sold more than 75 million games worldwide.

➤ Remember Dr. Erno Rubik, the Hungarian engineer and mathematician who invented the Rubik Cube? During its three-year hot streak, this innocent-looking, two-and-a-quarter-inch puzzle with more than 43 quintillion possible combinations but only one true solution, sold an estimated 100 million authorized copies, plus another 50 million knock-offs and at least 10 million books explaining how to solve it.

➤ Monopoly was brought to Parker Brothers in 1933 by the late Charles B. Darrow, who developed the game while he was unemployed during the Depression. It was initially rejected as having "52 fundamental errors," but was later published in 1935 and is now licensed in 33 countries and printed in 23 different languages. Over 300 million sets of Monopoly have been sold worldwide.

➤ Crayola Crayons will celebrate its 100th birthday in 2003. Alice Stead Binney conceived the name Crayola for her husband Edwin's crayons in 1903. She derived it from the French word "craie" (stick of color) and the word "oleaginous" (oily). Each year, the company Binney & Smith produces more than two billion Crayola Crayons. That would be enough crayons to circle the globe four and a half times or produce a giant crayon 35 feet wide and 400 feet tall—100 feet taller than the Statue of Liberty. Kids ages two to eight spend an average of 28 minutes a day coloring. The average child in the United States will wear down 730 crayons by age ten.

Notable Quotables

"Play is at the heart of learning, so good toys can put learning in the hands of a child."

—Lynn Cohen and Sandra Waite-Stupiansky, early childhood experts

➤ Cincinnati barber Merle Robbins came up with the card game Uno and licensed it to International Games in 1972. Today Uno, published by Mattel, is sold in 26 countries and is available in 12 languages, with sales of over 80 million units worldwide.

➤ The Hula Hoop, introduced by Wham-O in 1958, set the standards by which all fads are measured. Within four months of its introduction, more than 25 million Hula Hoops were sold. The Hula Hoop was inspired by childrens' bamboo exercise hoops from Australia.

➤ A game invented by a wealthy Canadian couple to play aboard their yacht was so popular with their friends that they approached Edwin S. Lowe, most famous for publishing bingo games in the 1920s, to make samples of "The Yacht Game" for them to give as gifts. Lowe liked the game so much that he offered to buy the rights from the couple and they agreed. He eventually changed the name of the game to Yahtzee. In 1973, Milton Bradley acquired the E.S. Lowe Company.

➤ The world's best-selling top, one that can hit speeds of 10,000 rpms, the Wiz-z-zer, was invented by Paul L. Brown, the sixth child in a family of 12. His parents were so poor that, when Paul was seven years old, they had to send him and four of their other children to the Clark County Children's Home in Springfield, Ohio for care. A high school dropout, Paul graduated first in his class from Fenn College Engineering Defense Training Program. In 1970, Mattel licensed his top and named it the Wiz-z-zer. To date the top, manufactured today by Duncan, has surpassed 25 million units sold.

Notable Quotables

"Inventor product needs to have at least five out of the following six P's:

Product: originality; improved adaptation

Packaging: exciting/impactful point of purchase

Production: safe; foolproof

Promotion: consumer awareness

Price: you can't fool the customers

Patents: protection from competition"

—Fred Kroll, Hungry, Hungry, Hungry Hippos

New York Toy Fair: A Networking Mecca

In spite of the fact that Mattel, the world's largest toy maker, dramatically reduced its presence at the 98-year-old trade show in 2001, and Hasbro contemplates doing likewise in 2002, it is still the best place to see what's in and out and who's who in the industry. This is where the pulse of toy land is taken and contacts are made and nurtured. Toy Fair, as it is more commonly known, is the largest toy trade show in the United States.

In 2000, Mattel and its rival Hasbro each spent $10 million on their Toy Fair showrooms and presentations, according to *The New York Times*.

The 2001 Toy Fair featured 1,942 exhibitors, including 333 foreign companies from 31 countries, and was attended by 17,255 commercial retail buyers from 99 countries. It is also one of the most

Fast Facts

Wal-Mart sells more toys than Toys "Я" Us.

299

extensively covered trade shows in the United States; the 2001 Fair hosted over 1,000 national and international print and broadcast reporters.

Toy Fair is held in New York City, beginning on the second Monday in February. Exhibits are located in permanent showrooms in the Flatiron district and surrounding neighborhoods and concurrently in exhibit booths at Jacob K. Javits Convention Center.

For more information on Toy Fair, its exact dates, seminars, and so on, contact: The Toy Industry Association, 1115 Broadway, New York, New York 10010. Telephone: (212) 675-1141; Fax: (212) 633-1429. Or visit the Toy Fair section of the TIA Web site at www.toy-tia.org.

The Professional Edge

Most major toy companies, where the big money is made on TV-promoted products, depend upon the established, professional inventing community. You can be a part of it if you are smart about how you present yourself and your concepts. There are new inventors breaking into the business every year. See Part Two, "Getting High Marks," for advice in this topic.

The professional inventors know that ingenuity is just the first step, and not an end in itself. In the professional, creativity and imagination are guided and tempered by hard business reality and historical perspective. Toy inventing is far from child's play.

If you want to jump start your career, and learn the ropes, the best way is through the good offices of a toy broker. While not all toy manufacturers will recommend brokers, many, such as Hasbro and Mattel, frequently will if asked. Requests for broker lists should be made to each company's inventor relations department.

Professional agents typically expect 50 percent of any advances and royalties. This is fair. And it assumes that you have an acceptable "looks like/works like" prototype. If the agent has to invest money to further develop your idea, you may have to give up even more of the pie. There should be no up-front money required under such an arrangement.

The top agents not only have access to the toy companies at the highest levels, but they are in the loop to know who's looking for what. The best are professional inventors themselves and will make contributions to your concept. While you may have had the initial idea, the most successful brokers in this business are inventors with patents and products to their names. Many top inventors will quickly put on an agent's hat if they spot a promising product opportunity.

Before signing up with a broker, have a face-to-face meeting. Ask to see the products he or she has invented and/or had a hand in developing and/or licensing. Talk to the inventors behind these products and see what they think of the broker.

WACKY PATENTS

Dog Umbrella
Patented February 18, 1992
United States Patent Des. 324,117

Lastly, insist that the broker arrange for advances and royalties to be paid directly from the toy manufacturer to you. You want to be a party to contracts. Do not allow the broker to receive your money and then redistribute it. I say this not because I worry about the honesty of the broker, but because you want the path of least resistance for your advances and royalties. No toy company would deny a request to divide the money and send separate checks and reports. If the broker says the company won't do it, don't believe it, and you are outta there.

Prolific inventor Michael Satten summed up the odds: "Things have to pass through so many people. Imagine. You have to show it to a guy who has to like it; he has to take it back and show it to a group that has to like it; the engineering has to work; it has to work at a cost; it has to be tested with kids and tested with parents; the trade has to see it; the trade has to like it; the agency has to do commercials; the commercials have to be tested with kids and parents who have to like what they see; then the trade has to see the product again and like the commercial. And after all that, there is a problem in China. It's mind-boggling."

411

The Toy Industry Association, Inc. operates a year-round, 24/7, toll-free hotline and consumer Web site to assist consumers with questions and concerns about toy safety. Call 1-877-486-9723; Web site: www.toy-tia.org and click on 4TOY SAFETY.

Questions for Self-Analysis

Before you spend money on a prototype and approach a possible licensee, make sure that you have asked yourself the following questions. Toy companies do not license ideas or figments of your imagination; they license original, well-developed products that meet certain criteria.

1. *Is your idea original?* Talk to seasoned toy store managers. Attend New York Toy Fair. Read trade magazines. Conduct a patent search (See Part Three). You'll find the answer. All too often inventors with no memory for product reinvent something that has been done before. This wastes everyone's time and does nothing to forward your position. David Berko, senior vice president for inventor relations at Tiger Electronics, counsels, "Becoming an expert in a category will equalize your position with the people to whom you are presenting."

2. *Does your idea fit the company's line profile?* Tiger's David Berko cautions, "The biggest mistake is when the inventor does not understand the company's direction and its brands. We are anxious to see new products that compliment our brands. Our time is limited. We don't need to be looking at products that are not appropriate for our brands or target market."

See Part Two for how to find prospective licensees, get through the door, and make the pitch.

3. *Does your idea have visual appeal?* Hire an industrial designer if you do not possess the skills to design your concept. Toy executives are accustomed to a high level of professionalism. It must not only look good, it must have perceived value.

4. *Does Your item have play and repeat play value?* Child-test a breadboard or mock-up of the item. Make sure it works, and that it has the ability to sustain interest. In the case of games, it could take dozens of play sessions to fine-tune a concept.

5. *Does your concept have wide market appeal?* Major companies have no interest in small market segments. A small business to a major toy company could be $15 or $20 million. In order for a product to make the cut at larger manufacturers, it must have very broad appeal. In other words, it must sell to Toys " Я " Us, Wal-Mart, K-Mart, Target, and other mass-market outlets. If the company cannot sell hundreds of thousands of units the first year and then expand and build the item, it will not license the submission.

6. *Is your product safe?* All products selected for manufacture by United States or foreign toy makers must meet one or more of the following safety standards:

    ➤ CPSC Regulations

    ➤ ASTM F963-92

    ➤ DEHP Content

    ➤ CONEG

    ➤ EN-71 (1988)

    ➤ BS 5665 (1989)

    ➤ HD271 (for electrical toys)

    ➤ Perspiration and saliva test (Germany)

    ➤ Phenol Content (Germany)

411

Don't miss the award-winning Web site: www.drtoy.com, an invaluable resource on playthings and the toy industry. The site is designed and hosted by Stevanne Auerbach, Ph.D., director of the Institute of Childhood Resources, founded in 1975. You'll learn a great deal from the smorgasbord of information she serves up.

Bright Ideas

Barbie, the world's best-selling and most widely recognized fashion doll in history, celebrates her forty-third birthday in 2002. She is named after the daughter of the doll's inventors, Ruth and Elliot Handler. Since 1959, over 600 million Barbies and members of the Barbie clan (Ken is Barbie's real-life brother) have been sold in 67 countries throughout the world. Mattel sells over 20 million Barbie fashions annually, making the California toy maker the largest producer of "petite" women's wear in the world.

There is also a battery of functional abuse exercises which, depending upon the product, can include transit test, aging test, humidity test, drop test, torque and tension test, compression test, abrasion test, adhesion test, and life test.

7. *Can your product be manufactured, and at what cost?* You may have to build or hire someone to figure this out, and see if anything would render the concept infeasible. Play value and technical elegance mean little if your concept cannot be made or made for the right price. No matter how terrific your concept may be, the manufacturer must make sure that the product can be manufactured and sold at the right price. It's one thing to make a piece of something, and another to make two and a half million of them. That kind of development work is often just as creative as the idea itself.

WACKY PATENTS

Hat
Patented January 25, 1921
United States Patent 56,990

8. *Have you come up with a cost guesstimate?* In costing toys, we use this rule-of-thumb to reach the wholesale price: hard cost times four for nonpromoted items; hard cost times five for TV-promoted items.

9. *What competitive products are on the market?* Be able to tell your target licensee the category in which you envision your item as well as the competitive atmosphere. Buy competitive products, and tear them apart. Know what makes them tick.

10. *What "wow factors" make your concept unique?* Demonstrate to yourself what makes your item unique compared to other product in its category.

Once you have satisfied these issues, then and only then embark on building a "looks like/works like" prototype.

A Degree in Toy Design

The Fashion Institute of Technology in New York City began offering a Bachelor of Fine Arts degree in Toy Design, the first known program of its kind, in 1989. FIT graduated its eleventh class of toy designers in Spring 2001. At graduation almost all of the students had been placed in jobs at toy companies and inventor groups.

The FIT toy design curriculum emphasizes conceptual and technical design development supported by a knowledge of safety and regulatory requirements, child psychology and anatomy, production, packaging, marketing, and consumer motivation fundamentals, plus a general overview of the toy industry. A strong liberal arts component is included to broaden the designer's perspective as an interpreter of cultural trends. Industry internships with toy companies and working with children as teacher assistants are also important elements of this program.

For more information, contact Professor Judy Ellis, Fashion Institute of Technology, Toy Design Department, 227 West 27th Street, Room B231, New York, New York 10001. Tel: (212) 217-7133. E-mail: ellisjud@sfitva.cc.fitsuny.edu.

TIA Freebie

Toy Industry Association (TIA) publishes the *Toy Inventor/Designer Guide.* For a copy of this brochure, which describes ways to sell your invention/design or manufacture it yourself, please write to TIA's Communication Department *Toy Inventor/Designer Guide,* Toy Industry Association, 1115 Broadway, New York, New York 10010.

411

There are more than 100 separate tests and design specifications included in ASTM F963-92, a comprehensive voluntary toy safety standard developed jointly by private industry and government. For a copy of ASTM F963-92, call (610) 832-9585 or go to www.astm.org Cost: $40 per copy.

The Hit Parade

The toy industry's greatest natural resource is the outside, independent inventor who is responsible for its greatest successes. In an era of intense global competition, the inventor becomes even more important to the health of the industry. Here are some products that came from outside, though they never would have made it to market and hit pay dirt were it not for the dedicated and talented pros inside the toy companies. It is the combination of the outsiders and insiders that make it work.

Battling Tops	Othello
Big Wheel	Play Doh
Boggle	Pokemon
Cabbage Patch Kids	Risk
Candyland	Rubik's Cube
Clue	Scrabble
Connect Four	Shelby
Etch-a-Sketch	Super Soaker
Frisbee	Teenage Mutant Ninja Turtles
Furby	Tickle Me Elmo
Game of Life	Trivial Pursuit
Giga Pets	Twister
GI Joe	UNO
Monopoly	Upwards
Mr. Machine	Yomega
Mr. Potato Head	Water Babies
Nerf	

See Appendix B, "Resources," for a list of some toy makers who entertain outside submissions. If you want to see a complete list, go to the TIA Web site www.toy-tia.org and click on MEMBERS. The list is alphabetical. Each name takes you to another page with the company's address, etc. There you will find hot links to corporate Web sites.

The Least You Need to Know

➤ Never get caught with your trends down.

➤ Risk is more than a game.

➤ Color outside the box.

➤ Never grow up. Never give up.

Chapter 21

Inventor Organizations

In This Chapter

➤ The benefits of inventor organizations

➤ Joining an inventor organization

➤ Starting an inventor organization

➤ Beware of wolves in sheep's clothing

➤ You have options

"In 1899 the Commissioner of Patents recommended the abolition of the Patent Office on the grounds that everything had been invented. Yet on the horizon were such inventions as the airplane, radio, television, refrigerators, electric hair dryers, and rockets that would make possible the exploration of space, as well as improvements in such things as automobiles, cameras, ships and razors, to mention but a few. Inventions have transformed the face of America, stimulated its businesses, and enhanced the lives of its people and those of the world."

—Harold D. Langley, Curator Emeritus, The National Museum of American History, Division of the History of Technology, Smithsonian Institution

The best reason to join an inventor organization is fellowship, as it is with any association of people who have common interests and goals. Getting product from your workshop or drawing board to an end user can be a long, tough, and sometimes lonely haul. Isolationism is an inevitable drawback of being an inventor, and this can be particularly problematical if you are self-employed and at home.

Operating on the frontier of an emerging idea is difficult enough. But spearheading the development, licensing, and manufacture of an invention can leave even the most experienced players nonplused. It's nice to have a vibrant social network that is comprised of individuals who share a community and are striving for a similar goal.

Fast Facts

Intellectual Property Owners, Inc. reports that of 150 firms worldwide in eight industries that are ranked in the May 2001 issue of *Technology Review,* according to quality and quantity of their patents, at least one of the top three in each industry is an IPO member.

Bright Ideas

Independent inventor Frampton Ellis III of Arlington, Virginia, is the successful inventor of a new kind of sole for sports sneakers, which he has licensed to Adidas. According to an article in *The Washington Star,* Mr. Ellis says he spent seven years and thousands of dollars before signing a licensing agreement with Adidas, and it took nearly 10 years before he made any money.

Expanding Your Network

We inventors are no different than any other group of people who share a similar purpose. We love to get together, explore professional issues, and share experiences, success stories, heartbreaks, information, personal contacts, methods, techniques, and dreams. Nothing is more satisfying than the camaraderie provided by a club.

Membership can be particularly satisfying in a business like ours that finds people chained to the Wheel of Chance in ways no other enterprise does. Inventing and licensing is one of the most unstable, unforgiving, misunderstood, and risky businesses in the world. It is not for the faint of heart. It is an esoteric field, one in which imagination rules reason. It is understood by so few, and fraught with so many hazards. Most people outside the business don't understand it at all, or have very little comprehension of it. Through association with other inventors, successful and unsuccessful, you will get the benefit of what Hayakawa called "the best possible maps of the territories of experience."

Care to Share?

Membership in an inventor organization connects you to a network of like-minded colleagues, encourages you to exchange ideas and solutions, and gives you access to what's going on within the inventing community, locally, and by extension, nationally.

When you are a member of an inventor organization, you can frequently get free advice and information on virtually any aspect of ip by contacting other members, people who operate on the premise "if I can't answer your question, I know someone who can." Larger organizations are comprised of memberships that embrace experts in a wide range of specialties, including legal, prototyping, patent searching, drafting, engineering, industrial design, venture capital, Internet, marketing, and so forth.

I always remind executives that although on one level independent inventors compete against each other for the placement of product, we are generally very friendly toward each other as a group. We do not perceive each other as competition in the way K-Mart considers Wal-Mart competition or Ford does General Motors. In the toy industry, for example, we inventors help each other with everything from sharing contacts and insights to the best terms available in licensing agreements.

I called a friend the other day and asked what kind of a deal he received from a certain company. "Let me fax you my agreement," he offered. I frequently do similar favors for friends. It's one big *quid pro quo.*

411

If you want to learn how to start an inventor organization in your area, the Houston Inventors Association, one of the oldest and largest such organizations in America, tells you how on its Web site: http://www.inventors.org/invclub/h2start.htm.

Inventor Organizations Thrive on American Soil

Inventor organizations, typically nonprofit, often take root where inventors practice their trade, and there is no more fertile territory than the U.S.A. Seeking to establish relationships among themselves, independent inventors have formed organizations throughout the nation, groups that provide professional and social forums. For a list of such organizations see Appendix B, "Resources." This list was made possible by UIA, to which I am grateful. These organizations offer members all kinds of product development support, guidance, and resources. A common objective is to stimulate self-fulfillment, creativity, and problem-solving. Naturally, some inventor groups are more sophisticated than others; some are more organized. But all the legit ones have something positive to offer. Note: I have not personally contacted and become familiar with each group listed. You'll need to evaluate them yourself.

"Inventor organizations are the biggest bargain around for helping inventors to get their invention going, avoid scams, and meet people who have similar interests and have solved similar problems," says Ray Watts, former editor of the *Inventor-Assistance Program News.*

Chuck Mullen, Chairman, Board of Advisors, Houston Inventors Association (www.inventors.org), told me, "At our regular meetings, when a newcomer stands up and asks for help, there will be at least three or four members that will have the information and experience that he or she needs."

And Penny Becker of the Minnesota Inventors Congress feels the best free guidance and networking opportunities inventors can obtain are through the nonprofit inventor organizations.

John Moreland, publisher of *The Dream Merchant* magazine, had this to say: "Inventor organizations may prove to be an excellent means to meet or network with other inventors [and] learn of available resources.

"However, most clubs meet once a month or less frequently and *should not* be considered a substitute for diligence, persistence, and action.

"My biggest complaint about any organization is that many times the organization is more concerned about the welfare of the 'organization' than [about] individuals [in] the organization; this seems more true in larger national organizations. Also there seems to be some sort of rivalry between some clubs, much like the competitiveness of sports teams. Instead of working together to achieve a synergistic concept, they are more content with spinning their own wheels and trying to develop their membership."

WACKY PATENTS

Birthday Cake Candle Extinguisher
Patented September 29, 1964
United States Patent 3,150,831

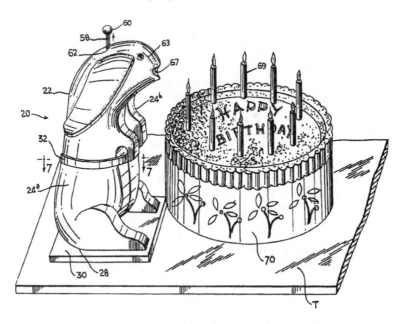

Truth in Packaging—Caveat Emptor

Be especially careful when selecting a national organization. I have found some organizations that are nothing more than wolves (invention marketing companies) in sheep's clothing. The Internet has made it especially easy for unscrupulous characters to ambush naïve inventors. But if you look hard beneath the surface, it's the same old shell game. Their con is to get as much money from you as they can without having to deliver any moneymaking results. They'll sell you marketing reports, patent work, insurance, self-published books, ads, expo booths, and even t-shirts. What they do not deliver is wise counsel or the kinds of personal contacts that get inventions licensed.

They can even fool the experts. I have a list published by the U.S. Department of Energy, dated August of 2000, that contains the names and numbers of some companies that I know were never qualified by DOE. The USPTO needs to put forth its best efforts to compile a list of organizations that it can represent as legit.

I found one inventor service company running a museum for inventions. If they cannot get your money one way, they'll get it in another way. And it is the money and what the organization is selling that usually gives them away.

Notable Quotables

"Perserverance! Overcome luck through diversity! The more good ideas, the less the need to be lucky."

—Rollie Tesh, Pente

Take Your Pick

I will now tell you those organizations with which I have had personal experience and/or know select members of an organization's leadership team. I cannot, however, vouch for most of the organizations listed and you should use your own judgment as to whether you feel a group meets your personal requirements, and as to its legitimacy. One of the best ways to qualify an organization is through references by satisfied members. See Appendix B for a full list of organizations.

There are several kinds of organizations:

➤ National

➤ State

➤ Local

➤ Informal

National Organizations

Here are two different types of national organizations.

United Inventors Association (UIA)

The United Inventors Association claims to be the largest nonprofit inventor organization in North America. It was established in September 1990 as an outgrowth of a

Department of Energy Conference organized to discuss the needs of our nation's independent inventors.

I know several members of its Board of Directors who rock like Gibraltar on behalf of independent inventors. They are ...

➤ Board President Jack Lander is a prolific inventor and self-employed mechanical engineer. He and his wife, Jini, founded the Innovators Network of Greater Danbury (Connecticut) and are a force behind Yankee Invention Exposition, Inc., an annual expo and workshop that takes place in Waterbury, Connecticut. Jack also teaches invention development, protection, and marketing to adults in the greater Danbury region.

➤ Board Vice President Joanne M. Hayes-Rines, one of the most influential thinkers and inventor advocates, is publisher and editor of *Inventors' Digest*, America's leading inventors' magazine. She created National Inventors' Month and made it happen. A board member and Vice President of the Academy of Applied Science, a national nonprofit organization which promotes creativity, invention, and scientific excellence through multilevel educational programs, Joanne has been honored frequently for her efforts on behalf of America's independent inventors.

➤ Director Pamela Riddle Bird is a nationally recognized commercialization expert who managed one of the largest publicly funded innovation centers in the U.S. and has provided advice to thousands of inventors and entrepreneurs for nearly a decade. She is the founder and Chief Executive Officer of Innovative Product Technologies, Inc.

➤ Director Gerald Udell is a Professor of Marketing and Executive Director of the Center for Business and Economic Development in the College of Business Administration, Southwest Missouri State University. Dr. Udell is the author of over 30 books and more than 200 articles and other publications. Prior to SMSU, he held positions at the University of Wisconsin, Purdue University, University of Oregon, and the University of North Dakota. He developed the Wal-Mart Innovation Network.

I know two members of UIA's Panel of Experts:

➤ Donald Kelly is Chief Executive Officer of the Academy of Applied Science. For more than 30 years, Don promoted American innovation and technological growth through his work as a career civil servant and member of the elite Senior Executive Service at the USPTO. He established and was first director of the Office of Independent Inventor Programs at the USPTO.

➤ Ronald J. Riley is president of Riley and Associates, Inc. He is an inveterate inventor who has been awarded seven patents, five related to electrified monorail controls, the others to exercise treadmills. He founded InventorEd, Inc., is President of the Professional Inventors Alliance, President of the advisory board of Washington, D.C.–based Alliance for American Innovation, a member of the Union of Concerned Scientists, the Planetary Society, and the Society of Manufacturing Engineers.

There is no finer or more impactful group of advocates for the independent inventor than these folks. They labor tirelessly on the front lines and behind the scenes, scrupulously watching out for the rights of the independent inventor.

UIA is actively involved in bringing fraudulent invention marketing companies to the attention of lawmakers, law enforcement agencies, and regulators. Robert G. Lougher, UIA's Executive Director, is founder of Inventors Awareness Group (IAG), an all-volunteer consumer group that between 1992 and 1998 spearheaded the work that brought eight invention marketing scams to justice.

I strongly encourage you to visit the UIA Web site at www.usuia.org. It is one-stop shopping for the independent inventor.

411

PatentCafe.com, Inc. is an Internet communications, commerce, and New Media company serving the intellectual property and business community, worldwide. In 1996, it (www.PatentCafe.com) established itself as the first-to-market online navigational directory for creators and professionals needing informational resources related to patents, trademarks, copyrights, and trade secrets. It has continued to expand its vertical content to maintain its market-leading position in terms of quality original and aggregated content depth, reliability and trust, and breadth of visitor demographic within the IP space. Bookmark it! PatentCafe.com has no equal in the vast wealth of information it delivers.

Intellectual Property Owners (IPO)

Intellectual Property Owners, Inc., often at odds with UIA on issues of patent law and patent policy, is a very fine organization, comprised of many more corporate members than independent inventors. IPO is not an inventor organization such as UIA.

It is a trade association (read: lobbyist) that serves the needs of owners of patents, trademarks, copyrights, and trade secrets throughout a wide range of industries and fields of technology. Members include many Fortune 500 companies, universities, patent law firms, independent inventors, and authors.

IPO was founded in 1972. Its *Daily News* is an awesomely informative summary of current ip news and tidbits. It is sent to members via e-mail and still available to anyone who visits the IPO Web site: www.ipo.org.

I served on IPO's board of directors—it has one seat for an independent inventor—and would encourage you to join for the kind of information available to members and to see other points of view.

IPO was founded by a group of individuals concerned about the lack of understanding of intellectual property rights in the United States. Members include nearly 100 large and medium-sized corporations (including Union Carbide, Monsanto, United Technologies, P&G, and AT&T) and more than 300 small businesses, universities, independent inventors, authors, executives, and attorneys.

Herb Wamsley, IPO's indefatigable executive director, says that applications for individual inventor memberships are on the rise. While IPO is definitely not for the casual inventor, it should be given consideration by professional inventors who have interest in up-to-the-minute information about intellectual property issues and who seek contacts within big business. For a full list of IPO's benefits and services, request a fact sheet and other background material from the organization.

IPO sponsors the National Inventor of the Year Award. Its purpose is to increase public awareness of current inventors and how they benefit the nation's economy and our quality of life.

For information contact Intellectual Property Owners, 1255 23d Street NW, Suite 850, Washington, D.C. 20037. The telephone number is: (202) 466-2396; the fax number is: (202) 466-2893. Or visit its Web site: www.ipo.org.

The Value of State and Local Organizations

Do not join a national organization at the exclusion of a state or local group. These organizations complement each other in terms of what they deliver. State and local organizations are typically smaller, warmer, and more friendly. You will be able to attend regular meetings. And because the membership is close by, the information shared will be highly targeted, e.g., where to: get prototypes made, find competent patent counsel, and so forth.

The big draws of nonnationals are also guest speakers, social events, and recreational activities.

Fred Hart, of the Department of Energy, advises, "Search out the nearest inventors' organization and join. If there isn't one, start one up. It's only through a mutual support group that you can safely get help."

WACKY PATENTS

Device for Producing Dimples
Patented May 19, 1896
United States Patent 560,351

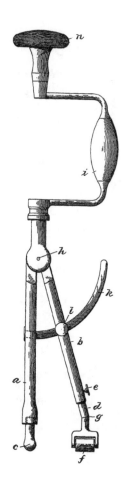

Chuck Mullen of the Houston Inventors Association explains that his organization runs a nonprofit initiative to grow inventor organizations nationwide in areas where there are none. "We see this as the first step to a strong and healthy national network of inventors, one which will reach out to school children, motivate and teach them how to invent. At the same time, we'll stress the importance of staying in school and mastering math and science so that they have the opportunity to grow up to become rich and famous inventors."

For the nominal cost of materials and postage, Mullen says HIA, which was founded in 1983, will furnish written materials about how to start a club plus send videotapes of their best guest speakers, tapes that groups can show at their monthly meetings. Inventors of the National Capital Area (INCA) was the first such clone organization.

To contact the Houston group, go to its Web site at: www.inventors.org. There you will find the information on how to start your own inventor organization.

Notable Quotables

"Do not protect yourself by a fence, but rather by your friends."

—Czech proverb

Informal Organizations

If you do not want to start a formal organization, think about informal get-togethers. A great example of one is what has become known as Toy Inventors Weekend in Vermont every September.

John Hall, a former vice president for R&D at Playskool, and his wife, publishing dynamo Nancy, first organized this weekend back in 1993, and it has become an annual, by invitation only, event that some 25 people attend. We take over a beautiful country inn and spend the weekend renewing friendships, sharing business stories and corporate intelligence, and enjoying the beauty of the Green Mountain State.

Toy inventors and their spouses or significant others come from as far away as California and England. It is restricted to independent inventors only. No currently employed corporate executives are invited, though some of the inventors once worked inside.

The Least You Need to Know

➤ It's not about giving; it's about sharing.

➤ There is strength in numbers.

➤ No man (or woman) is an island.

➤ Find an organization you like, and sign up.

➤ Start an organization. It need not be large to be beneficial and enjoyable.

Agreements

License Agreement

AGREEMENT made this _ day of ___, 20__ by and between _____, located at _____ (hereinafter referred to as LICENSOR) and _____, located at _____ (hereinafter referred to as LICENSEE).

Witnesseth:

WHEREAS, LICENSOR represents and warrants that it is the creator of _____ _____ (hereinafter referred to as the ITEM).

WHEREAS, LICENSOR hereby warrants that, to the best of its knowledge, it is the sole and exclusive owner of all rights in the ITEM, that, to the best of its knowledge, it has the sole and exclusive right to grant the license herein, and that it is not engaged in litigation or conflict of any nature whatsoever involving the ITEM; and

WHEREAS, LICENSEE is in the business of making and selling (enter type of product, e.g., shoes, faucets, toys, etc.); and

WHEREAS, LICENSEE wishes to obtain the sole and exclusive rights to manufacture and sell the ITEM (enter territories, e.g., worldwide, US and its possessions, Europe, etc.)

NOW, THEREFORE, for and in consideration of the sum of One Dollar (US$1.00) and other good and valuable consideration, receipt of which is hereby acknowledged, and for the performance of the mutual covenants hereinafter to be performed, it is agreed as follows:

DEFINITIONS:

Item: As used in this Agreement, the term ITEM refers to the ITEM described herein-above, and any Improvements, Accessories or Extensions thereto, whether developed by or for LICENSEE.

Improvements: As used in this Agreement, the term Improvements means any design or technical refinements or advances made by or for LICENSEE and reflected in the ITEM as marketed.

Accessories: As used in this Agreement, the term Accessories means any products making use of the ITEM, as well as equipment developed by or for LICENSEE designated for use with the ITEM.

Extensions: As used in this Agreement, the term Extensions means any products that are sold independently by LICENSEE under the ITEM trademark, i.e., products that trade on the name of the ITEM, but are not necessarily marketed as accessories to the ITEM.

Collateral Merchandise: As used in this Agreement, the term Collateral Merchandise means products that are sold under the ITEM trademark or trade on its good will. (Note: *You may not want to grant these rights. If not, omit this reference. Or, you may wish to allow for certain collateral merchandise and not others. If so, spell it out here. Collateral Merchandise could range from t-shirts to tennis rackets.*)

1.(a) LICENSOR hereby grants to LICENSEE the sole and exclusive right, privilege and license to make, reproduce, modify, use and/or sell, to have made, reproduced, modified, used and/or sold and to sublicense others to make, reproduce, modify, use and/or sell the ITEM and any images, representations, and material associated with the ITEM as well as the subject matter of a patent application which is to be filed on the ITEM pursuant to Paragraph 2(a) hereof.

(b) All rights and licenses not herein specifically granted to LICENSEE are reserved by LICENSOR and, as between the parties, are the sole and exclusive property of LICENSOR and may be used or exercised solely by LICENSOR. Included within this understanding is the right of LICENSOR to use whatever trademark LICENSEE markets the ITEM under; however, it is understood and agreed between the parties that LICENSOR will not license the concept to a third party for a product that would compete with the ITEM as marketed by LICENSEE.

(c) This Agreement shall continue for as long as the ITEM upon which royalties would be payable to LICENSOR, under provisions of this Agreement, shall continue to be manufactured or sold by LICENSEE.

2.(a) LICENSOR agrees to use its best efforts and to bear the expenses of obtaining patent protection in the USA, and any and all such patents will be in the name of and remain the property of LICENSOR during and following any termination or cancellation hereof.

(b) To the best of LICENSOR's knowledge, the ITEM does not infringe any patent rights.

3.(a) LICENSEE shall pay LICENSOR _ percent (__%) of the "Net Sales" of the ITEM, its Improvements, Accessories or Extensions. As used in this Agreement, "Net Sales" are defined as sales computed on prices charged by LICENSEE to its customers for the ITEM, less a deduction not to exceed seven and a half (7.5%) percent which provides for freight allowances, sales allowances actually credited, customary trade discounts (but not cash discounts), volume discounts (not to exceed usual industry practices), to the extent taken, directly applicable to the sale of licensed products, and less returns (but not for exchange) which are accepted and credited by LICENSEE. No deduction shall be made for non-collectible accounts. No costs incurred in the manufacture, sales, distribution, exploitation or promotion of the ITEM, its improvements, accessories or any adaptations thereof shall be deducted from any royalties payable by LICENSEE to LICENSOR, nor shall any deductions from due royalties be made for taxes of any nature. LICENSEE cannot barter or trade or do so-called "charge-backs" on the ITEM without computation of full royalties.

(b) In event LICENSEE sells FOB direct from a foreign manufacturing location, LICENSEE shall pay LICENSOR _ percent (__%) of all Net Sales, as defined hereinabove, of the ITEM.

(c) LICENSEE may grant foreign manufacturing sublicenses on the ITEM upon any terms and conditions which it wishes to grant and establish so long as said terms and conditions are competitive and market prevailing; and provided that in the event LICENSEE does grant such sublicenses to manufacture and market the ITEM, LICENSEE shall pay to LICENSOR fifty (50%) percent of any and all moneys received, including, but not limited to royalties (which shall be no less than 2½% of the sales of the ITEM), advances, guarantees, mold or pattern lease or rental fees, etc. as received by LICENSEE from any such sublicense or grant. LICENSEE agrees to send a copy of any sublicense agreement, or shall otherwise promptly inform LICENSOR in writing about the terms of the sublicense to manufacture the ITEM.

(d) In the event LICENSEE sells the ITEM as a premium, the royalty rate shall be _ percent (__%) of the revenue derived by LICENSEE from the sale of the ITEM as a premium. For purposes of this Agreement, the term "premium" shall be defined as including, but not necessarily limited to, combination sales, free or self-liquidating items offered to the public in conjunction with the sale or promotion of a product or service other than the ITEM, including traffic building or continuity visits by the consumer, customer, or any similar scheme or device, whose primary purpose in regard to each of the sales described above is not directed at the sale of the ITEM itself and the prime intent of which is to use the ITEM in such a way as to promote, publicize, and/or sell the products, services, or business image of the user of such ITEM rather than the ITEM itself.

(e) All royalties payable by LICENSEE to LICENSOR based upon LICENSEE's sales of the ITEM shall accrue upon LICENSEE's shipment and invoicing of the item.

(f) If payments are made to LICENSOR from a foreign country, LICENSEE assumes sole responsibility for procuring any permits and documents needed to make all payments under any exchange regulations, and all such royalties shall be made by LICENSEE to LICENSOR in U.S. dollars at the then prevailing rate of exchange as used by Chase Bank.

4.(a) Upon execution of this Agreement, LICENSEE shall pay to LICENSOR the sum of $____, as a non-refundable, guaranteed advance against royalties. In no event shall such advance be repaid to LICENSEE other than in the form of deductions from payments due under Paragraphs 3 and 9 hereof.

(b) Should LICENSEE, for any reason, and at any time, decide not to manufacture the ITEM, or if in any calendar year the ITEM fails to generate $_____ in royalties for LICENSOR, LICENSOR shall have the right to terminate this Agreement. And should LICENSEE cease to manufacture said ITEM, or should this Agreement be terminated for a breach of conditions by LICENSEE, then all rights to the development work done on the ITEM on behalf of and/or paid for by LICENSEE (e.g., breadboards, models, etc.) shall belong to LICENSOR free-and-clear and LICENSEE shall have no further claim to the ITEM.

(c) The receipt or acceptance by LICENSOR of any written statements furnished pursuant to this Agreement or of any payments made hereunder (or cashing of any checks paid hereunder) shall not preclude LICENSOR from questioning the correctness thereof at any time.

5. LICENSEE agrees to introduce the ITEM on or before (date). LICENSEE agrees that during the term of this Agreement it will diligently and continuously manufacture, sell, distribute and promote the ITEM and that it will make and maintain adequate arrangements for the distribution of the ITEM and satisfy demand for the ITEM.

6. LICENSEE has the right to change the form of the ITEM as submitted by LICENSOR, and to produce and sell it under new form(s); provided, however, that all the provisions of this Agreement shall apply to said new form(s) of the ITEM.

7.(a) LICENSEE shall mark the ITEM and its packages, containers and display cards with the words, "Patent Pending," if advised that a patent application is pending and until advised that a patent has been issued on the ITEM, at which later time LICENSEE shall mark the ITEM, containers and display cards with the specific patent number.

8.(a) LICENSEE shall annually furnish LICENSOR, free-of-charge, (enter number) samples of each ITEM and its packaging prior to its availability at retail for purposes of quality control. In the case of the ITEM as made by LICENSEE's foreign sublicensees, LICENSEE shall annually furnish, free-of-charge, to LICENSOR (enter number) samples of each and its packaging.

9.(a) The rights to sublicense the ITEM in foreign countries covered by this Agreement are conditioned upon introduction of the ITEM on or before (enter date). In the event LICENSEE has not entered into a fully executed sublicense agreement or made formal, documented arrangements to sell the ITEM through a distributor in a foreign country prior to (enter date, usually one year after domestic release), all rights with respect to such foreign country shall automatically revert to LICENSOR. However, LICENSEE shall be entitled, after expiration of any manufacturing sublicense agreement or distributor arrangement in any foreign country entered into prior to (enter a cut-off date) to enter into a new agreement or arrangement in such foreign country.

(b) When either party considers it necessary or desirable to obtain patent protection in a foreign country covered by this Agreement (other than the USA), it shall notify the other party of that decision and upon the agreement of said other party, LICENSOR shall, if obtaining the foreign patent protection is not barred by prior use or publication, promptly file such foreign application and the expenses thereof shall be shared equally by both parties. In the event the parties do not agree to share the expense of obtaining such patent protection, the party requesting the foreign patent protection may proceed alone, at its own expense, and all rights obtained shall belong to that party alone, notwithstanding any other provisions of this Agreement. If LICENSEE has not timely requested the filing of a patent application in a foreign country, LICENSOR is under no obligation to file such foreign application, and in the event that neither party has filed a patent application in a particular foreign country, or the parties have agreed not to file an application or have agreed to discontinue an application or patent, then the royalties for such foreign country shall be payable to LICENSOR as if the patent protection had been obtained in that country and the expenses shared equally by the parties.

(c) LICENSEE may sublicense its rights hereunder to use the ITEM on Collateral Merchandise under the terms and conditions it wishes to grant and establish as long as they are competitive and market prevailing; and provided that in the event LICENSEE grants such sublicenses, LICENSEE shall pay to LICENSOR the sum of __ percent (___%) of any and all moneys received, including, but not limited to, royalties, advances, guarantees and consultation fees it may receive.

(d) In the case of sublicenses of Collateral Merchandise, LICENSEE shall ensure that sublicensees cause the above trademark notices, if one or both trademarks are used by LICENSEE, to appear on all collateral merchandise, its packaging, containers, advertising, etc.

10.(a) LICENSOR agrees to indemnify, defend and save harmless LICENSEE against actions brought against LICENSEE with respect to any claim or suit that LICENSOR is not the originator of the Item.

(b) LICENSOR agrees to indemnify LICENSEE against losses, claims and expenses with respect to losses, claims or expenses that arise only from an act or omission by LICENSOR that is done in bad faith.

321

(c) LICENSOR shall not indemnify LICENSEE on claims whereby LICENSEE has been said to have been previously shown an ITEM similar to the ITEM by the claimant. LICENSEE warrants that it has never seen an item similar to the subject ITEM.

(d) LICENSOR agrees to indemnify and hold harmless LICENSEE from and against any claim of infringement of trade secrets arising out of LICENSEE's sale of the ITEM.

(e) LICENSEE will conduct its own patent, copyright and trademark searches and satisfy itself that the ITEM does not infringe anything in any of these fields, and once satisfied, LICENSEE agrees to indemnify, defend and save harmless LICENSOR from and against all damages, costs and attorney fees resulting from all claims, demands, actions, suits or prosecutions for patent, copyright, trademark based upon use of the ITEM or its components and all forms of the ITEM as produced and sold by LICENSEE, its subsidiaries, affiliates and sublicensees. LICENSEE shall be given prompt notice of any claim against LICENSOR and shall have the right to defend such claim with counsel selected by LICENSEE. LICENSOR agrees to co-operate with LICENSEE in connection with the defense of any such claim.

(f) LICENSEE agrees to indemnify, defend and save harmless LICENSOR from and against all damages, costs and attorney fees resulting from all claims, demands, actions, suits or prosecutions for personal injury or property damage. LICENSEE agrees to cover LICENSOR under its product liability insurance, with an insurance company providing protection for itself and LICENSOR against any such claims or suits relating to personal injury, product manufacture, property damage, or materials failure but in no event in amounts less than (enter a number) million dollars or the limits of its policy, whichever is greater, and within thirty (30) days before manufacture of the ITEM, LICENSEE will submit to LICENSOR a certificate of insurance naming LICENSOR as an insured party, and covering LICENSOR requiring that the insurer shall not terminate or materially modify such without written notice to LICENSOR at least twenty (20) days in advance thereof.

(g) In the event of infringement of any patent that may be issued to LICENSOR on the ITEM and upon notice thereof from LICENSEE, LICENSOR shall, within thirty (30) days, notify LICENSEE of its election to prosecute or not prosecute a suit for infringement. If LICENSOR prosecutes said suit, it may select legal counsel and pay legal fees and costs of prosecution subject to being reimbursed therefor from any recovery in said suit. The balance of any recovery shall be divided equally between LICENSOR and LICENSEE. If LICENSOR elects not to prosecute any infringement suit, LICENSEE may do so after notice to LICENSOR of that intention. LICENSEE may then select legal counsel and shall bear all the legal fees and costs subject to reimbursement therefor from any recovery in said suit. The balance of any recovery shall be distributed as follows: One-fourth (¼) to LICENSOR and three-fourths (¾) to LICENSEE.

11. LICENSEE shall, within thirty (30) days following the end of each calendar quarter, starting with the month following the quarter in which sales of the ITEM commence, submit to LICENSOR a report covering the sales of the ITEM during the

preceding quarter, and LICENSEE shall therewith send to LICENSOR payment of the amount due under Paragraphs 3 and 9 hereof. Such quarterly statements shall be submitted whether or not they reflect any sales.

12.(a) LICENSEE agrees to keep full and accurate books of account, records, data and memoranda respecting the manufacture and sales of the ITEM in sufficient detail to enable the payments hereunder to LICENSOR to be determined, and LICENSEE gives LICENSOR the right, upon notice, at its own expense, to examine said books and records, only insofar as they concern the ITEM and not more often than twice in any calendar year, for the purpose of verifying the reports provided for in this Agreement. In the event LICENSOR shall examine the records, documents and materials in the possession or under the control of LICENSEE with respect to the subject matter, such examination shall be conducted in such a manner as to not unduly interfere with the business of LICENSEE. LICENSOR and its representative shall not disclose to any other person, firm or corporation any information acquired as a result of any such examination; provided, however, that nothing herein contained shall be construed to prevent LICENSOR and/or its duly authorized representative from testifying, in any court of competent jurisdiction, with respect to the information obtained as a result of such examination in any action instituted to enforce the rights of LICENSEE under the terms of this Agreement.

(b) In the event that LICENSEE has understated Net Shipments or underpaid royalties by 5% or more for any contract year, LICENSEE shall forthwith and upon written demand also pay to LICENSOR all reasonable costs, fees and expenses incurred by LICENSOR in conducting such audit.

(c) Payments found to be due LICENSOR as a result of a delay or an examination shall be paid immediately at the prime rate quoted by Chase Bank at the close of business on the due date plus __% per annum until paid.

13.(a) LICENSEE agrees to send all payments and reports due hereunder to LICENSOR at address noted in this Agreement's preamble.

14.(a) If LICENSEE shall at any time default by failing to make any payment hereunder, or by failing to make any report required under this Agreement, or by making a false report, or for cause, and LICENSEE shall fail to remedy such default within ten (10) days for money, and thirty (30) days for reports, after notice thereof by LICENSOR, LICENSOR may, at its option, terminate this Agreement and the license granted herein by notice to that effect, but such act by LICENSOR shall not relieve LICENSEE of its liabilities accruing up to the time of termination. In the case of subsequent default, the time period which to remedy the default shall be reduced to fifteen (15) days.

(b) Should a third default take place, LICENSOR may, at its option, terminate this Agreement.

15. It is understood and agreed that if LICENSEE does not introduce the ITEM on or before (<u>enter date</u>) or does not sell the ITEM for a period of 90 consecutive days or

more except as provided in Paragraph 16 hereof, LICENSOR may give notice to LICENSEE of its desire to terminate this Agreement for that reason and if LICENSEE does not within thirty (30) days resume producing and selling of the ITEM, this Agreement and the license granted herein shall terminate as of the end of that thirty (30) day period.

16. It is understood and agreed that in the event an act of government, or war conditions, or fire, flood or labor trouble in the factory of LICENSEE, or in the factory of those manufacturing parts necessary for the manufacture of the ITEM, prevents the performance by LICENSEE of the provisions of this Agreement, then such non-performance by LICENSEE shall not be considered a breach of this Agreement and such non-performance shall be excused, but for no longer than a period of six (6) months on any single occurrence.

17. This Agreement shall continue for as long as the ITEM covered by this Agreement shall continue to be manufactured by LICENSEE, or unless sooner terminated under the provisions of this Agreement.

18. LICENSEE agrees that if this Agreement is terminated under any of its provisions, LICENSEE will not itself, or through others, thereafter manufacture and sell the ITEM and all rights to the ITEM and to any patents filed hereunder shall revert to LICENSOR.

19.(a) LICENSOR agrees that LICENSEE may assign this Agreement to any affiliate corporation; provided, however, that such assignee shall thereafter be bound by the provisions of this Agreement.

(b) LICENSEE may not assign this Agreement, or any part thereof, without the expressed written permission of LICENSOR, which shall not be unreasonably withheld, unless it is selling its entire business as a going concern, and the same restriction shall be binding upon successors and assigns of LICENSEE.

(c) Should LICENSEE wish to sell its rights in the ITEM or transfer this Agreement to any person or corporation that does not plan to purchase LICENSEE's entire business as a going concern, but has an interest only in said ITEM, then said prospective buyer will have to strike a separate deal with LICENSOR for its consent to the sale.

20.(a) In case of the Receivership or Bankruptcy of LICENSEE, by reason of which LICENSEE is prevented from carrying out the spirit of this Agreement, after written notice thereof by LICENSOR, LICENSOR may, at its option, terminate this Agreement and the license granted herein by notice to that effect, but such act shall not relieve LICENSEE of its liabilities accruing up to the time of termination.

(b) If LICENSEE, at any time after the execution of this Agreement and prior to and during the preparation of said ITEM for production, display and offering for sale, shall elect not to produce, display, offer or produce said ITEM, which election shall be in writing sent by Registered or Certified or Express Mail to LICENSOR, then LICENSOR's sole and exclusive remedy shall be to keep the advance against royalties, as provided for in Paragraph 4 hereof, for breach of this Agreement, and such Agreement shall thereafter be of no further force and effect, and the license shall be deemed canceled and neither party shall have claim against the other.

(c) Immediately upon expiration or termination of this Agreement, for any reason whatsoever, all the rights granted to LICENSEE hereunder shall cease and revert to LICENSOR, who shall be free to license others to use any or all of the rights granted herein effective on and after such date of expiration or termination, and to this end, LICENSEE will be deemed to have automatically assigned to LICENSOR upon such expiration or termination, all copyrights, trademarks and service mark rights, equities, good will, titles, designs and concepts, and other rights in or to the ITEM. LICENSEE will upon the expiration or termination of this license execute any instruments requested by LICENSOR to accomplish or confirm the foregoing. Any assignments shall be without consideration other than mutual covenants and considerations of this Agreement. In addition, for whatever reasons, LICENSEE will forthwith refrain from any further use of the trademarks or copyrights of any further reference to any of them, direct or indirect.

(d) In the event of termination of this Agreement, for any reason other than for failure to pay or make reports due hereunder to LICENSOR, LICENSEE shall have the right to dispose of its existing inventory for a period of 60 days. Further, upon termination of this Agreement, LICENSEE agrees to assign to LICENSOR the right to receive directly any royalties due to LICENSOR from any collateral merchandise sublicensee of the ITEM.

21. All notices wherever required in this Agreement shall be in writing and sent by Certified Mail, Registered Mail or Express Mail to the addresses first above written.

22. If any provisions of this Agreement are for any reason declared to be invalid, the validity of the remaining provisions shall not be affected thereby.

23. This Agreement shall be binding upon and inure to the benefit of the parties hereto and their successors and assigns as herein provided and said successors and assigns shall be libel hereunder. LICENSOR may assign its rights to receive royalties under this Agreement.

24. It is expressly agreed that LICENSOR is in no way the legal representative of LICENSEE and has no authority, expressed or implied, on behalf of LICENSEE to bind LICENSEE or to pledge its credit.

25. (Optional) It is a condition of this license that, if LICENSEE decides to market the ITEM under LICENSOR's trademark, (insert TM), LICENSEE shall cause the following notice to appear on the ITEM and its advertising, promotional, packaging and display materials therefor:

(insert trademark) is a TM of (insert name of TM owner)

Used with permission. All Rights Reserved.

26. This Agreement shall be construed in accordance with the laws of the State of
_____.

IN WITNESS WHEREOF, the parties have executed this Agreement in duplicate originals the day/year first hereinabove written.

LICENSOR _____

By _____

LICENSEE _____

By _____

Option Agreement

THIS AGREEMENT made as of this __ day of ___, 200__ between _____, located at _____ (hereinafter "LICENSOR"), and _____, located at _____ (hereinafter "LICENSEE").

WHEREAS, LICENSOR has invented a _____ (hereinafter "Item"), and

WHEREAS, LICENSOR has presented the Item to LICENSEE for evaluation and possible licensing; and

WHEREAS, LICENSEE wishes to review and evaluate the Item;

It is therefore agreed between the parties as follows:

LICENSOR agrees that LICENSEE may examine and evaluate the Item for a period commencing on the date of this Agreement and ending on (insert date) ("Review Period"). LICENSOR represents that, to the best of its knowledge, it has such rights in and title to the Item as to enable it to grant LICENSEE an exclusive license for its manufacture and sale. LICENSOR agrees that it will not license or disclose the Item or similar items during the Review Period to any other person, firm, corporation, or other entity in that would compete with LICENSEE.

LICENSOR agrees that should LICENSEE wish to license the Item, LICENSOR will enter into a mutually satisfactory licensing agreement for the exclusive use in the (define territory, e.g., US, Europe, worldwide, etc.) of the Item with LICENSEE or a subsidiary or affiliate designated by LICENSEE.

In consideration of the foregoing, LICENSEE agrees to pay to LICENSOR the sum of $_____, along with other good and valuable consideration, the receipt of which is hereby acknowledged. If LICENSEE decides to license the Item, it will so notify LICENSOR, by a written confirmation sent to LICENSOR at the address specified above, mailed no later than the last day of the Review Period, and both parties agree to negotiate a licensing agreement within thirty (30) days thereafter. In that event, LICENSEE may apply the above-referenced paid consideration against any royalties payable under the executed license agreement. In the event that LICENSEE does not elect to use the Item, it is agreed that LICENSOR shall be entitled to retain the entire sum payable hereunder.

IN WITNESS WHEREOF, the parties have executed this Agreement as of the date first written above.

LICENSOR: _____ LICENSEE: _____

Title: _____ Title: _____

Agreement to Hold Secret and Confidential

The below described invention, idea or concept (hereinafter referred to as INVENTION) is being submitted to _____ of _____ (hereinafter referred to as COMPANY) by _____ of _____ on ___ ___, 20___ (hereinafter referred to as INVENTOR) who is the inventor of record. The undersigned, in consideration of examining said INVENTION, with a purpose to opening negotiations to obtain a license to manufacture and sell said INVENTION, hereby agrees on behalf of himself/herself and said COMPANY that he/she represents, that:

1) He/she (during or after the termination of employment with said COMPANY) and said COMPANY, will keep said INVENTION, and any information pertaining to it, in confidence.

2) He/she will not disclose said INVENTION or data related thereto to anyone except for employees of said COMPANY, sufficient information about said INVENTION to enable said COMPANY to continue with negotiations for said license, and that anyone in said COMPANY to whom said INVENTION is revealed, shall be informed of the confidential nature of the disclosure and shall agree to hold confidential the information, and be bound by the terms hereof, to the same extent as if they had signed this Agreement.

3) Neither he/she nor said COMPANY shall use any of the information provided to produce said INVENTION until agreement is reached with INVENTOR.

4) He/she has the authority to make this Agreement on behalf of said COMPANY.

It is understood, nevertheless, that the undersigned and said COMPANY shall not be prevented by the Agreement from selling any product heretofore sold by said COMPANY, or any product in the development or planning stage, as of the date first above written, or any product disclosed in any heretofore issued U.S. Letters Patent or otherwise known to the general public.

The terms of the preceding section releasing, under certain conditions, the obligation to hold the disclosure in confidence does not however, constitute a waiver of any patent, copyright or other rights which said Inventor or any licensee thereof may have against the undersigned or said COMPANY.

IN WITNESS WHEREOF, the parties have signed this Agreement on the respective dates hereinafter written.

The INVENTION is generally described as follows:

Discloser: _____

Company Representative: _____

Date: _____

Resources

Toy and Game Manufacturers

This is a list of some companies that review and license outside concepts. There are fewer and fewer targets of opportunity in the toy industry because of acquisitions, principally by Hasbro and Mattel. This is not a complete list, but something to get you started.

For a complete list of the members of the Toy Industry Association, (formerly Toy Manufacturers of America, Inc.)
1115 Broadway, Suite 400
New York, NY 10010
TEL: (212) 675-1141, ext. 216
FAX: (212) 633-1429
E-mail: dianec@toy-tia.org
Web site: www.toy-tia.org

Bandai America, Inc.
5551 Katella Avenue
Cypress, CA 90630
TEL: (714) 816-9500
FAX: (714) 816-6713

Basic Fun
1080 Industrial Highway
Southampton, PA 18966
TEL: (215) 364-1665
FAX: (215) 364-9676

Blue Box Toys, Inc.
200 Fifth Ave.
New York, NY 10010
TEL: (212) 255-8388
FAX: (212) 255-8520

Briarpatch
150 Essex St., Suite 301
Milburn, NJ 07041
TEL: (973) 376-7002
FAX: (973) 376-7003

Cadaco
4300 W. 47th St.
Chicago, IL 60632
TEL: (312) 927-1500
FAX: (312) 927-3937

Cardinal Industries
21-01 51st Street
Long Island City, NY 11101
TEL: (718) 784-3000
FAX: (718) 482-7877

Decipher Inc.
253 Granby St.
Norfolk, VA 23510
TEL: (804) 623-3600
FAX: (804) 623-3630

DSI, Inc.
1100 W. Sam Houston Parkway N.
Houston, TX 77043
TEL: (713) 365-9900
FAX: (713) 365-9911

Duncan Toys Co.
15981 Valplast Rd.
P.O. Box 97
Middlefield, OH 44062
TEL: (440) 632-1631
FAX: (440) 632-1581

Endless Games, Inc.
22 Hudson Place
Hoboken, NJ 07030
TEL: (201) 386-9464
FAX: (201) 386-9471

Fundex Games
2920-A Fortune Circle West
Indianapolis, IN 46241
TEL: (317) 248-1080
FAX: (317) 248-1086

Funrise Toy Corp.
6115 Variel Ave.
Woodland Hills, CA 91367
TEL: (818) 883-2400
FAX: (818) 883-3809

Great American Puzzle Factory
16 South Main Street
S. Norwalk, CT 06854
TEL: (203) 838-4240
FAX: (203) 838-2065

Hasbro
1027 Newport Ave.
Pawtucket, RI 028
TEL: (401) 431-TOYS
FAX: (401) 727-5779

Hasbro Games Group
443 Shaker Rd.
E. Longmeadow, MA 01028
TEL: (413) 525-6411
FAX: (413) 525-1767

Irwin Toy Ltd.
43 Hanna Ave.
Toronto, ON M6K 1X6
Canada
TEL: (416) 533-3521
FAX: (416) 533-3257

Just Toys, Inc.
50 W. 23rd, 7th Fl.
New York, NY 10010
TEL: (212) 645-6335
FAX: (212) 741-8793

Larami Corp.
303 Fellowship Rd. Suite #110
Mt. Laurel, NJ 08054
TEL: (609) 439-1717
FAX: (609) 439-9732

Learning Curve Toys
311 W. Superior #416
Chicago, IL 60610
TEL: (312) 654-5960
FAX: (312) 654-8227

Lego Systems, Inc.
555 Taylor Rd.
Enfield, CT 06083-1600
TEL: (800) 243-4870
FAX: (203) 749-6077

Mattel Toys
333 Continental Blvd.
El Segundo, CA 90245-5012
TEL: (310) 524-2000
FAX: (310) 463-0571

The Ohio Art Co.
One Toy St.
Bryan, OH 43506
TEL: (419) 636-3141
FAX: (419) 636-7614

Playmates Toys, Inc.
16200 Trojan Way
La Mirada, CA 90638
TEL: (714) 739-1929
FAX: (714) 739-2912

Pressman Toy Corp.
200 Fifth Avenue, #1050
New York, NY 10010
TEL: (212) 675-7910
FAX: (212) 645-8512

Rose Art Industries, Inc.
6 Regent St.
Livingston, NJ 07039
TEL: (201) 535-1313
FAX: (201) 533-9447

Spin Master Toys
250 Esplanade, Suite 400
Toronto, ONT M5A 1J2
Canada
TEL: (416) 364-6002
FAX: (416) 364-8005

S.R.M.
5 Foxcroft Square
Jenkintown, PA 19046
TEL: (215) 572-6200
FAX: (215) 884-6525

Tiger Electronics Inc.
980 Woodlands Parkway
Vernon Hills, IL 60061
TEL: (708) 913-8100
FAX: (708) 913-8118

Tomy America, Inc.
18818 Teller Ave., Suite 210
Irvine, CA 92612
TEL: (949) 955-1030
FAX: (949) 955-1037

Tootsietoy-Strombecker Corp.
600 N. Pulaski Rd.
Chicago, IL 60624
TEL: (312) 638-1000
FAX: (312) 638-3679

Uncle Milton Industries
5717 Corsa Avenue
Westlake Village, CA 91362
TEL: (818) 707-0800
FAX: (818) 707-0878

University Games Corp.
2030 Harrison Street
San Francisco, CA 94110
TEL: (415) 503-1600
FAX: (415) 503-0085

WHAM-O
182 2nd Street, 3rd Fl.
San Francisco, CA 94105
TEL: (415) 357-4202
FAX: (415) 357-4292

Wild Planet Toys
98 Battery Street, Suite 300
San Francisco, CA 94111
TEL: (415) 705-8300
FAX: (415) 705-8311

Patent and Trademark Depository Libraries

To double-check phone numbers, addresses, etc., please call 1-800-786-9199, the PTO General Information Services number.

Alabama

Auburn University Libraries (205) 844-1737

Birmingham Public Library (205) 226-3620

Alaska

Anchorage: Z. J. Loussac Public Library (907) 562-7323

Arizona

Tempe: Noble Library, Arizona State University (602) 965-7010

Arkansas

Little Rock: Arkansas State Library (501) 682-2053

California

Los Angeles Public Library (213) 228-7220

Sacramento: California State Library (916) 654-0069

San Diego Public Library (619) 236-5813

San Francisco Public Library (415) 557-4488

Sunnyvale Patent Clearinghouse (408) 730-7290

Colorado

Denver Public Library (303) 640-8847

Connecticut

New Haven: Free Public Library (203) 946-7452

Hartford: Hartford Public Library (860) 543-8628

Delaware

Newark: University of Delaware Library (302) 831-2965

District of Columbia

Howard University Libraries (202) 806-7252

Florida

Fort Lauderdale: Broward County Main Library (305) 357-7444

Miami-Dade Public Library (305) 375-2665

Orlando: University of Central Florida Libraries (407) 823-2562

Tampa Campus Library, University of South Florida (813) 974-2726

Georgia

Atlanta: Price Gilbert Memorial Library, Georgia Institute of Technology (404) 894-4508

Hawaii

Honolulu: Hawaii State Public Library System (808) 586-3477

Idaho

Moscow: University of Idaho Library (208) 885-6235

Illinois

Chicago Public Library (312) 747-4450

Springfield: Illinois State Library (217) 782-5659

Indiana

Indianapolis-Marion County Public Library (317) 269-1741

West Lafayette: Siegesmund Engineering Library, Purdue University (317) 494-2872

Iowa

Des Moines: State Library of Iowa (515) 281-4118

Kansas

Wichita: Ablah Library, Wichita State Library (316) 689-3155

Kentucky

Louisville Free Public Library (502) 574-1611

Louisiana

Baton Rouge: Troy H. Middleton Library, Louisiana State University (504) 388-8875

Maine

Orono: Raymond H. Fogler Library, University of Maine (207) 581-1691

Maryland

College Park: Engineering and Physical Sciences Library, University of Maryland (301) 405-9157

Massachusetts

Amherst: Physical Sciences Library, University of Massachusetts (413) 545-1370

Boston Public Library (617) 536-5400, ext. 265

Michigan

Ann Arbor: Media Union, University of Michigan (734) 647-5735

Big Rapids: Abigail S. Timme Library, Ferris State University (616) 592-3602

Detroit Public Library (313) 833-3379

Minnesota

Minneapolis Public Library and Information Center (612) 630-6120

Mississippi

Jackson: Mississippi Library Commission (601) 961-4111

Missouri

Kansas City: Linda Hall Library (816) 363-4600

St. Louis Public Library (314) 241-2288, Ext. 390

Montana

Butte: Montana College of Mineral Science and Technology Library (406) 496-4281

Nebraska

Lincoln: Engineering Library, University of Nebraska-Lincoln (402) 472-3411

Nevada

Las Vegas: Clark County Library (Not Yet Operational)

Reno: University of Nevada-Reno Library (702) 784-6500

New Hampshire

Concord: New Hampshire State Library (603) 271-2239

New Jersey

Newark Public Library (973) 733-7779

Piscataway: Library of Science and Medicine, Rutgers University (908) 445-2895

New Mexico

Albuquerque: University of New Mexico General Library (505) 277-4412

New York

Albany: New York State Library (518) 474-5355

Buffalo and Erie Country Public Library (716) 858-7101

New York Public Library (The Research Libraries) (212) 592-7000

Rochester: Central Library of Rochester and Monroe County (716) 428-8110

Stony Brook: Melville Library, Room 1101, SUNY at Stony Brook (516) 632-7148

North Carolina

Raleigh: D.H. Hill Library, North Carolina State University (919) 515-2935

North Dakota

Grand Forks: Chester Fritz Library, University of North Dakota (701) 777-4888

Ohio

Akron-Summit County Public Library (330) 643-9075

Cincinnati and Hamilton County, Public Library of (513) 369-6971

Cleveland Public Library (216) 623-2870

Columbus: Ohio State University Libraries (614) 292-3022

Toledo/Lucas County Public Library (419) 259-5209

Oklahoma

Stillwater: Oklahoma State University Center for International Trade Development (405) 744-7086

Oregon

Portland: Lewis & Clark College (503) 768-6786

Pennsylvania

Philadelphia, The Free Library of (215) 686-5331

Pittsburgh, The Carnegie Library of (412) 622-3138

University Park: Paterno Library, Penn State University (814) 865-6369

Puerto Rico

Bayamon: General Library, University of Puerto Rico (787) 786-5225

Mayaguez: General Library, University of Puerto Rico (787) 832-4040, ext. 2022

Rhode Island

Providence Public Library (401) 455-8027

South Carolina

Clemson: R. M. Cooper Library, Clemson University (803) 656-3024

South Dakota

Rapid City: Devereaux Library, South Dakota School of Mines and Technology (605) 394-1275

Tennessee

Memphis & Shelby County Public Library and Information Center (901) 725-8877

Nashville: Stevenson Science Library, Vanderbilt University (615) 322-2775

Texas

Austin: McKinney Engineering Library, University of Texas at Austin (512) 495-4500

College Station: Sterling C. Evans Library, Texas A&M University (409) 845-5745

Dallas Public Library (214) 670-1468

Houston: Fondren Library, Rice University (713) 348-5483

San Antonio Public Library (Not Yet Operational)

Utah

Salt Lake City: Marriott Library, University of Utah (801) 581-8394

Vermont

Burlington: Baily/Howe Library, University of Vermont (802) 656-2542

Virginia

Richmond: James Branch Cabell Library, Virginia Commonwealth University (804) 828-1104

Washington

Seattle: Engineering Library, University of Washington (206) 543-0740

West Virginia

Morgantown: Evansdale Library, West Virginia University (304) 293-4695, ext. 5113

Wisconsin

Madison: Kurt F. Wendt Library, University of Wisconsin-Madison (608) 262-6845

Milwaukee Public Library (414) 286-3051

Wyoming

Cheyenne: Wyoming State Library (Not Yet Operational)

State and Local Inventor Organizations

The following list is current as of the date of publication. However, such organizations tend to come and go, so it's best to reconfirm the information before sending anything off to addresses noted. Again, I recommend the Patent Cafe's most excellent Web site for organization updates: www.patentcafe.com/inventor_orgs/assoc.html. I am told that the USPTO uses it as a reference, too.

Alabama

Invent Alabama
Bruce Koppenhoefer
137 Mission Circle
Montevallo, AL 35115
TEL: (205) 663-9982
FAX: (205) 250-8013
E-mail: BKOPPENHOE@aol.com

Alaska

Alaska Inventors & Entrepreneurs
Pam Middaugh
P.O. Box 241801
Anchorage, AK 99524-1801
TEL: (907) 563-4337
FAX: same
E-mail: inventor@arctic.net

Inventors Institute of Alaska
Al Jorgensen
P.O. Box 876154

Wasilla, AK 99687
TEL: (907) 376-5114

Arkansas

Inventors Congress Inc.
Garland Bull
Rt. 2 - P.O. Box 1630
Dandanell, AR 72834
TEL: (501) 229-4515

Arizona

Inventors Association of Arizona
P.O. Box 12217
Tucson, AZ 85732
TEL: 520-721-8540
FAX: 520-721-2488
E-mail: Tucson–Lisa Lloyd
Phoenix–Linda Schuerman
(800) 299-6787

California

Inventors Forum
Scott Gilzean
80 Huntington St. #9
Huntington Beach, CA 92648
TEL: (714) 540-2491
FAX: (714) 668-0583

Inventors Alliance
Andrew Krauss
P.O. BOX 390219
Mountain View, CA 94039-390219
TEL: (650) 964-1576
FAX: same
E-mail: andrewinvents@onebox.com

Central Valley Inventor's Assn.
John Christensen
P.O. Box 1551
Manteca, CA 95336
TEL: (209) 239-5414
FAX: same
E-mail: cdesigns@softcom.net

Contra Costa Inventors Club
Sherm Fishman
295 Stevenson Dr.
Pleasant Hill, CA 94523-4149
TEL: (510) 934-1331
FAX: (510) 934-1132

Inventors' Alliance of Northern
California
Jerry Richmond
737 Auditorium Drive, Suite A
Redding, CA 96001
TEL: (530) 225-2770
E-mail: jrichmond@scedd.org

Inventors Forum of San Diego
Greg Lauren
11190 Poblado Rd.
San Diego, CA 92127
TEL: (619) 673-4733
FAX: (619) 451-6154

Bruce Sawyer Center
Charles Robbins
520 Mendocino Ave., Suite 210
Santa Rosa, CA 95401
TEL: (707) 524-1773

American Inventor Network
Jeff McGrew
1320 High School Rd.
Sebastopol, CA 95472
TEL: (707) 823-3865
FAX: (707) 823-0913

Idea to Market Network
P.O. Box 12248
Santa Rosa, CA 95406
(800) ITM-3210

Inventors Forum (Whittier Chapter)
Anthony Harris
14034 Oval Drive
Whittier, CA 90605
TEL: (562) 464-0069
E-mail: AnthonyH@inventorsform.org

Colorado

Rocky Mountain Inventors Congress
Hal Linke
P.O. Box 36233
Denver, CO 80236
TEL: (303) 670-3760
E-mail: info@RMinventor.org

Connecticut

Inventors Association of Connecticut
Mary Ellroy
9-B Greenhouse Road
Bridgeport, CT 06606-2130
TEL: (203) 866-0720
FAX: (781) 846-6448
E-mail: gamebird@compuserve.com

Innovators Guild
Robin Faulkner
2 Worden Road
Danbury, CT 06811
TEL: (203) 790-8235
E-mail: RFaulkner@snet.net

Delaware

Delaware Entrepreneurs Forum
Colleen Wolf
P.O. Box 278
Yorklyn, DE 19736
TEL: (302) 652-4241

District of Columbia

Inventors Network of the Capital Area
Bill Kuntz
Building 31C at National Institutes for
Health (NIH)
Bethesda, MD
TEL: (703) 971-9216
FAX: same
E-mail: info@inca.hispeed.net

Florida

Inventors Society of South Florida
Joanna Zaremba
P.O. Box 4306
Boynton, Beach, FL 33424
TEL: (954) 486-2426

Edison Inventors' Association, Inc.
Gary Nelson
P.O. Box 07398
Ft. Myers, FL 33919
TEL: (941) 275-4332
FAX: (941) 267-9746
E-mail: drghn@aol.com

Tampa Bay Inventors' Council
David Kiewit
5901 Third Street South

St. Petersburg, FL 33779
TEL: (727) 866-0669
FAX: same
E-mail: KIEWIT@patent-faq.com

Inventors' Council of Central Florida
David Flinchbaugh
4855 Big Oaks Ln.
Orlando, FL 32806-7826
TEL: (407) 859-4855
FAX: (407) 438-3922

Emerald Coast Inventors' Society
Earnie DeVille
c/o UWF-SBDC
11000 University
Pensacola, FL 32514-5752
TEL: (904) 455-4641

Space Coast Inventors Guild
Angel L. Pacheco, Sr.
1221 Pine Tree Dr.
Indian Harbour Beach, FL 32937
TEL: (407) 773-4031
FAX: same

Georgia

Inventor Association of Georgia, Inc.
Bob Miquelon
1608 Pelham Way
Macon, GA 31220
TEL: (912) 474-6948
FAX: (770) 840-8814
E-mail: jrmiq@mindspring.com

Iowa

Drake University Inventure Program
Ben Swartz
SBDC-Drake University
2507 University Avenue
Des Moines, IA 50311
TEL: (515) 271-2655

Idaho

East Idaho Inventors Forum
John Wordin
P.O. Box 452
Shelly, ID 83274
TEL: (208) 346-6763
FAX: (208) 346-4388
E-mail: techhelp@srv.net

Illinois

Inventors' Council
Don Moyer
431 S. Dearborne #705
Chicago, IL 60605
TEL: (312) 939-3329
FAX: (312) 922-7706
E-mail: patent@donmoyer.com

Illinois Innovators & Inventor's Club
Phil Curry
P.O. Box 623
Edwardsville, IL 62025
TEL: (618) 656-7445

Illinois Group
Dr. Tom Honsa
3637 23rd Ave.
Moline, IL 61265
TEL: (309) 762-6936
FAX: (309) 762-6939

Indiana

Indiana Inventors Association
Robert Humbert
5514 So. Adams
Marion, IN 46953
TEL: (765) 674-2845
FAX: (765) 733-0579
E-mail: arhumbert@busprod.com

Inventors Council (Wabash)
Bud Pressler
2783 E. Old 24
Wabash, IN 46992
TEL: (219) 782-2511

Kansas

Inventors Association of South
Central Kansas
Richard Friedenberger
2302 No. Amarado St.
Wichita KS, 67205
TEL: (316) 721-1866
E-mail: rlfreid@southwind.net

Kansas Association of Inventors
Clayton Williamson
272 W. 6th St.
Hoisington, KS 67544
TEL: (316) 653-2165
E-mail: clayton@hoisington.com

Kentucky

Central Kentucky Inventors and
Entrepreneurs
Mohamed H. Nasser
117 Carolyn Drive
Nicholasville, KY 40356
TEL: (606) 885-9593
FAX: (606) 887-9850
E-mail: nashky@IBM.net

Louisiana

Louisiana Inventors Association
Kyle Rainey
14724 Vinewood Drive
Baton Rouge, LA 70816
TEL: 225-752-3783
E-mail: info@recyclecycle.com

341

Maine

Portland Inventors Forum
Att: Jake Ward
University of Maine
5717 Corbett Hall
Orono, ME 04469-5717
TEL: (207) 581-1488
FAX: (207) 581-1479
E-mail: jsward@maine.edu

Maryland

Inventors Network of the Capital Area
Bill Kuntz
Building 31C at National Institutes for
Health (NIH)
Bethesda, MD
TEL: (703) 971-9216
FAX: same
E-mail: info@inca.hispeed.com

Massachusetts

Cape Cod Inventors Association
Ernest Bauer
Briar Main
P.O. Box 143
Wellfleet, MA 02667
TEL: (508) 349-1629

Inventors Association of New England
Chris Holt
P.O. Box 577
Pepperell, MA 01463
TEL: (978) 533-2397
E-mail: crholt@aol.com

Innovators Resource Network
Dave Cormier and Karyl Lynch
Pelham West Associates
P.O. Box 137
Shutesbury, MA 01072-0137
TEL: (413) 259-2006
E-mail: info@pelhamwest.com

Worcester Area Inventors
Barbara Wyatt
132 Sterling Street
West Boylston, MA 01583
TEL: (508) 835-6435
FAX: (508) 799-2796
E-mail: barbara@nedcorp.com

Michigan

Inventors Clubs of America
Carl Preston
524 Curtis Rd.
East Lansing, MI 48823
TEL: (517) 332-3561

Inventors Association of Metro
Detroit
Peter D. Keefe
24405 Gratiot Ave.
Eastpointe, MI 48021-3306
TEL: (810) 772-7888
FAX: (810) 774-5848

Inventors Council of Mid-Michigan
Bob Ross
519 S. Saginaw, Suite 200
Flint, MI 48502
www.rjriley.com/icmm
TEL: (810) 232-7909
FAX: (810) 233-7437
E-mail: LFORD22649@aol.com

Inventors Club of Michigan
Tom Milgie
24685 Ravine Circle, Apt. 203
Farmington Hills, MI 48335
TEL: (810) 870-9139

Minnesota

Inventors' Network
Bill Baker
23 Empire Dr., Suite 105
St. Paul, MN 55103
TEL: (651) 374-5234

Society of Minnesota Inventors
Paul Paris
20231 Basalt St. NW
Anoka, MN 55303
TEL: (612) 753-2766
FAX: (612) 753-6817
E-mail: paulparis@uswest.net

Minnesota Inventors Congress
Sara Madsen, Coordinator
P.O. Box 71
Redwood Falls, MN 56283-0071
TEL: (507) 637-2344
TEL: (800) 468-3681
FAX: (507) 637-8399
E-mail: mic@invent1.org

Missouri

Women's Inventor Project
Betty Rozier
7400 Foxmount
Hazlewood, MO 63042

Mid-America Inventors Association
Carl Minzes
8911 East 29th St.
Kansas City, MO 64129-1502
TEL: (816) 254-9542
FAX: (816) 221-3995

Inventors Association of St. Louis
Robert Scheinkman
P.O. Box 410111
St. Louis, MO 63141
TEL: (314) 432-1291

Mississippi

Society of Mississippi Inventors
Bob Lantrip
University of Mississippi-SBDC
216 Old Chemistry Bldg.
University, MS 38677
TEL: (601) 232-5001
FAX: (601) 232-5650
E-mail: blantrip@olemiss.edu

Montana

Yellowstone Inventors
Warren George
3 Carrie Lynn
Billings, MT 59102
TEL: (406) 259-9110

Montana Inventors Assn.
Casey Emerson
5350 Love Lane
Bozeman, MT 59715
TEL: (406) 586-1541
FAX: (406) 585-9028

North Dakota

North Dakota Inventors Congress
Arvid Brockman
P.O. Box 1530
Jamestown, ND 58401
TEL: (701) 252-4959
FAX: (701) 252-4999

Nebraska

Lincoln Inventors Association
Roger Reyda
92 Ideal Way
Brainard, NE 68626
TEL: (402) 545-2179
FAX: same

Nevada

Nevada Inventors Association
Tony Patti
P.O. Box 11008
Reno, NV 89506
TEL: (702) 677-4824
FAX: (702) 677-4888
E-mail: rvrdl@aol.com

343

Inventors Society of Southern Nevada
Penny J. Ballou
3627 Huerta Drive
Las Vegas, NV 89121
TEL: (702) 435-7741
FAX: same
E-mail: InventSSN@aol.com

New Hampshire

New Hampshire Inventors Assn.
John Rocheleau
P.O. Box 272
Concord, NH 03202-2772
TEL: (603) 228-3854
FAX: (603) 227-0886
E-mail: john@nhinventor.com

New Jersey

Jersey Shore Inventors Club
Ed McClain
416 Park Place Ave.
Bradley Beach NJ 07720
TEL: (732) 776-8467
FAX: (732) 776-5418
E-mail: 2edeilmcclain@msn.com

National Society of Inventors
Shelia Kalisher
94 North Rockledge Dr.
Livingston, NJ 07039-1121
TEL: (973) 994-9282
FAX: (973) 535-0777

New Jersey Entrepreneurs Forum
Jeff Millinetti
325 Kimball Ave
Westfield, NJ 07090
TEL: (908) 789-3424
FAX: (908) 789-9761

New Mexico

New Mexico Inventors Club
Albert Goodman
P.O. Box 30062
Albuquerque, NM 87190
TEL: (505) 266-3541
FAX: same

New York

Inv. Alliance of America—Buffalo
Chapter
Mark Ellwood
300 Pearl St.
Olympic Twrs, Suite 200
Buffalo, NY 14202
TEL: (716) 842-4561
E-mail: ellwood@netcom.ca

NY Society of Professional Inventors
Daniel Weiss
P.O. Box 216
Farmingdale, NY 11735-9996
TEL: (516) 798-1490
FAX: (516) 799-1362

Long Island Forum for Technology, Inc.
Phil Orlando
P.O. Box 170
Farmingdale, NY 11735
TEL: (516) 755-3321
FAX: (516) 755-9264
E-mail: porlando@lift.org

Inventors Alliance of America—
Rochester Chapter
Jim Chiello
97 Pinebrook Dr.
Rochester, NY 14616
TEL: (716) 225-3750
FAX: (716) 225-2712
E-mail: InventNY@aol.com

Ohio

Inventors Network of Greater Akron
John Sovis
1741 Stone Creek Ln.
Twinsburg, OH 44087
TEL: (330) 425-1749
FAX: (330) 461-2416

Inventors Council of Cincinnati
Cookie McDonough
5840 Price Rd.
Milford, OH 45150-1425
TEL: (513) 831-3011

Inventors Connection of Greater
Cleveland
Murray Henderson
P.O. Box 360804
Cleveland, OH 44136
TEL: (440) 543-3594
FAX: (440) 543-0354
E-mail: icgc@usa.com

Inventors Network, Inc.
Bob Stonecypher
1275 Kinnear Rd.
Columbus, OH 43212
TEL: (614) 470-0144
E-mail: 13832667@msn.com

Inventors Council of Canton
Frank Fleischer
303 55th Street NW
No. Canton, OH 44720
TEL: (330) 499-1262
E-mail: fleischerb@aol.com

Inventors Council of Dayton
George Pierce
P.O. Box 611
Dayton, OH 45409
Tel: (937) 293-2770
E-mail: geopierce@earthlink.net

Youngstown-Warren Inv. Assn.
Heather Barnes
McLaughlin & McNally
500 City Centre One
Youngstown, OH 44503
TEL: (330) 744-4481
E-mail: mm@cisnet.com

Oklahoma

Oklahoma Inventors Congress
William H. Baker
3212 NW 35th Street
Oklahoma City, OK 73112
TEL: (405) 947-5782
FAX: (405) 947-6950
E-mail: w.baker@cwix.com

Week-End Entrepreneurs
Dale Davis
8102 S. Sandusky Ave.
Tulsa, OK 74137-1831
TEL: (918) 664-5831
FAX: same

Oregon

So. Oregon Inventors Council
Nancy Hudson
332 W. 6th St.
SBDC@ S. Oregon State
Medford, OR 97501
TEL: (541) 772-3478
FAX: (541) 734-4813
E-mail: Smartly2@aol.com

Pennsylvania

American Society of Inventors
Jay Cohen
P.O. Box 58426
Philadelphia, PA 19102
TEL: (215) 546-6601

Pennsylvania Inventors Assn.
Jerry T. Gorniak
2317 East 43rd St.
Erie, PA 16510
TEL: (814) 825-5820
E-mail: dhbutler@velocity.net

Northwest Inventors Council
Robert Jordon
Gannon University
Erie, PA 16541
TEL: (814) 871-7619
FAX: (814) 455-2631

South Carolina

Carolina Inventors Council
Johnny Sheppard
2960 Dacusville Highway
Easley, SC 29640
TEL: (864) 859-0066
E-mail: john17@home.com

Inventors & Entrepreneurs Association
of South Carolina
Charles Sprouse
P.O. Box 4123
Greenville, SC 29608
TEL: (864) 244-1045

South Dakota

South Dakota Inventors Congress
Kent Rufer
SDSU-EERC
P.O. Box 2220
Brookings, SD 57007
TEL: (605) 688-4184
FAX: (605) 688-5880

Tennessee

Tennessee Inventors Assn.
John Galkiewicz
P.O. Box 11225
Knoxville, TN 37939
TEL: (423) 869-8138
E-mail: bealaj@aol.com

Inventors' Association of Middle
Tennessee and South Kentucky
Marshal Frazer
3908 Trimble Rd.
Nashville, TN 37215
TEL: (615) 269-4346

Texas

Amarillo Inventors Association
Pauline Hefley
2028 S. Austin #901
Amarillo, TX 79109
TEL: (806) 351-0702
FAX: (806) 351-0170
E-mail: phefley@gateway.net

Houston Inventors Association
Chuck Mullen
2916 West TC Jexter #105
Houston, TX 77018
TEL: (713) 686-7676
FAX: (281) 326-1795
E-mail: kenroddy@nol.net

Laredo Inventors Association
Jorge Guerra
210 Palm Circle
Laredo, TX 78041
TEL: (956) 725-5863

Network of American Inventors
& Entrepreneurs
Alison McCaleb, President
P.O. Box 667113
Houston, TX 77006
TEL: (713) 523-3923
E-mail: mcalicat@netscape.net

South Texas Inventors &
Entrepreneurs Association
Andrew Taylor
P.O. Box 700287
San Antonio, TX 78270
TEL: (210) 491-6554
E-mail: hoh1@flash.net

Vermont

Inventors Network of Vermont
Joe Cammaratta
6 Bellows Rd.
Springfield, VT 05156
TEL: (802) 885-8094
E-mail: jtenter@excite.com

Virginia

Inventors Network of the
Capital Area
Bill Kuntz
Building 31C at National Institutes
for Health (NIH)
Bethesda, MD
TEL: (703) 971-9216
FAX: same
E-mail: info@inca.hispeed.com

Assoc. for Science, Technology &
Innovation
Robert Adams
P.O. Box 1242
Arlington, VA 22210
TEL: (703) 241-2850

Blue Ridge Inventor's Club
Mac Woodward
P.O. Box 6701
Charlottesville, VA 22906-6701
TEL: (804) 973-3708
FAX: (804) 973-2004
E-mail: mac@luckycat.com

Washington

Inventors Network
Rick Aydelott
P.O. Box 5575
Vancouver, WA 98668
TEL: (503) 239-8299

Tri-Cities Enterprise Assn.
Dallas Breamer
2000 Logston Blvd.
Richland, WA 99352
TEL: (509) 375-3268
FAX: (509) 375-4838

Wisconsin

Central Wisconsin Inventors
Association
Steve Sorenson
P.O. Box 915
Manawa, WI 54949
TEL: (920) 596-3092
E-mail: drheat@excite.com

Inventors' Network of Wisconsin
Jeff Hitzler
Green Bay, WI
E-mail: jhitzler@megtec.com

Political Letter

Write to Your Elected Officials in Washington, D.C.

Stop Picking the PTO's Pockets

The 106th U.S. Congress passed an omnibus government-funding bill that included the U.S. Patent and Trademark Office. The PTO is totally, 100 percent, funded by user fees (e.g., filing fees paid by independent inventors, and such). But the Congress controls how the money is spent. Boo! Hiss!

The subject bill made $1,039,000,000 available to the PTO for 2001. Based upon projected PTO income for the same period, this signifies that Congress will divert $161 million from the PTO and spend it elsewhere. Much of it will no doubt wind up in pork barrel projects in legislators' home districts.

Since 1992, Congress has diverted, rescinded, or otherwise not made available to the PTO more than $715 million. This is your money. And PTO fees continue to escalate to make up the shortfall. Urge your representatives to let the PTO keep what it earns, and then it will be able to hold its fees at present levels.

Richard C. Levy

Index

SYMBOLS

10 commandments for success, 12-19
10-K (SEC filing), 72-75

A

abandonment
    patent applications, 263
    patents, 271-272
Abstract of the Disclosure, non-provisional application, 178
"actions," patent applications, 258
admission prices, trade shows, 65
Advanced Technology Program. *See* ATP
advances
    licensing agreements, 121
    negotiating deals, 107
advantages
    licensing option (commercializing your invention), 49
    venturing option (commercializing your invention), 51-54
advertising, as element of presentation binder, 95
agents
    locating honest brokers, 40-41
    marketing, profile of reputable agents, 37
agreements, 317
    getting through the door, 87
    Hold Secret and Confidential, 327-328
    License, 317-326
    Option, 326-327
AIC (American Inventors Corporation), 24-25
AIRD (American Institute for Research and Development), 25
alternative marks (trademarks), 225
    certification marks, 226
    collective marks, 227
    service marks, 226
    trade and commercial names, 227
amending applications, patent applications, 260-261
American Institute for Research and Development. *See* AIRD
American Inventors Corporation. *See* AIC

American Inventors Protection Act, 28, 132, 141-142
    OIIP (Office of Independent Inventor Programs), 141-142
    outreach programs, 142
    workshops, 141
American
    mindset, 7
    ingenuity, 8
        Witcomb L. Judson, 9
    organizations, 309-310
annual reports, SEC, 72
Apley, Richard J. (Director of the Office of Independent Inventor Programs), 141
appeals, patent applications, 263
applications
    copyrights
        Form CA, 250
        Form RE, 250
        Form TX, 249
        Form VA, 250
    design patents, 203-211
        claims, 209-210
        drawings or photographs, 214-218
        figure descriptions, 213
        insurance against competitors, 204-205
        Preamble, 212
        single claim, 213
    federal trademark registration, 234
    patents, 257
        "actions," 258
        amending applications, 260-261
        appeals, 263
        assignment, 267
        final rejection, 260
        interference proceedings, 264-265
        responding to an examiner, 259-260
        time for response and abandonment, 263
    plant patents, 189-198, 201-202
        claims, 197
        cost, 194
        drawings, 197
        fees, 198
        growing business, 190
        infringement, 193-194
        oath/declaration, 197
        patent-protection limitations, 192

        specification, 195-196
        specimens, 197
        utility plant patents, 191
        who can apply, 192
    utility patents, 173-174
        nonprovisional applications, 175-185
        provisional applications, 174
Argonne National Laboratory, 46
asexual reproduction, plant patents, 199
assignment of patent applications, 267
Assistant Commissioner for Trademarks, 132
Association of University Technology Managers. *See* AUTM
ATP (Advanced Technology Program), 277
    partnerships, 278
    portfolio, 278-279
    proposals, 279-280
        Proposal Preparation Kit, 279
attorneys (patent), fees and scams, 22-23
AUTM (Association of University Technology Managers), 276
Automated Line/Status of TM Applications, 132

B

Background of the Invention, nonprovisional application, 177
best efforts (licensing agreement), 122
Biro, Laszlo (developer of ballpoint pen), 6
Board of Patent Appeals and Interferences, 133
broken lines, drawings or photographs (design patent applications), 216
brokers, locating honest brokers, 40-41
business options, commercializing your invention, 44
    costs, 57
    licensing, 46-50
    looking at exit strategies, 56-57

organizations to aid in decision, 57
prerequisites, 55
venturing, 51-55

C

cannibalizing, 56
categories, copyrightable works, 240-241
CCPA (Court of Customs and Patent Appeals). *See* Court of Appeals for the Federal Circuit
certification marks, 226
champions, selling your idea, 99
Chief Administrative Patent Judge, 263
claim limited knowledge (licensing agreement), 120
claims
    design patent applications, 209-210
    nonprovisional application, specification, 178
    plant patent applications, 197
classification system (patents), 157-158
co-ownership of patents, 266
collective marks, 227
color-coding sheet, plant patent applications, 195
colors, as a trademark, 222
commercial names, 227
commercializing your invention, 44
    costs, 57
    licensing option, 46
        advantages, 49
        disadvantages, 50
        manufacturers seek risk reduction, 47
        MBA syndrome, 48-49
        reinventing inventors, 46
        relationship with licensees, 47-48
    looking at exit strategies, 56-57
    organizations to aid in decision, 57
    prerequisites, 55
    venturing option, 51
        advantages, 51-54
        disadvantages, 54-55
companies, scams, 23-25
computer programs, patentability, 185
"conception of the invention," 265
conducting business (negotiating deals), 105
conferences, locating the right partner, 66
consultants, 40
Continental Ventures, 24

contract agreements, negotiating deals, 108-110
contracts, lawyers, 103
Copyright Office, 240-241
Copyright Office Electronic Registration, Recordation, and Deposit System. *See* CORDS
copyrights, 143-150, 240-249
    application forms
        Form CA, 250
        Form RE, 250
        Form TX, 249
        Form VA, 250
    categories, 240-241
    Copyright Office, 240-241
    CORDS, 246-247
    duration, 245
    eligible applicants, 243
    ineligible categories, 245
    investigating the copyright status of a work, 248-249
    Notice of Copyright, 243
    resources, 248
    searching copyright records, 247
        individual searches, 249
    securing, 241-242
    submitting registrations, 247
copies of patents (USPTO), 136
CORDS (Copyright Office Electronic Registration, Recordation, and Deposit System), 246-247
corporate culture, getting through the door, 85
corporate profiles, locating, 76
    Standard & Poors, 77
    Thomas Register, 77
correspondence·
    Federal Trademark Registration, 235
    trademark matters, 225
costs
    commercialization strategies, 57
    plant patents, 194
Court of Appeals for the Federal Circuit (former CCPA, Court of Customs and Patent Appeals), 185, 264
Court of Customs and Patent Appeals. *See* Court of Appeals for the Federal Circuit
court protection, trade secrets, 252
Critical Infrastructure Protection Grants Program, 279
cross-reference to related applications, nonprovisional application, specification, 177
customers, 163

D

databases, patent searches, 154
deal negotiations, 101
    advances, 107
    agreeing to agree, 106
    conducting business, 105
    contract agreements, 108-110
    guarantees, 107
    lawyering, 102
        approaching the company, 102-103
        contracts, 103
        patents, 104
    licensing agreements, 110-114
        fairness and flexibility, 115-116
        Management by Objectives, 116-117
        setting the scene and the mind, 118-124
        spirit of agreement, 117
        standard agreements, 114-115
    option agreements, 108
    patent and trademark ownership, 111
    royalties, 107
    winning at what cost, 105
declaration/oath
    nonprovisional applications, 179-185
    plant patent applications, 197
Department of Defense, federally funded research and development centers, 281
Department of Energy. *See* DOE
Department of Health and Human Services, federally funded research and development centers, 282
depository libraries, patents and trademarks, 332-338
description of invention (licensing agreement), 120
design patents, 128, 143, 203-204
    applications, 211
        claims, 209-210
        drawings or photographs, 214-218
        figure descriptions, 213
        Preamble, 212
        single claim, 213
    defining design, 209
    draftsmen, 206
    form over function, 204-205
    improper subject matter, 210
    insurance against competitors, 204-205
    patent attorneys, 206
    types of designs and modified forms, 209
    value, 207
    versus utility patents, 210

disadvantages
  licensing option (commercial-
    izing your invention), 50
  venturing option (commercial-
    izing your invention), 54-55
disclosure documents (USPTO),
  136-139
do-it-yourself patent searches, 149
  Internet Search, 151
  Scientific Library of the Patent
    and Trademark Office, 151
  USPTO Patent Public Search
    Room, 149-150
do-it-yourself trademark searches,
  232
DOE (Department of Energy), 283
  grants, 285-286
  I&I program, 286
    stages, 287
    success stories, 288
  OIT (Office of Industrial
    Technologies), 283-284
    success stories, 284-285
drafting symbols, drawings or
  photographs (design patent
  applications), 216
draftsmen, design patents, 206
drawings
  nonprovisional applications,
    179
  plant patent applications, 197
drawings or photographs, design
  patent applications, 214-218
  broken lines, 216
  surface shading and drafting
    symbols, 216
  views, 215
Driscoll's, 192
duration of copyrights, 245

E

EAST (Examiner Automated
  Search Tool), 150
EBC (Electronic Business Center),
  177
Edison, Thomas Alva, 11
education, 11
effective logos, characteristics,
  152
EFS (Electronic Filing System),
  177
Electronic Business Center. *See*
  EBC
electronic databases, patent
  searches, 154
Electronic Filing System. *See* EFS
elements
  design patent applications,
    211
    drawings or photographs,
      214-218
    figure descriptions, 213
    Preamble, 212
    single claim, 213

proposals, 93-94
  multiple submissions, 98
  presentation binder con-
    tents, 94-97
  taking products to tooling,
    97-98
eligibility
  application for Federal
    Trademark Registration, 234
  copyrights, 243
Employment Agreements, scams,
  36
Encyclopedia of Associations, 66
enforcement insurance, patents,
  269-270
English requirement, non-
  provisional applications, 181
evaluation criteria, SBIR programs, 291
examination, application for
  trademarks, 235-236
Examiner Automated Search Tool.
  See EAST
Examiners, patents, 133
exclusivity (licensing agreement),
  120
exit strategies, as factor when
  choosing commercialization
  strategy, 56-57

F

facsimile submissions, documents
  not accepted by the USPTO, 186
Fashion Institute of Technology,
  Toy Design degree, 305
Federal Trade Commission. *See*
  FTC
Federal Trademark Registration,
  227-228
  application examination,
    235-236
  correspondence, 235
  eligibility for application, 234
  foreign application, 235
  issuance of certification of reg-
    istration or notice of
    allowance, 236
  publication for opposition,
    236
  types of applications, 234
Federally Funded Research and
  Development Centers. *See*
  FFRDCs
fees
  copies of patents from USPTO,
    136
  kill, 9
  patents
    attorneys, scams, 22-23
    maintenance, 266
    plant patent applications,
      198
  up-front, 33

FFRDCs (Federally Funded
  Research and Development
  Centers), 281, 293
  Department of Defense, 281
  Department of Health and
    Human Services, 282
  National Aeronautics and
    Space Administration, 282
  National Science Foundation,
    283
figure descriptions, design patent
  applications, 213
filing date, provisional applications, 174
final rejection, patent applications, 260
Fire Research Grants, 279
firms
  patent search, 148-149
  scams, 23-25
first impressions, getting in the
  door to sell your invention,
  80-81
FirstGov Web site, 85
flexibility, licensing agreements,
  115-116
foreign applications, Federal
  Trademark Registration, 235
Foreign Rights (licensing agreement), 123
Form CA (copyright application),
  250
form over function, design
  patents, 204-205
Form RE (copyright application),
  250
Form TX (copyright application),
  249
Form VA (copyright application),
  250
forms of trademarks, 221
  colors, 222
  scents, 221
  translation considerations,
    222-224
frauds. *See* scams
fraudulent companies versus
  legitimate, 32-35
FTC (Federal Trade Commission),
  26, 267
  reporting problems, 37
  warnings, invention promo-
    tion firms, 30-31
  Web site, 26
function of trademarks, 227

G

games, manufacturers, 329-331
Gee Whiz Factor, 72
General Information Services
  (USPTO), 183
General Trademark Information,
  132

getting in the door (selling your invention), 80
  choosing your target and making your mark, 83-85
  corporate culture, 85
  first impressions, 80-81
  hooks, 85-87
    sources, 86-87
  N.I.H., 81-82
  signed agreements, 87
GIS (Greentree Information Services), 149, 231
Government Affairs Subcommittee on Regulation and Government Information, 27
grants
  Critical Infrastructure Protection Grants Program, 279
  DOE (Department of Energy), 285-286
  Fire Research Grants, 279
  Materials Science and Engineering Grants, 279
  Precision Measurement Grants, 279
Greentree Information Services. *See* GIS
guarantees, 87
  licensing agreements, 122
  negotiating deals, 107

H–I

Handbook for Inventors, 162
hiring a patent attorney
  interview questions, 164-165
  laying the groundwork, 169
  rules, 165-168
Hold Secret and Confidential agreement, 327-328
honesty, 90
hooks, getting through the door, 85-87
  sources, 86-87
Houston Inventors Association, 309

I&I (Inventions and Innovation) program of DOE, 286
  stages, 287
  success stories, 288
IAG (Inventors Awareness Group), 27
  Web site, 28
ideas, pitching, 5, 7
  champions, 99
  elements of a proposal, 93-98
  follow-ups, 28-29
  gaining attention, 90-92
  multiple submissions, 98
  PPP (Post-Pitch-Propulsion), 92-93
  unfavorable odds, 99

improper subject matter, design patents, 210
In on the Take-Off, In on the Landing (licensing agreement), 120
indemnifications (licensing agreement), 123
  licensee, 118
  licensor, 119
independence of Americans, examples of American ingenuity, Witcomb L. Judson, 7-9
Independent Inventor Program Office (USPTO), 29
independent inventors
  toy industry, 305-306
  trade secrets, 254
individual searches for copyright records, 249
ineligible categories, copyrights, 245
informal organizations, 316
infringement
  infringers, 159
  patents, 267-268
    plant, 193-194
    suing for damages, 268-269
ingenuity of Americans, Witcomb L. Judson, 8-9
innovation, USG labs, 281
inquiries, plant patents, 198
Inside Santa's Workshop, 297
insurance patents, enforcement, 269-270
intellectual property, 155
Intellectual Property Owners. *See* IPO
intentional abandonment of patents, 271-272
interference proceedings, patent applications, 264-265
Internet search
  do-it-yourself patent searches, 151
  trademark searches, 232
interviewing patent attorneys, 164-165
Inventions and Innovation program (DOE). *See* I&I program of DOE
Inventive Thinking Curriculum Project, The, 181
inventor organizations. *See* organizations
Inventor's Digest, 8
Inventor's Notebook, 129
Inventor's Workshop International. *See* IWIEF
Inventors Awareness Group. *See* IAG
investing in your invention, time commitment, 9-10
IP searches (licensing agreement), 123
IPO (Intellectual Property Owners), 162, 313-314

issuance of certification of registration, application for trademarks, 236
IWIEF (Inventor's Workshop International), 32

J–K–L

joint ownership of patents, 266
Judson, Witcomb L. (first patent on a slide fastener for shoes), 9

kill fee, 9

Lanham Act, 225
laws of patents, 131
law firm trademark searches, 230
lawyering, negotiating deals, 102
  approaching the company, 102-103
  contracts, 103
  patents, 104
legitimate companies versus fraudulent, 32-35
Library of Congress, Copyright Office, 240-241
License Agreement, 317-326
licensees, 62
  indemnification of, 118
licensing agreements, negotiating deals, 110-114
  fairness and flexibility, 115-116
  Management by Objectives, 116-117
  setting the scene and the mind, 118-124
  spirit of agreement, 117
  standard agreements, 114-115
Licensing Book, The, 230
licensing option (commercializing your invention), 46
  advantages, 49
  disadvantages, 50
  manufacturers seek risk reduction, 47
  MBA syndrome, 48-49
  prerequisites, 55
  reinventing inventors, 46
  relationship with licensees, 47-48
licensing partners, locating the right partner, 62-63
  big companies versus small companies, 67-71
  conferences and meetings, 66
  public companies versus private companies, 71-76
  trade shows, 64-66
licensors, 62
  indemnification of, 119
limitations of plant patents, 192-199
local inventor organizations, 314, 338-343

locating
  honest brokers, 40-41
  licensing partners, 62
    big companies versus small companies, 67-71
    conferences and meetings, 66
    public companies versus private companies, 71-76
    trade shows, 64-66
  product and corporate profiles, 76
    Standard & Poor's, 77
    Thomas Register, 77
    trade shows, 65-66
logos, 223
  characteristics, 152
logotypes. *See* logos
Lougher, Robert (founder of Inventors Awareness Group), 27

M

maintenance fees, patents, 266
Management by Objectives, licensing agreements, 116-117
Manual of Patent Examining Procedure, 186
manual patent searches (PSR and PTDLs), 156-157
manufacturers of toys and games, 329-331
Manufacturing Extension Partnership. *See* MEP
market analysis, as prerequisite for commercialization strategies, 55
marketing companies
  distinguishing between fraudulent and legitimate companies, 32-35
  locating honest brokers, 40-41
  profile of reputable company, 37
  things to do before signing with an invention marketer, 31
  warnings, 32
  what to do if you are a victim of a scam, 37
marketing plan, as element of presentation binder, 94
Materials Science and Engineering Grants, 279
mechanical advantage, 279
MEP (Manufacturing Extension Partnership), 280-281
models, nonprovisional applications, 180-181
modes of asexual reproduction, plant patents, 199
mothers of invention, 75
multiple submissions of proposals, 98

N

naming your product
  alternative marks, 225
    certification marks, 226
    collective marks, 227
    service marks, 226
    trade and commercial names, 227
  trademarks, 220
    do-it-yourself searches, 232
    Federal Trademark Registration, 227-236
    forms, 221-222
    function, 227
    Internet searches, 232
    law firm trademark search, 230
    professional trademark search, 230-232
    registerable marks, 229
    rights, 232-233
    searches for conflicting marks, 230
    symbols, 235
    terms, 234
    those not subject to registration, 228-229
    translation considerations, 222-224
    USPTO, 224-225
National Aeronautics and Space Administration, 282
National Institute of Standards and Technology. *See* NIST
national organizations, 310-311
  IPO, 313-314
  UIA, 311-313
National Science Foundation, 283
NDA (nondisclosure agreement), 88
negativity, overcoming naysayers, 4-5
negotiating deals, 101
  advances, 107
  agreeing to agree, 106
  conducting business, 105
  contract agreements, 108-110
  guarantees, 107
  lawyering, 102
    approaching the company, 102-103
    contracts, 103
    patents, 104
  licensing agreements, 110-114
    fairness and flexibility, 115-116
    Management by Objectives, 116-117
    setting the scene and the mind, 118-124
    spirit of agreement, 117
    standard agreements, 114-115
  option agreements, 108
  patent and trademark ownership, 111

royalties, 107
winning at what cost, 105
networking
  organizations, 308
  trade shows, 65
New York Toy Fair, 299
NewIdeaTrade.com, 182
N.I.H. (Not Invented Here), 32
  getting in the door to sell your invention, 81-82
NIST (National Institute of Standards and Technology), 263, 276-281
  ATP (Advanced Technology Program), 277
    partnerships, 278
    portfolio, 278-279
    proposals, 279-280
  MEP (Manufacturing Extension Partnership), 280-281
nonprovisional applications, utility patents, 175
  drawings, 179
  English requirement, 181
  models, 180-181
  oath or declaration, 179-185
  presentation requirements, 182-183
  specification, 176-178
  transmittal letter, 175
nondisclosure agreement. *See* NDA
Not Invented Here. *See* N.I.H.
notice of allowance, application for trademarks, 236
Notice of Copyright, 243

O

oath/declaration
  nonprovisional applications, 179-185
  plant patent applications, 197
Office of Independent Inventor Programs. *See* OIIP
Office of Industrial Technologies. *See* OIT
Office of Information Products Development (USPTO), 232
Official Gazette, 37
OIIP (Office of Independent Inventor Programs), 141-142
  outreach programs, 142
  workshops, 141
OIT (Office of Industrial Technologies), 283-284
  success stories, 284-285
one-stop shopping, trade shows, 64
operating instructions, as element of presentation binder, 94
Operation Mousetrap, 26-27
Optical Disk Products at PTDLs (electronic database), 154

355

option agreements, 326-327
  negotiating deals, 108
ordering copies of prior art,
  158-159
organizations (inventors)
  American, 309-310
  choosing a commercialization
    strategy, 57
  exchanging ideas, 308
  expanding your network, 308
  informal, 316
  national, 310-311
    IPO, 313-314
    UIA, 311-313
  state and local, 314, 338-343
ornamental design, 209
outreach programs, OIIP (Office
  of Independent Inventor
  Programs), 142
overcoming naysayers, 4-5

P–Q

partnerships (ATP), 278
Patent and Trademark Depository
  Libraries. *See* PTDLs
Patent and Trademark Office
  Public Search Library, 28
Patent and Trademark Office. *See*
  USPTO
patent attorneys, 161
  conducting patent searches,
    147-148
  design patents, 206
  fees and scams, 22-23
  hiring
    questions to ask lawyers
      you interview, 164-165
    rules, 165-168
  laying the groundwork, 169
  need for, 162-163
*Patent Attorneys and Agents
  Registered to Practice Before the
  U.S. Patent and Trademark Office*,
  166
Patent Public Search Room. *See*
  PSR
patent searches, results, 95
PatentAuction.com, 182
patents
  abandonment, 271-272
  American Inventors Protection
    Act, OIIP (Office of
    Independent Inventor
    Programs), 141-142
  applications, 257
    "actions," 258
    amending applications,
      260-261
    appeals, 263
    assignment, 267
    final rejection, 260
    interference proceedings,
      264-265

responding to an examiner,
      259-260
    time for response and
      abandonment, 263
  co-ownership, 266
  defining what is patentable,
    132
  depository libraries, 332-338
  design, 128, 203-204
    applications, 209-218
    defining design, 209
    draftsmen, 206
    form over function,
      204-205
    improper subject matter,
      210
    insurance against competi-
      tors, 204-205
    patent attorneys, 206
    types of designs and modi-
      fied forms, 209
    value, 207
    versus utility patents, 210
  enforcement insurance,
    269-270
  examiners, 133
  infringement, 267-268
    suing for damages, 268-269
  law, 131
  lawyers, 104
  maintenance fees, 266
  negotiating deals, ownership,
    111
  ordering copies of prior art,
    158-159
  patent pending, 17
  plant, 128, 189
    acceptable modes of asex-
      ual reproduction, 199
    applications, 195-202
    cost, 194
    growing business, 190
    infringement, 193-194
    inquiries, 198
    patent-protection limita-
      tions, 192
    plurality of inventors, 199
    provisions and limitations,
      198-199
    trademark replacement,
      194
    utility plant patents, 191
    who can apply, 192
  rights, 265-266
  searches, 145-146
    classification system,
      157-158
    do-it-yourself, 149-151
    electronic databases, 154
    manual searches at PSR and
      PTDLs, 156-157
    patent attorney directed
      searches, 147-148
    patent search firms,
      148-149
    PTDLs, 152-155
    studying the results of the
      search, 159

selling, 267
  submarine, 139-140
  top ten companies awarded
    patents in 2000, 80
  USPTO, 133-135
    copied documents, 136
    disclosure documents,
      136-139
    inventor applications only,
      135
  utility, 128, 173-174
    nonprovisional applica-
      tions, 175-185
    patentability of computer
      programs, 185
    provisional applications,
      174
personal resumé, as element of
  presentation binder, 97
pitching your idea, 5-7
  champions, 99
  elements of a proposal, 93-94
    multiple submissions, 98
    presentation binder con-
      tents, 94-97
    taking products to tooling,
      97-98
  follow-ups, 28-29
  gaining attention, 90-92
  PPP (Post-Pitch-Propulsion),
    92-93
  unfavorable odds, 99
plan, commercialization, as prerequisite for commercialization
  strategies, 56
plant patents, 128, 143, 189
  acceptable modes of asexual
    reproduction, 199
  applications, 195-202
    claims, 197
    drawings, 197
    fees, 198
    oath/declaration, 197
    specification, 195-196
    specimens, 197
  cost, 194
  growing business, 190
  infringement, 193-194
  inquiries, 198
  patent-protection limitations,
    192
  plurality of inventors, 199
  provisions and limitations,
    198-199
  utility plant patents, 191
  who can apply, 192
plurality of inventors, plant
  patents, 199
political letter, 349
portfolio (ATP), 278-279
Post-Pitch-Propulsion. *See* PPP
postcards, marketing companies,
  34
PPP (Post-Pitch-Propulsion), 92-93
Pre-Grant Published Applications,
  150
Preamble, design patent applications, 212

Precision Measurement Grants, 279
preferred certificates, 186
prerequisites, licensing and venturing as commercialization strategies, 55
presentations
  binder contents, 94-97
    advertising/publicity, 95
    marketing plan, 94
    operating instructions, 94
    patent search results, 95
    personal resumé, 97
    technical profile, 96
    trademarks, 95
    video, 95
  requirements, nonprovisional applications, 182-183
Principal Register (trademarks), 227-228
PrinTEAS, 232
prior art, 149
  ordering copies, 158-159
private companies, locating the right partner, 71-76
product identification (trademarks), 220
  alternative marks, 225
    certification marks, 226
    collective marks, 227
    service marks, 226
    trade and commercial names, 227
  do-it-yourself searches, 232
  Federal Trademark Registration, 227-228
    application examination, 235-236
    correspondence, 235
    eligibility for application, 234
    foreign application, 235
    issuance of certification of registration or notice of allowance, 236
    publication for opposition, 236
    types of applications, 234
  forms, 221-222
    colors, 222
    scents, 221
  function, 227
  Internet searches, 232
  law firm trademark search, 230
  professional trademark search, 230-232
    applying, 232
  registerable marks, 229
  rights, 232-233
  searches for conflicting marks, 230
  symbols, 235
  terms, 234
  those not subject to registration, 228-229

translation considerations, 222-224
  USPTO, 224-225
    correspondence, 225
product profiles, locating, 76
  Standard & Poor's, 77
  Thomas Register, 77
professional inventing community, toy industry, 300
professional trademark searches, 230
  applying, 232
Project XL, 181
Proposal Preparation Kit (ATP), 279
proposals
  ATP, 279-280
  elements, 93-94
    presentation binder contents, 94-97
    taking products to tooling, 97-98
  multiple submissions, 98
  unfavorable odds, 99
provisional applications, utility patents, filing date, 174
provisions, plant patents, 198-199
PSR (Patent Public Search Room), 149-150
  patent searches, guide to manual searches, 156-157
PTDLs (Patent and Trademark Depository Libraries), 142
  patent searches, 152-154
    guide to manual searches, 156-157
  publications, 155
public companies, locating the right partner, 71-74
publication for opposition, application for trademarks, 236
publications of PTDLs, 155
Putnam, Mande (Manager of the USPTO's PTDL Program), 153

R

records, Inventor's Notebook, 129
reference to a microfiche appendix, nonprovisional application, specification, 177
registered patent attorneys, 166
registration
  copyrights, 247
  trade shows, 65
  trademarks
    Federal Trademark Registration, 227-236
    registerable marks, 229
    those not subject to registration, 228-229
    USPTO, 224-225
rejection, patent applications, 260
Renewal registration form. *See* Form RE
reporting problems to the FTC, 37

research and development centers (federally funded), 281
  Department of Defense, 281
  Department of Health and Human Services, 282
  National Aeronautics and Space Administration, 282
  National Science Foundation, 283
resources
  copyrights, 248
  inventor organizations, state and local, 338-343
  patent and trademark depository libraries, 332-338
  toy and game manufacturers, 329-331
responding to an examiner, patent applications, 259-260
Richard C. Levy's Secrets of Selling Inventions, 6
Right to Audit (licensing agreement), 123
rights
  patents, 265-266
  states, 38
    Minnesota, 38-39
    Virginia, 39
  trademarks, 232-233
Rinehart, Pamela (Manager, Research & Administration and Patents Webmaster), 152
Rothschild Petersen Patent Model Museum, 258
royalties
  licensing agreement, 121
  negotiating deals, 107
rules for hiring a patent attorney, 165-168

S

SBA (Small Business Administration), 57, 288
  SBIR program, 288
    evaluation criteria, 291
    funding of research and devlopment concepts, 290
    state-supported programs, 290-291
    success stories, 292
  STTR program, 293
SBIR (Small Business Innovation Research Program), 279
  evaluation criteria, 291
  funding of research and devlopment concepts, 290
  state-supported programs, 290-291
  success stories, 292
scams, 21
  Employment Agreements, 36
  firms/companies, 23-25
  Operation Mousetrap, 26-27

357

patent attorneys, 22-23
what to do if you are a victim, 37
scents, as a trademark, 221
Scientific Library of the Patent and Trademark Office, do-it-yourself patent searches, 151
searches
  conflicting trademarks, 230
  copyright records, individual searches, 247-249
  patent, 145-146
    classification system, 157-158
    do-it-yourself, 149-151
    electronic databases, 154
    manual searches at PSR and PTDLs, 156-157
    patent attorney directed searches, 147-148
    patent search firms, 148-149
    PTDLs, 152-155
    studying the results of the search, 159
  trademarks, 159
    do-it-yourself searches, 232
    Internet searches, 232
    law firm searches, 230
    professional searches, 230
SEC (Securities and Exchange Commission), 72
  10-K, 72-75
  annual reports, 72
securing a copyright, 241-242
Securities and Exchange Commission. See SEC
selling patents, 267
selling your idea
  champions, 99
  elements of a proposal, 93-94
    presentation binder contents, 94-97
    taking products to tooling, 97-98
  gaining attention, 90-92
  getting in the door
    choosing your target and making your mark, 83-85
    corporate culture, 85
    first impressions, 80-81
    hooks, 85, 87
    N.I.H., 81-82
    signed agreements, 87
  honesty, 90
  multiple submissions, 98
  PPP (Post-Pitch-Propulsion), 92-93
  unfavorable odds, 99
service marks, 143, 226
services
  invention promotion firms, FTC warnings, 30-31
  things to do before signing with an invention marketer, 31

single claim, design patent applications, 213
Small Business Administration. See SBA
Small Business Innovation Research Program. See SBIR
Small Business Technology Transfer program. See STTR program
Small Claims Court, 38
small companies, locating the right partner, 67-71
sources, hooks to get in the door, 86-87
Special Processing Branch (USPTO), 180
specific performance (licensing agreement), 122
specification
  nonprovisional applications, 176
    Abstract of the Disclosure, 178
    Background of the Invention, 177
    claims, 178
    cross-reference to related applications, 177
    reference to a microfiche appendix, 177
    Summary of the Invention, 178
    title, 177
  plant patent applications, 195-196
specimens, plant patent applications, 197
spirit of agreement, licensig agreements, 117
split royalties, 66
Standard & Poor's, locating product and corporate profiles, 77
standard licensing agreements, 114-115
Stark Brothers, 192
state inventor organizations, 314, 338-343
state-supported programs, SBIR programs, 290-291
states rights, 38
  Minnesota, 38-39
  Virginia, 39
STTR program (Small Business Technology Transfer program), 293
studying the results of a patent search, 159
submarine patents, 139-140
submitting registrations for copyrights, 247
success stories
  I&I program of DOE, 288
  OIT, 284-285
  SBIR program, 292
  ten commandments for success, 12-19
  toy industry, 297-299

suing for damages, patent infringement, 268-269
Summary of the Invention, non-provisional application, specification, 178
surface shading, drawings or photographs, design patent applications, 216
symbols, trademarks, 235

T

Take an Interest in Late Payments (licensing agreement), 123
TEAS (Trademark Electronic Application System), 232
technical profile, as element of presentation binder, 96
Temporary Restraining Order. See TRO
terms of trademarks, 234
TESS (Trademark Electronic Search System), 154, 230
Thomas Register, locating product and corporate profiles, 77
Thomcat. See *Thomas Register*
Three Strikes and You're Out (licensing agreement), 124
TIA (Toy Industry Association), 296, 305
time commitment, investing in your invention, 9-10
time for response, patent applications, 263
title, nonprovisional application, specification, 177
Toy Design degree, 305
Toy Fair (New York), 299
toy industry
  New York Toy Fair, 299
  outside, independent inventors, 305-306
  overview, 296-297
  professional inventing community, 300
  self-analysis, 302-305
  success stories, 297-298
  Toy Design degree, 305
Toy Industry Association. See TIA
Toy Inventor/Designer Guide, 305
toys, manufacturers, 329-331
track records of marketing companies, 33
trade names, 227
trade secrets, 143, 251-252
  independent inventors, 254
  protection, 252
trade shows, 64-65
  admission prices, 65
  locating, 65-66
  networking, 65
  one-stop shopping, 64
Trademark Assistance Center, 132
Trademark Electronic Application System. See TEAS
Trademark Electronic Search System. See TESS

Trademark Search System
(X-Search), 154
Trademark Trial and Appeal
Board, 132
trademarks, 143, 220
alternative marks, 225
certification marks, 226
collective marks, 227
service marks, 226
trade and commercial
names, 227
as element of presentation
binder, 95
deposit libraries, 332-338
do-it-yourself searches, 232
Federal Trademark
Registration, 227-228
application examination,
235-236
correspondence, 235
eligibility for application,
234
foreign application, 235
issuance of certification of
registration or notice of
allowance, 236
publication for opposition,
236
types of applications, 234
forms, 221-222
colors, 222
scents, 221
function, 227
Internet searches, 232
law firm trademark search, 230
negotiating deals for ownership, 111
professional trademark search,
230-232
applying, 232
registerable marks, 229
replacing plant patents after
expiration, 194
rights, 232-233
searches, 159
symbols, 235
terms, 234
those not subject to registration, 228-229
translation considerations,
222-224
USPTO, 224-225
TRADEMARKS Pending
Applications, 232
translation considerations (trade
marks), 222-224
transmittal letter, nonprovisional
applications, 175
TRO (Temporary Restraining
Order), 268
T®ADEMARKS Assignment File,
232
T®ADEMARKS Registrations, 232

U

U.S. Patent and Trademark
Museum, 155
U.S. Patent and Trademark Office.
See USPTO
UIA (United Inventors
Association), 311-313
undercapitalization, as disadvan-
tage of venturing commercial-
ization option, 54
unfavorable odds, selling your
idea, 99
Uniform Trade Secrets Act. *See*
UTSA
unintentional abandonment of
patents, 271-272
United Inventors Association. *See*
UIA
Universal Consulting Service, 24
up-front fees, 33
USG labs, 281
USPTO (U.S. Patent and
Trademark Office), 37, 127,
133-135
copied documents, 136
disclosure documents, 136-139
documents not accepted by
fax, 186-187
EBC (Electronic Business
Center), 177
General Information Services,
183
Independent Inventor
Program Office, 29
Internet Search Systems (electronic database), 154
inventor applications only,
135
Office of Information Products
Development, 232
Official Gazette, 37
Patent Public Search Room. *See*
PSR
registered patent attorneys,
166
Special Processing Branch, 180
trademark registration,
224-225
Web Patent Database (electronic database), 154
USPTO Today, 44
utility patents, 128, 143, 173-174
nonprovisional applications,
175
drawings, 179
English requirement, 181
models, 180-181
oath or declaration,
179-185
presentation requirements,
182-183
specification, 176-178
transmittal letter, 175

patentability of computer programs, 185
provisional applications, filing
date, 174
versus design patents, 210
UTSA (Uniform Trade Secrets Act),
252, 255

V–W

value of design patents, 207
venturing option (commercializing your invention), 51
advantages, 51-54
disadvantages, 54-55
prerequisites, 55
Vice Chief Administrative Patent
Judge, 263
videos
as element of presentation
binder, 95
USPTO, 191
views, drawings or photographs,
design patent applications, 215

warnings
FTC, invention promotion
firms, 30-31
things to do before signing
with an invention marketer,
31
Web sites
AIG, 28
FTC, 26
inventors and invention, 282
Web-based Examiner Search Tool.
See WEST
WEST (Web-based Examiner
Search Tool), 149
Wilkness, Edith (Manager, USPTO
Public Search Room), 146
Winslow, Samuel (first patent
granted in North America), 94
WIPO (World Intellectual
Property Office), 151
WISC (Wisconsin Innovation
Service Center), 57
Wisconsin Innovation Service
Center. *See* WISC
wish list, 284
wooden stake letter, 76
workshops, OIIP (Office of
Independent Inventor
Programs), 141
World Book, The, 176
World Intellectual Property
Office. *See* WIPO

X–Y–Z

Yet2.com, 182

Zaiger Genetics, 191

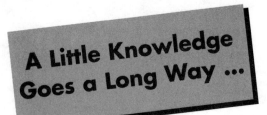
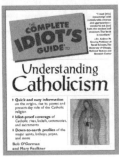

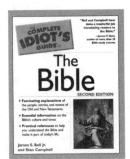

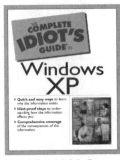